R

£4

A guide to the Roman Remains in Britain

R J A Wilson

A guide to the

Roman
Remains
in
Britain

With a foreword by
Professor J M C Toynbee

Third Edition

Constable London

To my Mother and my Father

who first encouraged my love
of Roman archaeology and
who tolerated countless
detours in search of Roman
Britain

First published in Great Britain 1975
by Constable and Company Ltd
10 Orange Street London WC2H 7EG
Second edition 1980
Third edition 1988
Copyright © 1974, 1980, 1988 Roger J A Wilson
Design Ivor Kamlish MSIA & Associates
Set in Monophoto Times New Roman
Filmset and printed in Great Britain by
BAS Printers Limited, Over Wallop, Hampshire

British Library Cataloguing in Publication Data
Wilson, Roger John Antony
A guide to the Roman Remains in Britain – 3rd ed
1 Great Britain – Antiquities, Roman
1 Title
936.1′04   DA145

ISBN 0 09 468680 7

Opposite; 1   Dorchester Museum, shale table-leg

Contents

List of illustrations

Maps

Photographs, plans and line-drawings

Foreword

by Professor J M C Toynbee

Archaeology, the study of the material, as contrasted with the written, evidence for history, is now firmly entrenched as an important element in a liberal education. It can be studied at school and as part, or even as the whole, of a degree-course in most universities; while the television, the radio, and adult education-classes have placed it within the reach of anyone who has not been confronted with it at the normal student stage. The majority of people would seem to be particularly impressed by the relics of the earliest periods, in this country by the monuments that ante-date the Norman Conquest. And of such series of early monuments none are more rewarding or exciting to investigate than those of Romano–British times, of the 400 years during which this island was a province of a highly-civilised world, at once unified and intensely diversified, that stretched from the Euphrates to the Tyne and Solway, from the Sahara to the Rhine and Danube.

In our present age, with its passion for reality and urge to be ever on the move, no one who is interested in Romano–British archaeology can be content to look at photographs and read descriptions in books. He must be up and out to see the actual monuments, whether in town or country or within museum walls. He must have first-hand knowledge of the things he has heard about; and it is the purpose of the present work to help him (particularly if he is a 'layman') to find how that knowledge may be gained. No Romano–British earthwork or building or collection of objects has escaped the author's net: those most worthy of the reader's attention are given full descriptions in the text, and the rest can be pursued with the help of information given in the appendices. Nearly every site he has personally visited and checked in 1971 or 1972. These journeys he has done by car –

a possession now so almost universal that probably most of the users of this guide will follow him on wheels. But his minute and crystal-clear instructions as to how to find a given site will be just as valuable to the humbler, but no less energetic, non-car-owner, travelling by train, bus, and finally on foot. The present book is, in fact, unique for the comprehensiveness of its contents and for the detail contained in its directions. Quite a number of items little-known even to specialists are noted in its pages. If the Introduction covers ground with which some will already be familiar, it will usefully draw the threads of their knowledge together and provide the neophyte with the basic information, succinctly set out, for appreciating what he sees. The numerous illustrations are a very welcome and conspicuous feature.

As the author states, the substance of this guide is primarily factual. But his always lucid and unpedantic and often vivid style of writing brings all the facts to life. He will certainly succeed in kindling his readers' interest and enthusiasm by his personal approach – an approach in which a living scholarship and a controlled imagination are happily blended.

JMCT

From the Preface to the First Edition

In writing this book I have received help from many people. They include Graham Tingay, Elizabeth Dwiar, Stephen Johnson, Sheppard Frere, Cecilia and Roy Dyckhoff, my brother Donald, Patricia Drummond and Kevin Shaughnessy. I am equally grateful to those who gave me access to land, answered queries and contributed, usually unwittingly, to the contents of this book. Several museums have given permission to reproduce copyright material: this is acknowledged in the list of illustrations above.

My greatest debt is to the two people who have read the typescript in full. Firstly, my friend John Crawshaw, who spent countless hours ironing out the inconsistencies and aberrations of my English style, always with alarmingly keen perceptiveness. Secondly, Professor Jocelyn Toynbee, who made many useful comments on my manuscript and has kindly contributed a generous foreword. But my debt to her is also a much wider one: from the time I went up to Oxford as an undergraduate she has always taken a warm interest in my studies, and encouraged and helped me in numerous ways. To all these, and many others, I am deeply grateful.

A book of this kind is unfortunately doomed to be out of date in some respect even before it appears in print; to the best of my knowledge everything is correct at the time of going to press. In case the book should have a second edition, I shall be very grateful to receive any information about omissions and mistakes.

RJAW, *Palermo, March* 1973

Preface to the Second Edition

In the seven years which have elapsed since the preparation of the first edition, Romano-British archaeology has expanded as never before. The sheer volume of excavation work has been enormous, and there have been corresponding advances in knowledge. Most sites have been dug in advance of destruction and do not therefore feature in this book, but the pace of modern development, particularly construction of new roads, together with archaeological changes, made it evident that a second edition could not be prepared from the armchair. At a time when my research interests have been wholly directed overseas, I am grateful to a number of friends and colleagues who have kept me abreast of recent developments and checked over a dozen sites: they include Roger Goodburn, Stephen Johnson, Christina Hooi, Brian and Elizabeth Merriman, Kenneth Milne and Peter Wiseman. But of the remaining 217 places selected for the first edition, 183 were visited by myself over a period of twenty-five days in September 1978 and March 1979. Six sites in the first edition have been removed or relegated to Appendix One, but thirteen make an appearance for the first time. Few of the other entries have been left unaltered, and sometimes the changes have been substantial. This is, therefore, I hope, as fully revised an edition as circumstances will allow. I should like to thank all those who have taken the trouble to write to me with information about changes, omissions and mistakes, and I would be grateful to readers for further information in case the book should ever go into a third edition.

RJAW, *Trinity College Dublin, 1st July 1979*

Preface to the Third Edition

The past nine years have not seen quite the same amount of
hectic archaeological activity which marked the heady days of
the 1970s, but excavation and research have of course
continued to make major advances in our knowledge of
Roman Britain, necessitating substantial alterations in this
book. To keep the price within bounds the publishers have
allowed me to make text changes provided that the pagination
was not affected, and to include a section of supplementary
material at the end of the book (pp. 375–407). The signal to
turn to this section is a double asterisk (**) in the margin of
the main text at the appropriate places. Sixteen new sites are
included for the first time, but five places mentioned in the
second edition can now be excluded, three because they are no
longer regarded as Roman (Carisbrooke, Blackpool Bridge,
Blackstone Edge), two because they have been backfilled
(Kingscote, Combley). If the main text of this edition looks
superficially similar to that of the second edition, appearances
are deceptive: more than 60 per cent of the pages have received
some alteration, and in many cases this has been substantial.
Opening hours have also been revised in accordance with the
latest available information, and the select bibliography has
been thoroughly updated. My debts as usual are many;
warmest thanks go especially to Sally Stow, Heather Goodhue,
Roger Ling, Tim Potter and above all Max White, most
enthusiastic and regular of correspondents. The finishing
touches were put, and the proofs read, in the congenial
surroundings of the Archäologisches Institut in Bonn, where
I owe much to the hospitality of Professor Nikolaus
Himmelmann and the generosity of the Alexander von
Humboldt Stiftung.

RJAW, *Bonn, October 1987*

Introduction

Purpose

This book is intended to be a guide to the visible remains of Roman Britain. It does not pretend to give a balanced or complete picture of Britain under the Roman Empire; for that the reader must turn to one of the books listed at the beginning of Appendix Three. It is designed primarily for the ordinary individual who has an interest in his Roman past but no prior specialized knowledge (some background information has therefore been provided in the second half of this introduction); but I also hope that the book may be found useful by those who have been confronted with Roman Britain in the classroom or lecture-hall and who want to know precisely how much of the places they have learnt about remains permanently accessible.

I have also tried to make this guide a comprehensive survey of *all* the antiquities of Roman Britain which are visible *in situ*, with the following exceptions:

(a) Roman linear works, e.g. roads, frontiers, canals. It has been impossible to describe *every* visible portion of these. Readers interested in Roman roads will find a complete record in I D Margary, *Roman Roads in Britain* (Baker, rev. ed. 1973), and only a few outstanding stretches have been included in this book. Further details about the two Walls can be found in the works listed in the relevant sections of Appendix Three.

(b) The vast majority of native settlements inhabited during the Roman period, as there are many thousands of these. A handful of them, however, has been included (in chs. 2, 6 and 7), in order to give a slightly more balanced picture of the countryside in Roman times.

(c) Sites such as mines and quarries which were used in

Roman times but also later, and where it is not certain which, if any, of the workings visible today are Roman.

(d) Antiquities claimed as Roman but of which the Roman date is unlikely or unproven.

Ground-plans of Roman buildings marked out in modern materials, and Roman remains removed from their original positions, are not normally included. Some museums are described, others merely mentioned in passing: few have received the space they deserve. Most of the important collections are listed in Appendix Two.

Because of the vast number and diversity of our visible Roman remains, this book sometimes becomes little more than a catalogue. For each site I have tried to give answers to the question that I think will be asked by the visitor, i.e. when was it built, why was it built, and what was the purpose of x and y. This means that nearly all my account is purely factual, and I have rarely had the space to provide 'atmospheric colouring'. This I hope the reader will supply for himself at each individual site. For imagination *is* required when visiting Romano–British remains: if you treat knobbly little bits of wall as knobbly little bits of wall you are going to be disappointed. There are no Roman monuments in this country which can compare with the Pont du Gard in Provence, the aqueduct at Segovia in Spain, the temples at Baalbeck in the Lebanon or the amphitheatre at El Djem in Tunisia; Roman buildings in Britain are generally reduced to little more than their foundations. The reason is partly that few such colossal structures were ever built here, partly that our country has been intensively inhabited and cultivated since Roman times, and partly that the British climate deals unkindly with ancient structures. I hope, therefore, that with the knowledge of a little background history, and with some idea of their original appearance (aided by Alan Sorrell's excellent drawings), you will be able to picture these places when they were not dead relics but thronging with people and alive with activity.

How to Use this Book
The main text. I have found from experience that to link all the sites in a given area with a single itinerary is impractical. It is infuriating if you happen to be doing the route in the

reverse order; and often you will want to see places other than those with Roman remains, and so the itinerary carefully provided by the author becomes useless. In each chapter of this book, therefore, (with the exceptions mentioned below) I have paid little attention to the geographical proximity of one site to another, but have grouped them according to the nature of the remains, i.e. forts, towns, villas. When you wish to see some Roman sites, first look at the map on p. 1 which will show you which chapter covers the area you are interested in. Then turn to the beginning of that chapter, where a map is given showing all the sites discussed in the section, and work out your own itinerary from there. If, before doing this, you want to know what there is to see at each place, either use the index or flip through the pages of that chapter, looking at the names in bold type.

In some cases it has proved impossible to treat each site in isolation, especially where several exist very close together. This applies in particular to the Stainmore Pass (ch. 7), Dere Street from Corbridge to the Scottish border (ch. 9, §1), and to Hadrian's Wall (ch. 8) and the Antonine Wall (ch. 9, §2). Here I have had to link sites together to form a coherent itinerary, and I can only apologise to those who have to visit these places in the reverse order. I hope that some, at least, of my direction will still be helpful after they have been 'translated' (i.e. for 'left' read 'right' etc.).

Particular stress has been laid on giving directions to monuments. The only map I assume you will have is one such as the Bartholomew's $\frac{1}{4}''$ map available as a separate Atlas, or any Road Atlas of similar scale, of which many are now available. I do *not* expect readers to have any 1:50,000 Ordnance Survey maps, except in a few instances where I have explicitly said so. You will, of course, find them helpful if you do have them, and a 4-figure National Grid reference is therefore included in brackets after the name of every place. Very occasionally I have provided 6-figure references for greater accuracy (mainly in Appendix One for some remains not marked on current 1:50,000 maps). At each site I have talked about 'left' and 'right' wherever practicable, but this is often not possible and points of the compass are the inevitable alternative.

Outstanding remains which I consider deserve a special

effort to see have been given an asterisk (*). The standard, however, is only set in relation to the other sites *in the same chapter*, and not to the book as a whole. Thus, High Rochester (p. 316) would have no chance of an asterisk if it were situated on Hadrian's Wall; it receives one because it preserves stone remains, in contrast to most of the other sites of ch. 9, which are earthworks.

Inevitably, technical expressions keep recurring in a book of this nature. Rather than waste space explaining these each time they occur, I have grouped them together in a Glossary at the end of this Introduction (p. 26). Roman names of forts and towns are usually given where they are known: note that in Latin V is used both as a consonant and as the vowel U.

Plans and photographs. I have *only* included a plan of a site when I think that it is impossible to understand the remains without one. This means that unimportant sites, usually earthworks, sometimes receive a plan when major monuments do not. For monuments situated in towns of which I have not supplied a plan, I have assumed that you will have access to town-plans in a road handbook such as that published by the AA; if you do not, you can at least ask directions locally.

Photographs of most of the well-known monuments occur here, but I have also tried to include illustrations of the less famous sites. The ranging-rod which appears in many photographs to give an idea of the scale is six feet long, divided into measures of one foot. The caption of each illustration is necessarily brief: further details are given in the list on pp. vi–xi.

Appendix One. All the visible Roman antiquities in Britain which are not described in the text are listed in Appendix One, usually referred to as App. I (pp. 408–419). These cannot be found without the help of 1:50,000 OS Maps, and the grid reference and the map number are therefore given in the first two columns. (*s*) or (*e*) is added after the type of antiquity has been noted (column 5). In the case of (*s*), which means that stone remains are visible, it may be assumed that these are so fragmentary as to be of interest only to the most avid enthusiast. This is not always so in the case of earthworks (*e*). In the north of England, Scotland and Wales many fort-platforms and other military antiquities are still prominently visible, and it has been impossible to include all of them in the text. (It must be remembered that 'earthwork' (*e*) only describes the present state of the site and is no indication of its original condition: many rampart-mounds cover stone defensive walls which are not now visible.) What constitutes 'visible' is a difficult problem, and obviously some will think that there is nothing to see at some of the sites that I have listed, whereas other sites that are faintly visible I may have omitted. My guideline has normally been the relevant symbol on the 7th series 1″ OS map, though occasionally some places have been included that the OS considers 'site of' (i.e. nothing visible), and vice versa. There has been a drastic reduction in the number of antiquities shown on the 1:50,000 maps.

Access

Some of the most important monuments of Roman Britain in England are in the care of the Historic Buildings and Monuments Commission (HMBC), more popularly known as English Heritage. These are indicated in the text by 'AM' in square brackets after the name of the site, and by the following letters which correspond to these times of opening:

A: at any reasonable time. S: standard hours:

	Mon.–Sat.	*Sunday*
15 March–15 October	9.30–6.30	2–6.30
16 October–14 March	9.30–4.00	2–4.00

SM means that, in addition to the above hours, the monuments are open on Sunday mornings from 9.30 in the 15 March to 15 October period. Ancient Monuments in Wales are the responsibilty of Cadw, Heritage in Wales, and generally have the same opening hours except where otherwise stated. In Scotland Ancient Monuments are in the care of the Scottish Development department, and opening hours are different; all such sites included in Chapter 9 are, however, accessible at any time.

Opening hours of sites not in the custody of the State are also supplied, and as far as possible are correct at the time of going to press. In the case of museums where I give vague closing-times, e.g. 4.00 or 5.30, it may be assumed that the later hour applies to the summer months only (usually May–September).

The vast majority of the places described in this book, or

listed in Appendix I, are on private land. In cases where I
know from whom permission to visit can be obtained, I give
this information. But in places where I do not, you must NOT
assume that you are free to wander. Most landowners are
proud of their ancient monuments and are happy to let
interested visitors see them, but *only* if the latter make the
effort to enquire first, and *only* if they shut gates, keep dogs
on a lead, do not trample down standing crops, and do not
damage fences or dry-stone walls. A little courtesy will go a
long way, and will make things easier for yourself and the
other would-be visitors who will come after you.

The Roman army in Britain

Under the Empire, the Roman army consisted of two distinct
forces, the legions and the *auxilia*. A **legion**, with a nominal
strength of 6,000, was originally recruited only from men with
full Roman citizenship (i.e. Italians and men from Roman
colonies during much of the first century AD), but the rule was
relaxed in the second century and in the third all provincials
were given Roman citizenship. The main body of fighting men
was organized into *centuriae*, centuries, of 80 men under the
command of a *centurion*. Six centuries formed a *cohort* (about
480 men), and 10 cohorts made up a legion, but the first
cohort was bigger (about 800 men). The legionary soldier
would normally serve about 25 years before being discharged
as a *veteran*. The commander of the legion, the *legatus*, or
legate, was a Roman senator, and under him were six *tribunes*,
or junior officers. Like the legate, they were not full-time
professional soldiers, but held the post as part of their public
career.

The **auxilia**, or auxiliary troops, were not Roman citizens,
but were recruited from the provinces of the Roman Empire.
They usually took their names from the areas in which they
were originally levied (e.g. first cohort of Thracians from
Bulgaria), and I have often given these areas when naming
auxiliary garrisons. Do not, however, be misled into thinking
that British forts were all manned by foreigners from many
lands; for each unit, though retaining its original native name,
would have received fresh recruits from the area in which it

was stationed, i.e. from the local British population.

The auxiliaries were organized into *cohorts* if they were infantry, or *alae* (wings) if they were cavalry. Both generally had a nominal strength of 500, but units of 1,000 men are also known. A cohort could either be composed entirely of infantry or contain a contingent of 120 (or 240) men on horseback. The *auxilia* were generally commanded by Romans of the equestrian rank (a class below that of senator), who had the title of prefect (*praefectus*) if the cohort was 500 strong, or tribune (*tribunus*) if 1,000 strong; *alae* were commanded by prefects.

Auxilia were placed in forts and were expected to bear the brunt of fighting and frontier-duty. Legions were placed in fortresses behind the main frontier areas, and were the crack troops used only in emergency. In addition to being a soldier, the legionary was also a considerable technician and he was often away from his fortress constructing auxiliary forts or frontier-works.

The original *auxilia* had come from what at the time were the fringes of the Roman-controlled world, but by the third century they were an integral part of the Roman army. In the Later Empire, the tribes on the fringes were also organized into military units, but to distinguish them from the *auxilia* they were called **numeri**. Not attested in Britain before the third century, these forces were composed of light-armed infantry (the cavalry equivalents were called **cunei**). They always served away from their place of drafting. An example of a *numerus* was that stationed at South Shields in the fourth century.

Roman Remains in Britain

Military Remains
Marching Camps. The words 'camp' and 'fort' must be carefully distinguished: the former is used only of temporary earthworks, the latter applies to permanent posts, whether constructed in turf or stone.

An army on the march always defended itself when it stopped for the night by erecting a camp. These are called *marching camps* or *temporary camps*. Their plans are often irregular, to suit the terrain. They consist of an earth rampart, originally perhaps 5–6 feet high and crowned with a timber palisade. Outside was a single ditch, not always dug when the ground was too hard. Poles for the palisade were carried in the soldiers' kit-bags; and the tents which housed the men inside the ramparts were carried by mules. The entrances of temporary camps are of two types: those defended by *titula*, which are short pieces of rampart and ditch set a few yards in front of the gap in the main rampart (in theory they would break the charge of an enemy); and those defended by *claviculae*, which are curved extensions of the rampart (and sometimes its ditch), usually inside the area of the camp, though external and double *claviculae* are also known. Dating evidence from these camps is slight: both types of gateway are found in the first century, but from the second century onwards *claviculae* seem no longer to have been used (Chew Green III, dated to the mid-second century, is the latest known; plan, fig 104). Very occasionally *titula* are found protecting the gates of forts (Hod Hill, Bar Hill) and fortlets (Durisdeer). The best examples of marching camps are: Rey Cross (*titula*, fig 70), Y Pigwn (*claviculae*, fig 55).

Practice Camps. Troops also built earthworks as part of their training, but these were never meant to be occupied. The rounded corners and the gateways are the most difficult features of a camp to build, and practice camps are often, therefore, very small, avoiding the need for unnecessary lengths of straight rampart. Today these earthworks are rarely more than 1 foot high; examples near Castell Collen, Gelligaer and Tomen-y-Mur. Others are of normal size and may be built as part of a mock-siege (as Burnswark). At Cawthorn is an example of what appears to have been a 'labour camp', housing troops engaged on fort construction.

Legionary Fortresses. These are larger versions of the fort (see below), and contain similar buildings similarly arranged. They hold a legion and normally cover about 50 acres. There were several short-term legionary fortresses, with turf ramparts and timber buildings, but the three permanent bases, later rebuilt in stone, were at Caerleon, Chester and York.

Vexillation Fortresses. These were short-term store-bases and quarters for both legionaries and auxiliaries during the conquest period in the first century. Fourteen examples are known, all between 20 and 30 acres; only Clyro (App. I) is partly visible.

Forts. These were the permanent bases of the auxiliary units, and except as a temporary measure (Hod Hill is one example) rarely housed even a detachment of legionaries. Their size varies according to the type of garrison, but most forts in the first and second centuries cover between $2\frac{1}{2}$ and 8 acres. Their shape is almost universally like that of a playing-card, with straight sides and rounded corners.

Defences. The earliest forts in Britain had a rampart of turf or clay, on average about 18 feet wide at base, which was crowned with a breastwork and wall-walk of timber. Gateways and towers at intervals round this rampart were also of timber. The best examples of first-century forts in Britain are Hod Hill (fig 15) and the restored Baginton (see figs 40 and 41), but neither represent typical types.

From early in the second century onwards, the front of the rampart was usually cut back and a stone wall inserted in front of it. Henceforth all new forts were usually, but by no means always, built with a stone wall from the beginning, although an earth rampart nearly always accompanied it. This stone wall was originally about 15 feet high, and included a parapet at the top. Today the facing-stones have usually been robbed away, revealing the irregular core of the wall; and in many places the stone wall is now buried beneath a broad mound which marks the line of the defences. There were normally four gateways, consisting of either one or two arched carriageways, often flanked by guardrooms. Internal towers, perhaps with open crenellations (fig 2) rather than with sloping roofs (fig 48), were placed at the four rounded corners, and at intervals between the latter and the gateways.

Outside the ramparts there were one or more ditches, usually V-shaped. Each had a narrow drainage-channel in the bottom and was never meant to be filled with water like a medieval moat.

Internal Buildings. These conform to a standard pattern. In the earliest forts they were timber-framed with walls of wattle-and-daub, but all visible examples are of stone. In some forts, only the central buildings are made of stone, while the barracks are entirely of timber. Stone foundations need not always imply stone superstructures.

In the centre of each fort is the *principia*, or headquarters building (1 on fig 2). The front part consists of a large courtyard, usually surrounded on three sides by a colonnade. It leads to the covered *cross-hall* which stretches the full width of the building. This was capable of holding the complete contingent standing shoulder to shoulder; here it would have assembled for an address by the commanding officer, who spoke from the raised platform, or *tribunal*, at one end. At the back of the building are some smaller rooms, often five in number. The central one is the *sacellum* or *aedes*, the shrine where the regimental standards and the statue of the emperor stood (see fig 85). Below its floor the pay-chest was kept, sometimes (from the mid-second century onwards) in an underground strong-room. The rooms on either side were used for administrative purposes.

On one side of the *principia* is the *praetorium*, or commandant's house, usually consisting of a range of rooms round a central courtyard (2). Private bath-suites seem to have been a luxury installed only in the late empire. On the other side stand two or more *horrea*, granaries (3). These are always buttressed and have raised floors to keep their contents dry. A *fabrica*, workshop (4), and sometimes a *valetudinarium* hospital (5), also occupy the central area of a fort.

The rest of the area is taken up by *barrack-blocks* (6), with the provision, too, of *stables* (7) if the regiment was cavalry or part-mounted. A single barrack-block was designed to hold a *centuria* of 80 men. The main part of the building is divided up into approximately 10 portions. Each is further subdivided into two (not always by stone partitions): in one cubicle the men ate and slept, and in the other they kept their weapons and other equipment. There was a verandah running down one side of the building. The centurion and his junior officer(s) lived in the more spacious accommodation provided at one end. The most instructive barrack-block in Britain is the legionary example at Caerleon.

The road running from the front of the HQ to the front
gate is called the *via praetoria*; from the back to the back
gate, the *via decumana*. The road joining the gates in the long
sides and running along the front of the HQ is known as the
via principalis. There was also a road going all round the fort
in the *intervallum*, or the space between the back of the
rampart and the internal buildings.

Outside the ramparts lay the garrison bath-house (p. 14)
and usually a civilian settlement.

The best examples of Roman forts in Britain are Chesters,
Housesteads, Hardknott, Caernarfon and South Shields.

<u>Tactics</u>. Early forts are meant to house garrisons trained to
fight in the open: they would sally forth from their gates and
meet the enemy outside. Later, there is a trend towards
making the fort more of a stronghold impregnable to attack:
ditches increase in number, and the ramparts are sometimes
furnished with catapult emplacements, *ballistaria*, from which
artillery could bombard an attacker. The final move towards
the medieval notion of a 'castle' came in the third and fourth
centuries with the Saxon Shore Forts.

<u>Saxon Shore Forts</u>. These abandon the conventional (playing-
card) shape and layout. They have massive stone walls,

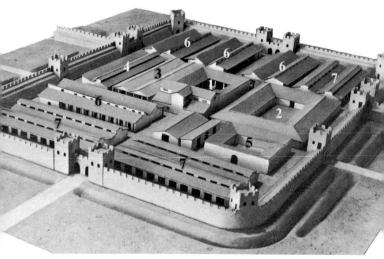

2   Model of a Roman fort

probably 30 feet high, usually without an earth bank behind.
Most are defended by projecting bastions, to have maximum
view of and control over an attacker. Gateways are narrow.
These are the forts built along the coastline from the Wash to
Southampton to defend SE Britain from Saxon pirate raids
(hence their name). The remains of Richborough, Pevensey
and Portchester are perhaps the most spectacular monuments
of Roman Britain. Similar late forts were built in the west,
and the restored example at Cardiff gives an excellent idea of
the formidable nature of these strongholds (see fig 60).

Fortlets. These are small guard-posts, often filling gaps
between forts. Their size varies: each probably held between
50 and 150 men. Defences usually consist of a rampart broken
by a single gate, and surrounded by one or two ditches. Some
(e.g. Maiden Castle) had stone walls, but most were
earthworks (e.g. Castle Greg).

Signal-Stations. Fire, smoke and semaphore were all used by
the Romans in transmitting messages, and there are many
examples of signal-stations in Britain. Most consist of a
timber tower, surrounded by an earth rampart and ditch (e.g.
Bowes Moor), but some first-century towers (e.g. Gask Ridge)
have no rampart. Stone towers are also known (e.g. one later
incorporated into Hadrian's Wall, p. 305). In the late fourth
century, a row of strongly-defended stone signal-stations was
built along the Yorkshire coast.

Civilian Remains

Towns. The Romans were the first to build towns in Britain,
with streets laid out in a regular chess-board pattern (street-
grid). Most of the sites they chose are still flourishing cities
today, but by modern standards Roman towns were small
(the population of the whole of Britain at the end of the
second century is unlikely to have much exceeded two million
people). Very little is visible of the class of minor settlements
called *vici*, except for those which grew up around the forts of
Housesteads and Chesterholm (VINDOLANDA). More
important were the small market-centres and roadside
settlements, but these too have not left many visible remains
(ch. 5, pp. 181–187, for the best examples). Most of the towns

described in this book, therefore, belong to one of the
following two categories:

(i) *coloniae*. These were special foundations for veterans,
retired Roman legionaries, and were composed of Roman
citizens. Colchester, Lincoln and Gloucester were founded in
this way. The title later became an honorary one, conferred
on a prosperous town already in existence. We know that
York's civilian settlement received this honour, and it is a fair
guess that at least London (ch. 10) did so too. *Coloniae* were
intended to act as civilizing influences on the surrounding area.
They were self-governing communities, with a city-council
(*ordo*) and a system of magistrates modelled on that of Rome.

(ii) *tribal* or *civitas capitals*. The pre-Roman tribal
organization was not obliterated by the invaders, and towns
were founded to serve as the new market and administrative
centre of each *civitas*. These, too, were self-governing
communities, and their magistrates would have been elected
from among the local aristocracy. Their size varies from
Cirencester, 240 acres, to Caistor St Edmund, 35 acres.
Inhabitants of tribal capitals were not awarded the privilege
of Roman citizenship (though all provincials became citizens
by a decree of Caracalla in 212 or 214).

<u>Public Buildings</u>. The centre of a *colonia* or a tribal capital
was occupied by the administrative unit, the forum and
basilica. The *forum* was the civic centre and market-place, and
consisted of a large courtyard surrounded by a colonnade.
The *basilica* was a long hall, sometimes with apsidal ends,
where justice was dispensed. It lay along one end of the
forum. Adjoining it were administrative offices. The plan of
the forum and basilica is derived from the military *principia*.
Unfortunately, no complete example is exposed in Britain
today: the colonnade on one side of the forum at Wroxeter is
the most notable relic.

The *bath-house* was an indispensable part of Roman life,
and examples are found in every town and villa of any note
and also outside every fort. They varied enormously in
elaboration. The system was close to the present-day Turkish
baths, and consisted of a series of rooms heated to different
temperatures. The bather first took his clothes off in the
apodyterium (undressing room), proceeded to the *frigidarium*
(cold room), started sweating in the moderately-heated

tepidarium (warm room), and perspired profusely in the
caldarium, the room of intense sticky heat. Here he would
scrape himself down, to remove dirt from the skin, with an
oiled metal instrument called a *strigil*, a sort of blunt 'cut-
throat' razor. He could also take a plunge in the small hot
bath which usually adjoined the *caldarium*. He would then go
through the rooms in the reverse order, taking a dip in the
cold plunge-bath in the *frigidarium*, to close the pores and so
avoid catching cold. This was the most common system, and
depended for its effect on moist heat: steam was created by
sprinkling water on the floor, which was heated by a
hypocaust (see Glossary, p. 27). A more rigorous experience
was sweating in dry heat, when the hot room was known as
the *laconicum* (Spartan room) or the *sudatorium* (sweating
room). A complete bath-house contained both systems, and
the public establishments also had *palaestrae*, exercise-courts.
Swimming-baths as we know them were rare. The best
example of a public bath-house is at Wroxeter, and of a
military one, Chesters. The thermal establishment at Bath is
exceptionally grand; the Caerleon legionary baths are also
instructive.

Other public buildings within a town included *temples*
(below, p. 18), a *mansio*, or inn (partly for the use of officials
travelling on public business), and (sometimes) *theatres*. The
only completely excavated and visible example of the last, at
St Albans, is described in its proper place (p. 145). The theatre
was a D-shaped building and must be distinguished from the
amphitheatre. The latter, nearly always outside the built-up
area, consisted of an elliptical arena surrounded by tiers of
wooden seats erected on earth banks. These banks were
usually revetted in stone or timber, but no monumental
structures built entirely of stone, like the amphitheatres of
Arles or Nimes or the Colosseum, have yet been found in
Britain. Gladiatorial combats and animal sports were staged
here. Today, civilian amphitheatres survive usually as earth
banks (e.g. Silchester, where stonework is now also visible).
The legionary amphitheatres at Chester and Caerleon have
been more extensively exposed, but here weapon-training came
before gladiatorial entertainment, and the arenas were
consequently larger in relation to the seating space than in their
civilian counterparts.

Water-supply. *Aqueducts* raised on great arches are unknown in Britain. Where water was brought from a distance it was conducted in an open channel, following natural contours. Dorchester has the best example. Examples of *sewers* have been found at Lincoln, Bath, St Albans and recently at York. *Latrines* are common: the public lavatory at Wroxeter can be seen, but more instructive are the military ones such as that at Housesteads (fig. 93). Wooden seats were mounted over a deep sewer, and running water in a gutter in front of the seats washed the sponges which were the Roman equivalent of toilet-paper.

Private houses. The simplest dwelling was a long, narrow building, with one end fronting the street (often a shop, with living-quarters behind). This type was sometimes expanded and had a wing or wings added at the back. The largest house consisted of a series of rooms ranged about a courtyard. The most elaborate were decorated with mosaics and painted wall-plaster. Few town-houses have been preserved in Britain: Canterbury, St Albans and Caerwent have the best examples; the one at Dover lay in a civilian settlement outside a fort.

Defences. All the large towns, and many smaller settlements, were equipped with defences at some time before the end of the Roman occupation. Some, such as St Albans, received an earth bank and ditch soon after AD 43, and the *coloniae* had stone walls before the middle of the second century. On the other hand, some very small towns did not receive ramparts until the fourth century. The defences of most other Romano–British towns show three distinct phases: an earth bank, a stone wall inserted in front of it, and projecting bastions added to that. Excavation at different sites has produced different dates for each of these phases, as will be noticed by comparing my account of one town-wall with another. It is most unlikely, however, that such diversity in dates is real. Most towns were given earth defences with a wooden stockade or breastwork at the end of the second century. These must have been erected on the command of a central authority, probably in response to, rather than in anticipation of, a crisis, either that of *c*. 180, or, more likely, that of 196–7 (see p. 23). In most places the stone wall was inserted in front of the earth bank at a later period, probably at various times in the third century. The third phase, the

addition of projecting bastions, is given various dates in the
fourth century, but it too may be the product of a single policy.
A date nearer to 350 rather than in the late 360s (Theodosian)
now seems probable, at least for some. Bastions gave more
complete control over an attacker, and although there is no
certain evidence that they were provided with artillery
machines (*ballistae*), it is hard to explain otherwise the new
broad ditches (to keep an attacker at artillery range?) which
frequently accompany such defences. The best example of
urban stone defences can be seen at Caerwent.

Villas

These are the most popular and familiar monuments of
Roman Britain because of the spectacular mosaics which
often adorn their floors. Nearly all the mosaics, however,
belong only to the last phase of a (usually) complicated
development. The simplest houses of just a few rooms have
not generally been preserved, though Lullingstone in its final
form is a luxurious, expanded example of a very compact
house, without projecting wings or spacious courtyards. Most
of the villas visible in Britain belong either to the 'corridor-
type', in which several rooms open off a long corridor and are
often flanked by short wings on either side (e.g. Newport), or
the extensive 'courtyard-type', in which blocks of rooms
forming separate wings are grouped around one or more
courtyards (e.g. Chedworth; North Leigh). Most villas were
not pleasure-palaces but the centres of agricultural estates,
and farm-buildings are usually found on the outskirts of the
main living-area (or in the outer courtyard of some courtyard
villas). The courtyard-type, usually a development from
simpler dwellings, belongs (in the visible examples) to the
fourth century. The first-century palace at Fishbourne is quite
exceptional.

Even the smallest villas had hypocausts, mosaics or plain
tessellated floors, and painted wall-plaster. A bath-house or
suite (above, p. 14) was also normal.

Native Settlements

A high proportion of the population of the countryside,
especially in Wales and N and SW England, remained largely
uninfluenced by Roman civilization. They used Roman

pottery and coins and sometimes even had refinements such as painted wall-plaster, but the settlements they inhabited belonged mainly to the pre-Roman tradition. The dwelling-place was usually a circular hut, though in the Roman period rectangular huts often replaced or co-existed with those of a circular plan. Some of the very few native settlements mentioned in this book are built of stone (Chysauster, Tre'r Ceiri), and are therefore substantial monuments, but most survive only as earth ridges (e.g. Ewe Close). It is always best to visit the latter on a sunny evening, when long shadows pick out the surviving banks and make the remains more intelligible.

Temples
The true classical-style temple was built on a lofty platform (*podium*) and approached by a flight of steps. The shrine (*cella*) had a front porch of free-standing columns supporting a triangular pediment. This type is rare in Britain: Colchester has one.

The most common type is called Romano–Celtic. The ground-plan of the visible examples consists of two squares, one inside the other. The inner wall enclosed the *cella*, the outer wall supported a colonnade and was an ambulatory. The appearance of this type is suggested in fig 3. The best example is at Maiden Castle.

Other temples were of the 'basilican' type, an early forerunner of the Christian church. The outer walls of these are solid, and the interior may be divided into a nave and

3   Suggested appearance of a Romano-Celtic temple

side-aisles. Lydney and the London temple of Mithras are examples. The Carrawburgh Mithraeum is much smaller and simpler. Undisputed Roman churches are rare and in any case not visible; but there is an early Christian baptismal font at Richborough.

Roads

Most Roman trunk roads were built in a series of straight stretches, usually changing direction on hill-tops. But straightness was not always possible and in mountainous terrain a Roman road can wind as much as a modern one. The composition of each road varied a great deal: generally there was a foundation of large slabs or stones and the final surface consisted of rammed gravel. The latter has usually been washed away, leaving the foundation-slabs exposed (e.g. Wheeldale Moor, fig 67). Sometimes iron cinder was used for surfacing (Holtye), but a paving of stone blocks was apparently not used in Britain. To ensure good drainage (a vital element when roads lacked the cohesion afforded by modern macadamized surfaces), Roman highways were often built on raised embankments (*aggeres*), and were sometimes accompanied by ditches on either side.

Burials

By Roman law burial was prohibited inside a city, except for infants; in cases which appear to contradict this, e.g. Canterbury, the burial must have preceded urban expansion. Both cremation and inhumation were practised in Roman Britain: the former was predominant in the first and second centuries, the latter in the fourth. Most burial-places were simple graves perhaps marked by tombstones, and many of such stones are on display in museums. Larger, monumental tombs have remains left *in situ*, and these fall broadly into two categories:

(i) the earth barrow, or *tumulus*, which has a steep, high, conical profile. These are particularly frequent in SE Britain, and are a direct descendant of pre-Roman burial-mounds. Most date from the first and second centuries. The burials, usually cremations and often associated with grave-goods, were placed in a receptacle in the middle of the barrow. *Tumuli* often occur in groups, e.g. The Bartlow Hills. The most instructive single example is probably Mersea.

(ii) stone-built tombs. The circular structures at Keston and High Rochester were probably merely retaining-walls for a central mound of earth, perhaps with a conical top. Those at Stone-by-Faversham or Harpenden, however, definitely have internal chambers and were freestanding.

Historical outline

55–54 BC	Caesar raids Britain.
AD 43	Invasion of Britain under Aulus Plautius with four legions, II Augusta, IX Hispana, XIV Gemina and XX Valeria, and auxiliaries (about 40,000 men in all). Landing at Richborough. Battle on the Medway. Native chieftain Caratacus flees to Wales. Plautius pauses to await the emperor Claudius before advancing to Colchester.
44–60	Division of the invading army: legion II advances SW, legion IX towards Lincoln, legion XIV and part of XX through the Midlands. Rest of legion XX is kept in a base-fortress at Colchester. Early frontier-line marked by Fosse Way, the Roman road from Exeter to Lincoln.
47–52	Ostorius Scapula governor. Campaigns against the Silures (S Wales) and the Ordovices (mid- and N Wales), who are inspired by Caratacus. Beaten in battle in AD 51 he flees to N Britain, where Queen Cartimandua of the Brigantes hands him over to the Romans.
52–7	Aulus Didius governor. Further campaigns in Wales. Civil war among the Brigantes and Roman intervention there.
61	King Prasutagus of the Iceni (East Anglia) dies. Rapacity of Roman administrators causes revolt of Boudica (Boadicea). Petillius Cerialis with part of legion IX is ambushed by Boudica – infantry massacred, but he himself escapes. Suetonius Paulinus, governor, rushes back from Anglesey but not soon enough to save Colchester, London and St Albans from going up in flames. 70,000 inhabitants massacred.

Poenius Postumus, acting commander of legion II, refuses Suetonius' call for assistance and falls on his sword after hearing news of the final battle, when 80,000 Britons are killed. Julius Alpinus Classicianus comes to Britain as the new financial administrator (procurator). Disagreement over policy leads to the recall of Suetonius.

66   XIV Gemina withdrawn from Britain for service in the East.

71–74   Petillius Cerialis, now governor, arrives with new legion, II Adiutrix, and campaigns against the Brigantes; the huge native fortress at Stanwick near Scotch Corner is one of their strongholds.

74–8   Julius Frontinus, governor, finally pacifies the Silures. Legionary fortresses established for II Augusta at Caerleon near Newport c. 74, and for II Adiutrix at Chester c. 78.

78   Arrival in Britain of Gn. Julius Agricola, most famous of the governors of Britain, because of the surviving biography written by his son-in-law Tacitus. Final mopping-up in Wales. Base for legion IX probably established at York c. 78–9, on site of earlier fort.

79   Advance to the Tyne-Solway isthmus.

80   Advance to the Forth-Clyde isthmus, and reconnaissance as far as the Tay.

81   Consolidation, building of forts and roads.

82   Invasion of SW Scotland.

83–4   Agricola pushes up to the Spey, building forts behind him, including a legionary fortress for legion XX at Inchtuthil. Battle of Mons Graupius, in which 30,000 Caledonians under their leader Calgacus are crushed. Roman fleet circumnavigates Britain.

84   Recall of Agricola.

c. 87   Withdrawal from Scotland north of the Forth-Clyde isthmus. II Adiutrix withdrawn from Britain about now. Legion XX moves to Chester.

c. 105 Complete withdrawal from southern Scotland, perhaps after a disaster. Frontier now the

Stanegate, Agricola's road across part of the Tyne-Solway isthmus.

c.118   Revolt in Britain, perhaps among the Brigantes. Suppressed by 119.

122   Emperor Hadrian visits Britain. Hadrian's Wall and its attendant works begun, under the supervision of the new governor, Aulus Platorius Nepos, who brings another legion to Britain, VI Victrix. Disappearance of legion IX, last recorded in 107/8. Probably withdrawn from Britain c. 121–2, eventually to perish in a disaster in the East, possibly in 161.

139–42   Antoninus Pius, emperor, orders a new advance in Britain, under Lollius Urbicus. Reoccupation and refortification of S Scotland. Building of the Antonine Wall.

c. 155   Serious revolt, possibly of Brigantes, in N Britain with heavy Roman casualties. Antonine Wall temporarily evacuated. Gn. Julius Verus arrives as governor with legionary reinforcements, and rebuilding of Pennine forts burnt in the revolt is begun.

c. 156/8 Antonine Wall recommissioned.

c. 163   Another crisis causes the final abandonment of the Antonine Wall and of S Scotland, probably after enemy destruction. Hadrian's Wall fully recommissioned. More rebuilding of forts in N Britain under Calpurnius Agricola (governor c. 162–166).

c. 169   Possible unrest in Wales.

c. 180   The historian Dio records a war in Britain and the death in battle of a Roman general. Invading tribes cross 'The Wall'. If this refers to a barrier in commission, and if the Antonine Wall had been evacuated c. 163, this must mean Hadrian's Wall, and the forts at Corbridge and the adjacent sector of the Wall were probably destroyed now. Ulpius Marcellus is sent to Britain, and victory is achieved by 184 (coins).

193–7   Clodius Albinus (governor of Britain from c. 191) claims the imperial throne in 193 and is recognized as assistant (an office with the title of Caesar) by Septimius Severus, who becomes emperor. Growing tension between the two. In 196 Albinus stripped Britain of troops and crossed to France. Defeated and killed by Severus near Lyon in February 197. Many forts in N Britain burnt, probably by Brigantes, but it is far from certain that Hadrian's Wall was destroyed now; if so, reconstruction was delayed 10 years. Probably as a reaction to this crisis (rather than that of 180) most of Britain's towns were equipped with earth defences in c. 197–200.

197–201/2   Virius Lupus sent to Britain to restore the situation. Many Pennine forts rebuilt now. Britain divided into two provinces (*Superior* and *Inferior*, Upper and Lower).

205–8   L. Alfenus Senecio, governor, restores Hadrian's Wall and its forts, sometimes from foundations, after a long period of neglect. Further rebuilding of Pennine forts where reconstruction had begun earlier, in 197.

208–9   Emperor Severus campaigns in N Scotland to punish the invaders.

210   Caracalla, his son, conducts campaigning because Severus is too ill.

211   Severus dies in York, February 4th. Complete withdrawal from Scotland, but probably not before 213.

c. 213–70   Period of peace. Rebuilding and reorganization of forts in N Britain continues (until c. 230). Towns given stone walls. From 259 Britain is part of a Gallic separatist empire.

c. 275–85   Increasing insecurity of SE England because of Saxon pirate raids. Most of the Saxon Shore forts built either now or under Carausius.

286–7   Carausius, commander of the British fleet, declares himself Emperor of Britain and N Gaul. Loses control of the latter in 293.

294   Carausius is murdered by his finance-minister Allectus.

296   Constantius (the emperor Maximian's Caesar)

recovers Britain, and Allectus is killed in battle in S Britain. Constantius sets in hand a lot of rebuilding on Hadrian's Wall, in the Pennine forts and at the legionary fortresses of Chester and York. Perhaps natural decay mainly the reason for the reconstruction. Britain divided into four provinces. Office established of *Dux Britanniarum*, commander of all land-forces in Britain.

306   Constantius returns to Britain, now as emperor, and campaigns in N Scotland (little archaeological trace). Dies at York, July 25th. His son Constantine proclaimed emperor there.

313   Christianity tolerated by the edict of Milan, and three British bishops attend Council of Arles in 314.

300–42   Peace and prosperity in Roman Britain.

342–3   Trouble north of Hadrian's Wall; remaining outpost forts abandoned. Emperor Constans comes to Britain, and pacifies the Scottish tribes. Strengthening of the forts of the Saxon Shore (Pevensey added) under newly created 'Count of the Saxon Shore'. Bastions on some town walls.

360   More trouble with the tribes north of the Wall, the Picts of Scotland and also with the Scots of Ireland. Peace settled by one Lupicinus.

367/8   Britain is overwhelmed by a great barbarian conspiracy: concerted attacks by Picts, Scots and Saxons according to Ammianus. Nectaridius, Count of the Saxon Shore, is killed, and Fullofaudes, *Dux Britanniarum*, is besieged or captured. Much of the countryside of lowland Britain probably unaffected, though some villas are deserted now.

369   Theodosius comes to Britain to restore the situation. A fifth province, called Valentia, is established (probably in NW Britain). Hadrian's Wall restored and its forts patched up. Some forts in N Britain rebuilt, others abandoned. Signal-stations built on the Yorkshire coast, either now or a decade or so later. The Theodosian

reconstruction is evidently effective, for towns and villas continue to show signs of prosperity until the end of the fourth century and beyond.

383   Magnus Maximus, probably *Dux Britanniarum*, revolts, removes troops from Wales and N Britain, and crosses to the continent. Irish raids in Wales, but Hadrian's Wall probably remains intact.

395   Stilicho, general of the emperor Honorius, orders some sort of expedition against Scots, Picts and Saxons.

c. 400   Final end of Hadrian's Wall.

401   Troops withdrawn from Britain to defend Italy.

407   Constantine III, a usurper, removes the garrison from Britain, and crosses to the continent.

410   Emperor Honorius tells the British cities to look to their own defence.

c. 446   British cities appeal for military assistance to Aetius, the leading general in Italy at this time ('The Groans of the Britons').

Some Roman Emperors

The dates of some Roman Emperors mentioned in this book:

Claudius	41–54	Caracalla	211–7
Nero	54–68	Geta	211–2
Vespasian	69–79	Gordian III	238–44
Nerva	96–98	(Carausius	287–93)
Trajan	98–117	Constantius	293–306
Hadrian	117–138	Constantine I	
Antoninus Pius	138–161	(the Great)	306–37
Severus	193–211	Constans	333–50

The adjectives *Hadrianic, Severan* and *Constantian* refer of course to the years when Hadrian, Severus and Constantius respectively were emperors. *Antonine* refers to the period 138–192, but most of the structures so described in this book belong to the first Antonine phase, i.e. 138–54. *Agricolan* refers to the years 78–84 (Agricola's governorship) and *Theodosian* to 369–70.

Glossary

A page-number in brackets gives a reference to the Introduction, where a fuller explanation of the relevant term may be found.

abutment: masonry platform or earth embankment supporting the central structure of a bridge

agger: cambered embankment-mound carrying a Roman road

ala: unit of cavalry in the Roman auxiliary army (p. 8)

ambulatory: covered portico surrounding the inner shrine of a temple (p. 18)

apodyterium: undressing room in a bath-suite (p. 15)

architrave: the horizontal member above two columns (piers, etc.), spanning the interval between them

bailey: fortified enclosure in a medieval castle

ballista: artillery-weapon discharging arrows and stone balls

basilica: town hall (p. 14)

berm: in military defences, the level space between two features (e.g. ditch and rampart)

bonding-course: bands of brickwork (or occasionally stone slabs) which alternate with wider sections of regular stonework; they normally run through the entire thickness of the wall, presumably to give cohesion and stability to the mortared rubble-core; they were also useful as levelling-courses during construction

breastwork: the vertical timber-work built on top of the earth rampart of a fort to provide screening for the sentry; see fig 40

caldarium: hot room (moist heat) in a bath-suite (p. 15)

cella: inner shrine of a temple (p. 18)

centuria: unit of 80 legionary soldiers, commanded by a centurion (p. 7)

chi-rho: Christian symbol composed of the first two letters of the Greek name for Christ (Χριστός); see fig 118

civitas: tribal unit (p. 14)

clavicula: in a Roman camp, curved extension of rampart (and ditch) protecting a gateway (p. 9)

cohort: unit of infantry soldiers, legionary or auxiliary (p.7)

colonia: settlement of retired legionaries; for York a title of honour (p. 14)

crop-mark: colour-differentiation in standing crops or
  vegetation (best seen from the air), indicating the presence
  of buried ancient features

cross-hall: covered assembly-area in the headquarters building
  of a fort (p. 11)

culvert: drainage-channel

curtain: wall of fortification

dado: continuous border round the lower part of a wall
  decorated with painted plaster

field-system: regular pattern of rectangular fields attached to
  an ancient farming settlement

flue-arch: underfloor arch in a hypocaust (qv) allowing hot
  air to pass from furnace to room, or from one heated room
  to another

flue-tiles: open-ended, box-shaped tiles built in the thickness
  of the walls of a room heated by hypocaust (qv)

frieze: horizontal band above an architrave (qv), sometimes
  carved with sculpture

frigidarium: cold room in a bath-suite (p. 15)

graffito: writing scratched on tile, pottery, plaster, etc.

guilloche: on mosaics, decorative feature consisting of two or
  more intertwining bands

herringbone: descriptive of a style of construction in which
  stonework or tiles are set in zig-zag pattern

hypocaust: Roman method of central heating: see fig 4. The
  floor was raised, usually on *pilae* (qv), and flue-tiles (qv)
  acting as 'chimneys' were built in the thickness of the walls.
  The draught created by these flues enabled hot air to be
  drawn from the stoke-hole (qv; on the right in fig 4),
  where brushwood or other fuel was burnt, to circulate
  under the floor, and to escape up the wall-flues to the air
  outside. In the channelled type of hypocaust, the hot air
  circulated not around *pilae* but through narrow channels
  built under the floor

imbrex: semi-circular roofing-tile, linking two flat tiles
  (*tegulae*)

in situ: in its original position

jamb: side-post of a doorway or window

keep: central stronghold of a medieval castle

laconicum: hot room (dry heat) in a bath-suite (p. 15)

latrine: lavatory (p. 16)

leet: aqueduct-channel

lintel: wooden beam or stone slab lying horizontally above a doorway (or window)

mansio: an inn, especially for government officials

monogram: set of letters combined into one (used of Chi-Rho, qv)

mosaic: floor composed of pieces of coloured *tesserae* (qv) to form geometric or figured designs

motte: earth mound marking site of a small medieval castle

offset: point at which the thickness of a wall is reduced, forming a 'step' in the structure

palaestra: exercise-yard of a public bath-house, in Britain sometimes covered

parapet: top of a Roman fortification consisting of a wall-walk (qv) and battlements

pediment: triangular gabled end of a roof (usually used of temples)

pilae: pillars of brick (or stone) supporting the floor of a room with a hypocaust (qv)

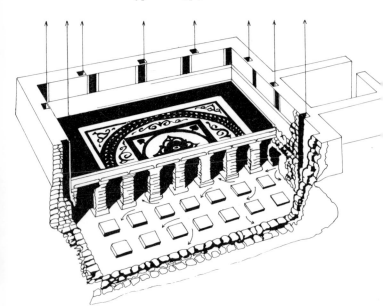

4 *The working of a hypocaust*

pilaster: column or pillar incorporated in, but projecting from, a wall

piscina: swimming-bath in a public bath-house

plinth: projecting course at the foot of a wall; also used of a base, e.g. for an altar

podium: raised platform (especially used of temples)

portal: doorway or carriageway, especially of a fort-gateway

post-hole: hole dug to receive a wooden upright

postern: minor gate or door in a late Roman town- or fort-wall

posting-station: small town on a main road, where travelling officials could find an inn (*mansio*, qv)

principia: headquarters building of a Roman fort (p. 11)

procurator: government financial administrator

putlog holes: row(s) of square or rectangular holes in a masonry wall which held horizontal scaffolding timbers during construction; on completion of the work they were plugged with loose material, since fallen out

relieving-arch: arch built as part of a solid wall to take the weight of the construction above, and to divert it from weak points such as doors and windows lower down

revetment: facing of one material given to a structure of a different material (eg stone wall given to an earth bank)

roundel: circular panel containing a design (eg on mosaics)

sacellum: shrine in a fort's headquarters building (p. 11)

samian: high-quality, red-coated pottery, imported from the continent (mainly from France)

sarcophagus: coffin of stone or lead

Saxon Shore: coast of SE England exposed to Saxon pirate raids (p. 12)

sleeper wall: low wall supporting a raised floor, especially in a granary

springer: the voussoir (qv) which rests on the cap above a jamb (qv) and marks the beginning of an arch

stoke-hole: furnace-area for a hypocaust (qv)

street-grid: regular pattern of streets crossing at right-angles

sudatorium: hot room (dry heat) in a bath-suite (p. 15)

tepidarium: warm room (moist heat) in a bath-suite (p. 15)

tessellated: composed of *tesserae* (qv), usually of a floor without decoration

tesserae: small cubes of coloured stone, glass or tile, of which a mosaic (qv) or tessellated (qv) floor is composed

titulum: short detached stretch of rampart (and ditch) protecting the gateway of a marching camp (p. 9)

tribunal: platform for commanding officer in *principia* (qv) (p. 11), or on a parade-ground

triclinium: dining-room

tumulus: burial-mound (p. 19)

vexillatio: detachment of a legion (normally 1,000 men)

vexillation fortress: campaign base for legionaries and auxiliaries (p. 9)

via decumana: road in a fort running from back of *principia* (qv) to back gate

via principalis: road in a fort linking the gates in the long sides and passing in front of the *principia* (qv)

vicus: small civilian settlement, especially one outside a fort

voussoir: wedge-shaped stone forming one of the units of an arch

wall-walk: level platform for the sentry on top of a fortification (see parapet)

wattle-and-daub: wall-construction consisting of wickerwork plastered with mud

Chapter 1

South-East England

Kent and Sussex

(Appendix I only – Surrey)

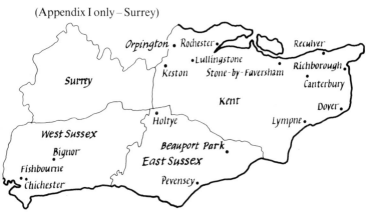

In 55 and 54 BC, Gaius Julius Caesar made his famous
invasions into Britain. On the second expedition he crossed
the Thames and penetrated into what is now Hertfordshire;
the great ditch known as Devil's Dyke at Wheathampstead is
probably part of the fortress of the native king
Cassivellaunus, which Caesar successfully assaulted. But there
was no permanent Roman occupation, and the marching
camps which Caesar must have built have never been found.

We have, therefore, to turn to **Richborough*** (TR 3260)
[AM;SSM] for the earliest visible traces of Roman Britain.
The site lies 1½ m NW of Sandwich in Kent and is reached by
taking a minor road to the right just before the level-crossing
on the Canterbury road (A257) out of Sandwich. It is difficult
to imagine the place as it was in AD 43, the year of the Roman
invasion under Aulus Plautius, as the coastline is much
changed: the whole of the NE corner of Kent, the Isle of
Thanet, was indeed an island, and Richborough itself lay on a
small peninsula attached to the mainland. In particular, the
steep escarpment on the east, where the railway-line and river
Stour now lie, has carried away the east wall of the later stone

fort, and in AD 43 the ground must have extended flat for some way beyond this.

On arriving at the fort, ignore for the moment the massive walls and go straight into the interior; leaving the triple ditches on the right, head northwards and you will see (1 on plan, fig 5) a line of double ditches interrupted by a causeway, just inside the west gate of the later stone fort. These ditches (and a now vanished rampart) have been traced in both directions for a total length of 2,100 feet, but only this short portion has been dug out and left visible. Everything that is described in this book – all the villas, towns and forts of the Roman occupation – are later than these ditches, dug by the invading army in AD 43 to defend their beach-head.

These ditches were soon filled up once the progress of the invasion had ensured that a defended base was no longer necessary at RVTVPIAE (as the Romans called Richborough). The area then became a supply-base; several buildings, all of timber, are known, and the plans of three of them have been marked out in concrete on the site. One of them, marked 2 on fig 5, is immediately adjacent to the early ditches: it had a row of posts (now concrete circles) forming a verandah. Now turn towards the centre of the site (4), noting the outlines of the two other timber buildings, granaries (3), to your right.

By about AD 85, the area of the storebase had been cleared for the erection of a great marble-faced monument, of which all that remains is an enormous cruciform mass of concrete rubble and part of the surrounding precinct wall (4). What you have to imagine here is a magnificent four-way arch, towering nearly 90 feet high, sumptuously adorned with bronze statuary and marble imported from Italy, fragments of which are visible in the museum. The earth now piled up between the arms of the cross masks the full mass of the concrete but makes clearer the original rectangular shape of the structure: the concrete cross was the platform for the marble-paved passageway between the arches, reached by four flights of steps, but the massive masonry piers of the arch itself have been completely removed by stone-robbing. Richborough was the chief port of Roman Britain, at least during the first century, and the monument was evidently a piece of propaganda, probably celebrating the completion of the conquest of the province and designed to impress the many visitors passing through. About the middle of the third century, the monument was stripped of all its ornament and served as a signal tower, surrounded by an earth rampart (not visible) and the triple ditches which surround it on three sides. Shortly afterwards the monument was totally levelled and the triple ditches filled in when the walls of the Saxon Shore fort were built in the late third century.

The other buildings immediately adjacent to 4 can be dealt with briefly. Building 6 belongs to the fourth century but its function is uncertain. Note the difference in surface-level: this and the top of the monument-platform represents the ground-

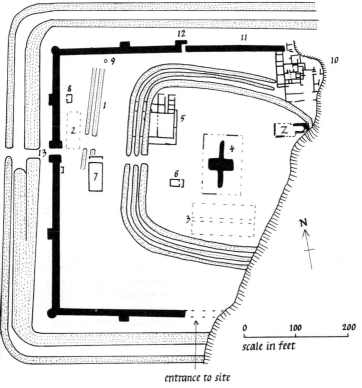

entrance to site

5 *Plan of Richborough*

level of the Saxon Shore fort. Building 5 was interpreted as a
block of shops rebuilt in stone in the second century. It
consisted of three large rooms, with corridor in front and
smaller rooms for living quarters or storage behind. Half of it
was destroyed when the triple ditches were dug in the third
century, and the rest was buried beneath the now-vanished
earth rampart of the fortlet. Z is the ground-plan of a Saxon
church. The substantial stone building in the NE corner (10)
had a long history. The earliest building of c. AD 85 (plan
marked by brown concrete-dressing) was rebuilt on a larger
scale in the second century (white concrete). It was clearly an
official building of some sort, perhaps a *mansio* or inn, as it
was respected by the ditches of the third-century earth fortlet
which stopped short of it. It remained in use until the
construction of the Saxon Shore fort, when a small military
bath-building (the remains on a higher level, including a
hypocaust and semi-circular plunge-bath) was built on the
site.

From here you can easily reach the outside of the walls of
the Saxon Shore fort. This was one of a series of forts,
running from the Wash to Portsmouth, which was designed to
protect SE England from Saxon pirates. It is usually believed
that Richborough was put up by Carausius (287–293), who
revolted from Rome and made himself master of an
independent empire of Gaul and Britain; but it has recently
been suggested that it belongs to the decade before him. At
some time towards the end of the third century, at any rate,
these massive walls were built, probably 30 feet high and
faced, as can be seen, with rows of squared stones separated
at intervals by bonding-courses of tiles. This facing is best
preserved on the north side, which presents other interesting
features; you can study here, for example, the various sections
in which the wall was built: the join is very clear (11) to the
east of the north postern – note the row of patterning in chalk
and ironstone blocks, which are not on the same level in each
section. Next you reach the first bastion (12), which has an
opening for a postern gate; its outer face contains a large reused stone, now much worn, once representing the head and
mane of a lion. Just beyond the bastion a sharp eye will spot
that the bottom tiling-course changes its level at one point,
indicating another section-break in the building of the wall.

Now go back inside the fort through the postern gate (12) and follow the inside of the wall to the NW corner. On your way you will pass a hexagonal structure of brick, covered by a perspex dome. Of fourth-century date, it was interpreted by the excavator as a water-tank, but it is much more likely to have been the baptismal font of a Christian church, the main construction of which is visible in some of the excavation photographs but was entirely removed without proper record. This was of course a church of Roman date, not to be confused with the Saxon church already noted. Further on you will pass no. 8, an early second-century cellar, the only surviving part of an otherwise timber building. Then make you way to the west gate, noting to the left the outline of building 7, a fourth-century structure of unknown purpose like no. 6: they may have been meeting-rooms for military clubs, but this is no more than a guess. Now pass to the outside of the fort, through the west gate (13), a single passageway defended by a guard-chamber on either side, one of which is visible. Here began the Roman road later called Watling Street, which ran through London and the Midlands to Chester. Rounding the SW corner bastion, you arrive back at the entrance to the site. The area beyond the fort-walls was also intensively occupied in Roman times, but no surface features are visible except for the amphitheatre, now an unimpressive hollow; it is difficult to find, lying in a field to the west of the minor road where the track to Richborough Castle joins it.

Richborough is only one of four Saxon Shore forts in Kent; others were at Reculver, Dover and Lympne. **Reculver**, the Roman REGVLBIVM, (TR 2269) [AM; A], lies 3m east of Herne Bay, and is signposted from A299. Here too the coastline has changed dramatically, but whereas Richborough is now some way inland, the fort at Reculver has been eroded by the sea and only the south half of the original eight-acre enclosure remains. A fortlet connected with the Roman invasion in AD 43 was built here, but the surviving walls belong to the first half of the third century. This was confirmed by the finding in 1960 of a fragmentary but important inscription referring to the building of the *principia* and cross-hall under a certain Rufinus, probably Q. Aradius Rufinus, who was governor of Upper Britain *c.* 240. The fort is therefore considerably earlier

than that at Richborough, and the absence of bastions and
tile bonding-courses at Reculver confirms this. Excavations
since 1952 have shown that it was supplied with the
customary buildings of a Roman fort, but these were much
robbed and are not now visible. Coin evidence shows that
occupation ceased about 350–60. The garrison was the first
cohort of Baetasians from Brabant, on the Belgium–Holland
border.

To see what remains of the defences (and if you have just
come from Richborough be prepared for disappointment),
take the path from the seashore car-park which leads up to
the twin towers of the Saxon and medieval church. Passing
this, you reach the east gate, excavated in 1967, with a single
guardroom on its north side. Turning right, the path follows a
stretch of wall, about 8 feet high, but only rubble-core
remains, as nearly all the facing-stones have been robbed
(some are visible near ground level south of the east gate).
About 130 feet from the SE angle a rough bit of projecting
masonry indicates a repair to the wall in late Roman times.
Along much of the south side the wall has now been freed of
shrubbery, and its line can be followed (except at the SW
corner) right round to the inn opposite the car-park. Only a
few blocks remain of the south gate, excavated in 1964, but
the plan of the rest, and the position of the timber gateposts,
have been marked out in concrete. It consisted of a single
passageway 9 feet wide with a guardroom on the west side
only.

The village of **Lympne** (TR 1134) lies on B2067, 3m west
of Hythe. To find the remains of the Saxon Shore fort, known
today as Stutfall Castle but as PORTVS LEMANIS under the
Romans, take the turning in the village to Lympne Castle;
where the road turns 90° to the left, by a building called 'The
Cottage', walk down the path which leads straight on. After
climbing a stile, continue down a narrow path between two
barbed-wire fences, over three more stiles, and after ten
minutes you will see the forlorn Roman walls in a field on
your right. They have been much tossed around by landslides, and the sea has now retreated far away, but the
overgrown ruins have an air of impressive, almost romantic,
solitude. Some fragments are still about 25 feet high and 14
feet thick, even though fallen from their original position. The

walls originally formed a pentagon enclosing about ten acres. Tile-courses and bastions (one good example survives on the NW, near the solitary tree on the far side of the field) make it likely that they are contemporary with those of Richborough (mid to late 270s AD), although pottery indicates the presence of a naval base here in the second century. Excavations in 1976–8 revealed some further details of the fort, but these have been backfilled. Part of the east gate has, however, been left exposed, including the large flagstones of the entrance passage and the more southerly of the two semicircular towers which flanked it (now about two feet high and lying at a 45° angle because of subsidence and landslips). To reach this, continue on down the slope from the footpath, keeping the wire fence to your right. The gate is situated at the beginning of the last stretch of walls, just before the bottom of the slope.

The fourth of the Kentish Saxon Shore forts was at **Dover*** (TR 3141), DVBRIS, but until rescue excavations in 1970–1 along the path of the inner relief-road, its exact position was uncertain. Now, however, the south and west walls of the fort are known, together with three bastions – a later addition and not, as at Richborough, of one bond with the wall. A totally unexpected find was that of another fort on a slightly different site. This was built in the second century and, on the evidence of tile-stamps (CL BR), it is almost certainly one of the headquarters of the British fleet, the *Classis Britannica*; another has recently been uncovered in Boulogne. Unfortunately, nothing of the Dover fort is now visible, as the new road covers the remains. One discovery of 1971 has, however, been salvaged: parts of five rooms and a corridor belonging to a building in the extensive civilian settlement which grew up in the second and third centuries north of the *Classis Britannica* fort. All five rooms have hypocausts and it is presumed that they are part of some well-appointed private house, built *c.* 200 AD over an earlier building. The walls, still standing nine feet high in places, are covered with brightly coloured painted plaster, exceptionally well-preserved in one room and part of a second. A green or red dado below is surmounted by a series of panels separated by columns. The panels contain different motifs, including a kind of reversed torch or wand, and a winding, stunted tree. Their preservation is due to the fact that they lay under the earth bank piled

behind the wall of the Saxon Shore fort, the building of which
c. 270 AD removed most of the rest of the house. Because of
our climate, substantial finds of painted wall-plaster are rare:
Dover can in fact boast of by far the largest area of Roman
wall-plaster – over 400 square feet – visible *in situ* in this
country. The so-called 'Roman Painted House', opened to the
public in 1977, is clearly signposted from York Street on the
inner relief road (daily except Mondays, Apr.–Oct. only, 10–5).

As well as this spectacular new find, Dover possesses
another monument unique in Britain. This is the Roman
pharos, or lighthouse [AM; A], which adjoins the church of St
Mary close to the car-park in the grounds of Dover Castle

6   *Dover, the lighthouse*

(reached from the old Dover–Deal road on the east side of the town: avoid the new A2 eastern ring road, Jubilee Way). The top 19 feet are entirely medieval, but the lower 43 feet are good Roman work, built of flint-rubble, originally faced in ashlar blocks, with external tile bonding-courses (fig 6). The outer face, octagonal in plan, is now much battered by decay and by medieval refacing (especially on the NW); in Roman times it rose in a series of eight vertical stages, with a set-back of about one foot at each stage. It was probably about 80 feet high, or 20 feet higher than the whole monument is today; and from the top a beacon of fire would have risen by night, to guide ships using the Channel. The Roman entrance survives on the south, and some of the upper windows retain their stone voussoirs interlaced with brick. The square interior, now a roosting-place for pigeons, is equally impressive. The lighthouse was probably built in the second century. The church, which incorporates Roman material in its walls, also has a small collection of finds to the right of the entrance.

A second lighthouse was built at Dover, on the Western Heights. Paintings show that it was still standing at the end of the seventeenth century, but a drawing of 1760 depicts a mere shapeless chunk of masonry, known as the Bredenstone. What was left was mutilated when the Western Heights fortification was built in 1805–6. All that survives today is a long stretch of flints and tile-course encased in stonework of 1861 and, on the surface above, three chunks of concrete propped up against one another. At present these pathetic remnants are not accessible, the staircase to them being dangerous; but the fortifications are in the care of English Heritage (also called HMBC) who may , one day, tidy up the area and allow visitors to see where the western *pharos* stood. Re-used material, including stamped tiles, indicates that this lighthouse belongs to the later Roman period.

One more Saxon Shore fort belongs to this chapter, and it is even more impressive than the examples in Kent. It is at **Pevensey*** (TQ 6404) [AM; A], which lies between Eastbourne and Hastings on the A27. This, too, now lies inland; in Roman times the walls were built on a peninsula, with the sea coming right up to the south wall and the harbour situated to the east in the area of the present car-park. The Roman walls enclose an oval area of about nine acres. That on the south has entirely gone except for two bastions, incorporated into the keep and the outer walls of the medieval castle which lies at the SE angle. Going through the east postern, which is on the site of a Roman gate (the existing masonry is medieval or modern), you reach the interior of the fort, where excavations in the early years of this century found only a few timber buildings and hearths. On the right, near the trees just before the gap where the wall has fallen away, the internal face has been cleared down to Roman ground-level. Here you can see that the thickness of the wall is reduced by offsets; note, too, how the lowest eight feet retain their facing-stones, as this part of the wall was covered by earth in the post-Roman period and so escaped the later stone-robbing and weathering which have battered the top part. Return to the path and go on to the west gate. This consisted of a central arched entrance nine feet wide, with two guardrooms on either side, of which only the lowest courses of one survive; the whole was then flanked by the two gigantic bastions (the existing gate-jamb is medieval). In front of this entrance a ditch was dug across the isthmus joining the peninsula on which the fort stood to the mainland, and part of it is visible. From here you can follow the walls right round to the east gate again: they are about 12 feet thick and stand virtually to their original height except for the parapet. Facing-stones and bonding-courses are well preserved, and the few patches of flintwork used in the facing (where the parapet survives, for example) show how little repair the Roman walls needed during medieval times. From the west gate you first reach three bastions; here, as elsewhere, they are bonded into the wall and therefore were built at the same time. Then comes a magnificent stretch of wall (fig 7) where section-joints between building-parties can easily be spotted (note how the rows of green sandstone or brick bonding-courses do not tally with those of adjacent sections). Next, immediately before the fallen sector, was a small postern-gate, a simple curved passage in the wall; it is now obscured by a 1939–45 gun turret. Between here and the east gate are three more bastions; the herringbone patchwork especially clear on the last one is due to Norman repair-work.

ANDERITVM, as the Romans called it, was not built until the

fourth century (as a coin of *c*. AD 335 found *under* a bastion shows), although earlier occupation of the site cannot be ruled out. Most of the coins date from the late third and early fourth centuries. Two brick stamps, previously taken as evidence for reconstruction under the Emperor Honorius (AD 395–423), have now been shown to be fakes. They were probably 'planted' during excavation work by a well-known forger, Mr Charles Dawson, who exhibited them to the Society of Antiquaries in London in 1907. The Anglo-Saxon Chronicle relates how a vain defence of the fort was made in 491, ending in a terrible massacre. The site then lay derelict until the Normans used the walls as an outer bailey for their castle.

So far, I have dealt almost exclusively with military antiquities, and this may have given the impression that SE England was predominantly a garrisoned area. This was not the case; the forts described belong to the later phase in the Roman occupation of Britain when the peace and security of SE England was threatened by Saxon pirates. Both before and

7   *Pevensey, the north wall*

after the erection of the forts civilian life continued in the towns and villas, and to these I must now turn.

Two trunk-roads, both built in the early years of the occupation, served SE England. One was Watling Street, which started at Richborough and reached London by way of Canterbury and Rochester; the A2 follows the Roman road for much of its course. The other was Stane Street, which linked London and Chichester (for the posting-stations en route to Alfoldean and Hardham, see App. I). From Canterbury there were roads to Reculver, Dover and Lympne, the last one surviving as the B2068 (Stone Street); and another road branched off Watling Street near London and headed for the south coast near Lewes, enabling swift transport to the Thames of corn from the Downs and iron from the Wealden mines. The road is unusual in being metalled for many miles with iron slag, and a portion of this has been preserved by the Sussex Archaeological Trust. It is reached by a footpath just south of the A264 East Grinstead to Tunbridge Wells road, 1m west of the crossroads with the B2026, and about 100 yards east of the White Horse Inn at **Holtye** (TQ 4638). The road was exposed in 1939, since when frost has loosened the smoothness of the cinder surface. The shallow hollow running diagonally across the road marks the site of a ford.

The Holtye road was metalled with iron slag for convenience, because of the proximity of major Roman iron works in the Sussex Weald. Three dozen sites have been identified between the East Grinstead area on the west and the Battle-Sedlescombe area on the east. Iron working and smelting was already in operation at many of these by the end of the first century, but the real boom for the industry came in the second century. Decline and abandonment had set in by the mid-third century, possibly because of over-exploitation or because deforestation made fuel for the furnaces more expensive and more difficult to obtain: in both cases working will have become uneconomic. The largest of these sites was at **Beauport Park** (TQ 786140), 3m E of of Battle. Much of the huge iron slag-heap here was taken away for road metalling in the nineteenth century, but what remains is still quire impressive; it has been estimated that there were originally about 100,000 tons of it, representing an iron production of some 50,000 tons. Even more impressive is a small but excellently preserved bath-house on the slope above the slag bank. Its carefully constructed walls stand over seven feet high in places and the lower part of a window also survives. Five rooms had hypocausts, two with *pilae*, three of the channelled variety. The bath-house was built in the first quarter of the second century and was repaired and extended in the early third, before being abandoned and systematically stripped *c*. 250, at the time of general decline in the whole Wealden iron industry. The discovery of over 1,300 tiles stamped CL BR here (as well as on other Wealden sites) demonstrates the direct involvement of the British fleet, the *Classis Britannica*, in the operation of the iron workings. It must be stressed that at present (1987) the bath-house is covered and there is nothing whatever to see. Consolidation and preservation are not expected to take place for some time, and as private funding is now required to enable the structure to be displayed, the future of this monument is uncertain.[1]

At Beauport Park a settlement of some twelve acres is indicated by surface finds across the stream from the bath-house. This of course was only a small mining village; the major settlements of the south-east were at Chichester, Rochester and Canterbury, but none of them have left much of their Roman past to see.

Canterbury (TR 1457) was DVROVERNVM CANTIACORVM, the tribal capital of the Cantiaci. Excavation since the war has revealed many new features of the Roman town, but little is now visible. The medieval walls follow the line of their Roman predecessors, but little Roman masonry is now exposed. One tiny fragment of a gateway (the 'Quenin Gate'), consisting of two large ragstone blocks and a few courses of bricks marking the turn of an arch, can be seen embedded in the medieval wall about 4 feet from the ground, at the most northerly (right-hand) end of the car-park in Broad Street, very close to the last square tower in this NE sector of city-wall (1 on fig 8). Further west, in St Radigund's Street (2), the removal of plasterwork on the north wall of the church of St Mary Northgate has revealed that the city wall,

[1]Information about access may be supplied by the excavator, Gerald Brodribb, Esq., Stubbles, Ewhurst Green, East Sussex, *on receipt of a stamped addressed envelope*.

incorporated in it, stood to its full height of 29 feet. A very sharp eye may detect faint traces of corner stones marking the position of the crenellations, now blocked, on a level immediately below a small round-headed window. The latter belongs to the twelfth century and so the city wall below is earlier: it has been suggested that much of the visible facing is even of Roman date, but the use of flintwork at all periods in

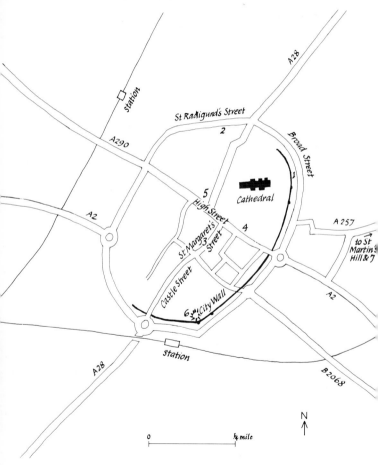

8 *Canterbury, plan*

this part of England makes it very difficult to be certain that
this is Roman rather than Saxon or Norman. Excavations in
1977 on the base of the city wall immediately adjacent showed
that the Roman flint core, still visible in part, had been
refaced and rebuilt in the fourteenth century. Work here has
also confirmed the results from elsewhere, that the Roman
walls and a contemporary earth bank behind them were not
built until *c.* 270–90, later than their counterparts in most
other Romano–British towns.

Of public buildings, we know most about the theatre which
lay at the junction of St Margaret's Street and Watling Street.
This was of two main periods: about AD 80–90, when the first
building was erected with timber seats on banks of gravel;
and about 210–20, when the whole theatre was rebuilt in stone
on a larger scale. To the later period belong the two fragments
of the theatre which are the most easily accessible: a portion
of the back wall is visible in Alberry's wine and food bar next
to 39, St Margaret's Street; and an imposing fragment, 4 feet
high, of the curving outer wall of the auditorium can be seen
in the 'Cellar Romana' of Slatter's Restaurant on the opposite
side of the street (3 on fig 8). For the fanatic, other
fragments are visible on private property in the cellars of 23,
Watling Street and 5 and 6, St Margaret's Street.

Much less disappointing are the remains of part of a
town-dwelling preserved in a basement in Butchery Lane off
High Street (4 on fig 8) (Mon.–Sat. only, Apr.–Sept. 10–1 and
2–5, Oct.–Mar. 2–4). The most impressive feature here is a
corridor paved by a tessellated floor, with two mosaic panels
with leaf- and flower-motifs and fragments of a third.
Excavation in 1946 showed that the corridor itself was a
second-century addition to a late-first-century stone house,
but that the mosaic was added later, probably in the third
century. Another mosaic panel, in what was probably the west
wing of the same house, was revealed during emergency work
in The Parade in 1976. A block of limestone visible on the left
of the corridor represents a Roman repair. The other main
feature of the site is a room with a hypocaust, of which only
the *pilae* supporting the vanished floor remain. The skeleton
of a baby and a small hoard of bronze coins (*c.* AD 270) were
found in the area of the hypocaust. The central part of the
basement, now covered with concrete but originally a

courtyard open to the sky, has showcases of small finds; note in particular a lamp showing a slave with a wine jar. Around the walls are tiles, pots and a small mosaic from Burgate Street.

The main collection of finds, however, is housed in the Royal Museum, High Street (weekdays 10–5; 5 on fig 8). This is small and at present very cramped: eventually it is intended to transfer the Roman collections to Butchery Lane. Note especially the collection of pre-Roman coins; two fine Roman swords, found in 1977 in a second-century burial of two men whose bodies had been hastily thrown in on top of each other (a Roman murder?); the reconstruction drawing of the theatre; some superb glass, especially a beautiful flagon from Bishopsbourne with ornate handles; and above all, the hoard of silver-ware deposited in the late fourth century and found in 1962. It includes 11 silver spoons, one with the Chi-Rho monogram and another inscribed VIRIBONISM (= ? 'I belong to a good man'); also a curious silver implement with a prong and another Chi-Rho.

Two other Roman relics in Canterbury deserve a brief mention. One is the Dane John, probably a Roman burial-mound of the first or second century, much obscured and altered by landscape-gardening (6 on fig 8). This and an attendant cremation cemetery originally lay outside the Roman town but were later incorporated within the third-century defences. The other is St Martin's church, which lies on a hill to the east of the city on the Sandwich road (A257, 7 on fig 8). Inside, a wall of Roman brickwork is clearly visible on the right-hand side of the chancel, pierced by a Saxon doorway. More impressive is the rear wall of the nave which, though much repaired, contains unmistakable Roman tile bonding-courses. Bede, writing in 731, mentions 'a church built in honour of St Martin while the Romans still lived in Britain'. The presence of Christianity in Roman Canterbury is confirmed by the silver hoard mentioned above; it is uncertain whether these walls are part of a Roman church, or of another Roman building only later converted to Christian worship, or are of Saxon date and merely incorporate Roman material (no Roman features were found in a 1985 dig nearby).

The remains of DVROBRIVAE (TQ 7468), Roman **Rochester**, need not detain us long. The town, 23 acres in size, defended the important crossing of the Medway by Watling Street. An earth rampart and ditch of the late second century was fronted, probably at the beginning of the third century, by a stone wall. The SW corner of this wall, faced with ragstone but without tile-courses, stands to an impressive 10 feet in a public garden called Eagle Court, which is reached by an alleyway between the Eagle Tavern (public house) and a butcher's shop (Kemsley's), at the east end of High Street at its junction with the inner ring road which swings round the north side of the town. All the facing-stones are present. Note that just after the Roman wall begins to turn the corner, the medieval wall carrying straight on abuts onto it. Then cross High Street and follow the medieval walls along the ring road. After turning the corner you will see, under a hideous stretch of modern brickwork, the core of the Roman wall. Other bits of core, unimpressive and difficult to reach, are visible in the Deanery Garden and elsewhere in the Cathedral precinct; and another forms part of the bailey-wall of the Norman Castle fronting the Medway.

Of Roman **Chichester** (SU 8604), the NOVIOMAGVS REGINORVM (the 'New Place of the Regini'), even less is visible. Fragmentary remains of timber buildings suggest that it had a military origin, and legionary belt buckles, a sword (found in 1977) and other evidence suggest it may possibly have been a base for the Second Legion during its thrust to the west (ch. 2). But further phases of timber building with associated industrial activity (c. 55–70) may be civilian rather than military. At any rate the street-plan does not seem to have been laid out until c. 75–85, and from then onwards Chichester developed into a flourishing town. Little is known in detail of its buildings. Parts of houses have been excavated from time to time, and the bath-house in the area of Tower Street, excavated in 1972 and 1974–5, is known to have covered an area of some 95 by 70 yards, but none of this is now visible. The museum in Little London contains the best of the small finds (Tuesdays to Saturdays, 10–5.30, all year round; 1 on fig 9). The site of the amphitheatre (2 on fig 9) is visible as a hollow surrounded by a low elliptical bank in a recreation-area on the east side of the city, reached by a passage called Whyke Lane from A259 (The Hornet); according to its excavator in 1934, it was built about AD 80

and abandoned at the end of the second century. The walls
follow the Roman line but no Roman masonry is visible.
There is a portion of second-century mosaic on show *in situ* in
the south aisle of the Cathedral's retrochoir (3 on fig 9).
And, for the record, Messrs Morant's shop in West Street has
a fragment of black-and-white mosaic from a bath-house; and
part of a massive flint foundation is visible in the cellars of the

9   *Chichester, plan*

Dolphin and Anchor Hotel (perhaps belonging to a
colonnade on the south side of the forum). Much more
important is an inscription (4) found in 1723 and now placed
in the wall under the portico of the Assembly Rooms in North
Street (fig 10). This records a temple to Neptune and
Minerva erected by a guild of artisans (*collegium fabrorum*) on
the authority of Tiberius Claudius Cogidubnus, who is
described as *rex magnus Augusti in Britannia*, 'great king of the
emperor in Britain'; the title is paralleled on inscriptions
elsewhere in the Empire. This Cogidubnus established his
kingdom in the Chichester region and did his best to foster
romanization in the early years of the conquest. In return the
Romans respected his authority as a native client-king and only
after his death was the area formally assimilated into the Roman
province. He is recorded by Tacitus as one 'who maintained his
unswerving loyalty down to our own times'. It was as a
reward for this loyalty that the next site, Fishbourne, was
erected.

Fishbourne* (SU 8404) is one of the success stories of post-
war British archaeology. It has, rightly, attracted enormous
publicity and brought renown to its excavator Barry Cunliffe,
who began digging here as an undergraduate in 1961 and was
a professor before it was opened to the public in 1968.
Visitors should be equally grateful to the late Ivan Margary,
whose generosity saved the area from housing-development

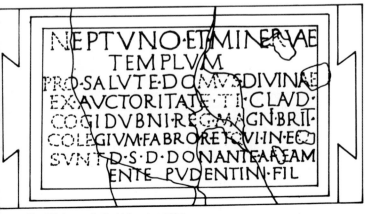

10   Chichester, the Cogidubnus inscription

and allowed the modern cover-building to be erected. The site lies 1¼m west of Chichester on the A27 to Portsmouth, and can be visited every day from 10 a.m. (March to November), closing at 4 p.m. in November, 5 p.m. in March, April and October, and 6 p.m. from May to September; from December to February it is open on Sundays only, 10–4.

The first occupation at Fishbourne was military: the remains of two timber store-buildings excavated under the east wing of the later palace belong to what is probably a supply-depot for the fort underlying Chichester in the early years of the conquest. The depot was soon cleared away, and sometime in the late 40's or early 50's a timber house with a

11 Fishbourne, first-century mosaic (polychrome)

separate building (perhaps a servants' range) was constructed. It had clay or mortar floors, and there were traces of painted plaster, so a man of some status must have lived here. Then, in the 60's, the first masonry building was erected at Fishbourne. Its site lies astride the main road and so could not be completely excavated, but trenching was able to show that it comprised a large colonnaded garden, a bath-suite, a set of living-rooms and servants' quarters. The whole was elaborately decorated with stucco and painted plaster; its floors were paved in mosaic or marble. It was no ordinary building; yet its magnificence was to be far outstripped by what was to come.

Sometime after 75, a start was made on the building of the great palace which has made Fishbourne famous. It is important to realize that only a small portion of the whole complex is visible today: it originally consisted of four wings arranged around a formal garden. The main living-rooms of the owner lay on the south, and are now largely under the A27; this wing had a colonnade on both sides, overlooking the formal garden on one side and a natural garden stretching down to the sea on the other. The official wing was on the west; its chief room, in the centre, was an apsed audience-chamber where the owner would have received official visitors. The east wing contained an entrance-hall designed to impress (as, indeed, was the whole palace), and suites of rooms arranged around courtyards, probably for visitors of lower rank as the standard of comfort was less than that of the north wing. The latter, protected in its entirety by the modern cover-building, had a sumptuous series of guest-rooms ranged about two private courtyards. Servants' quarters must lie elsewhere, still to be uncovered.

We have here, then, a palace of some ten acres – a staggering complex of colonnades, halls and rooms magnificently adorned with painted plaster, stucco, and mosaic, built by an army of skilled craftsmen from the continent, at an estimated cost in modern-day terms of about two million pounds. It is true that some British villas approached the size of Fishbourne, but that was not until the fourth century: for the first century AD the Fishbourne Palace is entirely without parallel not only in Britain but in the whole of Europe outside Italy: it is a piece of Italy transplanted into a distant, newly-conquered province. Who, then, could be the owner of such a palace – a high-ranking Roman official, or a local landowner of great distinction? This is where Cogidubnus (above, p. 49) fits into the picture. For a Roman official residence to be built so close to the capital of a loyal ally would have been an intolerable snub; and it is therefore more likely (though we shall never know for certain) that the palace was the home of king Cogidubnus in his old age, and that the earlier structures at Fishbourne (the timber house and the first masonry building) represent the earlier stages of his rise to luxury.

Drastic changes occurred *c.* 90/100 AD, no doubt soon after Cogidubnus' death. A bath-suite was inserted into the north wing, and another into the east, suggesting the splitting up of the palace into separate units (the palace baths lay at the SE corner – convenient for the owner, but a long way for his guests in the north wing!). Various other modifications to the north wing, including the laying of more mosaics, will be

12   Fishbourne, the garden (1969)

noted in turn below; the villa, though lacking its former
grandeur, still maintained a level of affluence markedly higher
than elsewhere in the contemporary Romano–British
countryside. Finally, at the end of the third century, a
disastrous fire brought the life of Fishbourne to a close until
its resurrection in 1960, the year of the laying of a water-main
which caused its discovery.

On arriving at the site, first pay a visit to the museum where
all the phases described above are imaginatively set out and
illustrated with photographs, models and plans; here too are
the principal small finds. In the main concourse is a model of
the palace as it may have appeared in about AD 80. From here
you can begin your tour of the north wing.

The first room (labelled 1) which you see on the left of the
viewing-platform was also the last addition: this hypocaust
was still being constructed when fire destroyed the whole
building at the end of the third century. No trace of the floor
above was found, and it had probably never been laid. The

floor-level here was in the process of being raised: fragments of the mosaic laid when the palace was first built can be seen on the right. Of the floor in 2, of second-century date, little remains, but the adjoining room (5) has preserved its polychrome floor (also second-century) which can be viewed either as a pair of scallop-shells or as the splayed tail of a peacock, the main body of the bird destroyed but the feet (?) surviving. On the other side of the catwalk (rooms 3 and 4) are two simple geometric mosaics and a solid dividing wall which *do* belong to the original palace; these floors seem to have survived later use without the need for replacement. (The masonry in the corner of room 4 represents the flue of a second-century oven.) Moving on, you reach a courtyard of the palace-phase, originally open to the sky. Its stone gutter has been largely replaced in modern materials. The tiles seen here are part of the collapsed superstructure. Opposite (behind you) is (7) the best-preserved mosaic at Fishbourne, of mid-second-century date and again, therefore, laid when the palace had ceased to operate as a single unit: remember that only half of the visible mosaics belong to the original palace. The central roundel depicts a winged cupid riding a dolphin, with sea-panthers and sea-horses in the surrounding semi-circles. Compare the two sea-horses: that nearer the catwalk is much more skilfully executed. Note, too, how the guilloche border which surrounds the mosaic changes its colour-composition. Clearly several craftsmen were at work
** on the same mosaic. At the same time as the laying of this floor, the little rooms on either side (6 and unnumbered) were given hypocausts; only the *pilae* bases remain, the heating proving so ineffective that they were destroyed in the third century, when the mosaic in an adjoining room (8) was laid. This is a simple knot-motif and a guilloche circle surrounded by dolphins.

Now come down the steps and examine room 12, which contains the best preserved of the first-century palace mosaics – a pleasing geometric design – as it was never refloored even when a timber partition chopped it in two. The success of the design is shown by the poor imitation of it which was laid in the mid-second century in the room beyond (14). Return to the cat-walk now, which skirts rooms 9–11. The skeleton in 9 was buried in the ruins of the building some time after its final destruction. 10–11 have plain or simple mosaic floors laid in the second or third century. After this, on the right, is the mosaic already mentioned (14). The primary interest of the room beyond (13) is that it displays two superimposed mosaics, the original floor being replaced about AD 100, when the palace first changed hands. The centre of the new mosaic depicted a head of Medusa, of which part of her right eye and eyebrow and some of her snaky hair can be made out (upside-down from this angle). The floor has been much damaged by medieval ploughing, but enough remains to show its rather poor technical standard, and it is perhaps the work of a local, not a foreign, mosaicist. Behind you is the site of another of the open courtyards of the original palace.

Of the north wing beyond this point very little remains, as before the mid-second century the whole of it, including a newly-inserted bath-suite, was demolished because of serious subsidence. Parts of three mosaics, however, which belonged to the original palace, still survive. Little is left of one (19), largely destroyed by the water-main trench of 1960. The next room (20) has a fine, if fragmentary, polychrome mosaic (fig 11). The central portion is destroyed, but enough remains of the surrounding rosettes and ivy-leaves, the band of guilloche, and the corner vases, to show the skill of the mosaicist both in his mastery of composition and in his use of colour. The adjoining mosaic (21) is much simpler but quite effective. The small white diamond on its border is clearly not part of the design and may be the craftsman's signature. A few fragments of the early-second-century bath-suite survive at the far end of the cover-building.

Now you should go out into the garden, flanked by parts of the east and west wings. The plan of the former is marked out in modern materials (note especially the entrance hall with its fountain), but the latter is at present grassed over. What you see here is not guesswork: excavation revealed the pattern of the bedding-trenches, and these have been followed in the reconstruction. Although pollen analysis could not determine what shrub was used, box is the most likely and that is what has been planted (fig 12). At the west end of the central path (remember that only half the formal garden is visible today), just in front of the steps leading up to the site of the audience-chamber, is a square construction made of tiles, probably the base for a statue. Finally, going back towards the modern entrance along the outside wall of the west wing, you reach the NW corner, where the gutter, column-bases, and the projecting corner of the stone foundation for a water-tank (to feed the fountains which adorned the garden), can be seen. Here your visit to this extraordinary site ends. Nowhere else in Britain will you see a Roman garden, nowhere else will you see mosaics laid as early as some of those in the north wing: such is the uniqueness of Fishbourne.

Another villa-site can easily be reached from Chichester: it is at **Bignor*** (SU 9814), a village situated about 14 miles away, midway between the A285 and the A29, but more conveniently approached from the latter (minor road via West Burton, leaving the A29 near the inn at the foot of Bury Hill). It is open from 1st March to 31st October, every day except Monday, 10–6, except in March and October when it closes at 5; also on Bank Holidays and Mondays too, June to September. In contrast to Fishbourne, Bignor has long been known. It was found in 1811 and the entire plan of the villa was uncovered in the following years. But it was not until partial re-excavation in the late 1950's and early 60's that anything of its historical sequence was revealed. We now know that the first stone building, a simple rectangular construction, was not erected before about AD 225, though a timber house or houses preceded it. It was given a corridor and small wings later in the third century, but only in the fourth was the villa expanded to enclose a courtyard. To get some idea of its size in this last phase, stand with your back to the modern huts and face the driveway up to the villa. On your right the west wing has been marked out: in front of you, part of the corridor serving the south wing is exposed. The south wing ended at the point where a modern hut covers the Medusa mosaic (far left, by the trees), and another corridor then turned to join up with the north wing, half of which is represented by the huts behind you. The present car-park covers about two-thirds of the area of the Roman courtyard. Farm-buildings lay further still to the left, and the whole complex was enclosed by a boundary wall. A model of the villa, together with some of the finds, can be seen in a room, still floored with its Roman mosaic, to the right of the

present entrance. Here too, in the corner at the far end, is a
reconstruction-drawing showing the villa on fire and the
inhabitants escaping to safety: but there is no evidence of
destruction by a looting party, and it is more likely that the
great house declined gradually until its final abandonment in
the early fifth century.

The glory of Bignor is its splendid series of mosaic
pavements laid in the mid-fourth century. The mosaic in the
first room (left of entrance) is divided into two parts: one
represents a large well-drawn eagle carrying off the shepherd
Ganymede to serve as Jupiter's cup-bearer on Mount
Olympus; Ganymede, naked except for boots, a red cap and a
red cloak, carries his shepherd's crook. The rest of the room
contains six hexagonal panels of dancing girls, now much
destroyed, with an ornamental stone water-basin in the centre.
If symbolism is to be looked for in these mosaics, perhaps the
soul's ascent to heaven (Ganymede) and the joy that awaits it
(the dancers) is the meaning here.

Moving to your left from the room with the mosaic of the
dancers, you come to an 80-foot length of well-preserved
geometric mosaic, uncovered in 1975. This is the western part
of the villa's north corridor, which was 230 feet long in all.
The lead water-pipe here carried excess water from the basin
in the previous room. At the far end of the corridor, on the
left, two steps inadequately bridge the difference in level
between the north wing and the beginning of the west wing. A
very naive and badly decayed mosaic here represents a head
of Medusa in the centre and busts of the Seasons (heavily
restored) in the corners. Next, on the right, is a fragment of
mosaic with a dolphin and the letters TƎR: this is probably
the signature of the mosaicist, whose name was Terentius or
something similar. Further on another mosaic depicts a
powerful head of Winter, heavily muffled in cloak and hood,
with a bare twig over her left shoulder. Now come out
of the hut and go right round the back of it. Laid out on
the grass here is the plan of the west wing, marked out in
different colours to distinguish separate building-periods. The
next hut you reach, on the left, contains the best-preserved
pavement, restored in 1929 partly with modern materials. The
main portion of the floor is destroyed, exposing the hypocaust
pilae and flue-tiles in the walls. Of the mosaic here only parts

of five dancing cupids survive, but in the apse is a superb, delicate rendering of the goddess Venus, with head-dress and halo, flanked by birds and festoons. Below it is a charming panel of winged cupids engaged in gladiatorial combat. After this the final door leads you to a room with a pleasing geometric mosaic in excellent condition, and then back to the Ganymede room, but there was no opening between the two in antiquity.

Finally, do not forget to cross the car-park to the trees at the far side to see the cold plunge-bath, and beyond it, the floor of the undressing room. This has a central panel depicting the snaky head of Medusa, which is often used on floors as a charm to ward off evil (according to the myth, a single gaze on it would turn you into stone).

The third outstanding villa-site in SE England is at **Lullingstone*** in Kent (TQ 5365) [AM; SSM], reached by a road (signposted) off the A225 in Eynsford. That a Roman building stood here had been known from the eighteenth century, but systematic excavation began only in 1949 and continued for 12 years. The first stone house, with a simple

13 Lullingstone in the fourth century, reconstruction-drawing

range of rooms served by a back corridor, was built towards
the close of the first century. A major change occurred about
100 years later when a new owner added a bath-suite to one
end of the villa and a series of cult-rooms to the other. He was
a man of some distinction and wealth, his rooms being
adorned with two portrait-busts of his ancestors, finely
executed in Greek marble. About AD 200 the villa was
suddenly deserted: the owner had to leave in a hurry, for even
the busts were left behind. After lying derelict for over
50 years, it was reoccupied by a new family in the last quarter
of the third century. The cult-rooms were demolished and a
long heated room built over them; the baths were refurbished;
and a large granary (no longer visible) was built between the
house and the river. From now until the early fifth century the
villa was continuously occupied. Mosaic floors were laid in the
mid-fourth century in the new apsidal dining-room and in the
main living-room. Then, about 360–70, the owner became a
Christian, and part of the villa was converted to Christian use.
At the same time the baths were filled in, and a little later the
granary was pulled down. Finally, in the early fifth century, a
fire destroyed the villa, whether deliberate or accidental is
unknown.

Passing the ticket-office and moving clockwise, turn the
corner and pause in front of the Deep Room, labelled no. 3. It
was probably first used for storing grain, but in the late
second century a pit containing ritual water was sunk into the
centre of the room and a niche built in the left-hand wall,
labelled 4. This was decorated with a fine painting of three,
now two, water-nymphs; the head of one is still in good
condition, with green leaves in her hair and water falling from
her breasts. The room was presumably dedicated to the
worship of these water-goddesses, and was connected on the
right to another cult-room, surrounded by a corridor on all
four sides (one side of the corridor is marked out in pink
gravel, labelled 2, but the rest is now under the modern
concrete concourse). All this was swept away in later
alteration and only the tiled stairway which served the cult-
rooms is clearly visible now (to the right of and behind the
Deep Room). In the late third century the Deep Room was
blocked off and the niche containing the water-nymphs
covered up: one of them was totally destroyed and the central

portion of what remained was marred by the erection of a shelf, as can be seen from the plain plaster (restored) in the middle of the fresco. The busts belonging to the previous owner were also placed here, on the steps labelled 5; the originals are now in the British Museum, but casts may be seen in a showcase at Lullingstone. Meanwhile, a new long heated room was constructed to the right of the Deep Room, concealing the second-century staircase and cult-rooms. Its floor was of timber supported on wooden rafters and therefore, of course, no longer visible: all we can see now is the area below the floor where the hot air circulated, passing from one compartment to another through the flue-arch prominently visible here. Flue tiles built in the thickness of the walls can be seen in the farther room.

In the second half of the fourth century, as we know from a reconstruction of the painted plaster which was found in tiny fragments among fallen debris in the Deep Room, the room on the first floor above the latter was converted into what was probably a Christian house-chapel, although no specific object was found to *prove* its use in Christian worship. Along the

14   Lullingstone, mosaic of Europa and the bull

end-wall facing us were painted six human figures in beaded robes, with arms outstretched (the way early Christians prayed), separated by ornate columns resting on a dado. Next to the figures, on the left-hand wall, was a large painted representation of the Christian Chi-Rho monogram within a wreath. Perhaps there was also an altar on the wooden floor, but no sign of it was found in the collapsed debris. The chapel was approached by an anteroom (labelled 8), which had another Chi-Rho, and a vestibule (7, top right hand corner). This house-chapel, and the probable churches at Silchester and Richborough, constitute the earliest known Christian shrines in Britain. The original wall-plaster is now in the British Museum (fig 118), but copies can be seen at Lullingstone on the wall by the exit.

Moving on, and passing the reconstruction-drawing (fig 13), you reach the bath-house at the far end, built at the close of the second century and demolished 200 years later. The various rooms – hot, cold, and tepid – are labelled, and there are two plunge-baths at one end (underneath the walk-way), the smaller being a fourth-century addition. Turning the corner, and passing the well which supplied the house with water, you can go up the balcony and look down on the whole building from above. In one room a large fourth-century pot, made at Farnham in Surrey, marks the site of a courtyard-cum-kitchen (11), but the main feature which strikes us is, of course, the splendid mosaic floors laid in the mid-fourth century. That nearer us is the dining-room: the couches would have been arranged on the semi-circular border to look down on the main panel of Europa being abducted by Jupiter in the guise of a bull, accompanied by winged cupids on either side (fig 14). The smiling bull, evidently delighted with his prize, leaps over the sea (the dark blue portion of mosaic) with lively charm. Above is a Latin verse-couplet referring to a passage in the Aeneid of Virgil – a reflection of the owner's literary tastes – and can be translated: 'if jealous Juno had seen the swimming of the bull, she might have more justly gone to the halls of Aeolus'. Juno was the wife of Jupiter; Aeolus was ruler of the winds and therefore capable of producing a tempest to upset Jupiter's amorous adventure. Part of the mosaic has been disfigured here by burning rafters in the final conflagration.

The mosaic in the principal room (9) has a skilfully-executed central panel. It depicts the hero Bellerophon, seated on the winged horse Pegasus, killing the Chimaera, which is a monster with a lion's head and serpent's tail. Surrounding this and much less realistically drawn are four dolphins and two opened-out mussel-shells, representing the sea-journey which Bellerophon had to make in order to carry out his task. Heads of the Seasons fill out the four corners – Winter, an old woman with a hooded cloak (top left); Spring, a girl with a bird on her shoulder (top right); and Summer, a middle-aged woman with corn in her hair (upside down). Autumn was destroyed when a fence was being put up in the eighteenth century. The rest of the mosaic is composed of a medley of geometrical patterns, poorly designed and laid, and clearly the work of the craftsman's assistants. The finding of these pagan mosaics so close to the almost contemporary Christian rooms suggests a symbolic meaning for them, and it is significant that Bellerophon also appears on a Christian mosaic in the British Museum. His killing of the Chimaera represents the triumph of life over death and good over evil – the Roman equivalent of St George and the dragon; and the rape of Europa probably symbolizes the freeing of the soul from the body at death.

Showcases at Lullingstone give a selection of the many finds from the site. One of the most interesting is a complete set of gaming-pieces displayed on the ground floor near the exit. They were part of the grave-goods of a young man and woman, and the skeleton of one of them, in a lead coffin, is also displayed here. They were buried in a mausoleum constructed in the early fourth century on the terrace behind the villa, but not now visible. One other structure there, a small circular temple erected c. AD 80–90, can be made out from the window nearest the exit on the balcony, by looking towards the hollow on the right.

The three villas so far mentioned are among the most luxurious of their type known in Britain. A more typical building of the Romano–British countryside is represented by the more modest structure uncovered in 1972–8 in the Fordcroft district of **Orpington** (TQ 467676). This is probably a small villa standing on a slight slope above the river Cray, and although Roman sites are thick on the ground in the Orpington area (for another see Appendix 1, p. 408), they are

more likely to be individual farms rather than part of a
nucleated settlement. The building visible at Fordcroft
measures approximately 42 feet by 21 feet and its walls still
stand up to four feet high. It incorporates a small bath-suite
including rectangular and apsed plunge baths and two
heated rooms, but the floors and *pilae* of these have been
completely robbed. The building probably dates to the third
century, but coins and pottery indicate occupation on the site
from the late first to the fourth century. Later the area was
used as an Anglo-Saxon burial ground, of which 75 graves
were uncovered nearby in the 1960's and more during recent
work in the immediate vicinity of the Roman building. To
reach the site from the centre of Orpington, go north from
High Street and follow the one-way system, turning right at
Perry Hall Road, then left, and left at the traffic lights
(signposted Central London, A2). Turn left at the next traffic
lights (Poverest Road) and you will see the cover-building
almost immediately on the left. The site is not, however, ever
open on a regular basis, and intending visitors should make
prior arrangements with the Bromley Museum, Church Hill,
Orpington (tel. 0689 31551), which contains a selection of local
finds (daily except Thurs. and Sun., 9–5).

Another villa, somewhat larger, is known five miles to the
south-west at **Keston** (TQ 4163), and although nothing of it is
now visible part of an adjacent Roman cemetery is. It lies in
the grounds of what is now private property, and although the
site is owned by Bromley Council access to it is private;
permission to visit, therefore, should be sought at the house on
arrival. The site is situated on the west side of the A233,
the Bromley Common to Westerham road, on a sharp bend
just south of its junction with the B-road from Hayes
Common, adjacent to the drive to the house named Warbank.
The site has been known for over 150 years and sporadically
dug on a number of occasions, but proper excavation and
consolidation was not carried out until 1967–8. The main
feature is a large circular tomb strengthened by six buttresses,
originally rendered externally with red plaster and perhaps 20
feet high. It was clearly a monumental tomb, probably for the
family who owned the villa, which was situated on the lower
part of the hill. Adjoining it is a rectangular tomb with a large
buttress on one side, and from it came the stone coffin set up

nearby on the perimeter of the site. This coffin has quite a history of its own: it was found about 1800 and performed a variety of tasks in the district, including that of a garden-box and a horse-trough; in 1941 it was smashed by a German bomb and only in 1968 was it restored and brought back to the site. A third tomb had eluded all the earlier excavators as it lay between two buttresses of the large circular tomb. It consists of a small chamber covered by a vault made of tiles set in mortar; a lead casket with the remains of an adult cremation was found inside. This tomb is now protected by a plastic cover. A number of simple graves were also found in the area but are not now visible. Pottery from them suggests a mid-second- to mid-third-century date for the cemetery, but the monumental tombs may be later.

Another burial site is at **Stone-by-Faversham** (TQ 9961), which lies by a group of trees in a field 100 yards north of the A2 opposite a minor road leading to Newnham; this is at the foot of Judd's Hill, $\frac{1}{2}$m west of Ospringe and $1\frac{1}{4}$m west of Faversham. Most of the masonry here belongs to a medieval church, but it incorporates a square Roman building into the west part of its chancel. The Roman work is unmistakable, consisting of regularly-tooled stones separated after each layer by tile bonding-courses. This is especially clear on the exterior south face (that nearest the road), where the break between the neat Roman work and the medieval masonry without the tile-courses is obvious. The Roman building is entered on the west by a massive stone sill, and the pivot-hole for the door is clearly visible. It was built in the fourth century and is most probably a mausoleum. No trace of a burial was found in the excavations of 1967–8, but it may have been robbed in medieval times or in later probes at the site. Finds from many other burials in and around Ospringe are displayed in the Maison Dieu Museum (open irregularly, summer only), $\frac{3}{4}$m east (junction of A2 with Water Lane). The Roman settlement of DVROLEVVM has been sought hereabouts, but the earthworks on Judd's Hill, sometimes claimed to be the site, are probably due to landscape gardening, and large-scale excavation in 1977 near the Maison Dieu in Ospringe village revealed no trace of a Roman settlement. Others would place DVROLEVVM further west, near Sittingbourne.

Chapter 2

Wessex and the South-West

Hampshire, Wiltshire, Dorset, South Somerset, Devon and Cornwall

(Appendix I only – Berkshire) For map see pp. 66–7

In AD 44, with SE England reasonably secure, the invading army split up into separate units to attempt the subjugation of the rest of Britain. The division chosen to advance south-westwards was the Second Augustan Legion, then commanded by the man who was later to become the Emperor Vespasian. His biographer Suetonius has left us the bare information that he fought thirty battles, overcame two powerful tribes and more than twenty hill-forts, and reduced the Isle of Wight to surrender. Archaeology, however, has been able to shed light on the nature of the opposition offered by the two tribes mentioned, the Durotriges of Dorset and south Somerset, and the Dumnonii of Devon and Cornwall; and this opposition resulted in the building of a series of forts which held the area in check during the early years of the Roman occupation. Few of these have left any features traceable on the ground today. Even the base of the Second Legion is still not known, but a 42-acre fort near Wimborne Minster in Dorset (not visible) is one possibility. By about AD 55, however, the Legion was in Exeter, where important excavations have revealed its fortress.

Ramparts of the smaller forts, designed for auxiliary forces with perhaps a sprinkling of legionaries, are visible at Hod Hill (see below) and, less impressively, at Waddon Hill in Dorset, Wiveliscombe in Somerset, North Tawton and Bury Barton in Devon and Nanstallon in Cornwall (Appendix I). Excavation at the last indicated an occupation of *c.* AD 55–80. Better preserved are two fortlets on the north Devon coast, at **Old Burrow** (SS 7849) and **Martinhoe** (SS 6649). Excavation in the early 1960's showed them to be successive, not contemporary, constructions. The former was the earlier, with occupation beginning perhaps about AD 48 and lasting only a short time. It was abandoned in favour of the slightly less exposed site at Martinhoe, where a fortlet was built about AD

60 and excavated on the final subjugation of the Silures of South Wales in 78: for these posts were designed to patrol the Bristol Channel as well as to keep an eye on possible trouble in Devon. Accommodation at Martinhoe was provided by a couple of timber barracks for about 80 soldiers, but at Old Burrow the men lived in tents. All that can be seen at either site today are the earth defences, which in both cases consist of an outer, circular rampart and ditch with an entrance on the south, and an inner square rampart and ditch or ditches with an entrance on the north. The position of the entrances ensured that an attacker who had stormed the outer gate would have to traverse half the circuit of the outer compound before attempting the gate to the fortlet proper. The earthworks at Old Burrow are better preserved than those of Martinhoe, where part of the outer rampart has slipped over

Martinhoe   Old Burrow

Devon

Exeter •

• Trethevy
• Tintagel

Cornwall

Gwennap Pit

Chysauster   St Hilary
• Breage

Carn Euny

to the
Scilly Isles

the cliff. The former is reached from the A39
(Minehead–Lynmouth), by the first path on the right (north)
of the road ½m after crossing the Somerset–Devon border at
County Gate (if you are coming from Minehead). The hamlet
of Martinhoe is reached by a minor road leaving the A39 at
Martinhoe Cross, 4m west of Lynton. Follow the track

leading north out of the village, keeping the farmyard to your
right, and then take the right fork, going through two gates
on each side of a cattle pen. When this track finally ends walk
across two fields to the fortlet.

The most interesting of the early Roman military works in
the area covered by this chapter is the fort built, unusually,
inside the ramparts of the prehistoric hill-fort of **Hod Hill*** in
Dorset (ST 8510). Take the Shaftesbury road (A350) for three
miles out of Blandford Forum, turn left at 'The White Horse'
in Stourpaine and right again at the crossroads. Keep straight
until the road peters out at a stream, and then follow the path

along the stream to the right for 250 yds and so up the track to
the SE corner of the hill-fort, which is here entered by a breach
of medieval or modern origin. The main pre-Roman entrances
were at the NE and SW, while the gap in the middle of the
eastern side was made by the Romans. Once inside the
ramparts, the visitor will notice in front of him a mass of
circular platforms and depressions. These mark the sites of the
huts occupied by Iron Age peoples immediately prior to the
Roman invasion; and excavation has shown that one of them,
surrounded by a hexagonal enclosure, was the target for
Roman artillery-fire during the assault on Hod·Hill in AD 44.
It is assumed, therefore, that this was the chieftain's hut and,
as no evidence was found of fighting at the gates or of
massacre within, this bombardment alone was apparently
sufficient to secure the surrender of the hill-fort's inhabitants.
The Romans then proceeded to build a garrison-fort inside
the NW corner of the hill-fort (diagonally opposite the corner
at which you entered), using the prehistoric ramparts to form
its north and west sides, but building their own defences on
the south and east. The latter have been damaged by
ploughing over the centuries, but are still impressively
preserved. The Roman rampart consisted of packed chalk,
faced with turf back and front, and was originally 10 feet high
to rampart-walk; it still stands to about five feet near the NE
angle. Outside the rampart were three ditches, all only about
five feet deep but skilfully designed. The innermost two each
had a nasty ankle-breaking channel at the bottom. Then came
a flat platform 55 feet wide before the outer ditch, which was
so shaped as to be easy to cross in attack but deceptively
difficult in retreat. These ditches are interrupted by causeways
leading to the south and east gates, both defended by *titula*
(visible in fig 15). The entrance in the NW corner of the hill-
fort is also Roman, as is the causeway crossing the ditch here.
It was made to provide the garrison with convenient access to
water from the River Stour below.

The entire plan of the interior of the fort was recovered in
excavations between 1951 and 1958. These revealed the
foundation-slots cut in the chalk to receive the timber-framed
buildings of which the fort was composed. The layout of these
indicates that the garrison consisted of about 600 legionaries
supplemented by an auxiliary cavalry-unit 250 strong. It was

evacuated after a fire had destroyed some of the buildings, probably by accident, and coins and pottery show that this cannot have happened more than about eight years after the original building of the fort in AD 44 or 45.

Hod Hill, as we have seen, can be included among the twenty hill-forts which Suetonius records as being captured under Vespasian's command. Much more dramatic evidence, however, was found in excavations in 1934–7 by Sir Mortimer Wheeler at the most famous and impressive of all British hill-forts, **Maiden Castle*** (SY 6688) [AM; A]. It is reached by the signposted road off the Weymouth road (A 354) in the southern outskirts of Dorchester. The massive triple ramparts which surround the site were erected in the early first century BC, and the defences are even more intricate at the two entrances. The west gate (that nearer the car-park) is the more strongly defended and has not been excavated. It is not, therefore, known if the Romans attacked it, but it seems more likely that Vespasian concentrated his assault at the less complex east gate. Here, in contrast to Hod Hill, the Romans met with tough resistance. First their artillery fired some rounds of

15   *Hod Hill from the air, looking south*

arrows, one of which landed in a defender's spine; the
vertebra and arrow-head are now in a case in the Dorchester
Museum. Then an advance party gained access to the interior
and set some huts on fire, and the resulting smokescreen
enabled the gate to be stormed by the rest of the troops. It
cannot have been easy: try running up and down the slopes at
the east gate today, then imagine determined natives raining
sling-stones down on you, and you will appreciate that even
for tough, well-disciplined Roman soldiers the battle cannot
have been a walk-over. This is confirmed by the fury they
showed on gaining entrance: the inhabitants, regardless of age
or sex, were brutally hacked down before a halt to the
slaughter was called. The natives were left to give a hasty
burial to their dead. The evidence for all this can be read in
Wheeler's report and some of it is displayed in Dorchester
Museum. No trace of the battle can be seen at the site today.

There are, however, Roman remains visible at Maiden
Castle, though they date from nearly 350 years later than the
battle of AD 44. In the closing years of the fourth century, at a
time when Christianity was the official religion but paganism

16   Maiden Castle, the Roman temple

still apparently flourished, a new temple was built in the
eastern half of the hill-fort. It is one of the best examples of
the typical Romano–Celtic temple to be seen in Britain, and
consists of the normal central shrine and surrounding
ambulatory (fig 16). Next to it is a tiny two-roomed
construction interpreted as the priest's dwelling. The name of
the deity worshipped is not known, but as representations of
several were found in the excavation there may have been a
plurality of deities. The very slight remains of another Roman
temple can be seen a short distance away, on **Jordon Hill**
(SY 6982) [AM; A], dug in 1843 and 1931–2. Here, however,
the outer wall is not visible and has not in fact been found:
the stone-work had probably been completely robbed and its
position escaped the notice of the excavators. Coins indicate
that it flourished, like the one at Maiden Castle, in the second
half of the fourth century. To reach it, follow the A353 out of
Weymouth, and keep straight on where the A-road swings
inland by a filling-station (DOE signpost missing in 1979).
The temple lies on the brow of the hill, to the left of the drive,
after ¼m.

The native occupation of Maiden Castle did not cease
immediately after the battle of 44, but it does not appear to
have continued beyond AD 70. We must assume that by that
date its inhabitants had been shifted elsewhere, probably to
the new town which the Romans founded in the valley below,
at **Dorchester*** (SY 6990). Finds and topography make a
military origin certain, but no structural remains of a fort
have yet been identified, unless a defensive ditch located in
1972, allegedly of late-first-century date, belonged to it. The
town which took its place was known as DVRNOVARIA and
served as a tribal capital for the Durotriges, though in the
fourth century it may have shared this role with Ilchester in
Somerset (Appendix I). At any rate it was then that both
towns reached the height of their prosperity, and the many
mosaics found in and around Dorchester indicate the
existence of a flourishing school of mosaicists in the town at
that date. To the fourth century, too, belongs the town-house
in Colliton Park, situated behind County Hall in the extreme
NW corner of the Roman walled area. It is reached by a path
from the Hardy Statue, and can be visited at any time. The
building consists of two separate ranges, both built in the

early fourth century but enlarged *c*. 340. The south range (that nearer the entrance-gate) first consisted of the three central rooms only, but in the enlargement the big room (nearest the gate), the corridor and the heated room at the end were built. A dwarf column, found amongst rubbish in the adjacent well, has been re-erected on the corridor wall. The heated room is an excellent example of a channelled hypocaust. Some of the paving-flags of the floor are in position and the hollows once containing flue-tiles for the escaping hot air can be seen in the walls. Opposite this room is the shed covering a geometric mosaic. Next to this is a rare survival from Roman Britain – the splayed opening for a window, originally closed by a wooden frame and glass. Fragments of this had collapsed, together with the stone framework, into the room below. Mosaics were laid in all the rooms of this western range, but except for the one on show only fragments survived. Another hypocaust is visible in one of these rooms. Coins cease *c*. 375, when the cobbled path by the well was built, but slum occupation went on, perhaps into the fifth century. Another mosaic panel, found in 1967, has been preserved *in situ* in the Wadham Stringer showrooms at 26, Trinity Street and can be viewed on request to the management. But little is known in detail about this or other houses in Roman Dorchester, and the only public building extensively excavated is the public baths, found in 1977 in the grounds of Wollaston House. These, however, have had to give way to modern development and have not been preserved.

The course of the defences of Roman Dorchester is not precisely known over their entire circuit, but they enclosed an area of between 80 and 90 acres. An earth bank and ditch came first, towards the end of the second century, and this was fronted with a stone wall at some later date, probably just before AD 300. A rather wretched fragment of this, penned behind railings and capped by a modern brick wall, is visible in West Walk, a short distance south of the Hardy Statue. Only the core of the wall is left, at most eight feet high, and displaying a double course of limestone bonding-slabs near the top. Nearby, in High West Street, is the Dorset County Museum's important archaeological collection (Mon.–Sat. 10–5, closed Sundays and Sat. 1–2). The most interesting items to note are the finds from Maiden Castle, the coin-hoard from South Street, the table legs (fig 1, Contents page) and other products from the Kimmeridge shale industry, and the mosaic floors which reflect the opulence of fourth-century Dorchester. A new archaeology gallery was opened in 1984.

The rest of the Roman remains in the Dorchester neighbourhood lie outside the walled area of DVRNOVARIA. The most impressive is the amphitheatre, known as Maumbury Rings, which lies on the left (east) side of Weymouth Avenue just before the railway bridge in the southern outskirts of the town. The earthworks started life as a Neolithic monument c. 2,000 BC, when the banks were about 11 feet high. The Romans converted it into an amphitheatre by lowering the ground level to create an arena floor and raising the banks to their present 30 or so feet. There was a timbered gangway round the arena, which had its principal entrance on the north, less wide than the present gap, and a lesser entrance on the south. It appears to have been built during the second half of the first century, surely c. AD 70–80 rather than earlier, and had an active life of no more than 80 and possibly as little as 50 years. Later ages employed it in other ways. In the seventeenth century it was used as a gun-emplacement and the internal terraces on the banks belong to this period. In the eighteenth century it was used as a place of public execution, and as recently as 1952 the people of Dorset assembled here to greet HM the Queen.

The second Roman feature outside the walls is interesting rather than spectacular. It is the aqueduct, built in the late first century, which carried water to the town over a winding course some twelve miles long. It is a puzzle to understand why it was ever necessary when water could easily be obtained by sinking wells; perhaps civic pride was responsible. It consisted of an open leat about five feet wide and three feet deep, now visible (in part) as an embanked shelf following the contours of the hillside. Take the Bridport road at the roundabout by the Hardy Statue and then turn immediately right along Poundbury Road. On the right, after you cross the railway bridge, are the ramparts of the prehistoric Poundbury Camp. Walk to the NW corner of the latter, and just outside, near the entrance to the railway-tunnel, you will see the shelf of the aqueduct. It is particularly prominent

curving round the hillside away to the left, by the river. After
¼m the road descends steeply and the aqueduct can be faintly
seen on the left on Fordington Down before returning close to
the road: it is particularly clear as the road climbs again, for
the aqueduct has become a field-boundary and a cattle-track.
The rest of its course is less well preserved.

Finally, mention may be made of two other relics in the
neighbourhood of Dorchester, this time to the east. One is a
finely-carved marble tombstone which was erected to a certain
Carinus, in the mid-second century, by his wife and three
children. It is now inside St George's church at Fordington, a
suburb of Dorchester. The other is what is almost certainly a
Roman milestone, nearly six feet high, which can be seen on
the south side of the A35 one mile NE of Dorchester. It is
situated on the verge immediately before the A-road makes a
left bend, at the point where a minor road turns off for
Stinsford village. The *agger* of the Roman road, at first in a
coppice, but then in the open, can be seen on the north side of
this lane before the latter also changes direction. The
milestone, no longer inscribed, was moved a short distance
from its original spot in the nineteenth century. It stands
beside the Roman road heading for the hill-fort of Badbury
Rings near Wimborne, where there was a small roadside
settlement.

Three other tribal capitals were founded by the Romans in
Wessex and the south-west, at Exeter, Winchester and
Silchester. The military origin of **Exeter** (SX 9192), long
suspected, was confirmed first by the discovery of a fort-ditch
near the south gate in 1964, and then of military buildings in
the centre of the city in 1971–3. These included barracks, a
workshop and a granary of timber and a fine stone bath-
house, and it is now clear that a legionary fortress was built at
Exeter during the 50's, presumably by and for the Second
Legion. At some stage, probably *c.* 75, the soldiery moved on,
and before the end of the first century the place was laid out
as a town-centre for the Dumnonii, ISCA DVMNONIORVM, with
a street-grid and the usual public buildings. At this time the
legionary baths were converted into the basilica: the
hypocausts were filled in, the floor-levels raised, and a range
** of steps provided to enter the basilica from the forum. The
only visible remains of ISCA, however, are the defences, which

enclosed some 93 acres, an average size for a Romano–
British tribal capital. As usual, a clay bank and
ditch came first, in the late second century, and in the early
third the bank was faced in stone. The walls have been much
repaired and altered in medieval and later times, and
consequently the Roman masonry is not everywhere apparent.
Look out, therefore, for regularly-coursed blocks of purple-
grey volcanic stone, with a projecting plinth at the base, and
you will know that you are looking at Roman work. The
plinth is often a few feet above ground and was underpinned
by medieval masonry when the ground-level was lowered.

The best place to start is in Northernhay Gardens, entered
from Queen Street opposite Northernhay Street. The walls
have been mostly refaced here, but the Roman plinth and a
few blocks above it are visible near the war-memorial 20 yards
south of the modern arched opening. The plinth is again
visible north of the opening, but is here four feet above the
present ground level. In the east corner of these gardens is the
former archaeological museum, now being redeveloped (1987)
as a costume museum; Roman finds from Exeter are not
currently on display. Go down to the end of Castle Street, then
turn left and first right by Eastgate House. Here the wall again
becomes visible, with plinth and about five feet of Roman
masonry above it. Continue on, past a much-botched portion,
until you reach the entrance to the underground car-park.
Immediately beyond this is a superb stretch of wall 15 feet
high, with plinth and 20 courses of Roman masonry above it.
Continue walking straight down Southernhay West, past the
Devon and Exeter Hospital (there is another piece of plinth
visible at the south end of the car-park opposite the hospital).
Then turn right (on foot only, since it is a one-way street) and
right again at the traffic-lights. The stretch of wall here has
been largely repatched, but part of the Roman plinth survives.
A green plaque on the modern wall behind points out the
foundations of a guard-tower of the Roman south gate,
adjoining the pavement. The rear face of the Roman wall is
well preserved here. Finally, on the other side of the inner by-
pass, there is a fine stretch of wall, with Roman facing-stones
impressively visible at first and medieval patching beyond.

Of Roman **Winchester** (SU 4829) virtually nothing is
visible. It was VENTA BELGARVM, the capital of the Belgae, the

tribe which occupied much of what is now Hampshire and
part of Wiltshire. There was a pre-Roman settlement here,
and the earthwork called Oram's Arbour in the western
outskirts of the town is now dated to this period (first century
BC). A Roman fort in the conquest period is a probability,
and a military defensive ditch found in 1971 in Lower Brook
Street possibly belonged to it. This was followed by several
phases of timber buildings before the town was properly laid
out with a street-grid about AD 90. Earlier than this, probably
c. AD 70, the town had received its first defences of earth with
timber gateways, a phenomenon appearing at Winchester so
much earlier than usual that the place must have enjoyed
privileged status, probably as part of the pro-Roman client-
kingdom of Cogidubnus (p. 49) or some other princeling. The
forum, situated immediately north of the Cathedral, was built
about AD 100 and enlarged 50 years later, and other public
buildings, including a small temple, also appeared in stone
c. 100. Private houses on the other hand were built of timber
until the mid-second century. Towards the end of the second
century new earth defences were erected to enclose an area of
144 acres, making it the fifth largest town in Roman Britain.
There was apparently decline in the fourth century, when part
of the forum fell into disuse and houses were demolished
without being rebuilt. The only readily accessible relic of
Roman Winchester *in situ* is a fragment of the third-century
city wall visible from a footpath called the Weirs, which runs
south from the river-bridge on the east side of the city. (There
is also some core of the Roman wall in the private grounds of
St Bartholemew's Maternity Home, Hyde Street.) A portion
of mosaic has been relaid on the floor beneath the entrance to
the Deanery, south of the Cathedral. Otherwise, the remains
of VENTA must be examined in the museum, at the NW corner
of the Cathedral Green, where finds from the city and nearby
are on display (weekdays 10–5; Sundays 2–4 or 5; closed Mon.
in winter). A near-perfect geometric mosaic from a villa at
Sparsholt is the outstanding exhibit.

To attempt to give coherent directions to the most famous
of all Romano–British towns, **Silchester*** (SU 6462), is
virtually impossible, for it lies in the middle of a maze of
minor roads in the extreme north of Hampshire, inside a
triangle formed by Newbury, Reading and Basingstoke. The

site is marked on most maps, and I will leave readers to make their own way there. It is a charming place, peacefully set in deep countryside far from the bustle of the twentieth century. It is truly a 'dead' city, for, whereas most Roman towns in Britain continue in occupation to this day, Silchester did not find favour with later town-planners and it remains deserted, with only a medieval church and a farm within its walls. Yet, paradoxically, the fact that it is dead makes CALLEVA ATREBATVM, as the Romans called it, very much alive with the spirit of the past, and most people find a visit to the spot, whatever the season and whatever the weather, a moving and uncanny experience.

The reason for Silchester's fame is that the area within the walls was totally excavated in 1864–78 and, more especially, in 1890–1909. Techniques were not scientific, and so the chronological development of the town was not revealed (a deficiency partly made good by the work of 1979–85). But the excavations did provide not only a wealth of objects but the complete plan of a Romano–British town – the forum and

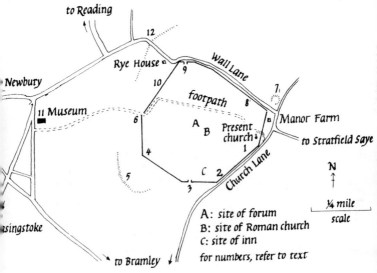

A: site of forum
B: site of Roman church
C: site of inn

for numbers, refer to text

17   *Plan of Silchester*

basilica in the centre, the baths to the SE where the ground slopes down to a stream, several temples and, of course, many houses. A tiny building, 42 feet by 33 feet, found near the forum in 1892 and re-excavated in 1961, was almost certainly a church, though no specific objects conclusively proved its use for Christian worship. All these buildings, however, unfortunately now lie under a blanket of soil; and apart from the forum, which was visible from 1875 to 1909, no attempt has been made to leave the remains open in an accessible form. Today the cost of conserving anything but a tiny area would be prohibitive.

Despite the lack of visible remains within the walls there is still plenty to see at Silchester today. Apart from the town-walls a series of earthworks once encircled the site; the dating of these is still disputed. The earliest seems to have been the inner earthwork, not marked on the plan (fig 17). It was erected about AD 30/40 around the pre-Roman settlement of the Atrebates, and enclosed a slightly smaller area than that of the later town-walls. The earthwork soon became redundant

18   Silchester, the Roman town-wall

and was levelled. The outer earthwork (5 and 12 on fig 17) has until recently been considered Roman (*c.* 70), but there is no evidence that it was continuous, and a pre-Roman (first century BC) date seems more plausible. The Roman town was not formally laid out with a street-grid until the end of the first century, even though the baths (*c.* 55/65), the forum and basilica (built in stone probably *c.* 130/40 to replace a timber predecessor of Flavian date), and some other buildings were earlier than it. The planning was a little too ambitious, for the earth defences of the late second century enclose a smaller area than that envisaged by the original street-grid. Finally, some time between about 260 and 280, the front of the earth bank was cut back and the existing stone wall erected.

The church provides a car-park and a good starting-point for a tour of the visible remains (1 on fig 17). By the path behind the church is a sun-dial, supported on part of a Roman column which comes from a temple-precinct underlying the churchyard. Walking south from here you will soon see the wall preserved to a good height, newly freed from its shrubbery and conserved by the Department of the Environment. Further on the wall becomes more impressive, even though, as usual at Silchester, almost all the facing-stones have been robbed, leaving visible the concreted flint-rubble core, separated at intervals by bonding-courses of large flat slabs. It is a spectacular sight, still standing 15 feet high, probably close to its original height apart from the patrol-walk (fig 18). Just before the wall changes direction (2), facing the iron gate on the road, is a postern-gate for pedestrians, erroneously interpreted as a sluice-gate in 1893 but re-excavated in 1976. It consists of a narrow inturned entrance, largely destroyed at the front, but with the brick piers of its single archway well preserved at the back. At some uncertain date the gate was blocked, and part of the blocking wall is still in position. Then the wall turns the corner and makes for the south gate (3). Its single arch rose from the mortared flint piers with brick facing at front and back that can be seen at the rear of the passage. Excavation here in 1975 showed that the stone gateway was contemporary with the earth rampart of the late second century, and that the outer part of the passage was formed in the third century by inturning the new curtain walls. A similar sequence occurred at the SE postern, but there an earlier timber gate is also known. From here you have a fine view of the interior of CALLEVA. Close to the walls on your right you have to imagine a large inn with rooms ranged round a courtyard; in the middle distance a polygonal temple; and beyond, in the centre of the town, close to the footpath on the skyline, the forum with, along its western side, a basilica rising 70 feet above the ground.

Visitors pressed for time should now return to their cars, and resume the itinerary from the beginning of the next paragraph. Others may like to continue following the walls right round to the west gate. This stretch is much less impressive, but the ditch accompanying the wall is visible here. At the SW corner (4) a detour can be made to Rampier Copse, where the outer earthwork survives to an impressive height of 20 feet (5). After the wall changes direction again and heads for the west gate, a short stretch of wall-facing can be seen, a rarity at Silchester. It is about three feet high, with neat rows of flints separated by bonding slabs. At the west gate (6), now a simple breach, but originally a twin-portalled gate with guard-chambers, you should go inside the wall and follow the footpath back across the buried city to the churchyard.

From here the amphitheatre (7) is only a short distance away. Its tree-grown elliptical banks are still 18 feet above the level of the arena, where the stone retaining wall is also now ****** visible. The adjacent stretch of city-wall (8), which near the amphitheatre stands to an impressive height and displays the base-plinth marking the original front face of the wall, can be viewed over the hedge from Wall Lane. Next, pause at the barbed-wire farm-gate (where a notice informs would-be visitors that the property is private) to view the north gate (9) which, like the south gate, consisted of a single carriageway; it is now a total ruin. Should you wish to see the remaining sector of city-wall (on the NW (10)), you must ask permission at Rye House. The most interesting feature is the long sag which the wall displays here; this is because the inner earthwork and ditch, now invisible, passed obliquely under the line of the later wall and the foundations of the latter have settled into the earlier ditch. Otherwise go on to the museum (11), passing through a well-preserved section of the outer earthwork (12) on your way. This tiny museum, refurbished in

1976, contains some objects as well as plans and photographs of the excavations, but the main collection is excellently displayed at Reading Museum (weekdays 10–5.30, Sat. 10–5). The objects in the showcases there speak for themselves; many of them, especially the iron tools, look remarkably similar to their modern counterparts. The inscriptions, too, are interesting: one has the word CALLEVA inscribed on a stone slab, a confirmation of the Roman name for the town; others scrawled on tile, such as 'Clementinus made this box-tile', show a high standard of literacy among the ordinary inhabitants of the town. Another *graffito*, reading *conticuere omnes* (the opening words of Aeneid II), suggests that Virgil was read in Romano-British schools.

Turning now from the towns to the countryside, we find a complex pattern of settlement. Romanized villas are absent west of Exeter and on the downs of Wiltshire and Dorset. Instead, they stick to the more cultivable and better-watered valleys, especially around Ilchester in south Somerset (App. I), Winchester, and, to a lesser extent, Dorchester. Apart, however, from the examples in the Isle of Wight, described below (p. 90–96), only the villas at Rockbourne in Hampshire and Littlecote in Wiltshire have something visible, though an outstanding mosaic from another site deserves a mention here. It was uncovered in 1946 at a villa at Low Ham near Langport (Somerset) and is now in **Taunton** Castle, the home of the Somerset County Museum (Mon.–Sat., 10–5). Unfortunately it has been displayed on the wall, and only one of the five scenes can be viewed in comfort. The mosaic tells the story of Dido and Aeneas as recounted in the Aeneid and presumably reflects the literary tastes of its owner. A detailed explanation of the panels is given in the museum and further comment here is unnecessary, except to say that the figure on the right in the bottom panel is not Anna but Dido herself, as her obvious interest in Aeneas on the left amply demonstrates (fig 19).

The **Rockbourne** villa (SU 1217) (early Apr. to early Oct., Mon.–Fri. 2–6, Sat., Sun. and Bank Hols. 10.30–6; July and Aug., daily 10.30–6), is signposted from the A354 5m SW of Salisbury and can also be reached by turning right off the B3078 at Sandleheath, 2m west of Fordingbridge. Its late owner and excavator, a retired architect, kept the villa open to the public during excavation, which continued each year from 1956 to 1974. The villa has now been largely backfilled for its own preservation, although some parts have been consolidated and left exposed; the rest has been marked out in modern materials. The earliest structure, in the courtyard of the later villa, was a circular Iron Age hut, replaced by a three-room cottage in the later first century. This was demolished and replaced by a new house in the second century, later incorporated into the west wing. A bath-suite was added to it perhaps *c.* 150-200; of it the highly unusual hypocaust, with *pilae* built of semicircular roofing tiles (*imbrices*), has been left exposed. The north wing was added in the third century, but the visible mosaic is not much before *c.* 300. The wing had its own tiny baths, replaced by a new and larger bath-suite (partly visible), also *c.* 300. The long corridor was the cold room, the room in the middle of its south side its original cold plunge; later, in the fourth century, this became the *tepidarium* and a new octagonal plunge bath was added on the other side of the *frigidarium*. The south side of the yard contained farm buildings including an aisled barn; a T-shaped corn-drying

19 *Taunton Museum, the Low Ham mosaic (detail)*

oven is exposed here. The museum, displaying the spacious but not luxurious villa's copious finds (some of them exceptional), deserves close inspection.

The villa in **Littlecote Park*** (SU 2970) is situated in the grounds of the sixteenth-century Littlecote House, signposted from B4192 2½m NW of Hungerford (every day from 10 a.m. to 6 p.m. from early April to the end of October only). A spectacular mosaic, described as 'the finest pavement that sun ever shone upon in England', was uncovered in 1728 and recorded in an embroidered tapestry, still hanging in the 'New Chamber' in the House. An engraving in the Ashmolean Museum, Oxford, on which it was based, adds no fresh information. The mosaic, presumed lost, was laid bare anew in 1978, but although there is every reason to think that it had originally been found intact (it lay beneath seven feet of soil), neglect, building work and rodent activity in the intervening two and a half centuries had destroyed over half the original floor. The mosaic you see today, therefore, has been largely recreated from the tapestry design, and although overall it makes a striking impression, it is a pity that the portions of Roman original have not been clearly distinguished from the modern work. The floor, a work of undistinguished draughtmanship, is in two parts. One is a rectangular area containing geometric designs, which are flanked by two strips depicting sea-beasts and panthers respectively, arranged either side of centrally placed chalices. The other, principal, part of what was presumably a reception room or dining room has figured scenes in the central square and, around it, three semicircular apses floored with scallop-shell motifs. The figured scenes feature Apollo (or, less likely, Orpheus) in the centre and a female figure on the back of an animal in each of the surrounding quadrants, probably the Seasons. The three-apsed room (*triconchos*) is an ambitious architectural conception unmatched in Britain. It first appears in town-houses in north Africa in the late third century and is then found soon afterwards in Italian and Sicilian country villas. This may provide a clue that either the owner or the architect had close links with the central Mediterranean world or at least was aware of contemporary architectural thinking there. The room with the Apollo mosaic had been added, probably in the middle of the fourth century, to an earlier structure

which contained a small bath-suite. A separate building has been located further south, including part of a corridor and rooms with hypocausts. Excavations are at the time of writing (1987) still continuing, and it is planned to uncover and consolidate even more of the Roman villa over the next few
** years.

In additon, however, to romanized villas there are hundreds of native settlements, which could be mentioned, ranging in size from single homesteads to large villages and displaying varying degrees of romanization. Their economy was based on small-scale mixed farming, consisting of both corn-growing and sheep- or cattle-raising. In Cranbourne Chase, immediately west of Rockbourne, however, a change seems to have been introduced in the late third century, if not before, when the area may have been appropriated as an imperial estate. At this time several of the settlements were deserted, field-systems fell into disuse, and new cattle-enclosures were erected. It looks, therefore, as if government-controlled sheep- and cattle-farming replaced arable farming – a theory supported by the record that there was an imperial weaving-mill in the fourth century at VENTA, probably Winchester rather than Caistor in Norfolk. One such cattle-enclosure, known as **Soldier's Ring** (SU 0817), is close to the Rockbourne villa. To reach it from the latter, take the road towards the village of Rockbourne, and turn first left and then right (signposted Martin). Continue along this road for 1¼m, and take the first track on the left after South Allenford Farm (double wooden gates). The polygonal enclosure's slight earthworks, now crowned by wire fences, lie in the field at the end of this track.

Several other Roman sites can be visited in close proximity on Cranbourne Chase, and so I will describe them in geographical, not chronological, order. Continue along the minor road at Soldier's Ring through the village of Martin to the A354. Turn left at this junction and keep going for 1¼m until you cross the Hampshire–Dorset border, where there is a lay-by on the right. Running alongside the left of the road here for 100 yards, before it changes direction, is a bush-covered stretch of the impressive barrier known as the **Bokerley Dyke** (SU 0319). It was designed to protect the downland of NE Dorset against marauders from the north by running across a neck of land four miles wide, flanked on either side by forest, of which some remnants exist. In its first phase, the bank and ditch stopped some 500 yards east of the A354, having started from Martin Wood, 3m SE, and run over Blagdon Hill and Martin Down. This sector, still visible over its entire length though difficult to reach, is dated to *c.* AD 325–30. Later, in phase II, the barrier was extended up to and across the modern road, though west of the latter the dyke is not now visible. It was even built over the Roman road at this point, and the road's *agger*, heading northwards towards Old Sarum, is clearly visible on the right (west) of the modern road. The fact that the new extension was built across the Roman road, thus blocking the major trunk route to the south-west, suggests a period of crisis; and the archaeological evidence makes the barbarian invasion of 367 the most likely occasion. A year or two later, however, the road was reopened through it: the crisis had clearly passed. Finally, sometime after 395, in the closing days of Roman rule, the dyke west of the road was replaced by another on a different and more commanding line. To sum up, then, the Bokerley Dyke belongs to three periods: west of the road it dates to the end of the fourth century; east of the road for just over ¼m it dates to *c.* 367; and the long sector beyond was thrown up about 330.

I have already mentioned the *agger* of the Roman road visible here near the Bokerley Dyke. Its alignment touches the A354 at this point and joins it at the village of Woodyates for one mile, before the modern highway swings away towards Blandford and leaves the Roman line altogether. The best place to examine the Roman road is a little further south. Continue along the A354 for another mile and turn left for Ringwood along the B3081. The *agger* of the Roman road, known here as the **Ackling Dyke** (SU 0116), crosses the B-road after ¼m (first field-boundary on the left) and forms a striking sight. From here it strides magnificently over the downland, dead straight and visible for miles, aiming for the hill-fort of Badbury Rings, over eight miles away. The whole of this stretch is a right-of-way and it provides a wonderful walk. Here the *agger* is at its best, 40 feet wide and 5 or 6 feet high. Such an embankment is unnecessary on this dry ground, and it has been suggested that the road was deliberately built in this fashion to impress the natives.

Return now along the B3081 and cross the A354 to Sixpenny Handley. Two miles beyond this village is a turning to the left, signposted Cashmoor and Dean, and immediately after this, on the right by a telephone-booth, is a grass track. In the field at the end of this lies the classic native settlement of **Woodcuts** (ST 9618). Excavated in 1884 by General Pitt-Rivers, the pioneer of scientific archaeology, and later reinterpreted by Professor Christopher Hawkes, the site is now known to have had three separate phases. The first lasted from the early first century, before the Roman invasion, to the third quarter of the second century, and was entirely non-Roman in character. The homestead was surrounded by a circular bank and ditch within which were 80 storage pits for grain, though only a few were dug at a time. From the late second century Roman influence was certainly present in the form of wall-plaster, two wells (now marked by modern stone slabs), and corn-driers, the latter in one of the two separate enclosures tacked on to the original perimeter-bank. There was further remodelling of the enclosure-banks at the end of the third century, and in the later fourth the place was deserted. The visible earthworks, restored by Pitt-Rivers, belong to all periods, but still give some idea of the level of native occupation under Roman rule.

Of the many hundreds of similar settlements in which Wessex is so rich, I will mention just three more – sites which I have visited and which are generally reckoned to be among the best-preserved of their kind. Giving directions to these is not easy and readers will find it better to locate them with the help of the 1:50,000 series OS maps. At none of them is there anything to see beyond some confusing ridges, mounds and building-platforms, but they ought to be visited for the sake of reminding ourselves that it was only a minority of the inhabitants of Roman Britain who enjoyed the plush luxury of the stone-built villas, with their hypocausts and mosaics, that are popularly associated with the countryside. Very close to Woodcuts, and reached from the bridleway leading due north from Tollard Royal on the B3081 (turn right at the pillar-box and telephone-booth, and then bear right up the hill) is the native settlement on **Berwick Down** (ST 941197). It adjoins the right-hand side of the track one mile from Tollard, at the point where the pylons cross over it from left to right. There are three separate areas here: behind the beech trees is a U-shaped bank enclosing an oblong hut-enclosure which has yielded finds of the first century AD; 100 yards to the north, where the trees end, is a circular enclosure over two acres in extent, with a mass of rectangular building-platforms, certainly of Romano–British date; and north again is a concentration of pits and a large circular hut which belongs to pre-Roman times. ½m due east, across the other side of the valley and on the edge of another wood, is **Rotherley** (ST 948196), which is very remote and best reached by another path from Tollard (see OS map). It was excavated by Pitt-Rivers in 1885–6 and, like Woodcuts, restored by him. The main layout of the earthworks must be dated to the immediate pre-Roman period, but occupation continued with few changes, except for the introduction of Roman coins and pottery, until about AD 300. The main features are a large circular enclosure where the principal house was situated, a smaller enclosure to the NE, where there was a granary, and other hollows, working-areas and gulleys to the east. The settlement never seems to have been more than a single community with at most two or three dwelling-huts.

Finally in Wessex I will mention the settlement on **Meriden Down** (ST 802049), as visitors are welcome even though the land is private, and there is a plan of the earthworks displayed on the site. There is very little of interest to see, but it is set in some of the most peaceful and delightful countryside in Dorset, and the walk alone should make the visit worthwhile. Take the minor road signposted Milton Abbas in Winterbourne Whitchurch on the A354, 5m SW of Blandford Forum. Keep straight on without going into Milton, and then turn left at the fork (signposted Bulbarrow). Go on for two miles until you see a gate marked 'Delcombe Manor'. Two hundred yards further on, on the right, a track goes off through the woods. Follow this, forking left where it forks, through a gate, and you soon come to an exercise-ground for horses. The site lies at the far end of this field and the plan, now somewhat battered, is displayed near the trees on the right. Part of the settlement lies behind these trees, and three embanked loops, probably the compounds for three large buildings, are clearly visible here. The main part of the settlement is honeycombed with banks and level platforms indicating the site of working-areas and building-structures. Four roads (a–d on the site-plan) lead to open spaces outside the nucleus; one of the western roads (f) is accompanied by four small mounds of unknown purpose. To the south is a large area of perfectly-preserved contemporary fields, tilled by the inhabitants of the settlement.

An interesting sidelight on Romano–British Wessex is shed by the **Cerne Giant** (ST 6601), a chalk figure (given a face-lift in 1979) cut into the hillside above the village of Cerne Abbas on the A352, a few miles north of Dorchester. He is a powerful muscular figure, 180 feet high, emphatically displaying his potency and wielding a knotted club above his head. Nipples and six ribs are also rather crudely shown. The club makes it almost certain that the figure is a native representation of the god Hercules, carved by the local population to promote the fertility of their crops. Its precise date is unknown, but its Romano–British origin seems generally accepted, although both this and the identification of the god as Hercules have been questioned.

In the Cornish peninsula, Roman influence was virtually non-existent, and only a single example of a romanized house is known in Cornwall, at Magor, Camborne (not now visible). For the vast majority life must have been little changed by the Roman conquest. The classic native settlement in this part of Britain is **Chysauster** (SW 4735) [AM; S] on the Land's End peninsula. It is signposted from the B3311 Penzance to St Ives road at Badger's Cross and from the Penzance to Zennor road at Newmill. The well-preserved remains consist of eight oval stone-built houses arranged in pairs, with another to the right of the path near the entrance-stile. Pass this and go to the next two houses, no. 3 on the left and no. 5 on the right. It is best to study house 5 first, since its plan is simple and characteristic of the 'courtyard-house' of which this and other similar villages are composed. The entrance-passage leads into a courtyard, open to the sky, in the centre of the enclosure. On the left is a recessed portion, perhaps covered by a lean-to for cattle, and on the right is a long narrow room, perhaps used as a workshop or for storage. The living-room was the round or oval hut at the far side of the courtyard opposite the entrance, and its roof was supported by a central beam in a stone socket (here *in situ*). There are sometimes other small rooms or recesses opening off the central courtyard, but the other houses all display these same basic features. No. 3, however, is more complicated as it is 'semi-detached': there are two entrances, two round rooms and two recesses on the left, all enclosed in the single unit. Many of the houses have terraced area (?gardens) adjacent. Pottery indicates that the Chysauster village goes back to the first century BC, but the main occupation occurred in the first and second centuries AD until peaceful abandonment *c.* AD 300. The inhabitants existed on small-scale mixed farming, and the custodian, if asked, will point out the remains of the nearby field-system.

Another peculiar feature of some Cornish settlements is a subterranean chamber known as a *fogou*, apparently used as a cellar for keeping food cool and dry. There is a very ruinous example at Chysauster, reached from the main area by a separate footpath, but the best *fogou* is at a nearby village, **Carn Euny** (SW 4028) [AM ; A], 4m west of Penzance and signposted from the A30 at Drift. It is approached from one of the houses by a roofless stone-lined passage, which leads to the main curving gallery, five feet wide and six feet deep, still roofed with massive stone slabs. Opening off it at one end is a tiny tunnel leading to a circular chamber which probably originally had a timber and turf roof. It is believed that the *fogous*, like the villages themselves, are of pre-Roman origin, but continued in use during the Roman period. Carn Euny also has four stone 'courtyard-houses' and four smaller stone dwellings. Excavations between 1964 and 1972 showed that these replaced earlier timber huts from the first century BC onwards; the farming settlement was peacefully abandoned *c.* 400.

Analogous round houses occupied during Romano-British times can be seen in the Scilly Isles, most notably at Halangy Down on St Mary's (SW 9011) and, if you can arrange for a boat to take you there, on the uninhabited island of **Nornour** (SV 9414). The last has produced a wealth of objects, some quite exotic, including Roman rings, over 300 brooches, coins and glass-beads as well as good quality Romano-Gaulish clay figurines, all *c.* 80–220. It seems that the most westerly hut there became a shrine in Roman times: to whom is unknown, but the figurines feature Venus and a mother goddess. The

finds throw particularly fascinating light on the penetration of
Roman artefacts into an area remote from mainstream Roman
influence and culture.

Apart from the early invasion-period, official Roman
interest in the far west was confined to the exploitation of the
tin-streams of central Cornwall in the third and fourth
centuries AD, after the Spanish tin-mines, Rome's previous
major source, were exhausted. The workings themselves have
been largely destroyed by later activity, but five crudely-cut
Roman milestones, all of them just a few yards from their
original find-spots, bear witness to road-building or repair in
Cornwall, though actual traces of these roads have not been
found. Two milestones imply a short stretch of road on the
north coast: one, dated to 251–3, is at St Piran's, **Trethevy**
(SX 0588), a hamlet midway between Tintagel and Boscastle
on the B3263; and the other, which is dedicated to Licinius,
emperor between 308 and 324, is in the south transept of
Tintagel Church (SX 0789). Further west is a better example,
found in 1942 and now erected in the garden of Mynheer
Farm at **Gwennap Pit** (SW 7241), a hamlet 1m due east of
Redruth, south of the minor road to St Day (ask for
directions locally). It is dedicated to the Emperor Caesar
Antonius Gordianus Pius Felix (AD 238–44) and belongs
either to a road running down the spine of Cornwall or to a
cross-road linking the north and south coasts, to assist in the
transport of tin from the mines to the ports. In south
Cornwall two more milestones are known: one erected to
Postumus, emperor 258–68, is now in the church at **Breage**
(SW 6128), a village north of the A394, 4m west of Helston;
and the best-preserved of all the Cornish milestones is now
cemented into the floor of the south aisle of the church at **St
Hilary** (SW 5531), which lies north of the B3280, $1\frac{3}{4}$m east of
its junction with the A394 near Marazion. It was set up in
AD 306–7 'To the Emperor Caesar Flavius Valerius
Constantinus Pius, most noble Caesar, son of the deified
Constantius Pius Felix Augustus' (fig 20).

I have stayed long enough on the fringes of Roman Britain
and it is time to return and deal with a more familiar
monument of the Romano–British countryside, the villa. The
Rockbourne and Littlecote villas have been noted above, but
two more are clearly visible in Wessex, both of them on the Isle

of Wight, or VECTIS as the Romans called it. **Brading*** Roman Villa (SZ 6086), open only from April to the end of September (daily 10–5.30, Sun. 10.30–5.30), is signposted from the A3055 in the southern outskirts of the town. The excavations, conducted during the 1880's, paid little attention to chronology, but pottery finds indicate that the site was occupied from the first century AD onwards and there is even a hint of pre-Roman (Belgic) occupation. In its final form, in the fourth century, it consisted of a main residential block of 13 rooms and two subsidiary wings arranged around a courtyard. The main block of the villa is completely visible and is chiefly notable for the remarkable fourth-century figured mosaics in four of its rooms. The first mosaic seen on entering lies in the middle of a long corridor and represents Orpheus charming the animals with his lyre: on the left is a monkey, on the right a bird and a fox. Eight other British examples of this scene are known, but only the Brading mosaic puts charmer and charmed within the same circle. To the right, a corn-drier has been inserted into the floor, presumably at a time when this part of the villa no longer

20   St Hilary, Roman milestone

mattered as a residence while the site continued in use as an agricultural centre. Moving now to the left, you come to the second mosaic, which is unfortunately badly damaged. The central roundel has a bust of Bacchus, and there is another Bacchic bust in the one surviving corner, but of the side-panels only one is substantially complete. On the left is a cock-headed man dressed in a tunic, in the centre is a small hut approached by a ladder, and on the right are two griffins (fig 21). This extraordinary scene has no parallel anywhere and is perhaps symbolic of some mystic rite of initiation connected with the after-life, in which the ladder represents the soul's ascent to heaven and the griffins are guardians of the dead. The cock-headed man is thought to have connections with Gnosticism, a philosophical sect which believed that through knowledge (*gnosis*) man could gain everlasting life. The adjacent panel depicted a gladiatorial combat, of which a man with a trident and sword survives: it too must surely have an allegorical meaning, perhaps of the ordeals which the soul has to suffer in life on earth.

Other rooms nearby have little of note except for a neatly-displayed selection of finds. There are some interesting metal objects, including ploughshares, a fine bronze linch-pin from a wheeled vehicle, and a bronze lock-plate. Note also the painted plaster with a bird and a bowl of fruit, found in the corridor and presented to the British Museum on discovery, but recently returned to the site; and also the fragmentary trays or table-tops of Kimmeridge shale from dorset (cf. p. 73 and fig 1), found in the north wing. Nearby, in the room projecting at the back of the block (8), a section of roofing-slabs of local Bembridge stone has been reassembled: this was an important export commodity for the Isle of Wight in Roman times, as Bembridge stone has been identified in Roman buildings as far away as Essex. Fragmentary remains of an 'oven' here, still visible, made the original excavators interpret the room as a kitchen, but its size makes it likely that it was planned as a living room. A crucible and metal slag discovered during recent investigations (on display in one of the cases) may indicate the oven is rather a furnace and that the industrial activity belongs, like the corn-drier, to a period when the block no longer functioned as the landowner's residence. Now mount the wooden catwalk again, and pass on the right a simple geometric mosaic and, on the left, a couple of small rooms. The first of these, paved with tiles, has a masonry bench or shelf round two walls. But it is the magnificent mosaics of the remaining two rooms which will claim your attention. The floor of the larger has mostly disappeared, but one side-panel is nearly complete. It represents Andromeda (on the left) being rescued by the hero Perseus, who holds aloft the head of the newly-slain Medusa. To the right of this panel is the bust of Summer, and of the other seasons Winter (diagonally opposite) and Spring also survive.

Go now to the far end of the shed to admire the superbly preserved mosaics of the remaining room. In the foreground is a lively strip showing tritons and mermaids. The central roundel of the main section contains a sad-looking, snaky head of Medusa and the four oblong panels which surround it depict the following mythological scenes (clockwise, starting with left-foreground): (i) Lycurgus, carrying his two-headed axe, pursues the nymph Ambrosia, who in response to her cry for help is being swallowed up by the earth, while Lycurgus is entwined by a vine-tendril and throttled; (ii) Attis (Phrygian cap, crook, pipes) chats up a river nymph (reeds in hair, upturned vase); (iii) Ceres, goddess of the crops, gives seed to Triptolemus, the inventor of the plough; (iv) nymph pursued by a man. In the triangles between these scenes are busts of the Four Winds, each blowing a conch. Finally, in the panel separating the two parts of the room, is the enigmatic figure of an astronomer pointing to a globe, above which is a pillar surmounted by a sundial. Once again, symbolism must be intended here: the astronomer perhaps signifies that by wisdom man could become immortal, and other symbols of immortality can be read into the Perseus-Andromeda and the Lycurgus-Ambrosia scenes (victory over death and evil), Ceres' gift to Triptolemus (bread and wine sustain us both on earth and in the after-life), the Winds (carrying the soul to heaven), etc. Such a significance cannot be proved but seems highly probable. In addition the pavement contains symbols of the elements: earth (e.g. Ceres), air (the Winds), water (mermaids) and the heavens (astronomer). At any rate, though the standard of figure-drawing is far from masterly, the peculiarity of the subject-matter puts these Brading mosaics in a class of their own, and indicates an owner well-versed in classical philosophy and mythology.

Of the north wing only two separate elements, a hypocaust and a well, are now visible. This and the south wing (on the other side of the car-park, now re-buried) seem to have been largely agricultural buildings, but the west end of the north wing with the hypocaust and other rooms with painted plaster may have been the living quarters of a farm manager or bailiff. The villa was very probably the centre of a large estate, and the ancient fields visible on the hillside 600 yards to the NW are probably contemporary.

The second villa on the Isle of Wight, at **Newport** (SZ 5088), deserves to be better known. It is open from Easter to the end of September, Sundays–Fridays, 10.30–4.30. The entrance is in Avondale Road, a turning to the west off the A3056 on the Sandown road. It is an excellent example of the corridor-type of villa, the corridor itself and four of the rooms which led from it lying outside the modern shed. The path leads first into a heated room through the foundations of a brick flue-arch: hypocaust *pilae* found here when the villa was excavated

21   *Brading villa, cock-headed-man mosaic*

in 1926 have since disappeared. This room leads into the corridor along the front of the building, from which it can be appreciated that the house faced left (south). At the far end a door into the shed leads to the bath-suite, entered also from the corridor in antiquity. The changing-room connects with a cold room and its cold plunge with lead pipe *in situ*. The visitor then crosses the site of a masonry base, outside the villa but inside the modern shed; it is believed to have supported a water-tank. The three rooms of varying heat beyond still have hypocaust *pilae* standing to a good height, but the floors they once supported are missing. At the far end is a semi-circular hot plunge-bath, with box flue-tiles still jacketed in the thickness of the walls, and the furnace for the baths beyond. Then follow three rooms with tessellated floors, of which the largest has the unusual feature of a fireplace, built of tiles, projecting from the far wall. The walls of the villa are preserved to almost their full height, for the superstructure is likely to have been of timber, except for the bath-suite which was probably entirely of stone. The house was built towards the end of the second century and seems to have had an active life of little more than a hundred years.

A third villa, first explored in 1910–11 and re-excavated in 1968–75, is enclosed within a recreation-park called Robin Hill at Combley, Arreton Down (SZ 5387). The park, which is open from March to October, 10–6, is entered by a gate on the minor road between Wooton on the A3054 and Arreton on the A3056, near 'The Hare and Hounds' Inn. The main features excavated here were a small bath-house and an adjacent rectangular building. The baths had been badly robbed, except on the uphill side, where a long room with a mosaic featuring dolphins, and an adjacent semi-circular cold plunge-bath, were well preserved, the walls here standing over four feet high. Until a few years ago (*c.* 1981), this bath-house was still visible, although badly neglected; unfortunately plans to erect a cover-building over it came to nothing, and the site has now been backfilled. The adjacent building comprised an aisled barn and four living rooms, three with red tessellated floors and a fourth with geometric mosaic. These have also been reburied and the whole area given over to an enclosure for wallabies (!), clearly a more crowd-pulling attraction than evidence for the life-style of Romano–Britons. The paltry finds indicated a possible period of occupation *c.* 230–350 AD, with a final abandonment soon after, probably because of flooding. It seems likely that the principal residential block of the villa has yet to be found, presumably in the woods further south.

Other villa-sites are known on the island at Rock and Carisbrooke, but neither is worth visiting now. At Carisbrooke Castle (SZ 4887) [AM, SSM, but opens 11 a.m. on Sun., Apr.–Sept.] a defensive wall of uncertain date is visible. Go out into the castle-bailey by the small gate below the keep on the east side and you will see, embedded in the lower banks of the later castle-ramparts, a stretch of walling five feet high, and a small round turret. In this east side there is also a gateway, 22 feet wide, visible to the right where the wall curves inwards. These walls are also exposed along the whole of the west side of the castle, both in the grounds of the tea-rooms and on the other side of the Gatehouse. A late-Roman date for this enclosure has for long been held likely, largely because of the presence of the projecting 'bastion', but there is no regular series of them, the gate does not match closely any of the normal late Roman types, and unlike the rest of the late Roman forts in south-east England, Carisbrooke is not on the sea. The Saxon date now suggested is plausible; precise dating evidence has unfortunately not been found. A small collection of Roman material is displayed in the Carisbrooke Castle Museum.

22 Portchester, the south wall

There is no uncertainty, however, about another of the forts in this series, **Portchester*** (SU 6204) [AM;A], which is one of the best-preserved and most impressive Roman structures anywhere in Britain. It is signposted on the A27 between Fareham and Portsmouth. The entire defensive wall of this fort, 10 feet thick and over 20 feet high, together with 14 of the original 20 bastions, still survives, except at the NW corner where the Normans built their keep. In many places medieval refacing has covered up the Roman work, but it can be spotted by the neat rows of coursed flints separated at intervals by stone and tile bonding-courses. The bastions are hollow and were originally floored with timber to mount artillery. In addition, each was provided with a tiled drain at the bottom to allow water to escape, and this drain can be seen in places, for instance in the east side of the second bastion from the keep along the north wall. The inner face of the walls has been largely cut back in medieval times, but the original Roman width can be seen in the places where the walls have been excavated down to Roman ground-level, as for example south of the Landgate. The battlements are mainly Norman work.

The fort was defended by four gates, of which only part of one is visible. In the north and south walls there were simple posterns, now blocked up, but the main gates in the middle of the west and east sides were formed by in-turning the curtain-walls to form a forecourt 45 feet wide and 36 feet deep, and closing the inner end of this passage with a gate 10 feet wide flanked by two square guard-chambers. The idea of this arrangement is that an enemy attacking the gate would be surrounded on three sides by defenders on the battlements above. The east gate is entirely buried beneath the medieval Watergate, but part of the lower courses of the west gate are traceable immediately south of the Landgate, inside the walls. Part of the Roman ditch-system is also visible and on the east the water still laps up to the walls as it did in Roman times. This magnificent site hardly qualifies for the description 'ruin', such is its state of preservation, and, unlike the majority of Roman sites in this country, it needs little imagination to visualize the fort in its heyday (fig 22).

Inside the walls excavation has revealed some traces of timber barracks and pits, but the Roman levels have been much disturbed by later occupation. First-century finds have been made, but the walls belong to the end of the third century. It was disused for a time in the early fourth century but reoccupied on a large scale again *c.* AD 340. It was finally abandoned *c.* 370, in favour of a different site with a better harbour, a few miles away. This was Bitterne, probably Roman CLAVSENTVM, where a promontory jutting into the river Itchen, the site of a small settlement in the first and second centuries, was fortified with a stone defensive wall about AD 370. Virtually nothing is visible at the site today, which is a suburb of Southampton, except for the fragmentary remains of a tiny second-century bath-house (Appendix I).

Chapter 3

Mendips and Cotswolds

Gloucestershire, Oxfordshire, North Somerset, Avon

(Appendix I only – Hereford and Worcester)

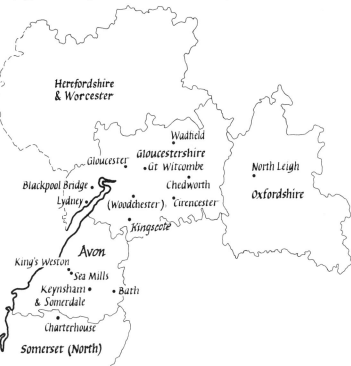

The tribe that inhabited the area of the Cotswolds and the Upper Thames in the pre-Roman period was known as the Dobunni. They appear to have caused little or no trouble to Roman armies in the early years of the invasion, but forts were established in their territory to protect them and the province behind from the aggressive Silures of South Wales. There was one at Cirencester and probably another at Bath, both places on the great trunk-road, the Fosse Way, which formed the earliest boundary of the new Roman province.

Much of its course in the area covered by this chapter is
followed by modern A-roads, but, for a three-mile stretch
going north from Shepton Mallet over Beacon Hill, the
Roman highway has become no more than a track, and plenty
of traces of the original metalling survive. Other forts were
established beyond the frontier road, notably at Gloucester
and Sea Mills, but hardly anything from this military phase is
visible anywhere now.

The Roman invaders did not waste much time before
exploiting the Mendip lead-mines around **Charterhouse**

23   *Charterhouse, plan*

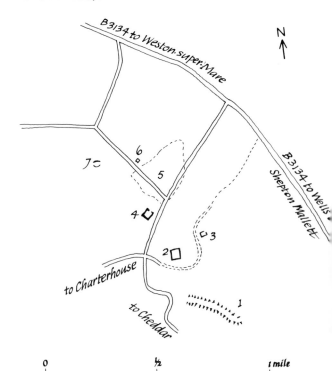

(ST 5056), which were already in operation only six years after the conquest. Lead was important not only in itself (eg to make water-pipes and coffins) but also for the manufacture of pewter and especially for the extraction of silver by a process known as cupellation. The lead remaining after the silver had been removed was cast in the form of ingots, often inscribed with the emperor's name, the date, and the authority in control of the mines. These ingots, therefore, furnish valuable historical information: one, now lost, is dated to AD 49, so that we know when mining was started; one was found near Southampton and another two in north France, and so we know they were exported to the continent. Indeed metallic tests have shown that a cistern in Pompeii, buried by the eruption of Vesuvius in 79, was made of British lead, probably from Charterhouse. One French ingot also tells us that the Second Augustan Legion was in control of the mines in Nero's reign (AD 54–68), but another in the British Museum dated to AD 60 is marked 'from the lead-silver works of Gaius Nipius Ascanius', making it clear that early military control soon gave way to private lessees. Finally, several Mendip ingots read BRIT.EX.ARG.VEB., 'British lead from the Veb . . . lead-silver mines'. VEB may be the abbreviation of the Roman name for Charterhouse, but the full name we do not know. The last securely datable ingot (in Taunton Museum) was made between 164 and 169, but another from Lillebonne (Normandy) of AD 195/211 is probably also of Mendip lead. Coin finds anyway at Charterhouse indicate that occupation continued into the fourth century.

Very little of the Roman mines or the associated settlement can be seen today; the former have been worked for a long time, especially in the nineteenth century, and the latter has never been adequately explored. A few earthworks, mostly of uncertain date and purpose, are the main features. The site is most conveniently approached from Cheddar. Take the road through the famous gorge (B3135), and then fork left along the B3371. One mile after the fork, turn left at the crossroads, signposted Charterhouse. After another mile, on the right of the road as it bends to ascend the hill to Charterhouse church, on land which is now included within a nature reserve and recreation area, deep trenching and pitting are visible and these probably belong to the Roman exploitation (1 on fig

23). Just beyond the church is a crossroads where you should turn right. After 200 yards, on the left-hand side of the road just beyond a group of trees, are the faint traces of a small earthwork (2 on fig 23) about 70 yards square; the south and east sides are largely destroyed. This is very probably the ploughed-out earthworks of a small Roman fort created to guard the lead-mines, and samian pottery dating to before AD 75, found here in 1975, did nothing to dispel the theory; excavation has not, however, been attempted. Further on, to the right of the track, is another small earthwork, but its date and purpose are uncertain (3 on fig 23). Now return to the crossroads and turn right; after $\frac{1}{4}$ mile take the track which goes off to the left. Just before this, on the left of the minor road, is another small earthwork (4), which is usually reckoned to be medieval. The site of the Roman town (5) lay on the right of the track at its junction with the road, in 'Town Field', but nothing is traceable now, although aerial photography has revealed something of the street-plan. Trial excavation between 1960 and 1967 found pottery of mid-first to late-third-century date as well as lead waste, charcoal, slag and other indications of industrial activity, but the investigations were too limited to reveal the plans of buildings or yield any detailed information about the settlement. A small earthwork enclosure can just be traced on the ground immediately next to an iron stile on the right of the track, where the stone wall stops; selective trenching seemed to indicate a medieval date for it (6). Finally, and most conspicuous of all, is the small amphitheatre (7), which can easily be spotted away to the left a little further on. The banks are still about 15 feet above the arena floor, and the entrances at either end are clear. The field in which it lies is entered by a gate $\frac{1}{4}$m further on, marked by a radio transmitter. The amphitheatre was inconclusively excavated in 1908. Finds from here and other sites in Charterhouse can be found in Bristol and Taunton Museums.

Charterhouse was not a normal Roman settlement in so far as its position was dictated by the nearby lead-mines. Another Roman town which owes its existence to natural phenomena – this time hot springs emerging from the ground at 120°F. – is **Bath*** (ST 7564), where the thermal establishment (winter: 9–5, Sun. 10–5; Summer: 9–6 or 7 daily) is Rome's most famous witness in Britain after Hadrian's Wall. And rightly so, for it was no ordinary bathing-station: it was a spa designed on the most elegant and ambitious scale.

The deity of the natural spring had probably been worshipped before the Roman period, and, although no pre-Roman occupation has ever been found, the name of the place, AQVAE SVLIS, indicates that the waters were sacred to the native goddess Sulis, whom the Romans identified with Minerva. There was probably a fort here in the period of the Roman conquest, as the spacing of forts along the Fosse Way demands it, but of this, too, not a trace has been found. Towards the end of the first century, the centre was laid out with an outstanding series of monumental buildings. The focus of the whole complex was clearly the sacred spring itself, surrounded by its reservoir; into this, now under the later King's Bath, all kinds of votive offerings were thrown. The spring was viewed from a hall in the baths (where the Circular Bath now is), and beyond it, on the same axis, the bather would catch a glimpse of a great altar, its corners richly carved with figures of deities. One of these was found in 1790, another in 1965 (both on display), and a third, now much weathered, is built into a buttress of the church at Compton Dando, seven miles to the west. While the altar lay on a north-south axis from a bather's viewpoint, it also lay on an east-west axis in front of a splendid temple dedicated to Sulis Minerva. Part of the plan of this temple was plotted in 1867–8 on the west side of Stall Street, but the precise dimensions, including the position of the bottom steps leading to the temple-platform (*podium*), were only established in 1964–5; much more was learnt during the extensive work of 1981–3. This was not the usual Romano–Celtic temple with central *cella* and lean-to ambulatory: it was a full-scale classical-style temple on a lofty *podium*, approached by a flight of steps, and fronted by a porch four columns wide and two deep supporting a frieze, architrave and pediment. The centre of the pediment was formed by the striking head of Medusa, found in 1790, and now in the Museum. The temple and altar were set in a large paved courtyard enclosed by a colonnade. Of this magnificent temple-complex a good deal, as we shall see, has been made accessible to visitors since 1984.

The baths themselves were at first quite simple, though on a monumental scale. From the central hall (*frigidarium*), with its vista of the spring and the altar, the bather could either turn right to the Great Bath and to the two smaller swimming-baths at its east end, or he could turn left and indulge in the artificial heat of the conventional Roman baths, which at this stage were very simple in layout. This set of baths with damp heat ('turkish' baths) was found insufficient, for in the second phase (probably early second-century) they were modified by the addition of a circular *laconicum* of the dry-heat (sauna) variety, and a large circular plunge-bath was inserted in the former *frigidarium*. At the same time, the last swimming-pool at the far end was replaced by a second set of turkish baths. The third period, also second-century, saw the entire re-roofing of the Great Bath with a grandiose barrel-vault and of the plunge- and swimming-pools at either end of it, but only minor alterations elsewhere. Some years later (period IV) extensive reorganization occurred: the eastern baths were rebuilt on a much larger scale; the alcove north of the tepid plunge-bath at this end was converted into an immersion-bath; and at the west end the heating systems were rearranged, and a new heated chamber as well as a cold swimming-bath were added. Later still, in period V, minor modifications were made, including the insertion of some small immersion baths at the west end. Finally, before the end of the Roman period, there was trouble with the drainage, and in the late fourth or early fifth century the flooding became serious: the baths were abandoned, the area became a marsh, the vault of the Great Bath collapsed. Not until the eighteenth century was something of Bath's former grandeur and popularity to be regained.

Nearly the whole of this elaborate and complicated sequence of baths is now laid open on permanent show: of the Roman establishment as so far known, only a few rooms on the west and south-west side are inaccessible below modern buildings. Your visit starts with the Museum, now superbly lit and displayed after total reorganization in 1983–4. Only a few outstanding exhibits can be mentioned here. You are first confronted with the famous Medusa head (fig 24) and the other surviving elements of the temple's pediment. The snaky-headed Medusa appeared on Minerva's shield and so is an appropriate subject for the temple, but the native sculptor has

24   Bath, the medusa head

turned her into a male, with craggy face, penetrating gaze and luxuriant moustache. It is an odd synthesis, but the effect is striking: 'it represents,' as J M C Toynbee has put it, 'the perfect marriage of classical standards and traditions with Celtic taste and native inventiveness.' After passing the King's Bath and finds from the reservoir below it (p. 109), you come to the notable gilt-bronze head of Minerva, now lacking the helmet she would have once worn. Usually thought to belong to the cult statue (if so one on the small side), it is executed in good classical style in striking contrast to the sculptured pediment. Make sure you go up the steps behind the head to see the temple steps themselves, worn by the tread of Sulis' devotees. You now descend to the paved precinct in front of the temple. To the right of the catwalk, the wall at the rear (brick bonding courses) was constructed when the sacred spring was enclosed by a vaulted roof *c.* 200; note the steps up to it and the two massive stone bastions built later to prevent the wall from settling. On the other side of the catwalk is a dedication to Sulis from L. Marcius Memor, a *haruspex* (inspector of sacred entrails). The letters VSP have clearly been added later to the centrally-placed HAR, presumably because nobody could understand the original abbreviation. Beyond are two of the corner slabs of the Great Altar mentioned above (p. 103) now reset in their original positions. Further on are displayed more votive offerings as well as the sculptural fragments of the facade of the Four Seasons and a pediment with Luna, goddess of the Moon (perhaps belonging to it); they decorated some other part of the temple precinct (its unexcavated north side?). Finally comes a selection of the altars and tombstones of others who 'took the waters': the presence of a sculptor from the Chartres area of northern France, a lady from Metz and a man from Trier in Germany emphasizes the 'international' reputation of AQVAE SVLIS.

Now come down the steps to study a model of the baths and, to the right and left, the outflow-arch and impressive vaulted drain which took excess water from the reservoir. From here you reach the most impressive feature of the Roman remains at Bath, the Great Bath, which until 1880–1 was still covered by houses of the Georgian city. It belonged to the original scheme and remained the chief feature of the establishment throughout its life. It is one of the rare

Romano–British structures which need no description, for its
appeal is immediate and obvious: a great rectangular
swimming-bath still lined with its Roman lead and still fed by
the constant flow of water from the sacred spring. But
although the bath is still intact, the hall that enclosed it is not,
and the present open-air effect is misleading. From the
beginning it was roofed over, at first with a simple timbered
ceiling supported by twelve simple piers lining the bath and
the exterior walls. In the third period, sometime in the second
century, the whole area was re-roofed with an enormous
barrel-vault, over 50 feet high – much higher than the modern
colonnade. It was made of hollow box-tiles, to lessen the
weight, and was left open at either end to allow the steam to
escape. At the same time, the piers lining the bath had to be
strengthened to take the extra thrust of the vault; and if you
look carefully at them you will see that the middle (original)
portion was cut back at this period, and extra masonry added
both in front and behind it (fig 25). Additional piers also
strengthened the inner and outer corners of the alcoves which
face on to the ambulatory. Other details are worth noticing:
in front of you a fountain rested on the block projecting over

25   Bath, pier alongside the Great Bath

the Great Slab; a semi-circular, shrine-like structure lay on the slab at the NW corner (to your right), where the water enters the bath; and, between the two, a water-pipe of Charterhouse lead inserted into the paving in period IV (third–fourth centuries) was designed to take water from the spring direct to a new immersion bath (see below).

Retrace your steps to the museum entrance and go past it to the far end (the East Baths), where a smaller swimming-bath and a series of rooms with a complicated history, are reached. A pool built in period I was replaced by a small set of turkish baths in period II, and this set was rebuilt on a much larger scale in period IV, when an immersion-bath was also added in the apse opposite the end of the swimming-bath (the lead pipe noted above was heading for here). A portion of mosaic in the far left-hand corner is reflected in a mirror. Now go out to the other side of the Great Bath and down to the opposite end. Part of the huge vault, with its hollow box-tiles and its neat brick facing, is displayed here, to the right. But keep straight on and you enter a double arcade on the south side of the Circular Bath. The Roman masonry here is very well preserved: the inner arcade, to your right, is now filled up with modern concrete, but to your left an entire pier and two voussoirs of an arch still survive. Through the window at the far end can be viewed a drain and two stoke-holes: you will see the room they heated presently. Now pass from the corridor to the Circular Bath, which served as a cold plunge for the dry-heat sauna baths added in the early second century; before this the room was a simple *frigidarium*. In the re-roofing phase of the later second century, it was provided with a vault springing from new piers fitted between the bath and the side walls.

From the Circular Bath a few steps lead up to the viewing point over the King's Bath. As you duck your head to look at this, you are passing under one of the most substantial pieces of Roman architecture in Britain: the rounded arch above and the square-headed arch to the right, both now partially blocked with modern stonework, still display superbly jointed masonry in the same position as it was when built in the first century AD. They form two of originally three vast windows to the central *frigidarium*, designed to give an impressive view over the sacred spring and the altar of the temple-complex

beyond. Of the Roman reservoir enclosing the sacred spring
nothing can now be seen, as the King's Bath covers it.
Excavation in 1880 and 1979–80 when the spring was
temporarily diverted not only revealed an astonishing array of
votive offerings (including gemstones, brooches, pewter vessels,
12,000 coins and 90 lead 'curse-tablets' in which Sulis' help was
invoked to bring disaster to an enemy), but also the remarkable
engineering skill needed for the reservoir's construction:
massive stone blocks, laid on a foundation of rammed oak piles
and held firm by iron clamps, were covered with lead sheets
sealed at the bottom by thick waterproof mortar.

From here move to your left and through the doors
beyond. This part of the baths, first uncovered in 1885–7, was
re-excavated in 1969–75 since when it has been made
accessible. On the right is an oblong swimming bath of cold
water, with rounded ends. This was inserted only in period V
(probably fourth century) into a rectangular room (with
recesses) which in all preceding periods from the very
beginning of the baths had served as a hot room (*caldarium*)
in the moist-heat suite here. The adjacent *tepidarium* to your
left, however, survived in use throughout the life of the baths,
although it went through various modifications, including a
rebuilding of the hypocaust and alteration of the furnace-
flues. Most of its *pilae* but none of its floor is still *in situ*, and a
flue and a blocked doorway are visible in the far wall. It was
the furnace area to this room which you saw earlier through
the glass window. Finally, beyond the *tepidarium*, a small room
on the left which had a hypocaust in periods III and IV was
demolished in period V (only the impressions of *pilae* remain)
and the area used as a new furnace-room for the adjacent
tepidarium. Thus ends your visit to one of the most
remarkable witnesses of the presence of Rome in Britain. Here
is an establishment not conceived along the normal lines of
Romano–British provincial architecture, but an offspring of
the mainstream classical tradition which would have been
readily acceptable in Italy itself.

Of the rest of Roman Bath, nothing is visible except a
feeble black-and-white mosaic in the basement of the Royal
Mineral Water Hospital (enquire at the entrance). There may
have been a theatre under the Abbey; there was another
bathing-establishment south-west of the main baths; and

there was certainly a Roman town-wall on the line of its medieval successor. But whether Bath was an administrative centre is uncertain – no trace of a forum has ever been found – and the town's precise status is obscure.

The status of the two remaining towns in this region is not, however, in doubt: Gloucester was a *colonia*, a settlement of retired Roman legionaries and their families, whereas Cirencester was the tribal capital of the Dobunni. **Gloucester** (SO 8318) has been the scene of important rescue excavation during the past decade, but not a great deal has been preserved *in situ*. The recent work has done much to clear up problems surrounding the early history of the site. It used to be thought that an early legionary fortress (now known to have been for the Twentieth Legion) lay under the area of the later *colonia*, but then it was suggested that its site was at Kingsholm, one mile north of Gloucester, where a good quantity of military equipment has been found. It has now been established, however, that there *was* a legionary fortress under the *colonia*, but coin evidence firmly indicates that it cannot be earlier than AD 64. Where, then, was the earlier fortress, presumed on the evidence of Tacitus to have been founded *c*. AD 49? Excavations in 1972 at Kingsholm produced timber buildings and more military objects, and the latest coin was one of AD 64; now (1985) the defences have been found, so it now looks certain that the earliest fortress was at Kingsholm, where scattered finds have been recorded over some 50 acres. It may have had a mixed garrison of both legionaries and auxiliaries: a decorated bronze cheek-piece found in 1972 was part of an auxiliary cavalryman's helmet, and Rufus Sita, whose tombstone is in the museum, belonged to a cohort of Thracians (from Bulgaria). Otherwise, one has to postulate in addition a normal auxiliary fort of which no trace has yet been detected.

Military occupation of the Gloucester site seems to have faded out in the 80's, but the earliest civilians still lived in the military barracks before the site was properly cleared in the second century. Yet the formal settlement as a *colonia* was made under the emperor Nerva (96–98), as we know from an inscription giving its full title as *Colonia Nervia Glevensium*. The peak of the town's prosperity seems to have been in the second century, and it is now known that there was

considerable occupation, including monumental buildings,
outside the 43 acres enclosed by the defences. The old view
that Gloucester was something of a 'failed town', stunted by
the proximity of flourishing Cirencester, may now be
discounted.

The visible remains of Roman Gloucester are not plentiful:
medieval and modern development has hit them hard. Inside
the walls there are fragments of relaid Roman mosaic in the
Eastgate Market Hall, in the National Westminster Bank in
Eastgate Street, and in the entrance of the Friends' Meeting
House in Greyfriars. Northgate and Southgate Streets run on
the lines of Roman predecessors. More substantial are the
stretches of Roman city wall which have been preserved. One
of these includes part of the East Gate below Boots' store at
38–44 Eastgate Street, which is partly visible through a window
at street level or, at closer quarters, between Whitsun and
September only (Wed. and Fri., 2–5; Sat. 10–5). Excavation
here in 1974 revealed three distinct Roman phases: fragments
of the timber gate-tower of the legionary fortress of *c.* AD 65;
the stone gate-tower (six feet high) and the first *colonia* wall
built late in the first century, which was of drystone
construction, partly reused in the later wall; and the base-
plinth of the late-third-century city wall above which rose the
conspicuous large limestone blocks of the final Roman
rebuilding which replaced the earlier wall. The large circular
** tower belongs to the thirteenth century. Other portions of the
defences on the east side can be viewed in King's Walk (25
July–30 Aug. only, times as Eastgate) and below the Midlands
Electricity Board Centre in King's Square,[1] and also in the
Gloucester Furniture Centre, 71–3 Southgate Street. More
accessible is the length of wall incorporated in the archaeology
gallery in the City Museum, Brunswick Street (Mon.–Sat.
10–5). Of the fine collection of sculpture here note especially
the tombstone of Rufus Sita, mentioned above, riding down his
barbarian foe; that of L. Valerius Aurelius, veteran of the 20th
Legion, found in 1983; and that of Philus, standing in his
hooded cloak under a very classical-looking pediment. The
head with huge bulging eyes, once taken to be Romano–Celtic,

[1] Apply to the District Manager, Midlands Electricity Board, Hammond's Way,
Barnwood, Gloucester.

is more probably medieval. Other exhibits include a Bacchus
from the Spoonley Wood villa (an imported piece, probably
from Italy) and the fascinating altar of Romulus, as usual in
the guise of Mars, of which both dedicator (Gulioepius) and
sculptor (Iuventinus) are recorded.

Cirencester* (SP 0201), CORINIVM DOBVNNORVM, has the
distinction of being the second largest town of Roman Britain
after London; but its medieval and modern successor is
considerably smaller and so large areas within the walls
remain free from buildings. Very little, however, of the
Roman town is visible, though rescue excavations over the
past decade have contributed an enormous amount to our
knowledge. Once again, the place had a military origin: a first
fort (or possibly a 30-acre fortress – its exact size is
unknown), which was established in the area of the
Watermoor Hospital, was found to be too close to marshy
land, and so another fort was built, about AD 49, on better-
drained soil, on a site bounded by The Avenue, Chester Street,
Watermoor Road and St Michael's Fields. By the late 70's,
when the military moved on, the civilian settlement which had
grown up around this fort became the new administrative
centre for the *civitas* of the Dobunni. It was laid out on an
ambitious scale with a forum and basilica (only London's was
larger), what is possibly a theatre, and later an amphitheatre
too. Development continued in the second century, despite a
setback to the basilica, which had to be entirely rebuilt: the
first building, erected over the filled-in ditches of the early
fort, had badly subsided. At the end of the second century
Corinium received her first earth defences, and these were
faced in stone in the third century, when her prosperity
continued. Nor was there any slackening off in the fourth
century: the town almost certainly became the capital of
Britannia Prima when Britain was divided into four separate
Roman provinces. The evidence is an inscription in the
museum (see below). Her wealth during the fourth century is
manifestly demonstrated by the splendid mosaics (in the
Corinium Museum) laid by a school of mosaicists centred in
the town. Civic life continued well into the fifth century, when
the forum was still kept clean. Finally, however, discipline
broke down and the time came when unburied bodies were
left rotting in the street-gutters.

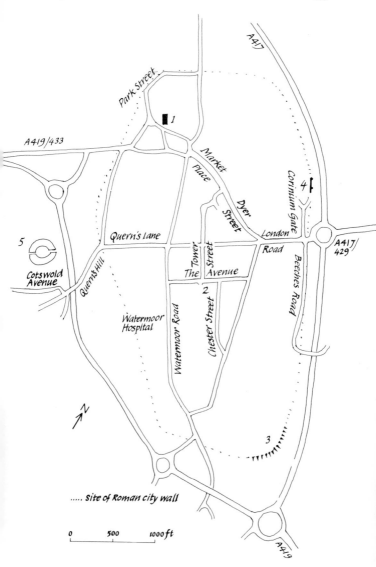

26 Cirencester, plan

The Corinium Museum in Park Street (1 on fig 26)
contains a splendid display of material which vividly
demonstrates the prosperity of the Roman town (Mon.–Sat.
10–5 or 5.30, except closed Mon., Oct.–March; Sun. 2–5 or
5.30); it is now one of the outstanding collections in the
country. The first Roman room contains some of the evidence
for the military origins of the town, including the tombstones
of two cavalry troopers, belonging to different regiments (the
ala Indiana and the *ala Thraecum*), who, like Rufus Sita at
Gloucester (p. 111), are shown trampling their foe. Further on
you reach the hall with the fourth-century mosaic of the hare,
discovered in a compact and well-equipped town-house in
Beeches Road in 1971. In the next room, after the
reconstructed section of Roman plaster, comes the first of
three more mosaic pavements which amply display both the
taste and the wealth of the inhabitants of CORINIVM. The first
depicts hunting-dogs chasing a (lost) prey in the central
roundel, with sea-beasts, and heads of Medusa and Oceanus,
in the surround. Opposite this floor, be sure not to miss the
word-square scratched on a piece of wall-plaster. It reads
ROTAS OPERA TENET AREPO SATOR, which means 'Arepo the
sower holds the wheels by his effort'. The words are set out
one above the other, so, most ingeniously, the line reads the
same from left to right, right to left, bottom to top and top to
bottom. The first words of the Lord's Prayer, *Pater Noster*,
are contained twice over in the formula (with two A's and O's,
alpha and omega, the beginning and end of the Greek
alphabet, left to spare; cf. *Rev.* I.8). This seems too
extraordinary to be coincidental, and the *graffito* may
therefore attest the presence of Christians in CORINIVM. The
date of this is unfortunately not certain, but the first three
words of another example, found in Manchester in 1978, were
scratched on a broken amphora datable *c.* 175/185 AD, and it
has been claimed as the earliest archaeological evidence for
Christianity in Britain.

The mosaic in the second bay, which was very probably
laid, like the hunting-dogs floor, in the late second century, is
part of an elaborate composition of which five roundels
survive complete. Three contain Seasons (Winter is missing)
and the other two portray mythological events – Actaeon
being torn to pieces by his dogs (for seeing the goddess Diana

at her bath) (fig 27), and Silenus, one of Dionysus' attendants riding on a donkey. The imaginative reconstruction around this floor gives an excellent impression of what a Romano–British interior may have looked like. The third mosaic was laid in the fourth century and depicts Orpheus with his lyre, charming the birds and animals which proceed in stately fashion round him. The idea of putting the animals and birds in concentric circles around the central figure of Orpheus seems to be peculiar to the Corinium mosaic-school, and the subject appears on several mosaics known from the neighbourhood: Woodchester is one of them, but the rest are covered up or lost.

At the far end of the museum is a huge Corinthian capital with the heads of four native deities, and next to it a dedication to Jupiter by Septimius, governor of Britannia Prima (PRIMAE PROVINCIAE RECTOR), evidence which suggests that Corinium was capital of this new province in the fourth century. The Venus mosaic from Kingscote (p. 117) is now also displayed here. Several sculptures illustrating the diversity of deities honoured in the town close the Roman section of the Museum.

27 Cirencester, mosaic of Actaeon

Apart from the objects in the Museum, Cirencester does not
have much of its Roman past on show. The apse of the
basilica (2 on fig 26) is marked out in modern materials in a cu
de-sac which opens off The Avenue; but nothing else is at
** present visible within the walls. The defences are visible as a
large bank on the south-east side of the town, in Watermoor
recreation-ground (3 on fig 26). North of London Road,
however, a stretch has been fully excavated and conserved (4).
It is reached from the housing-estate of Corinium Gate, and is
signposted from the footbridge on the right. The first feature
to notice here are the foundations of two projecting bastions.
One is square, the other polygonal, but the superstructure of
both was probably polygonal. These bastions belong to the
latest phase of the defences and were probably added about
AD 330. Now climb the bank and survey the defences from
above. There was a floodbank here in the late first century
(not now visible), but the first proper defences were erected
towards the end of the second century. These consisted of an
earth bank, and a square internal tower of stone, which is
visible roughly half-way along the bank. At least some of the
gateways were also built in stone at the same time. The earth
defences themselves, however, were not given a stone front
until *c.* 220 at the earliest. It was only about four feet wide, as
can be seen from the section of it still standing, south of, and
adjacent to, the tower. But you will also notice that elsewhere
the wall is much thicker, between seven and nine feet wide.
The reason for the variation is obscure, but presumably such
parts of the original wall which were in danger of collapse
were rebuilt as occasion demanded.

Finally, the amphitheatre is well worth a visit (5). Turn left
at the end of Querns Lane, right immediately after crossing
the by-pass, and then right at the fork, along Cotswold
Avenue. The footpath to the amphitheatre [AM;A] is opposite
Martin Close. It is now a large grassy depression, with
entrance gaps at either end and banks still standing to an
impressive height of about 25 feet above the arena floor.
Excavation has shown that the earliest building, probably
erected late in the first century, had entrance walls of timber
posts with dry-stone walling, and this was rebuilt in mortared
masonry, together with the arena wall, around the beginning
of the second century. There were several other rebuildings but

the amphitheatre apparently remained in use into the fifth century. The seats throughout were of timber, but shallow stone terracing walls in the banks provided some stability. No stonework has been left exposed.

The prosperity of Cirencester must have been largely due to the wealth of the surrounding countryside. The town formed the market-centre for the agricultural products of the many villas which are known in the Cotswold region, but it was not the only market-centre. Here, as elsewhere in Roman Britain, other nuclei of habitation sprang up at focal points, especially on or near lines of communication, to act as collecting centres and service areas for the surrounding countryside. All too little is known about such settlements, but fieldwork and aerial photography suggest that they were normally unwalled, sprawling centres of population which grew spontaneously and lacked the regularly-planned street-grid of the 'official' towns established by central authority. That such villages need not have been merely a collection of peasants' huts has been amply demonstrated by recent excavation at one example, The Chessals near Kingscote (ST 806960) in Gloucestershire. Excavation here in 1975–80 revealed several rooms of a well-constructed building ranged around a courtyard, which seems to have been an expansion, in the late third or early fourth century, of an earlier, smaller structure. Three of the rooms had hypocausts, two of them excellently preserved, and one of these had a largely intact mosaic floor featuring a bust of Venus in the central roundel and an aquatic scene in an adjacent panel. Found collapsed on top of this floor were substantial portions of painted wall-decoration which have now been reconstructed: it shows a figured scene from classical mythology, probably the story of Achilles on the island of Scyros. It is of astonishingly high artistic quality for a fresco from Roman Britain – the heads in particular are superb, delicate renderings – and there is some reason for thinking that it may be the work of a Greek painter. Other rooms contained a large number of hearths and ovens, and it appears that the building had an industrial use with some parts set aside as living-quarters. The mosaic and especially the wall-painting, together with other finds such as chip-carved stone table-tops, suggest an owner with wealth and a degree of sophistication. This building forms part of a settlement spread over at least 150 acres, approaching the size of some of the largest towns of the province. This surprising fact presumably bears witness to the prosperity that was to be gained from the rich farming land of the region, but we are still largely ignorant of the precise economic basis of these villages and their relationship to the surrounding villas. The site of Kingscote is reached by the first track on the south side of A4135 Tetley to Dursley road west of its junction with the road signposted Frocester and Gloucester, itself ½m west of 'The Hunters' Hall' in Kingscote. Since the second edition of this book (1980), however, the site has been backfilled, and there is nothing whatever to see on the ground today. The Venus mosaic has been lifted and is on display in the Cirencester museum (p. 115), next to the Orpheus mosaic from Barton Farm, but the splendid wall-painting mentioned above is unfortunately in store at present. The building excavated at Kingscote provides above all a salutary demonstration that not all dwellings in these lesser, unwalled, sprawling agricultural settlements were unsophisticated and unadorned: the standard of living enjoyed by the man who commissioned the Venus mosaic and the Achilles wall-painting is one which is more usually associated either with wealthy houses in the fully-fledged towns or else with the richer self-contained country estates of the Romano–British countryside.

About the villas of the countryside much is also still to be learnt, especially the stages in their development and the details of their farming economy: many of them were excavated at a time when mosaics and hypocausts were of greater interest than the less spectacular evidence of farm-buildings or industrial activity. The vast majority of villas have been reburied, but the area covered in this chapter has, in fact, more visible villa remains than anywhere else in Britain. It is convenient to deal with these in two main groups – those around Bristol, and those around Cirencester.

Bristol itself was not a Roman town, though the City Museum has a superbly-displayed collection of local finds. There was, however, a settlement known as ABONA in the suburb of **Sea Mills** (ST 5575). It probably began as the *vicus* of an early Roman fort, but by the end of the second century shops and houses in stone had been constructed. The foundations of one building, probably a house, are visible on

the north side of Portway (A4) at its junction with Roman
Way, opposite a bus-shelter about 2m south of Avonmouth.
There is a small courtyard with rooms surrounding it.

About 2m NW of Sea Mills is the Roman villa of **King's
Weston** (ST 5377). From the roundabout (M-spur) in
Avonmouth take the B4054 for ½m, then turn left at the traffic-
lights along King's Weston Avenue. The Roman villa lies on
the right after another ½m. The key must be obtained from the
Blaise Castle Museum in Henbury (Sat.–Wed., 10–1, 2–5; from
the villa keep straight as far as you can, then left for the centre
of Henbury). The part of the villa still accessible was built some
time between AD 270 and 300, and saw various alterations
before its abandonment towards the end of the fourth century.
It was excavated in 1948–50. The entrance leads immediately
to the four rooms of the east wing, of which the largest had
a hypocaust inserted into the floor some time later than the
original building. The threshold of this room leads to a long
corridor which gave access through columns (a few bases are
visible) to a gravelled court on the right. The building was
entered by a small porch which projects from the south (left-
hand) wall of the corridor. The west wing is covered by a
wooden shed. The room on the left has a mediocre geometric
mosaic, but the floor of the other room had largely perished
and the present mosaic comes from another Bristol villa (at
Brislington) which was found in 1900. Beyond are the remains
of a small bath-suite. The apsidal heated room belonged (with
an adjoining room to the right, now destroyed) to the original
building, but the other two compartments – on the left an
undressing-room, and, in the centre, a room with steps leading
down to a cold bath – are of later date.

On the other side of Bristol (to the SE) are two more villa-
sites close to one another. Leave Bristol on the Bath Road
(A4); at the roundabout avoid the Keynsham by-pass and
take the B-road for the town itself. After ¼m you will see a
cemetery on your left behind some trees. This is the site of the
Keynsham (ST 6469) villa, a spacious example of the
courtyard type, as proved by excavations in 1922–4. Only
fragments of the north wing, together with a few displaced
and broken columns, are visible today, near the mortuary
chapel. Mosaics from the Keynsham villa, however, are kept
at nearby Somerdale: continue on towards Keynsham, and

fork left by the church. Immediately after bridging the A4 and the railway-line, you will come to the entrance to Fry's chocolate-factory at **Somerdale** (ST 6569). Facing the entrance-lodge are the foundations of a small Roman house, discovered in 1922 when the factory was being built and untidily laid out here 300 yards south of its original position. Finds from the villas are displayed in the museum at the entrance-lodge (6 am–10 pm, Mondays to Fridays only), but the best mosaics from Keynsham, including a representation of Europa about to be abducted by Jupiter disguised as a bull (cf. fig 14), are preserved in a hall in the factory proper, and can only be visited by prior arrangement.

Of the villas situated around Cirencester, the least worth visiting is at **Wadfield** (SP 0226). It lies on the left of the Winchcombe to Andoversford minor road, 2m south of the former and 200 yards beyond the AM sign to Belas Knap Long Barrow. The villa is situated in a small enclosure of trees in the middle of a field, reached by first taking the public footpath signposted Humblebee and Winchcombe, and then, when it bends round to the left, by following the field-wall on your left until you reach a gate. The entrance to the villa-enclosure lies immediately before you. The villa was first discovered and partly explored in 1863 and again later in the nineteenth century. Some of the walls, now overgrown, are still traceable, but the overall ground-plan, consisting of two wings ranged about a courtyard, is not now distinguishable; that on your left (south) contained the bath-suite. One room of the villa is still floored with red *tesserae* (note also a moulded stone capital nearby), but the main room, covered by a wooden hut, has a partly-restored geometric mosaic, of which half is in position. The rest was presumably lost soon after discovery, for of some mosaic it was written that 'its speedy removal was found to be absolutely necessary in order to preserve it from the Winchcombe public, who in the space of one Sunday afternoon carried off a large portion, in small pieces, as souvenirs.' The mosaic may belong to the second century, in contrast to the other visible villa-mosaics of this region, which are of the fourth century. Another villa is situated in Spoonley Wood, only a mile away across the valley, but it is in a totally ruined state and not worth a visit (App. I).

Much better preserved is the **Great Witcombe** villa
(SO 8914) [AM]. Like so many villas, it is situated in a
beautiful position close to a source of water; but here the
water is a little *too* near, for the whole hillside is riddled with
springs, and the owners had great difficulty in preventing
these from undermining the whole house and carrying it away
down the slope. Most of the visible walls, which belong to
rooms arranged round three sides of an open courtyard, were
built c. AD 250–70, but alterations were made thereafter, in the
period 270–400. Traces have also been found of an earlier
dwelling on the site, dating back to the late first century.

The villa is reached by a mile-long road on the right (the
south) of the A417 (Gloucester–Cirencester) immediately east
of the roundabout where it is crossed by the A46
(Cheltenham–Stroud); do not take the turning to the
Witcombes. There is normally an AM signpost, but it is not
always clearly visible. There are also frequently problems over
access to the locked, covered rooms; a key is not available at
all times. First walk over to the far corner to the remains of
the bath-house, most of which belongs to the secondary phase,
although its development is likely to have been more
complicated than shown on the plan (fig 28). In the hut on
the left is a hot plunge-bath (8; there is another at 8a),

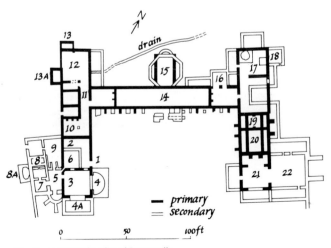

28   Great Witcombe, plan of Roman villa

associated with the hottest room of sticky damp heat
(*caldarium*, 7), under the square cover. The wooden bridge
passes over the hypocausted *tepidarium* (5) with apse to the
right and stoking area to the left (9). Note the two slabs
immured on the left of the entrance to the second hut: this
was a doorway, built on the skew, to link the *tepidarium* to
the *sudatorium* of dry heat (6). Another well-preserved
doorway links the latter with the *frigidarium* (3), which is
floored with a crude but lively sea-creature mosaic. You have
now gone through the baths in the reverse order to that used
by the Roman bather, who would have entered the suite from
the courtyard (1), changed in 3, moved into 5 with its tepid
heat and then either chosen the moist heat of 7 or the more
rigorous dry heat of 6 before returning to 3 for a cold
plunge in 4 or 4a. 2 appears to have been a latrine.

The next room on the uphill side (10) has a central basin
and three niches in the walls (fig 29). It is believed to have had
a religious function, perhaps the worship of the local water-
nymphs, who no doubt needed appeasing to prevent
landslides (cf. the Deep Room at Lullingstone, p. 59). The

29   *Great Witcombe villa, shrine*

end of this wing, at the top of the slope, was the area first planned as the original baths; 12 once had a hypocaust and 13/13a are the foundations of plunge-baths. The latter were probably demolished when the more spacious bath-suite was built further south, but 12 may have been retained as a heated living-room. Turn right along the corridor (14) and note, away to the left, a drain and, on the right, a series of buttresses designed to prevent the foundations from settling. In the centre of the corridor, on the left, is an octagonal construction, added in the second period to replace the original rectangular room, visible beneath (15); it may have been the dining-room.

The rest of the villa, first uncovered in 1818–19, has little of interest. The rooms grouped around 16 seem to have been the entrance area, 17 was the kitchen with ovens and hearths, and a latrine (18) beyond. 19 and 20 are massive substructures for what are presumed to have been living-quarters above; if they were not here it is hard to see where else they can have been in the villa, unless the SW wing had an upper storey. Rooms 21–2 have been interpreted as a barn, but if so one curiously close to the presumed living area and possessing an architectural solidity uncharacteristic of such structures.

The outstanding Cotswold site, however, is at **Chedworth*** (SP 0513), which is widely regarded as the finest preserved villa in the country. It is certainly one of the most beautiful, lying at the head of the peaceful wooded valley of the Coln in an utterly charming position. The site is open as follows: Mar.–Oct., Tues.–Sun. (and Bank Holiday Mondays), 11–6; Nov.–Dec. 9, Wed.–Sun., 11–4. It is closed on Good Friday and from 9 December to the end of February.

The villa is best approached from the Fosse Way (A429) 1m south of the crossroads with the A40: take the road to Yanworth (*not* Chedworth village) and then to the site (signposted). The other approach is from the north: take the turning to Withington from the A436, $\frac{1}{2}$m west of Andoversford and then follow signposts to the villa. It was discovered accidentally in 1864 by a gamekeeper digging for a lost ferret, and has been National Trust property since 1924. Only excavations since the 1960's, however, have clarified the history of the site, and four major phases are now known. In the first, dated to the first half of the second century, the

house consisted of two separate buildings on the west and
south and a detached bath-suite to the north. In the early
third century (phase II) the west and south wings were rebuilt
after a fire, the baths were enlarged, and a few rooms were
added on their east side (now forming the middle of the north
wing). In the early fourth century the villa took on its present
appearance: the existing elements were united with a covered
verandah, and an inner garden and outer courtyard were
created. At the same time the dining-room received its
mosaics and the north half of the west wing was converted to
take a second set of baths (damp-heat); meanwhile the
existing baths were modified into dry-heat sauna-baths.
Finally, in phase IV (late-fourth-century), the north wing was
further extended by the addition of a new dining-room.
Occupation continued to the end of the century.

The path first leads to the latrine (labelled 4) with its usual
sewer (now gravel-filled) and channel for running water. This
and the nearby 'steward's room' (2), so-called because a large
number of coins were found here, were added in the fourth

30   *Chedworth villa, mosaic of Spring*

century to the original south wing, which once began just
before the steps (plaque). Now retrace your steps, passing
through the kitchen (3) with an oven-base. The latter served
the heated dining-room (*triclinium*) (5), which is reached by
turning right along the corridor of the west wing. In its
present form it dates to the first half of the fourth century.
The most striking feature is the mosaic floor, laid by the
Cirencester workshop. The main portion is partially
destroyed, but originally it contained a central octagon
(perhaps with a representation of Bacchus) surrounded by
eight main panels. These were filled with figures of nymphs
and satyrs, and the greater portion of three remain. Perfectly
preserved, however, are three of the Seasons, represented as
charming little boys: Spring wears only a scarf and holds a
bird and flower-basket (fig 30); Summer, who is completely
naked and also winged, holds a garland and flower basket;
and Winter wearing a hood, cloak and leggings, holds a twig
and a dead hare. This part of the room probably formed an
antechamber; the dining-room proper lies beyond the
projecting piers and has an ordinary geometric floor bordered
on two sides by superb floral scrolls springing from vases.
Note the drain in the far left-hand corner, for swilling
rubbish away after a meal.

The next three rooms (6, 7, 8) have nothing of interest and
were probably ordinary day-rooms or possibly bedrooms; 6
had a hypocaust (note recesses for the wall-flues). Next we
enter the baths of damp heat, which once again only belong to
the fourth-century expansion of Chedworth. They are a very
well-preserved example and give an excellent idea of the
Roman bathing system. First (10) is the undressing room with
a mosaic floor relaid in 1978; it has a hypocaust underneath
and box-shaped flue tiles in the walls. Visible here is a tree-
stump marking the 1864 ground-level. Next (11) is the little
tepidarium, with flue-tiles and hypocaust *pilae* clearly visible
and mosaic floor in position; but the floor of the *caldarium*
(12) has gone, leaving just the *pilae*. A semi-circular hot bath
opens off it. Then the bather would return to the mosaic-
floored room where you are now standing, the *frigidarium* (4),
to cool off before taking a plunge in the cold bath (15), still
complete with its steps and drainage-pipe. He would then go
back to 10 to put his clothes on. The heavy wear on the door-

sill of 11 shows the popularity of these baths with the owner
and his guests. The furnace for heating the baths can be
studied outside (turn left and left again); you cross the
drainage-pipe from 15 en route.

Now go up to the far left corner to the shrine of the water
nymphs (17), with curved back and octagonal pool; this was
the villa's natural source of spring-water. Its prominence has
partly prompted a recent theory, quite unfounded, that the site
is not a villa but a religious cult-centre. A worn Christian
monogram carved later on the rim of the pool is in the Museum
(left of entrance).

The first part of the north wing contains another bath-suite,
the original baths of the villa. These were originally quite
simple, were then extended in phase II, and then partly
demolished. The plan of the demolished rooms is marked out
in modern concrete. The final, fourth-century alterations
included the building of the colonnade, of which the column-
stumps are visible (fig 31), and the conversion of the baths to
the dry-heat variety to supplement those in the west wing.
Mount the steps into room 21, which was the undressing-

31 Chedworth villa, the north wing

room of the final baths (previously the *tepidarium*). On your
left you can peer through the glass to see two small hot
rooms, originally with apsidal plunge-baths later disused (22).
Straight ahead (23) is a large cold plunge-bath and two
flanking immersion baths, all added in the fourth century.
Now come down the steps and note on your left (24), an
apsed room with a hypocaust of which only a few *pilae*
remain intact; then (25), two rooms with channelled
hypocausts, the larger probably being some kind of reception-
room.

The rest of the north wing can be summarily dealt with.
Don't, incidentally, be misled by the tiresome modern 'roofs'
which the walls have been given here, as elsewhere: they are
designed to protect the ancient structure from rain and frost.
Rooms 26–29 belong to the early-third-century extension of
the north wing. 26 shows its hypocaust *pilae* but the floor has
gone. The rest of the wing (30–32) was constructed in the
villa's closing years at the end of the fourth century. The very
last room was the largest in the villa, heated by a channelled
hypocaust. One end was raised on a dais as the hypocaust is
on a higher level here: it is probably another dining-room. A
visit to the little Museum completes a tour of this lovely site.

Brief mention must also be made of another villa, one of
the largest and most luxurious found in Britain, though, as in
all cases except Fishbourne, the summit of prosperity was not
reached until the fourth century. It lies at **Woodchester**
(ST 8403), a village 2m south of Stroud off the A46. 64 rooms
grouped round two courtyards were found at the end of the
eighteenth century. There is nothing whatever visible today,
but the uncovering of its chief mosaic, 49 feet square, every
twelve years or so, justifies its inclusion in this book: the last
time it was exposed was in 1973. It is a magnificent portrayal
of Orpheus charming the birds and animals, a larger version
of the mosaic in the Corinium Museum and, like that one,
laid by Cirencester mosaicists in the early fourth century AD.
It is greatly to be hoped that money can soon be found to
** keep the Woodchester mosaic open on permanent display.

Further away from the area I have so far dealt with, but
still in the Cotswolds, is the villa at **North Leigh** (SP 3915)
[AM] in Oxfordshire. It was first discovered and excavated
in 1813–16 and again before the First World War; further

examination and consolidation has recently been completed. In
its final fourth-century form, North Leigh is an excellent
example of the courtyard type of villa, with wings on three sides
and an entrance-gate on the fourth. This was, however, only the
last stage in a long and complicated development: the earliest
villa, built in the second century, consisted of a small main
house, under the later north wing, and a detached bath-house
at the NE corner. Further buildings, discovered by aerial
photography but as yet unexcavated, lie to the SW of the
main villa: they very probably include the agricultural
buildings of the villa-estate.

The site is signposted from the A4095, 3m NE of Witney
(East End; ignore directions to N. Leigh village; open Apr.
–Sept., 9.30–6.30. Sun. 2–6.30; officially closed Oct.–March,

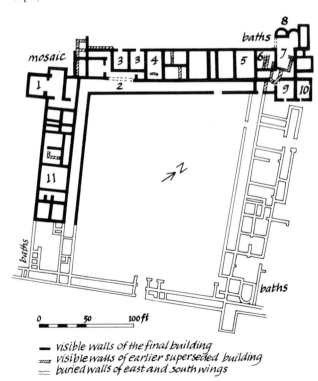

32 North Leigh, plan of Roman villa

but in effect viewable at any time). You first arrive at the main heated room of the villa (under cover; 1 on fig 32). This is floored with a geometric mosaic that was laid by Cirencester mosaicists at the beginning of the fourth century, as is known from stylistic comparisons with other mosaics (fig 33). The hypocaust is still in perfect condition, and part of the floor has been cut away to reveal the *pilae* beneath. Now walk along the corridor (2) of the north wing, the main living-quarters, towards the modern cottage at the NE corner. On your left is another heated room (3), this time with a channelled hypocaust, as distinct from the pillared type in the mosaic room. Beyond this the walls of some more living-rooms have been consolidated, but not all the visible remains belong to the same period. Thus the curved wall in room 4 and the wall built of stones pitched at an angle both belong to earlier phases in the villa's history, and would have been buried below the floors of the final building. Room 5 has another channelled hypocaust, after which begins the main bath-suite of the NE angle. The rooms here have a

33 North Leigh, mosaic

complicated structural history, elucidated during
consolidation work in 1975–7. The earliest structures are the
apsed room underneath 7 and the two parallel walls under
room 6. They were part of a bath-house, probably of the
second century, which originally stood detached from a much
smaller north wing. The north wing (as far as 5) was itself
substantially rebuilt at a later period (perhaps towards the end
of the third century), and extended some years afterwards by
the addition of the unheated living rooms 6 and 7. Finally
rooms were created around these in the mid fourth century to
form a new bath-suite, with a semicircular plunge-bath at
8 and a pair of rooms with channelled hypocausts (9 and 10),
heated by stoke-holes on their south side. Now walk down
towards the river, following the site of the east wing, which
contained another set of baths. Turning right, past the site of
the gateway leading to the courtyard, you reach the
foundations of the west wing, perhaps the servants' quarters.
Room 11 once had several ovens or furnaces in it, at least one
used for smelting. Again, not all the visible walls belong to the
same period.

It will have been noted that nearly all the villas mentioned
above reached the height of their prosperity during the fourth
century. Their owners must clearly have been very wealthy to
be able to afford the sumptuous mosaics of which such
impressive vestiges remain to this day. An equally rich
patronage, presumably by the owners of these same villas, is
implied by the building of an elegant temple-complex at
Lydney (SO 6102) in the early years of the fourth century. The
site has long been known, and was extensively excavated by Sir
Mortimer Wheeler in 1928–9; more recent work (1980–81) has
clarified its chronology. The temple itself was dedicated to
Nodens, who was certainly connected with hunting and
perhaps also with the sea: the main mosaic in the temple, now
lost, depicted sea-monsters and fish and was dedicated by a
naval officer. In addition, Nodens appears to be connected with
healing, and the discovery of numerous votive figures of dogs
in the excavations supports this, as dogs are often associated
with healing sanctuaries in the ancient world. In addition to the
temple, there was a long building of eleven rooms opening out
onto a verandah (apparently for patients to spend the night in
the hope of a visitation from the god); a large guest-house with

numerous rooms ranged about a courtyard; and a fine set of baths. The sanctuary was clearly built by and for worshippers of some standing. Coins indicate that the cult was still popular in the second half of the fourth century when Christianity was growing in popularity at the expense of paganism. The sanctuary is, in fact, the best visible example of a pagan Romano–British cult-centre, of which many examples are known through fieldwork or excavation.

The existing remains of the Lydney complex, situated within a prehistoric hill-fort amidst the luxuriant foliage of a private deer-park, are very overgrown and are unlikely to prove of great interest except to the enthusiastic visitor. In 1987 they were open on Sundays, Wednesdays and Bank Holidays between late April and mid-June, and every day for the last week in May, 11–6. At other times between Easter and September only, visits are permitted by prior appointment only with the Lydney Estate Office, Lydney, Glos. (Tel. 0594 42844). You should ask for directions from the Office, reached by a drive off the A48, immediately east of the village of Aylburton (gate piers). Remember to wear old clothes and take a torch if you wish to explore the iron-mine (see below). The temple is of unusual plan, being neither strictly classical nor Romano–Celtic in type: it consisted of a rectangular outer wall with bays or 'chapels' and an inner shrine with three small sanctuaries at the far end (nearer the path). In the first building the roof of the inner shrine was supported on six piers, but when one of these subsided, some time between 367 and 375, with the consequent collapse of the temple, the spaces between the piers were blocked up in the rebuilding to make a continuous wall. In addition, L-shaped walls were built round three of the bays in the ambulatory, but the purpose of these side-chapels is unknown: presumably they were connected with some temple-rite, perhaps healing. The site of the long dormitory building is behind the temple, on the left side of the track, under the trees. The remains of the guest-house, which are also filled in, were found to the right of the track, opposite the bath-house. Most of the latter is still visible, including several heated rooms and stoke-holes. At one point the Roman floor-level is marked by a massive door-sill still in position, linking the *tepidarium* with the large, apsed *caldarium*. The metal covers here close off the entrance to an exploratory iron-mine, of which a better example will be seen presently. Continue along the track a little further and you will see on the left, next to the large tree, the foundations of a water-tank which supplied the baths. Now strike through the bracken to the right of the track, over to the ramparts of the prehistoric hill-fort. These, erected some time in the first century BC or AD, are at their most impressive here. With a bit of searching you will find the metal covers that close off another Roman iron-mine, which in many ways is the most exciting of the present remains at Lydney. By the light of a torch you can climb down the steps and examine the walls of the narrow passage, still bearing the pick-marks of the Roman miners. The mine was never fully operational: this passage was only a test-dig in the hope of finding a body of iron-ore rich enough to be worth extracting. It was probably made in the third century AD when Roman activity inside the hill-fort prior to the building of the temple seems to have been

** at its height.

The Romans exploited iron in many parts of the Forest of Dean, and the centre of the industry was the small town of ARICONIVM, now Weston-under-Penyard near Ross-on-Wye (nothing visible). The road which linked Weston with Lydney has long been thought of as Roman, and earlier editions of this book directed readers to the preserved stretch of it at Blackpool Bridge (SO 6508), reached by taking the Coleford road (B4431) just west of Blakeney on the A48 and turning left after two miles ('Soudley, scenic road'); the ancient road is on the left after the railway bridge and cattle-grid. Questions have been raised from time to time about whether it really was a Roman road, and neither the kerb stones, nor the paved surface, nor its exceptionally narrow width (eight feet) conformed to the behaviour of Roman roads elsewhere in Britain. In 1985 a section cut across the road at Soudley found that the paving rested on a foundation of charcoal, samples of which were sent for radio-carbon dating. The conclusion from the laboratory results is that the road is not earlier than the seventeenth century.

Chapter 4

East Anglia

Buckinghamshire, Cambridgeshire (part of), Essex,
Hertfordshire, Norfolk and Suffolk

In about AD 10 Cunobelinus, better known as the Cymbeline
of Shakespeare's play, became king of the Trinovantes, the
tribe occupying the area of modern Essex. Very rapidly his
influence extended over the whole of SE England, and his
capital at Colchester became the most important centre of
pre-Roman Britain, defended by a complicated series of dykes
still traceable to the west and south of the modern town. It is
not surprising, therefore, that the Roman invading army
under Aulus Plautius in AD 43, three years or so after
Cunobelinus' death, made for Colchester after crossing the

Thames. Before advancing on the capital, Plautius sent for the Emperor Claudius, and the triumph over Camulodunum, 'the fortress of Camulos' (a war-god), was duly completed in imperial company.

The first Roman occupation of **Colchester*** (TL 9925) took the form of a legionary fortress situated under the western half of the later town. A military origin, first proved in 1965, was further confirmed in the excavations of 1971–5, when part of the eastern legionary defences, as well as fragments of barrack blocks, were found under the new shopping precinct on the south side of High Street, and also the legionary ditch on the west side near the Balkerne Gate. Then, in AD 49–50, the first town was founded at CAMVLODVNVM. It was, as the historian Tacitus tells us 'a strong *colonia* of ex-soldiers established on conquered territory, to provide a protection against rebels and a centre for instructing the provincials in the procedures of the law'. Its official title was COLONIA CLAVDIA VICTRICENSIS. The town did not spring up overnight. The recent excavations have shown that, as at Gloucester (p 110), the earliest settlers lived in the legionary barracks, which were hardly altered to accommodate them, while the authorities busied themselves with erecting public buildings a little to the east of the former fortress. Chief among these was a vast classical-style temple raised on a lofty *podium* and approached by a flight of steps. It was dedicated to the Emperor Claudius and was viewed, in British eyes, as the *arx aeternae dominationis*, 'the stronghold of everlasting domination', according to Tacitus. The presence of this symbol and the alleged rapacity of the imperial financial administrator Catus Decianus were enough to spark off the famous revolt of the Iceni under their queen Boudica (Boadicea) in AD 60 or 61. The portents in Colchester immediately before the revolt are described by Tacitus in a graphic passage: 'the statue of Victory fell down, its back turned as though in retreat from the enemy. Women roused into frenzy chanted of approaching destruction, and declared that the cries of barbarians had been heard in the council-chamber, that the theatre had re-echoed with shrieks, that a reflection of the *colonia*, overthrown, had been seen in the Thames estuary. The sea appeared blood-red, and spectres of human corpses were left behind as the tide went out.' When the revolt broke, there was no hope for the Roman inhabitants of the *colonia*. Tacitus reports that the settlement was undefended: how the colonists must have rued the slighting of the legionary defences, a demolition demonstrated in the 1972–3 excavations. 'In the attack,' says Tacitus, 'everything was broken down and burnt. The temple where the soldiers had congregated was besieged for two days and then sacked.' Archaeological evidence of Boudicca's attack has been encountered usually in the area west of the Temple of Claudius, suggesting that the earliest *colonia* was confined to this western half of the later city. The evidence is generally a thick layer of ash and burnt wattle-and-daub, but in 1927 blackened samian pots, stacked together waiting to be sold, together with molten fragments of glass vessels which had fused into them, provided an even more vivid illustration of Tacitus' words. The Boudican fire has also uniquely preserved for us part of a bed or couch, the weave of its cloth mattress still visible in carbonized form. This was excavated in 1972.

Our knowledge of the later development of Roman Colchester is less complete. Recovery after the Boudican fire seems to have been slow, but by the beginning of the second century occupation had spread into most of the 108 acres later enclosed by the town wall. Excavation in 1970 and 1972–3 has shown that this was built early in the second century, perhaps *c.* 120/30, and was apparently at first free-standing, the bank behind being added *c.* 150. Colchester was thus provided with city walls a century earlier than most Romano–British towns, a proud witness of its prestigious rank as *colonia* (cf. also Gloucester, p 111 and Lincoln, p 166).

The best starting-place for a tour of Roman Colchester is the Museum, situated in the castle which the Normans built on the foundations of the Temple of Claudius (weekdays 10–5; Sun., Apr.–Sept. only, 2.30–5). There are many splendid objects displayed here and some must be singled out for comment. On the right of the entrance-passageway is the Beryfield pavement, the best-preserved mosaic so far to have come from the Roman town. Inside the main hall, on the left, are parts of two mosaics from Lion Walk and some fine second-century geometric mosaics from North Hill. Upstairs note the case illustrating Claudian Colchester and the Boudican fire and, on the other side of it, the group of

charming objects from a child's grave of *c.* AD 50, including
terracotta toys in the shape of a boar, a bull and other
animals, caricatures of reclining and reciting figures, and a
drinking-bottle. Further on in the corner is one of the best
bronze statuettes to survive from Roman Britain, an imported
figure of Mercury made about AD 200. In the centre of the
next wing is the Colchester Sphinx, a funerary monument
vigorously rendered in British stone, with a man's head (no
doubt the deceased) between her paws. Nearby is the
gladiator vase, produced by a local workshop about AD 200
depicting a combat between Memnon and Valentinus, as the
inscription round the top informs us. Finally, magnificently
displayed against the rich red curtain, are two famous
military tombstones from the early days of Roman
Colchester. One is that of Marcus Favonius Facilis, centurion
of the Twentieth Legion, and it contains a superb full-length
portrait of the dead man (fig 34). Great attention has been
paid to the details of his uniform, including his sword, his
dagger and the vine-staff, the symbol of his rank, which he
holds in his right hand. The other tombstone depicts an
auxiliary cavalryman from Bulgaria, wearing a metal-plated
jerkin. He is called Longinus, and his father goes by the
delightful name of Sdapeze, son of Matycus. The inscription
has been broken, and the face of the deceased mutilated, while
that of the grotesque barbarian under his feet survives intact.
It is reasonable to assume that this damage was done by
Boudicca's followers in the sack of Colchester in AD 60 or 61.

When you have finished looking at the Museum (and the
pottery collection of the next wing, one of the most detailed
in Britain (being re-arranged, 1987), deserves more than a
cursory glance), ask a custodian to take you down to the
vaults. They belong to the substructures of the massive
Temple of Claudius, and form one of the earliest and most
impressive monuments of Roman Britain. The superstructure
was entirely swept away by the Normans when they built their
castle at the end of the eleventh century, but a model of the
temple is on show near the entrance to the Museum. You may
think this is fanciful, but Roman temples of the classical type,
rare in Britain, are sufficiently stereotyped to allow a high
degree of confidence in their reconstruction. The vaults still
visible were designed purely to support the weight of the

**

34 *Colchester, tombstone of Facilis*

temple above; there was no access to them in Roman times, and they were filled with rammed sand until the seventeenth century, though the Roman date of the work was not recognized until 1919. The plan consists of two parallel vaults with one cross-wall off-centre. At one point the join between the Roman and the Norman masonry can be seen.

A few other Roman remnants can be traced in the castle grounds. On leaving the Museum turn right and follow the path running alongside the castle wall, which here, as elsewhere, displays plenty of re-used Roman tile. Near the NW corner, the path slopes down and cuts through a flint wall. This is a tiny fragment of one of the walls which enclosed the temple-precinct. Nearby, over in the shrubbery to the left of the path, near the fence, a section of Roman drain is preserved behind railings. West of the bandstand, a little further on, are some red tessellated pavements belonging to a town-house excavated over fifty years ago. Finally, two further portions of Roman drain are visible through grilles in the grass east of the castle, near the children's playground.

Nothing else of Roman Colchester is visible within the walls, but the latter survive for much of their original course; a walk round them takes about $1\frac{1}{4}$ hours. The Roman work is at its best on the west side of the town near the mighty Balkerne Gate. This is reached from the Museum by turning

35   Colchester, south part of Balkerne Gate (from inside)

right along High Street and going down the narrow lane at
the end by the 'Waggon and Horses'. The ruins of the
gateway, though much mutilated, are still impressive. Its
position, wholly in front of the line of the adjacent wall, and
its massive size (107 feet wide), set it quite apart from the
other city gates of Roman Britain, an anomaly which requires
explanation. Recent careful examination of the structure has
revealed that a free-standing monumental arch with two
passageways was first erected here, perhaps *c.* AD 75, and that
this was incorporated into the stone defences when these were
built early in the second century by the addition of narrower
pedestrian passageways and D-shaped guardchambers on
either side. The passageway and guardchamber on the south
side are still intact (fig 35), but the middle portion of the gate
is mostly invisible. The footings of the central pier, however,
and the positions of the north carriageway and the north
pedestrian passage, are clearly marked in the display area on
the outer side of the gateway. Also visible is a rough wall
which blocked the entire gateway, probably in the Saxon
period, thus causing the permanent shift southward of the
main road to London which had until then passed through
the Balkerne Gate. To the left the north bastion still stands
20 feet high, and from here the Roman wall can be followed
down Balkerne Hill. Only rubble-core is visible, and the
stretch is at present rather overgrown with foliage, but
nowhere else at Colchester does pure Roman work stand to
such a height.

    From the foot of Balkerne Hill to the traffic-lights the wall
is largely repatched with later material, but the tile bonding-
courses which occasionally appear make it easy to spot the
little Roman work that still remains visible here. Cross
straight over at the traffic-lights and walk along St Peter's
Street, where the wall is not visible. At the end of this is the
entrance to Castle Park, where the wall reappears, though
again much re-faced with later material. After a while you
come to the railed-in remains of Duncan's Gate, named after
its discoverer in 1853. It consists of a single passageway set
back a little from the line of the wall, which turns in to meet
it. You can appreciate here from the inturned wall footings
near the railings how much of the front of the Roman
defences has been removed. The fallen masonry here is from

the superstructure of the gate; it included part of the arches of two windows. The wall can now be followed round the NE corner and for much of the north part of the east side. Towards the end of this stretch the Roman core, although at present rather overgrown, survives untampered by later patching. Now leave the park and follow the alley towards East Hill. Turn right, cross the road and then immediately left down the alley bordering the church. Note the arched brick drain at the beginning of this good stretch of the Roman wall, with bonding-courses clearly visible at the far end. The site of the east gate, demolished in 1675, lies near here under East Hill. Retrace your steps down this and turn right into Priory Street. The wall again becomes visible rounding the SE corner and running along the car-park on the south side. After a breach filled with seventeenth-century brickwork, the Roman tile bonding-courses are again visible near the top of the wall. The bastions here are all medieval, though incorporating Roman materials: the bastion near the end of the car-park uses Roman tiles at its top. There is no evidence at present that the Roman wall had external bastions, but it had the usual internal turrets at intervals, some of which have been excavated.

On the left at the end of Priory Street is the eleventh-century St Botolph's Priory, built largely of Roman stones and tiles [AM; A]. Cross now into Vineyard Street, where the wall is again visible, much mutilated, along another car-park. Half way along, another well-preserved Roman arched drain can be seen issuing from the wall at ground-level. Soon after the recently-made breach for a service-road the wall disappears for a long time. Keep walking straight until you reach the dual-carriageway bypass, where you should turn right. Here is the most magnificent stretch of all, 15 feet high, broken at first by the stairs for the church, and then marred by patching. But nearer the Balkerne Gate it survives majestically, with four rows of quadruple tile bonding-courses clearly visible and even some of the facing-stones.

Three other monuments to the west of the modern town may be mentioned in conclusion, one pre-Roman, one Roman and one dubiously Roman. Take the A1124 out of Colchester for about 1½m and turn left down Fitzwalter Road. The low mound in the field on the left next to No.38

was excavated in 1924 and found to contain an exceptionally rich group of grave-goods, dated to the first half of the first century AD and now displayed in Colchester Museum. Clearly a native royal prince was buried here, possibly Cunobelinus himself. Much more impressive structurally, but less exciting in that it lacks any possible historical connections, is another *tumulus* a short distance away. Continue along the A1124 to the village of Lexden, and turn left along Church Lane. Then take the first turning on the right (Shakespeare Road) and right again down Thomson Avenue, then first left (Masefield Drive) and right (Wordsworth Road). The steep-sided burial-mound, this time of Roman date (second half of first century), lies in the back garden of the first house on the left beyond Marlowe Way. Partial exploration in 1910 yielded nothing of any note. Return once more to the A1124 and continue to the traffic-lights, where you should turn left along Straight Road (signposted Mersea). After 250 yards, on the left-hand side of the road is the so-called Lexden Triple Dyke [AM; A]. Excavation in 1961 apparently showed this to be of Roman date, but its purpose is unknown. Perhaps it was intended to provide temporary cover for the invading army before it built its fortress. But since it continues the line of a known pre-Roman defence, it seems more likely that it was thrown up immediately before Roman armies reached Colchester, and that it forms part of the complicated defences of the British settlement.

Another Roman town which, like Colchester, was both founded near a pre-Roman settlement and sacked by Boudicca, is one of the outstanding sites of Roman Britain. It is VERVLAMIVM near the modern **St Albans*** (TL 1307), the third largest Romano–British city and still largely free from later buildings. About one third of the 200 acres within the walls has been excavated, mainly in the campaigns of Sir Mortimer Wheeler between 1930 and 1934 and of Professor Sheppard Frere between 1955 and 1961. Thanks to these excavations, and especially to the latter, a very great deal is known about the development, prosperity and decline of this great Roman city.

The capital of the British tribe which inhabited this area, the Catuvellauni, lay to the west of the Roman city, in Prae Wood. Coins inscribed VERLAMIO were issued under King

Tasciovanus, the predecessor of the great Cunobelinus, and even when the latter shifted his capital to Colchester, the Prae Wood settlement continued to flourish and still minted coins. A fragment of coin-mould can be seen in the Museum.

The first Roman occupation of the site was a small military post in the area occupied by the village of St Michaels, guarding the crossing of the river Ver. This phase was short, and in AD 49 or 50 the first Roman town was laid out. This was a *municipium*, according to Tacitus, ie a self-governing community, the magistrates of which were given the privilege of Roman citizenship. In 1955 a first-century defence-circuit was located well inside the area later enclosed by the city-walls, and it is likely that this delineated the *municipium* from the time of its foundation. Many of the streets and a row of rectangular timber-framed shops belonging to this first town have been found by excavation, but Boudicca and her followers saw to it in AD 60 or 61 that the entire settlement was razed to the ground.

Recovery from this attack was slow, and rebuilding on a large scale was not in progress until the late 70's. The new forum and basilica were dedicated in 79, during the governorship of Tacitus' father-in-law Agricola, whose name partly survives on a fragmentary inscription found in 1955. By the beginning of the second century the town had overspilled the early defence-circuit, which had been filled in, and many of the public buildings had been erected in stone. Private dwellings, however, remained in timber until another fire destroyed the city in about AD 155. Whether this was accidental or caused by enemy action is uncertain, but it does not seem to have greatly interrupted the prosperity of Verulamium. Town houses were now built in stone for the first time, and many were floored with splendid mosaics: it is clear from finds here and at surrounding villa-sites that a school of mosaicists was operating in the town at this period. The theatre was built now, and about the end of the second century, too, an earthwork defence, known as the Fosse, was thrown up at the west corner of the city. This appears to be unfinished, but why is unknown. If it was begun at a time of crisis (see p. 23), maybe construction was still in progress when the danger passed, and it was thought unnecessary to continue. The monumental gateways on Watling Street, one facing London and the other Chester, probably belong to the end of the second century also. In the early third century, the visible stone defences with earth bank behind and internal turrets were erected to enclose a different area from that of the Fosse. The projecting bastions were probably added, as elsewhere, in the fourth century.

No mosaics and not many structural alterations can be attributed to the third century, but we need not assume from this that the city was in decline. A burst of renewed activity in both private and public building points to continued prosperity in the fourth century, and the abandonment of the theatre and the temples c. 380–390 was probably more for religious reasons (the advance of Christianity which disapproved of pagan ritual and barbaric games) than for economic ones. Private buildings continued to flourish in the fifth century, and dramatic evidence for the continuation of organized life well after the legions had left Britain was found by Professor Frere. Mosaics were still being laid c. 390, and one very large house was built from scratch after 380. One of its mosaics was used long enough for a worn area to be repatched, before the construction of a corn-drying oven destroyed it. This too was used for some time, for its stoke-hole was rebuilt. Only then was the house demolished, and a substantial barn built on its site. Even when that was demolished, a wooden water-pipe with iron joints at six-foot intervals was laid, testifying to the remarkable survival of both constructional skills and civic discipline. In the absence of coinage, which ceased about 430, the date of this pipe-laying cannot be established, but it must be around the middle of the fifth century. The story speaks for itself: the hoary myth of Britain dramatically perishing by fire and sword before a Saxon advance has clearly been exploded.

Verulamium lies to the west of the modern town of St Albans, which grew up around the shrine of Alban, executed for his Christian beliefs, perhaps in AD 304, on the hill where the Abbey now stands. You should start your visit to the Roman city by seeing the Verulamium Museum, which is signposted from the A414 (St Albans–Hemel Hempstead) [weekdays, Apr.–Oct. 10–5.30; Nov.–March, 10–4; Sun. 2–4 or 5.30]. It is one of the most outstanding Roman collections in the country, both for the quality of the display and the beauty of the objects, which amply demonstrate the taste and elegance of the people of Verulamium. Nearly every object deserves a paragraph to itself and I can do no more here than mention the best exhibits. First comes a model of the London gate, with two passageways for vehicles and two for pedestrians; its site will be visited presently. Along the left-hand wall a series of showcases illustrates the development of the city from its earliest origins. Note in particular, half-way along, the curious 'lamp-chimney' from one of the temples excavated by Wheeler. But your eye will have already caught the three superb floor-mosaics displayed against the end wall. The earliest and most unusual is the Scallop Shell mosaic, laid between AD 130 and 150, brilliantly designed and executed with subtle and pleasing use of colour. The two mosaics on either side, one entirely geometric and the other depicting at the centre a rugged deity with beard and claws sprouting from his head, belong to the later second century. A little earlier in date, but far less skilled, is the dolphin mosaic on the floor. Before seeing the rest of the main hall, move into the annexe on the left, which houses the chief finds of the 1955–61 excavations. The mosaic here, also perfectly preserved, is another extremely competent and pleasing piece laid in the second century. The central panel depicts a powerfully-drawn lion making off with the head and antlers of a stag. Equally impressive are the reconstructed panels of painted wall-plaster and, in one case, ceiling-plaster. These are finds which have added enormously to our knowledge of Romano–British interior-decorating. The best pieces are in the British Museum (fig 119). Watch out also, in the case on Religion, for the splendid little bronze statuette of Venus, with flowing drapery gathered round her hips. It was made in the second century, perhaps in Gaul, and was found in 1959 in a cellar below one of the shops near the theatre. Mercifully it was for some reason saved, together with other bronze vessels, from the melting-pot for which it was destined. The other important exhibit is the fragmentary basilica-inscription, dated to AD 79. The suggested restoration of the lost parts is not fanciful, as Roman epigraphy follows strict conventions and the gaps can be filled from other stones. One of the fragments contains part of the name of Agricola, governor of Britain from 78 to 85 and immortalized in Tacitus' biography. Only two other epigraphic records of his activity in Britain are known (both at Chester).

Turn right and then left on leaving the Museum and a three-minute walk will bring you to the Roman theatre, the only visible example in Britain (except for fragments at Canterbury). Discovered in 1847 and excavated in 1934, it is open every day from 10 am to 5 pm. It was built in the middle of the second century, after the fire of 155, on a site previously reserved for it, as no earlier structures were found beneath. The first building had only a tiny timber stage and the entertainment must have taken place mainly in the *orchestra*. This area was used as the dance floor in the ancient Greek theatre (*orchester* = dancer) and the modern use of the term is therefore misleading. The nature of the entertainment at this period is uncertain, but its close association with a large temple to the south (buried) suggests that the theatre was sometimes used in religious ceremonies. At a later period in the second century the stage was enlarged and rebuilt in stone. But the most important alteration took place in the early fourth century when the theatre was enlarged by the addition

36   *St Albans, reconstruction-drawing of the theatre*

of a massive outer wall. The building continued in use until the last quarter of the century.

Passing the ticket-office and turning left in front of the 'dressing-room', go up the steps to the mound which surrounds the remains: this is merely the excavation 'dump', made into a viewing platform, and is no part of the original design. You will see at once that the theatre consisted of a stage and an *orchestra*; the latter is encircled with earth banks, partially re-erected, which carried timber seating. The stage displays three periods of work: originally it was wooden, and the posts which supported it have been replaced by modern timbers. Then, before the end of the second century (phase II), it was rebuilt in stone on a more impressive scale and given a back-drop of columns; one has been reconstructed in modern materials, based on ancient fragments, to give some idea of the height of the stage-building. Then, about AD 200, another wall was added in front of the stage, forming a narrow slot into which the curtain was lowered and raised (the reverse of modern procedure). The wooden cross in the centre of the *orchestra* marks the position of what was probably some kind of pole. Perhaps it was a sort of maypole and had a religious significance, or else animals were tied to it in blood-sports. In phase II, timber seats were built in part of the *orchestra*; but in the early fourth-century rebuilding they were removed, and the area of the *orchestra* reduced a little by the addition of a curved wall in front of the previous one retaining the seating-banks. The banks would then have been enlarged to take more seats, but the retaining-walls of both periods are now visible. The *orchestra* was entered by the three wide passageways which interrupt the seating-banks, but these entrances would have originally been vaulted and the seats carried over them. Finally, there are the outer walls of the theatre, at the foot of the bank on which you are standing. The inner, buttressed wall was the outer wall when the theatre was first built in the second century. It is clearly visible in the reconstruction-drawing (fig 36), which represents the building in its third-century state, after the addition of the curtain-slot c. 200, but before the major alterations of c. 300. In these latter, the buttresses of the original wall were demolished to floor-level and a massive new outer wall was built, forming a corridor round the whole of the back of the theatre, and increasing its capacity still further as more seats would have been built above it. The path leads behind the stage and back to the ticket-office again, passing the base of one pier of a triumphal arch, built over Watling Street in the fourth century.

Between the theatre and the A414 some of the buildings excavated in 1957–60 remain exposed. On the left, marked out in concrete, is the plan of some timber-framed shops belonging to the original foundation of *c.* AD 50 and destroyed by Boudicca ten years or so later. This is the earliest ground-plan of a Roman building to be seen in Britain. The stark regularity of the plan and the timber-framed construction were far in advance of anything Britain had previously known, and it is likely that military construction-experts supervised the laying-out of the earliest town. The shops were separated from Watling Street, now under Gorhambury Drive, by a covered pavement-walk. This is not visible, as it lies buried beneath a flint wall of *c.* 300, which belongs to the last series of shops on the site. The shops themselves consist of a working-area in front and living-quarters (the part nearer you) behind. The labels here give the various trades of the occupants as suggested by finds from the excavations. After the destruction of AD 60, the area lay idle until redevelopment *c.* 75, but constant use until the fire of 155 entailed the rebuilding of the shops on four occasions in that period, resulting in a build-up of layers. This can be seen by comparing the left-hand part of this site, which represents the timber shops erected after 155, with the level of the pre-Boudiccan building, about $3\frac{1}{2}$ feet below.

A little further on, to the right of the path, are the foundations of part of a town-house built in stone after the fire of 155. An earlier timber house, which yielded the dolphin mosaic and the imitation-marble wall-plaster (both in the Museum), was found below. The only features of note in the visible remains are the pipes in one room belonging to a hypocaust, and the apse of a shrine, the rest of which lies under the road. The apse was presumably intended for a statue and the side-niche for a lamp, but the shrine does not appear to have been finished and it was used as a cellar until the late fourth century.

Now retrace your steps to the Museum and go into the car-park beyond. Laid out in the grass on the left of the entrance are some of the offices belonging to the basilica, which lies under St Michael's Church; the forum lay beyond, in the area of the vicarage. From the car-park follow the signs across the grass to the 'Hypocaust' (same hours as the museum, where you should ask if keys are required). Here a modern bungalow covers the *tepidarium* of the bath-suite of a second-century town-house. Part of the floor has been cut away to reveal the hypocaust beneath. The geometric mosaic consists of four rows of four motifs arranged in pairs. Stand on the long side of the room and note the third (horizontal) row away from you. The first and third panels, though identical in design, look different because they have been set on a different orientation: this was clearly due to a fault in the laying and provides evidence that the individual panels were manufactured elsewhere and merely assembled here by less competent craftsmen.

Bear right on leaving the bungalow, making in the direction of the Abbey. Soon you will come to the railed-in remains of a fragment of city-wall (fig 37). Turn right and follow the bump in the ground as far as the massive London gate, the plan of which has been marked out. It consists of two passageways for vehicles and two for pedestrians, with flanking towers on either side; a model is in the Museum. The date of this gateway and the defences as a whole has been discussed above (p. 142). From here stretches a long section of the stone wall, with the bank behind it, and the ditch, now tree-grown, on the left [AM; A]. The facing-stones of the wall have gone and the core is much battered, but it still stands 8–10 feet high, about half its original height. Half-way along are the foundations of a projecting bastion, and another stands to a good height at the corner. Here you should clamber up onto the top of the wall to see the remains of an internal tower. This is contemporary with the stone wall of the early third century, but the projecting bastion is probably a fourth-century addition, though, if so, its junction with the wall has been skilfully bonded in. The line of the defences, now overgrown, continues in the wood beyond. You will soon reach the A414 again and so back to the theatre and Museum. The Fosse earthwork lies on private land beyond the A414: it can be traced with the help of the map on sale in the Museum, provided permission has been obtained from the Gorhambury Estate Office.

When Boudicca's revolt had been crushed and her tribe, the Iceni, had been reconciled to the idea of Roman occupation, a small Roman town was founded for them as their tribal capital. It was VENTA ICENORVM near the village of **Caistor St Edmund** (TG 2303), some 3m south of Norwich. The site is reached by taking the Ipswich road (A140) out of Norwich and turning to the left (signposted Caistor St Edmund) just after the junction with the B1113. Turn right at the next cross-roads, and, after 300 yards, look out on the right for the gates to the parish church. The path to the latter crosses the broad ditch and then cuts through the prominent mound which formed the east defences of VENTA. From here you can survey the interior of the Roman town, now entirely under grass. The clarity with which the street-grid appeared as parched lines in the ripening corn on an air-photograph of 1928 caused some excitement, and funds were raised which enabled the excavation of some of the internal buildings in 1929–35. These have been filled in.

37   St Albans, Roman city-wall and the abbey

The street-plan of VENTA was laid out about AD 70, but buildings remained very modest until the second century. Then a forum and basilica were built, but nothing is known of its plan: the one recovered from the excavations belongs to the middle of the century, and the bath-house near the west gate is of a similar date. There were repairs to both after burning at the end of the second century, and the forum was totally rebuilt on a smaller and simpler scale *c.* 270–90. Two stone temples were also found, but private dwellings were very humble and even in the third century were still not constructed of stone. Air-photographs have revealed a defence-system of earlier date on the south side of the town, but when the town-walls were finally built, *c.* 200, they enclosed a smaller area than that envisaged by the street-grid. All this points to only a moderately successful town, and the 34 acres enclosed within the final defences make it one of the smallest tribal capitals in Roman Britain, smaller even than distant Caerwent in South Wales (44 acres).

Though nothing is visible within the defences, the latter are still prominent in their entire circuit. They comprised an external ditch and a stone wall, backed by an internal bank and strengthened by bastions. Presumably there were the usual two or three phases in the development of these defences, but excavation has yet to prove it.

Walk through the churchyard, keeping the church on your right (note Roman tiles built into the porch and elsewhere), and go through the gap in the hedge to the field beyond. You are soon at the SE corner. Flints poke out of the grass along the entire length of the south rampart and there is an impressive drop to the ditch below. A depression half-way along marks the site of the south gate, which consisted of a single portal and two guardrooms. It soon became choked with rubbish and the guardrooms were deliberately filled in before AD 300. Near the SW angle you must make the descent down the steep bank on the left and aim for the gap in the corner of the field (gate missing). Turn right on passing through this, and you will soon pick up the line of the west rampart. The ditch was omitted on this side as the river Tas flows nearby. A depression and a wire fence mark the site of the west gate. Just beyond this, by a clump of trees, an isolated bastion still stands to an impressive height of 10 feet,

displaying four courses of triple bonding-tiles. Another lump
of stone core appears at the NW angle and again at the
beginning of the north wall. Keep along the outside of the
defences, as considerable stretches of impressive flint wall,
standing in places 20 feet high (virtually its original height
except for the parapet), are still visible. This is especially so
east of the north gate, the site of which is marked by an iron
gate. In two places even small sections of the facing flints are
preserved, and part of the tile bonding-courses, here only
surface deep. At the NE corner the fence is at present (1979)
broken down, and you can make your way back to the church
drive along the line of the ditch. Alternatively, retrace your
steps to the north gate and follow the line of the prominent
rampart-mound on the inside of the walls.

Each of the three towns so far described in this chapter had
a different administrative status: *colonia, municipium,* and
tribal capital. The fourth and last town is different again, for
although it would have had some degree of self-government it
came under the wider control of the tribal capital (cf. 'county-
town') of VENTA. It is **Caister-on-Sea** (TG 5212) [AM ; A],
3m north of Great Yarmouth on the western outskirts of
the village, but east of the by-pass roundabout. The coastline
has changed a great deal since Roman times : Caister was then
at the mouth of a large estuary stretching some way inland, and
where Yarmouth now is would have been sea. The Roman
town was therefore founded primarily as a trading point about
AD 125. It may have had a semi-military importance in the early
third century, when its stone wall was built, but if so this must
have transferred to Burgh Castle (see below) when the latter
was constructed. The town was still flourishing in the fourth
century, and a Saxon settlement is represented by over 150
burials. The Roman name of the site, which was excavated in
the 1950's, is not known.

Immediately inside the entrance-gate to the remains are two
concrete circles and a long wiggly concrete line. The circles
mark the site of post-holes for the timbers which carried a
wooden bridge over the ditch outside the defences. The
concrete line represents the timber palisade which surrounded
the town from its foundation. This was replaced by the broad
stone wall, originally backed by a clay rampart, which was
erected to defend the town in the first half of the third

century. It enclosed a square area of 9–10 acres, but only this
portion of the south defences, and the western guardroom of
the south gate, are visible now.

Inside the town-wall are the remains of the south wing of a
large courtyard-building identified as a seamen's hostel. It was
built at the end of the second century, went through several
modifications, and was still in use in the fourth century. At
this time the fine cobbled corridor on the south had been filled
in. The small curved wall in one corner of the first room (end
nearest the Roman guardroom) is believed to have been a
latrine. There is a hearth in the centre of the next room. A
little further on is an unusual hypocaust, with the channelled
type in the centre and *pilae* set round the edges. The room is
curiously labelled 'granary'; but although the hypocaust was
filled with rammed clay mixed with quantities of wheat when
it fell into disuse, there seems no reason to doubt that the
chamber was originally built as a normal heated room. Its
furnace was in the adjoining cubicle, in one corner of which is
the brick base for a water-tank. The rest of the building is
now largely buried. The only other features to note on the site

38   *Burgh Castle, the south wall*

are two depressions, the sites of Saxon huts, and the pebbled main street, with central depression for drainage, leading down to the south gate and so out to the harbour.

In the second half of the third century the threat of attacks on SE England by Saxon pirates increased. The towns such as Caister-on-Sea were safe behind their stone walls, but the countryside and the smaller settlements needed protection. To co-ordinate resistance to these attacks, a series of strong forts, known as the Forts of the Saxon Shore, was built. Several have already been described in Chapter One and another in Chapter Two, and there were three more on the East Anglian coast. Those at Brancaster, near Hunstanton in Norfolk, and at Bradwell-on-Sea in Essex, have left little trace above ground (see App. I), but the site at **Burgh Castle*** (TG 4704), the GARIANNVM (less likely GARIANNONVM) of the Romans, is very fine (AM; A). The garrison was a detachment of Stablesian cavalry from what is now Yugoslavia. The fort lies on the river Waveney only a short distance from the remains of Caister-on-Sea, but in Roman times the two sites lay on opposite sides of a large estuary. Take the Lowestoft road (A12) for about two miles out of Great Yarmouth, until a roundabout is reached; Burgh Castle is signposted from there. (Turn right at the T-junction.) The footpath leads to the SE corner bastion and the short but picturesque portion of the south wall, part standing, part toppling, part fallen (fig 38). The standing part retains all its facing-flints, separated by rows of tile bonding-courses (at Burgh only surface-deep), and forms a magnificent stretch of Roman masonry, $10\frac{1}{2}$ feet thick at base and 15 feet high – probably its original height except for a parapet. The fallen bastion here has a socket in the middle of its top, either to support a superstructure of wood or, less probably, for anchoring a *ballista*, which hurled stone balls and other weapons onto the attacker; and the base shows traces of the timber framework used in the foundations of the wall. The use of timber posts is also implied by a series of vertical square holes which can be seen on the inside of the stretch of south wall nearest the river. From here you can walk round the inside of the three remaining fort-walls: that on the west has totally vanished, but what was presumably a timber wharf was found in the nineteenth century at the foot of the low cliff facing the river. The thickness of the wall was reduced on

the inside face by a series of offsets, which can be seen (partially
restored) in the eastern portion of the south wall. The main
gate of the fort was in the long east wall, but only a simple
gap remains today. Eventually you reach the centre of the
north wall and its leaning bastion. This originally protected a
narrow postern-gate, but hardly anything remains of it now.
The particular interest of this bastion lies in the curving
profile of its back, and in the matching mortar curve of the
main body of the wall from which it has fallen. The reason for
this is as follows. When the decision to build Burgh Castle was
taken, the plan was to have the conventional internal turrets
and no projecting bastions: one turret has been found in
excavations but is not now visible. After about seven feet of
the curtain-wall had been built, the order went out that
bastions were to be added. For this reason, only the top half
of each bastion is bonded into the wall; the lower half merely
stands up against it. The curving portion marks the joint
between the bonded and unbonded parts of each bastion, and,
having observed it with ease in this example on the north, you
can examine the rest of the standing bastions (fig 39) for this

39   Burgh Castle, a bastion on the east wall

feature as you make your way round the outside of the walls, back to the SE corner. Throughout, the walls stand to a spectacular height, even though many of the facing-stones have been robbed. The construction of the bastions as an afterthought gives a clue to the dating of GARIANNVM. It is later than the early examples of the series, such as Reculver, which have no bastions, but is earlier than the late Saxon Shore forts such as Richborough, Portchester and Pevensey, where bastions are an integral part of the scheme. A date around AD 275 is the most likely for the building of Burgh Castle. It was occupied up to the close of the fourth century.

The comparative lack of prosperity in the Icenian tribal capital is reflected by a similar situation in the surrounding countryside, where villas never reached the size or degree of romanized luxury displayed by those of the south-west. It is not surprising, therefore, to find no villa-site visible today in the territory of the Iceni. Further west, the Fens were drained for the first time by the Romans and the area extensively cultivated, but villa-estates are non-existent here and it has been suggested that the area may have been an imperial estate. The artificial drainage system, however, designed to link natural watercourses, remains to bear witness to Roman engineering skills in this region. The main channel is the Car Dyke, which excavation has shown to have been eight feet deep, 30 feet wide at the bottom and 50 feet at the top. It was probably cut at the beginning of the second century (some think a little earlier), and has long been interpreted as a canal for transporting grain to the north, for the network extended at least as far as Lincoln. Recent work, however, has shown that in parts the Lincolnshire Car Dyke was not continuous, but interrupted by gravel causeways making navigation impossible; and a survey of the Dyke further south has demonstrated that the central sector here is higher than at its confluence with the rivers Welland to the north and Nene to the south, suggesting that it was intended entirely as a catchwater drain. A navigable channel would have needed a level course throughout to maintain water at a constant depth. Long stretches of the Car Dyke can be traced both in Cambridgeshire and Lincolnshire with the help of OS maps, but it is rarely more than a wet ditch and hardly likely to rouse much excitement. One convenient place to view the

Cambridgeshire Car Dyke is near **Waterbeach** (TL 4867), a
few miles north of Cambridge. From the latter follow the Ely
road (A10) for six miles, until you reach a turning to the left
(just past the airfield) signposted 'Landbeach 1, Cottenham 3'.
Park here but continue walking along the A10 for a few yards
until you come to some white railings. The Roman drain
shows as a wet ditch below and beyond the railings.

    Villas become more plentiful and more imposing in the
territory of the Catuvellauni, especially around Verulamium,
** but only one site, Dicket Mead near **Welwyn** (TL 2315) has
been permanently preserved. A pair of buildings with front
and rear corridors, together with part of a third building, was
excavated here in 1970–1, 350 yards south of a Roman villa
discovered in 1930 on the other side of the river Mimram.
None of these structures is now visible except for the small
bath-house at the end of one of the long buildings, which has
been preserved *in situ* in a concrete vault beneath the A1(M)
motorway. The first feature you encounter on entering the site
is the superbly preserved stoking-area for the baths; the main
flue-arch (and relieving-arch above), together with a hot
water-tank situated over the flue, still stands about 5 feet high.
The hot room (*caldarium*) comes next, with a fragment of
floor *in situ*. Its supporting *pilae* look to be of more than one
period (one very burnt *pila* has been strengthened by an
additional pier alongside it). The *pilae* of the warm room
(*tepidarium*) have been entirely removed (only impressions
remain) and the wall separating this room from the hot room
was neatly robbed out after the baths ceased to function. The
tiled floor of the cold room has been relaid. The intact cold
plunge-bath, and the hot plunge with cement floor and wall-
flues, appear to have been additions to the original building:
note the straight joints in the masonry. The bath-house was
built around the middle of the third century and only in use
for fifty years or so. Opened in 1975 it can be visited only on
Sundays (and Bank Holidays) from 2 to 5 pm. Access (green
plaque) is from a roundabout on the west side of A1(M) just
north of Welwyn, on a slip road linking B197 with A1000
(from the motorway take the exit for the latter, to Welwyn).

    But if the East Anglian countryside does not bristle with
remains of villas, the area is rich in Roman funerary
** monuments. Most of these are in the form of earth burial-

mounds, or *tumuli*, but an exception is the stone mausoleum
at **Harpenden** (TL 1113). It lies in the private ground of the
Rothampstead Experimental Station, which is signposted to
the right (west) of the St Albans road (A6) just south of the
town. Casual visitors during working hours on Monday to
Fridays are usually not unwelcome, but it is best to write first
if you know you are going on a particular day. Enquire at the
reception-desk in the entrance and you will be escorted to the
site. Here you will see the foundations of a circular building
11 feet in diameter, with a plinth in the centre and a cross-wall
making an alcove. Fragments of a statue, presumably of the
dead person, were found during excavations in 1937, and this
probably stood in the alcove, while the plinth served as the
base of an altar. The thickness of the external walls suggests
that the superstructure of the mausoleum was quite
substantial, perhaps 20 feet high. It stood in the middle of an
enclosure, about 100 feet square, in which two cremation-
burials dating to the first half of the second century were
found. One side and two corners of the enclosure-wall remain
exposed.

Of the many sites in East Anglia where Romano–British
tumuli are visible I will describe only four here; one near
Colchester has already been mentioned, and the rest are listed
in Appendix I. The most interesting barrow is perhaps that on
Mersea Island (TM 0214), the sole British example where it is
possible to go underneath the earth mound to inspect the site
of the burial-chamber. Immediately after the B1025 crosses
the causeway onto the island, turn left along the East Mersea
road. The barrow lies behind railings on the left just beyond a
road to the right (Dawes Lane). The keys are obtained from a
house 200 yards further on ('Bower Haven'). A concrete
tunnel made by the excavators of 1912 leads to the middle of
the barrow; the site of the burial is marked by some tiles in
the floor of the last chamber. These Roman tiles formed a
cavity 18 inches high, and inside was a lead casket containing
a glass bowl with ashes of human bones. These finds,
probably belonging to the second half of the first century AD,
are now in Colchester Museum. The earth mound raised over
the burial is 110 feet in diameter and over 20 feet high, and
since 1966 has been cleared of undergrowth and carefully
maintained.

The Mersea example is an isolated barrow, but *tumuli* also occur in groups. At **Thornborough** (SP 7333) in Buckinghamshire two are found side by side. They are quite well preserved, one 16 feet high and 120 feet in diameter, and the other a little smaller. When opened about 1840, the larger barrow yielded second-century samian pottery, bronze jugs, a glass vessel and other finds; these are now in the Museum of Archaeology and Ethnology at Cambridge. From Buckingham follow the Bletchley road (A421) for about two miles until you reach the bridge over the river Twin; you will see the two *tumuli* in the field on the left beyond the bridge. Excavations in 1972–3 before the building of the new bridge found seven first-century cremations with grave-goods (pottery and glass vessels), and evidence of at least two parallel roads leading to a ford across the river. A third-century Romano–Celtic temple is known 100 yards south of the bridge.

A larger group, this time of six barrows arranged in a single row, can be seen at **Stevenage** (TK 2323) in Hertfordshire. Each is 60 feet in diameter and now about 10 feet high. One was dug into in 1741 when 'wood and iron' were found, but otherwise they have not been explored. The *tumuli* are situated by a roundabout near the police station on the south side of Stevenage, but the town is full of roundabouts and it is easy to lose your way. Ask first for Stevenage railway station. From the forecourt turn left and go right the way round the first roundabout and back along the dual carriageway (if you are going by car; if on foot turn right!). At the next roundabout take the third exit (Stevenage College) and you will see the Six Hills, as the barrows are known locally, on your right.

The largest and most famous group of Romano–British *tumuli* is at **Bartlow** (TL 5844), on the border of Essex and Cambridgeshire. Here there were two rows of three and four barrows respectively, but the former was destroyed in the nineteenth century. The surviving four are excellently preserved, but they are at present rather overgrown. They were explored in 1832–40, when many fine grave-goods were found. These indicated that the barrows were erected between the end of the first and the middle of the second century AD. Most of the objects unfortunately perished in a fire in 1847, but some remnants are in Saffron Walden museum (weekdays 11–4 or 5; Sun., summer only, 2.30–5).

Bartlow is signposted from the A604 (Colchester road) ½m east of the village of Linton, 10m SE of Cambridge. Turn right at the first crossroads and go straight over the second. The footpath to the Bartlow Hills, the name by which the barrows are known, is signposted on the left immediately after the former railway-bridge. On the left of the path is barrow 2, 25 feet high and the least overgrown. In it were found a lamp and mid-second-century pottery, and a wooden chest which contained a pot and cremated bones in a glass jug. Barrow 3, on the right, is the largest extant *tumulus* in Roman Britain, a massive heap 144 feet in diameter and 45 feet high. It is very steep, but can be climbed with the help of the trees growing on one side. Its grave-goods were elaborate – a wooden chest containing glass vessels (for holding perfumes, food and the cremated bones), an enamelled bowl, and a folding stool with bronze fittings and a leather seat. The adjacent barrow 4, which is 35 feet high, is overgrown and at present inaccessible, for it lies outside the fence surrounding barrow 3. It produced finds similar to those of barrow 2. Finally there is barrow 1, the northernmost of the row, which lies in private ground on the other side of the former railway. It can, therefore, only be visited with the permission of the owner, but one side of it, rising steeply, can be seen from the railway-footbridge. A bronze bowl, an iron lamp and a toilet-instrument were found inside.

Chapter 5

Central England

NW Cambridgeshire, Derbyshire, Leicestershire, Lincolnshire,
Shropshire, Staffordshire and Warwickshire

(Appendix I only – Northamptonshire and Nottinghamshire)

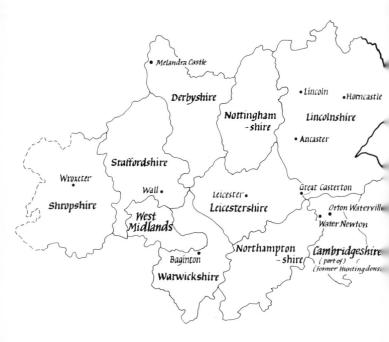

With the capture of Colchester in AD 43 and the establishment
of a base there for the Twentieth Legion, the invading army
split up. The Second Legion made for the West Country (see
Chapter Two), the Ninth advanced northwards towards
Lincoln, and the Fourteenth aimed for the Shropshire area.
The precise movements of these legions in the period AD 44–60
are still far from certain, but a vast addition to our knowledge
has been made by aerial discoveries and excavation during the
last two decades. It is now known that the Ninth Legion was
not established in its Lincoln fortress until about AD 60;

before that it was divided between a 28-acre ('vexillation') fortress at Longthorpe near Peterborough (p 180) and another of similar size at Newton-on-Trent near Lincoln. Smaller forts, garrisoned by auxiliary soldiers with some legionary detachments, are known to have existed at several places in the same area, but no trace of any of these early forts is visible on the ground today.

Less is known about the progress of the Fourteenth Legion. One part may have advanced through Cambridge and Godmanchester (near Huntingdon) to Leicester, where the size of the early fort is still undetermined but is possibly legionary in character. Another part of the Fourteenth may have followed the line later taken by Watling Street. In the 50's, when a temporary frontier had been adopted along the course of the Fosse Way, the legion's bases lay NW of this line, perhaps at Kinvaston near Penkridge (Staffs.), and at Wall. At both these places vexillation fortresses are known but are not visible on the ground. Eventually, about AD 58, the separated detachments were brought together and a fortress for the full Fourteenth Legion was established at Wroxeter.

The only one of these first-century forts worth visiting is that at the Lunt, **Baginton*** (SP 344752). Here an ambitious reconstruction-scheme, started in 1966, had turned a flat field into one of the most interesting and instructive sites of Roman Britain. The village of Baginton lies 2m due south of Coventry and is best reached by the minor road to Coventry airport. This leaves the roundabout joining the Coventry by-pass (A45) with the A423, SE of the city. At present the fort is open between late May and the end of September, daily except Mondays and Thursdays, 12–6. The site was occupied only between AD 60 and 79/80, but within that period its history is extremely complex. It was apparently constructed in the aftermath of the Boudiccan rebellion, for no finds at present point to the existence of a fort here in the earliest invasion-period. The first fort was much larger than the visible enclosure and its exact size has not yet been established. In the second phase the internal buildings were rebuilt on a different alignment. Then a curious circular structure was erected, covering in part two barrack buildings of the second stage of the fort. The original fort was then reduced in size, and the new eastern defences made a curious detour to avoid the circular structure; there is evidence too that the western defences were also far from regular. Finally, in period III, the size of the fort was apparently reduced once again, with a pair of ditches cutting through the *via principalis* of the period-II fort. In AD 77/8, when the coin-series from the site ends, the fort was abandoned, the defences dismantled, and the timber carried away for use elsewhere. There is also surprising evidence for a short-lived re-occupation in the late third century, together with fresh defences. A fort at that date in inland lowland Britain is quite exceptional and is presumably a reflection of local insecurity.

The first impressive feature at the Lunt is the magnificent east gateway to the period-II fort and the section of earth-and-timber defences rebuilt on either side of it (fig 40–41). The plan of the gateway was learnt from excavation in 1966–7; its elevation is based on evidence of a similar structure represented on Trajan's Column in Rome. It was prefabricated in modern army-workshops and erected by the Royal Engineers during three days in September 1970 without the aid of modern equipment. The defences were refurbished, and a further long section built, in 1984–7.

From here the *via principalis* leads you to the centre of the fort where the plan of the period-II HQ building has been marked out. It lacks a cross-hall but has the usual central courtyard and five administrative rooms along the back. The

40 Baginton, on the rampart-walk

41 Baginton, reconstructed fort-gateway (from outside)

room in the middle was the shrine for the standards, and sunk into its floor is a strong-room, a common feature of later stone forts (cf. Chesters and Chesterholm, Chapter 8). But the headquarters was presumably no longer used after the odd reduction of period III, for the fort's new south gateway, twin-portalled like the reconstructed one, was built over part of the HQ courtyard. The post-holes of this gate have been marked out in concrete. Reconstruction of the HQ is planned.

Next to the *principia* a timber granary, reconstructed in 1973, serves as the site museum (fig 42). The archaeological evidence for this was provided by the 105 post-holes at 5-foot intervals which represented the timber uprights for supporting the floor above ground-level, as customary in such buildings. Archaeology can provide a ground-plan but rarely evidence for a third dimension. The simulation at the Lunt, therefore, is an outstanding attempt at providing an illustration of that third dimension, the superstructure, even if evidence is scanty for details such as the pitch of the roof, the position and number of louvers, and the precise nature and appearance of the wall-finish. The Roman granary which stood here *c.* AD 67–77 is, however, unlikely to have looked very different from the one before you now.

The granary and the HQ are two structures which follow more or less predictable patterns known from other excavated forts in Britain and elsewhere. Few other features at the Lunt do, but none is more peculiar than the unique circular

42 *Baginton, the reconstructed timber granary*

stockade which the eastern defences bulge out to avoid. This, also reconstructed (in 1977), encloses a circular arena 107 feet in diameter, dug out to a depth of $2\frac{1}{2}$ feet below the rest of the interior of the fort. In the absence of parallels its purpose is uncertain; but the hypothesis that it is a *gyrus* or training-ground for horses and cavalry recruits seems convincing. Beyond it the plan of some barracks and granaries have been marked out in concrete.

The Lunt is therefore an impressive and fascinating site, but it is important to remember that it is not a typical Roman fort; it seems rather to have been an army training-centre. Having puzzled over the circular structure, do not go away thinking that every Roman fort had one. And having admired the splendid reconstructions of the gateway and portions of the earth-and-timber defences, remember that the sinuous course taken by the eastern rampart is a feature unique in Britain and very rare on the continent. Roman forts are almost always built to a regular playing-card shape with rounded corners and straight sides; and it is perhaps a pity that of all the Roman forts in Britain where such reconstruction could have taken place, it has been done at the most untypical example of all!

At five other fort-sites in central England something can be seen of the surrounding rampart-mounds, but at four of them the remains are not impressive and they are therefore relegated to Appendix I. Metchley was a large fort built soon after the conquest and burnt down *c.* 55–65; reconstruction was attempted here some years ago but it was vandalized, and only a burnt timber tower and an overgrown mound remain visible. Of a smaller, late-first-century fort nothing is visible. The other four were semi-permanent forts belonging to the garrisoned zone of Roman Britain. Greensforge and Wall Town were part of the garrison of Wales, while the two in Derbyshire belonged to the southern edge of the Pennine chain of forts. One of these, probably the Roman ARDOTALIA, is **Melandra Castle** (SK 0095); it lies just west of Glossop and is clearly signposted from A626 $\frac{1}{2}$m W of its junction with A57, at the top of the hill. The fort, which can be visited at any time, is situated on a magnificent spur with a steep escarpment on the west, down to the river, and an extensive command of ground to the north; erosion is, however, endangering the SW corner, and the site is also marred by rubbish tips and signs of vandalism. The banks covering the stone walls of the fort stand to a prominent height throughout their circuit, often over six feet high. Stonework is visible at the SE corner, opposite the car-park, where the fort-wall and corner tower are exposed, and a small fragment of the NW corner tower is also upstanding. The gaps at all four gates are clear, but apart from a few blocks at the north gate no stonework is visible. In the centre of the fort the foundations of the headquarters building, first exposed in 1899, have recently been re-excavated and consolidated. It is not a particularly instructive example of its type, as the footings were poorly preserved, but the entrance (to the north) and three rooms at the rear, including a central shrine (*sacellum*) which had a floor of crushed tile, can be made out. The small garrison bath-house was discovered in 1973 50 feet outside the fort between the N gate and the NW corner. Part of it had fallen down the slope, and the rest was excavated in annual campaigns up until 1984, but it has now been backfilled. Excavations have shown that the fort was an Agricolan foundation *c.* 79, its clay and timber defences being refurbished in stone *c.* 110/120. The *principia* foundations also date from then, but the bath-house was of stone from the beginning, although enlarged in the second century. The fort was then given up and systematically dismantled about AD 140, no doubt because of the renewed advance into Scotland under Antoninus Pius. A civilian settlement with timber buildings and its own defensive ditch, partly examined in 1966–9 before the housing estate was built, also showed that activity was limited to the period AD 80–140. Thereafter this part of Britain was reckoned peaceful enough not to warrant the presence of a permanent garrison.

Most of central England became civilian in character after the military had moved northwards and westwards in the last quarter of the first century AD, and many of the places which started life as forts were rebuilt as towns. The two legionary fortresses, Lincoln and Wroxeter, were no exception. The fortress at **Lincoln*** (SK 9771) was founded, as we saw above, in about AD 60 or 61 for the Ninth Legion, though there may well have been a smaller auxiliary fort on the site before that. About ten years later the Ninth was moved forward to

Yorkshire, and its place at Lincoln was taken by a legion
newly brought to Britain, the Second Adiutrix. The earth-and-
timber defences of this fortress have been found in
excavations, as well as part of the HQ building (*principia*). In
about AD 77 *Legio* II *Adiutrix* moved to Chester, and the
military phase at Lincoln was over.

The site was then resettled as a *colonia*, a town for retired
legionaries and their families. This first town clung to the hill-
top and when stone defences were erected in the early second
century, they followed the same line as the legionary
ramparts, and in fact used the latter to form the core of the
bank behind the wall. The *colonia* of LINDVM was a flourishing
town, and occupation also increased on the slope facing the
river. Before very long, probably at the end of the second
century, this quarter too was walled, and the area enclosed by
the defences was thus increased from 41 to 97 acres. The
defences of the upper town were rebuilt on a more massive
scale at the end of the second or beginning of the third
century, and most of the visible remnants of the wall belong to
this period, while the strengthening of the lower town was
carried out in the first half of the fourth century. Much less is
known about the interior of Roman Lincoln, but an
impressive sewerage-system and mosaic pavements point to a
comfortable standard of living.

Many fine stretches of the defences of LINDVM still exist, but
its chief pride are the three magnificent Roman gateways. A
convenient place to start a tour of the Roman remains is at
the Eastgate Hotel, opposite the Cathedral (1 on fig 43).
Here, in the forecourt of the hotel, the north tower of the
Roman east gate stands to a spectacular height. The
entrance-door, the jamb from which the arch sprang, and the
staircase giving access to an upper level, are all impressively
preserved. This semicircular bastion was matched by another
(buried beneath the pavement and part of the cathedral green)
which flanked the double carriageway of the gate proper, now
under the road. These massive remains, however, only belong
to the last phase of the gateway, in the early third century.
Excavation within the tower in 1959–66 revealed the post-
holes of the gateway of the timber legionary fortress of AD
61–77 and also the narrow stone wall, $4\frac{1}{2}$ feet wide, which was
built to front the timber gateway soon after the founding of

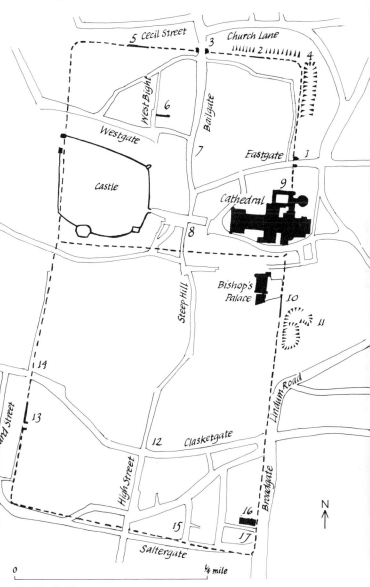

43   Lincoln, plan

the *colonia*. Both these earlier periods, labelled 1 and 2, are also visible and can be understood with the help of the plan displayed on the retaining-wall.

In the grounds of the hotel is a picturesque stretch of the Roman wall, part of which can be seen from the car-park on the other side of the hotel, near the hotel entrance. Now walk down the narrow lane adjoining the remains of the east gate. After turning the corner, in private grounds behind railings on the right of the road, you will see a massive lump of wall-core, 10 feet thick (2 on fig 43). It is backed by a large platform which formed the foundation for a water storage tank. The water came from a spring 1¼ miles to the north, whence it was pumped uphill in a sealed pipe-line. Next to it, attached to a piece of the original (narrow) gauge of stone wall, is an internal tower. The lane soon leads to the famous Newport Arch (3), the north gate of the town and the only Roman archway still standing in Britain (fig 44). Built early in the third century, it was restored at various times in the eighteenth and nineteenth centuries and again in 1964, when a lorry partly demolished it. It is a fine relic, looking a little squat because

44 Lincoln, the Newport Arch

of a build-up in road-levels, and consists of a main arch and a smaller one for pedestrians on one side, originally matched by a similar small arch on the other. Only the inner part of the gate is Roman; the rest of the masonry, including the pedestrian tunnel, belongs to the medieval structure. Like the east gate, it was flanked by projecting towers, and the lowest course of one of these, overlain by medieval work, can be seen laid out on the left (west) of the road. (If you want to be thorough, you may like to see a large but overgrown section of the ditch accompanying the wall (4). It lies on private property in the back garden of Fosse House, on the corner of Church Lane; go outside the Arch and turn right.)

When you have had your fill of the Newport Arch, turn left along Cecil Street. An arch on the left in Mary Sookias House leads to another fine stretch of city wall, 12 feet high, uncovered in 1976–7 (5). Here all but the lowest two or three courses of facing stones above the projecting base-plinth have been robbed. A row of putlog holes which held the scaffolding timbers during construction is also clear, 8 feet above the ground. Now return to the Newport Arch, go down Bailgate, and turn right along Westgate. At the back of the yard by the Castle Hotel is the so-called Mint Wall (6), 70 feet long and 18 feet high and, for Britain, an impressive enough piece of upstanding Roman masonry. It is almost certainly part of the rear wall of the city's *basilica*. The adjacent forum to the south was partly revealed in excavations of 1978–79, together with the cross-hall and part of the courtyard of the legionary HQ building below it. Part of a semicircular chamber and an adjacent well-shaft (with tile-built arches at the top) on the forum's east side can be seen by crossing Westgate from the Mint Wall; they are mid-second-century work built when the forum of *c.* 100/125 was refurbished, and the 275-foot-long colonnade further east (some of its columns are marked out in Bailgate) probably belongs to the same time (7). See also p. 383.

Continue now to the end of Bailgate and down Steep Hill. On the right, where a lantern has been affixed to the wall, is a piece of mellowed stone (8). This fragment is part of the south gate of the upper town; when the walls were extended in the mid-second century, there was of course another south gate, at the foot of High Street, facing the river. The upper gate, even before this, can hardly have been important, for the gradient here is too steep for wheeled traffic and difficult enough for pedestrians.

Now retrace your steps a little and turn right into the Cathedral precinct. Under a stairway leading off the NE corner of the cloisters is a portion of Roman mosaic, found nearby in 1793 (9). On the south side of the Cathedral are the remains of the Bishop's Palace [AM, open Mondays to Saturdays, April to September, 9.30–6.30, and Sunday afternoons from 2; closed daily 1–2 and from Oct. to March]. A good stretch of Roman town-wall at the extreme south end of this, bordering what was once the Palace garden, is still 14 feet high and formed part of the eastern defences of the lower town (10). Apart from other pieces of wall, described in the next paragraph, very little is visible of the lower *colonia*. A shapeless fragment of wall-ditch, also on the line of the eastern defences, and a flue-arch found in 1925 and perhaps belonging to a bath-building, are all that can be mentioned. The former (11) is in the grounds of the Usher Art Gallery, Lindum Road, and the latter can be seen, with permission, in the basement of the 'Roman Ruin' restaurant on the corner of High Street and Clasketgate (12).

Until the important excavations of 1970–1 very little was known of the walls of the lower Roman town, and none of its gates had been found. Now, however, a superb stretch, including the west gate, has been excavated and consolidated in the forecourt of the new Municipal Offices in Orchard Street (13). More of these defences were located in 1971 a few yards further north, on the site of the new Police Headquarters, but these have been destroyed. A plan of what was found there is, however, displayed on the façade of the new building in West Parade, and is marked out in cobbling on the footpath up Motherby Hill (14). As a result of this and other recent work we now know that the first wall surrounding the lower *colonia* was built at the very end of the second century and was only five feet thick. It was, however, well constructed and seems to have stood unrepaired until the fourth century. An interval tower was added on the inside of the wall in the early third century, but it was demolished a century later when the wall was pierced to make a gateway here. At first this formed a simple arched tunnel in the wall,

16 feet wide and 30 feet long, but some time later in the fourth
century the gateway was remodelled when the massive
projecting rectangular towers were built which form the
visible part of the gate today. The backs of these towers still
stand to a considerable height, and here can be seen the rear
portion of the two guard-chambers which each contained.
The fronts of the towers are less well preserved, but it can be
seen that their foundations incorporate material which has
been pirated from other buildings in the town. One piece built
into the south side of the north tower is a superb second-
century frieze, perhaps from a temple, replaced on site by a
cast (the original, viewable on request, is in the Municipal
Offices).

Soon after the gate-towers were built, the defences were
strengthened still further. North of the gate the old wall was
completely replaced at this time, but to the south new
masonry was tacked on to the back of the early wall, and to
save material the width was reduced by a series of offsets, thus
creating the present step-like effect. The wall here stands to a
height of 10 feet; the stonework was not robbed in medieval
times, because it was protected by the clay mound which
backed the wall and which was increased to a width of 80 feet
in these late-fourth-century changes. It has now been
removed, of course, to display the splendid masonry of the
rear face of the wall. Coins on the road-surface indicate that
the gate remained in use into the fifth century.

Another stretch of rebuilt *colonia* wall, presumably also
carried out in the late fourth century, was excavated in 1973
on the south side of the circuit, next to the Falcon Inn in
Saltergate (15). The Roman defences here, which also pirated
material from other buildings, including part of a
monumental inscription, stood over seven feet high and were
crowned by a further four feet of medieval wall. A narrow
postern gate for pedestrians was also found, but the main
south gate must lie further west, on the line of High Street.
The postern has been preserved in the basement of a modern
building, but at the time of writing (1987) access to it is
somewhat restricted: advance arrangements to view have to be
made with the museum in Broadgate (16), where there is a
small but well-arranged display of Roman exhibits (10–5.30,
Sun. 2.30–5). The Museum is next to the church of St Swithin's,

where a Roman altar is displayed (17).

Whereas the legionary fortress at Lincoln became a *colonia*, that at **Wroxeter*** (SJ 5608) [AM; SSM] was turned into the tribal capital of the Cornovii, VIROCONIVM CORNOVIORVM. Part of the ditches of the military fortress has been identified from the air, and timber buildings belonging to it have been excavated beneath the later bath-site. Finds indicate that the military phase lasted from about AD 58 to 87. The civilian settlement which must have grown up during this period then expanded and flourished. Later the city outstripped its second-century earth defences on the north, the third-century walls eventually enclosing some 170 acres, making it the fourth largest Romano–British town. Much has been learnt from air-photography (the site lies in open fields) and from excavation in the central sector.

The site is reached, if you are coming from the west, by turning off the A5 5m east of Shrewsbury, following the B4380 to Ironbridge, and turning right at the first crossroads. If you are coming from the east, leave A5 along B4394 and go straight across at the crossroads. Before entering the main site on the left, continue walking along the road a little further and look over the fence on the right. The long line of column-stumps which you see here formed part of a portico on the east side of the forum. The whole of the latter was excavated in the 1920's but only this part has been left exposed. The excavations produced one of the largest and finest inscriptions from Roman Britain, recording the erection of the building by the *civitas Cornoviorum* under the emperor Hadrian in AD 130. The original is in Rowley's House Museum, Shrewsbury (weekdays 10–5; Sun., Easter–mid-Sept. 12–5), but there is a cast in the site-museum. The excavations also showed that a bath-building had been planned for the forum area, but that it was demolished before completion.

Now enter the main site and visit the excellent site-museum. Apart from the cast of the forum stone, another inscription of great interest is displayed here. It reads: 'Cunorix, son of Maqqos-Colini' (Son of the Holly), and is dated on linguistic grounds to AD 460–75. Macus and Maqqos mean 'son' in ancient Irish, and Cunorix is probably an Irishman settled by the Romans in Britain to help stave off other invaders; such men were known as *foederati*, 'allied'. Other important exhibits in the museum include the painted plaster vault of the baths' *caldarium*, and the stack of samian bowls from the forum gutter, for long a key deposit in the understanding of the chronology of second-century samian pottery.

When you have finished visiting the museum, go out on to the verandah and look over the rest of the site. The most conspicuous feature is the fine upstanding piece of masonry known as the Old Work, which has miraculously survived medieval stone-robbing and over 1800 years of British weather. It is part of the south wall of a large aisled building which occupied all the area between the museum and the rest of the site, and which formed an exercise-hall (*palaestra*) for the baths. About AD 350 it collapsed, and in the building-rubble several timber structures, some of considerable pretensions, have been traced. Dating evidence is lacking, but life must have continued here into the fifth and possibly even the sixth century before Wroxeter was abandoned.

The *palaestra* excavations are still in progress (1987) and it is not yet clear how much of the remains will be consolidated and left open on permanent display. For the moment, therefore, a temporary walk-way leads to the rest of the site and the tour begins at its western end, near the road. At the end of the path is a small building consisting of a series of small rooms ranged about a courtyard, until 1985 under excavation. It is conventionally interpreted as a market-hall, and has a latrine in one corner. It was built, like the forum, in the Hadrianic period, over the levelled remains of the legionary defences and subsequent civilian timber structures, and was remodelled *c.* AD 300 when the corridor was floored in herringbone brickwork. For the moment, however, you leave this building to your right and pass through one of the two square rooms with central bases of unknown purpose, a narrow corridor, and then a public latrine. This can be recognized by the sewer, originally covered by wooden seats, which runs along the back wall of the building.

The rest of the remains on the site belong to the public baths. Unfortunately they have been left exposed since 1863 and a detailed history of their development cannot now be recovered. The *piscina*, however, has only recently been found. The baths themselves were not erected until the second half of the second century, and many of the visible walls belong to this period, but beneath there was an earlier civic building which was never completed. It is conceivable that the vast *palaestra* was built as the basilica of the new town, while the forum, planned for the site now occupied by the baths, was never completed and, in reorganization at the beginning of the second century, baths and forum changed places.

The bath-house was entered from the *palaestra* through the double doors which partially filled the present gap in the Old Work. On the underside of this gap can be seen the two rounded impressions left by the relieving-arches (now vanished) which lay above the lintels of the two doors; the doors were not, therefore, as high as the present gap in the structure. Higher up are three great tile arches which form deep recesses and were originally supported by pilasters. All these features can be better understood by a glance at the drawing of the suggested reconstruction (fig 45).

Now turn your back on the Old Work and examine the rest of the bath-complex. You are now standing in the *frigidarium*. On the left and right are cold plunge-baths and in front of you are the thresholds, one very worn, which led into the *tepidarium*. From here onwards you are walking below the original floor-level, for none of the baths' floors have survived. The *tepidarium* appears to be divided into two parts by a cross-wall. On the left are two smaller rooms, one with a few *pilae*-bases and an adjoining stoke-hole with firing

45   *Wroxeter, the Old Work reconstructed*

chamber and the steps down to it. Later the door to the firing chamber was blocked and a window, still extant, was inserted. The rooms this chamber heated formed a subsidiary set of intense dry heat and were matched by a similar set on the right, less well preserved. Ignore the latter for the moment and move from the second (main) part of the *tepidarium* into the *caldarium* (moist heat), on either side of which are recesses for hot baths. All the *pilae* here are modern, as all the original tiles had been robbed and only their impressions remained. The original walls of these rooms had also disappeared, and they too are marked out in modern materials. Soon after the baths were built, an outer wall of grey sandstone partly encased the *caldarium*, and this survives to its original height on the left (east) side. Probably cracks developed in the inner wall, and the new wall was then built to prevent heat-loss. At the end of the *caldarium* is the stoke-hole (fig 46); this was probably originally intended to heat both the warm rooms, but later the *tepidarium* was given a separate furnace, and part of its internal flue is represented by the lump of Roman masonry visible on the floor of that room.

Now turn right across the grass to see the small swimming-bath (*piscina*) with an apse at each end. This was not a regular feature of Roman baths, and it is in fact the only visible example in Britain, apart from one in the legionary baths at

46   Wroxeter, the baths and the Old Work

Caerleon and those at Bath. The latter were, however, enclosed and fed by natural hot springs; the Wroxeter example was open to the sky. It did not have a very long life, perhaps because the British climate never made it popular, and at the beginning of the third century it was demolished; most of its paving stones were ripped up for use elsewhere, and it became a rubbish tip. At the same time an extension to the main bath-suite prevented access to this corner of the establishment. The *caldarium* of this extension is clearly recognizable by the semicircular wall north of the *piscina*. Its stoke-hole is represented by the two large blocks on the left, while the room on the right, with another furnace-chamber approached by steps, was the *tepidarium* of the extension. This room was originally intended, however, to be one of a pair of dry-heat rooms flanking the *tepidarium* of the main suite, and matched by the similar pair of rooms mentioned earlier. The reason for building the extension is not known for certain, but it may have become an independent set of baths reserved for women.

The other tribal capital in central England was **Leicester*** (SK 5804), which was RATAE CORIELTAVVORVM, the capital town of the Corieltauvi. There was pre-Roman occupation of the site and a military post, possibly legionary, in the early years of the Roman conquest, but as yet very little is known of either phase. The later town-walls enclosed about 100 acres, but no scrap of them remains visible. One area inside the town has, however, been left exposed; like Wroxeter, it preserves a magnificent stretch of Roman masonry 30 feet high, the Jewry Wall.

The site, which lies in the western half of the modern town near the church of St Nicholas, was excavated in 1936–9. The intention had been to erect modern swimming-baths on the site, but as it was believed at the time that the Jewry Wall was part of the basilica and that the supposed adjacent forum was later covered by public baths, it was decided to preserve what was thought to have been the earliest administrative centre of Leicester. It is now known, however, that the forum and basilica lay on an adjacent site to the east partly under St Nicholas' Circle, and that the Jewry Wall, like the Old Work at Wroxeter, is part of the *palaestra*, or exercise-hall, of the baths.

It is best to visit first the excellent Jewry Wall Museum (10–5.30, Sun. 2–5.30, closed Fri.), which overlooks the Roman remains. The most spectacular exhibits are the two stretches of wall-plaster, recovered from a Roman town-house in 1958, which depict human figures, birds, garlands, etc. set in an architectural background (fig 47). There are also some notable mosaics, including a second-century floor featuring a peacock, and especially an outstanding geometric mosaic from Blackfriars, relaid in the Museum in 1977. Dated to *c.* 125/40 by pieces of samian pottery used as red *tesserae*, the pavement has a highly pleasing overall design and a restrained, tasteful use of colour. Outstanding among other finds are the weathered stone head of a boy, from Hinkley, fragments of moulded glass depicting a gladiatorial combat, and a Roman milestone of AD 119–20 recording a distance of two miles from Leicester – A RATIS II.

On leaving the museum, take a look at the plan of the Roman baths which is displayed on the terrace. It will be seen from this that the visible remains belong to two periods, the first about AD 125 (red labels), when the Jewry Wall itself and

47   *Leicester, Roman wall-plaster*

the rooms nearest to it were put up, and the second about
135–40, when the central area, including the three large halls
in front of you, was built. The apsed hot baths and furnaces
marked on the plan were filled in when the museum was
constructed. Keep to the right and make for the superb
Roman drain with a single capstone *in situ*. This marks
Roman ground-level: all the remains here except for the Jewry
Wall are reduced to foundations only. Beyond the drain, at a
higher level, is part of a town-house. Now walk over to the
impressive Jewry Wall, which may owe its preservation to the
fact that it was incorporated into a Saxon church. The origin
of the present name is unknown. It is an imposing stretch,
with tile bonding-courses and one of the two arches in a fine
state of preservation. The square holes were designed
to hold wooden scaffolding during construction, and would
have been plugged with other material which has now fallen
out. Below the Jewry Wall is another section of drain. At the
far end, close to the metal staircase, is an outfall-channel
leading into another drain from a tiny room at a higher level.
Now turn and face the museum. On the small mound in front
of you are some bases of hypocaust *pilae*. Finally, at a lower
level beyond, there are three rooms with apses for plunge-
baths on either side. The precise sequence of rooms which the
bather would have followed is not clearly understood, and the
Leicester site is not, therefore, as good an example of a public
bath-suite as that at Wroxeter.

After you have left the site, take a look at the other side of
the Jewry Wall. Four arches are visible here, and a niche,
presumably for a statue, in the middle. The lower courses of
the north wall of the *palaestra* hall can be seen from Welles
Street (follow St Nicholas' Walk to the far end).

The only other remnant of Roman Leicester is a stretch of
fairly impressive earthwork known as the Raw Dykes, usually
interpreted as part of an aqueduct but perhaps more likely to
have been connected with a docks-installation alongside a
Roman canal. It lies about 1m south of the Jewry Wall site.
Take the Rugby road (A426) out of Leicester and stop just
after the B5366 to South Wigston goes off to the left (Saffron
Lane). The earthwork is on the right of Aylestone Road
before the railway-bridge.

The rest of the Roman towns in central England did not

have colonial or *civitas*-capital status, and were generally much smaller in size. One settlement, however, at **Water Newton** (TL 1296) was quite extraordinarily large and complex, and it is possible that it was promoted to self-governing status in the later Roman period. It began, as with so many of the towns of Roman Britain, as a village outside a military fort, established in the conquest period (perhaps *c.* AD 45) to guard the crossing-point of the main trunk road to the north, Ermine Street, over the river Nene. When the army moved on *c.* AD 70 it flourished and expanded in piecemeal fashion, first as ribbon development along Ermine Street, but then over a vast area both north and south of the Nene: at its apogee in the fourth century, the town of DVROBRIVAE ('the fort at the bridge', indicating its military origin) sprawled over some 250 acres, a size rivalled only by Cirencester and London. But whereas the last two were carefully planned administrative centres, Water Newton was the product of spontaneous, unplanned growth, and aerial photographs show there was no neat grid-pattern of streets. Another difference was that the defences, when they came, enclosed only about 44 acres at the heart of the town. Limited excavation suggested that its earth rampart was of the late second century, as commonly in Romano–British towns, and that the stone wall in front of it was contemporary; this, however, seems unlikely (if both were really built at the same time, they probably belong to the third century at the earliest). Bastions, visible on air photographs, were presumably added in the fourth century. The site is easily accessible on the east side of A1, ½m N of its junction with A605 (Corby–Peterborough): there are parking-places on both northbound and southbound carriageways roughly opposite the site. Today there is very little to see of the Roman town. The defences can be made out as a low mound close to the road (and can be followed for most of their circuit), but particularly striking is the magnificent *agger* of Ermine Street striding up to the SE gate and right through the middle of the town: it will be appreciated that the modern road has swerved to the west and south of the Roman line at this point. Very little controlled excavation has been carried out within the defences, but aerial photos reveal a large public building, possibly an official inn for travellers, or else a market-place, and at least one temple, as well as other structures residential or commercial in character. But the shanty town spread far beyond the walls, and extensive excavation, especially over the past decade, has yielded detailed information about the building and activities there: this was one of the main industrial areas of Roman Britain, the centre of the most successful pottery works in the island. From the mid-second century onwards it produced a wide range of colour-coated vessels, both decorated and plain (known as Nene Valley or Castor ware), which was traded the length and breadth of the province. The mosaics of the surrounding countryside (DVROBRIVAE may have had a 'school' of mosaicists in the late fourth century), the silver plate of a Christian church or house-chapel in the town, now in the British Museum (p. 371), the high-quality small finds from even the humblest buildings – all are indicators of the prosperity and high living standards of the Nene valley region in late Roman times.

Some of the rich establishments in the hinterland of Water Newton, such as that underlying Castor village (App. I), may well have been connected in some way with the potteries, and perhaps owned by businessmen who had made their money in the industry; but others were traditional villas dependent on farming the fertile soils of the Nene valley. Few of these villas and farms have been excavated (many are known from the air), and of those that have, only one has something preserved *in situ*. That is the site at Lynch Farm, **Orton Longueville** (TL 149977), excavated in 1972–4. It lies in the recreation area known as Nene Park Ferry Meadows, which is signposted from the A605 (Corby–Peterborough) 2m E of its junction with A1 (near Water Newton), and 3m W of Peterborough. The Roman buildings are marked out, partly in modern materials, just past the information centre near the car-park, to the right of the path. The earliest feature here is the corner of a first-century military ditch, part of two multiple ditch-systems which may have belonged to marching camps or perhaps camps built in training, although neither type usually has more than one ditch. The earlier system is contemporary with the 28-acre vexillation fortress which lies facing you, immediately across the river at Longthorpe; it is now buried below a golf-course. This was a key base in the subjugation of the eastern Midlands, where legionaries and auxiliaries were brigaded together between *c*. AD 45 and 62, the base from which Petillius Cerialis made a desperate and disastrous attempt to stem the Boudiccan advance in 60/1 before Suetonius Paulinus could return from Anglesey (p 20). Later, probably in the third century, a large aisled barn was put up, built of timber on stone footings. Its roof was supported on two rows of posts, now marked out as concrete circles. The barn was used no doubt, like its modern counterpart, for storing crops and farm implements, but several furnaces were found (one is still visible), indicating as well small-scale production of ironwork. Such aisled buildings were extremely common in the countryside of Roman Britain, either as outbuildings in courtyard-type villas, or else as independent farm buildings, sometimes even with subdivisions for living accommodation; but apart from a portion of one example marked out in the south wing of the Rockbourne villa (p. 82), this is the only permanently accessible example of its type in Britain. A well and a small square timber building on stone footings with a timber verandah or colonnade (possibly a temple) are the other visible associated features, but a corn-drier, and a stone tank probably used as a fishpond, had to give way to the waters of an artificial pleasure-lake. These were clearly the outbuildings of a farming estate, possibly the same as the one which included ditched stockyards 400 yards further west, but the main villa buildings have not been excavated. In the fourth century decline set in here, probably because of flooding, and the stockyards were used as a cemetery for 51 burials (not now visible).

Towns such as Water Newton which were situated on trunk roads also served as 'posting stations', where the traveller could expect to find a hotel and a stable for his horses. Another example, this time on Watling Street, was LETOCETVM, now the village of **Wall** (SK 0906) [AM; S, but closed Mon. and alternate Tues.]. The earliest occupation at Wall was military, but the full details of a complex series of forts have yet to be unravelled. The earliest was about 30 acres in size and was presumably the base, from about AD 50–58, for part of the Fourteenth Legion. Finds however indicate that the same site continued in use until about AD 70. In the second century there was a small fort on the crest of the hill by the

church. The importance of Wall as a military site would have
attracted civilians to settle along Watling Street. The resulting
settlement was a sprawling one and does not seem to have
been enclosed by defences until a military strong-point was
established in the fourth century, and even then they did not
include the bath-house. Only this last building, compact and
well-preserved, together with an adjacent courtyard building,
can be seen at Wall today.

The bath-house was excavated in 1912–14. It is extremely
complicated in its present, final form, in which five separate
phases have been recognized. The first building, revealed by
excavation in 1956 but not now visible, belonged to the first
century and was presumably military. The phase-II bath-
house, perhaps early second-century, occupies about one third
of the area of the final building and is the part first reached
from the custodian's hut. In phase III (third-century) a new
undressing-room and cold plunge were added. In phase IV
there were internal changes, and in phase V (perhaps at the
same time as IV) the main stoke-hole was rebuilt. Visitors
who want to try and work out all these phases on the site
should study the plan displayed in the adjacent museum,
where a small collection of finds has been arranged.

The visitor first reaches the *tepidarium* and *caldarium*, built
in phase II. The floor has gone but many *pilae* are visible.
At first a small rectangular alcove projected from the
exterior wall in front of you, and the broken ends of it are
visible roughly in the middle of the long wall; it was
demolished in phase IV and the wall made continuous. Turn
right towards the hedge. The room next to the one with the
pilae was the entrance-hall and cold room of the phase-II baths
(floor missing). Next comes a tiny hot bath with brick seat
and lead outflow-pipe, and a small room for dry heat beyond.
The bath was inserted in phase IV; in the phase-II building
this had been a single room, and was in fact the southern limit
of the bath-house at this stage. The date of the room next to
the hedge is unknown. It has a stoke-hole to warm the
adjacent hot room, but the presence of five *pilae*-bases
indicate that it too was heated at some stage.

Now return to the other end of the bath-house and go
round the projecting stoke-yard which supplied heat to the
main rooms with the *pilae*. You can now examine the far side

of the wall running down the middle of the building, which
was the outer wall of the phase-II bath-house. Traces of three
of its external buttresses, designed to take the thrust of the
vaulted roof, can be seen here. The one nearest you is the
most conspicuous, and another will have been noted
projecting into the path on the other side. The wall here has
been much altered in later phases, and a new stoke-hole was
inserted in phase V. Now continue on round the outside of the
building, noting three parallel walls on your right. Two
belong to a verandah of the large adjoining exercise-
courtyard, added in phase IV, while the third wall (the one
nearest you) is part of an earlier building underlying the
courtyard. Rounding the corner you come to the broad
threshold blocks of the main entrance to the baths and so
cross into the courtyard. On the far side are three rooms
added in phase III, two still with their floors *in situ*. The one
on the right, with a slab in the centre, was a room of dry heat
(*laconicum*): the hypocaust-flues are visible beneath. The next
room also retains its original floor and is the undressing-
room. In phase IV a niche was inserted, presumably for a
statue; it is still covered with salmon-pink plaster. At the same
time also, the drain visible in this room was inserted to take
away water from the small hot bath already noted. Lastly,
between the undressing-room and the hedge is the fine cold
plunge-bath with an inlet and two outlets for filling and
emptying it with water.

A cobbled road separates the bath-house from a substantial
stone courtyard building still standing up to six feet high, first
uncovered in 1910–12 and re-excavated in 1974–7. Its small
and generally squarish rooms are arranged around a corridor
and a central court, where the semicircular apse once held a
fountain. The room at the far left-hand (north) corner has
fragmentary remains of a channelled hypocaust. Excavation
has shown that the building was constructed about AD 120
and replaced two phases of similar timber building on the
same alignment. The formal arrangement of the rooms, the
high quality of the construction work together with the
presence of painted wall-plaster and window glass, and the
comparatively early date for a building in stone at a civilian
settlement all strongly suggest some public function, possibly
as a small inn (*mansio*) for travellers; but it had a short life

and seems to have been destroyed about AD 160.

Another posting-station on a great trunk-road is the village of **Great Casterton** (TF 0009) on Ermine Street. It lies in the former county of Rutland, a few miles NW of Stamford. It is now by-passed by the A1; so if you are heading north, turn off for the Nottingham road (A606), and if you are going southwards, take the B1081 for Stamford. In the village, follow a lane signposted to Ryhall and Essendine, and you will see on your right, just after the farm, the surprisingly impressive remains of the town's defences. No stonework is now exposed, but the mound of the rampart is here five feet high and the enormous shallow ditch in front of it is 60 feet wide. Elsewhere the rampart has been largely ploughed away but the great ditch can be followed all the way down the east side of the town. Beyond the field wall, where it swings away to the right, it is much fainter. Excavations in the 1950's revealed that the town wall was first built, with a bank behind it, at the close of the second century, and that there was a deep V-shaped ditch seven feet in front of it. These walls enclosed about 18 acres but, of the buildings within, apart from a late-first-century bath-house, nothing is known. Soon after the middle of the fourth century the defences were drastically reorganized, and it was then that the wide ditch visible today was dug. The second-century ditch, which lay much closer to the wall, was then filled with the material excavated from the new ditch. The filling provided a foundation for rectangular projecting bastions which were added to the wall at this time. Some of these may have carried the Roman catapult machines, *ballistae*, which hurled stone balls and iron-tipped bolts at the enemy. The purpose of the new broad ditch, cut out of solid rock, was probably to keep the enemy at a range suited to the *ballistae*.

Outside the town, but close to the corner where the defences are visible, a temporary fort was discovered from the air in 1959. Excavation showed that it was built soon after the conquest and occupied until about AD 80, after a slight reduction in size *c.* 70. It is not visible from the ground. Further away to the east a villa has been excavated, now also filled in. It was built as late as *c.* AD 350–65, enlarged *c.* 370–80 and burnt at the very end of the fourth century. There is evidence that even then agricultural activity continued at the site, and it is likely that life went on behind the shelter of the town-walls well into the fifth century.

The next town of any size on Ermine Street north of Great Casterton was situated at **Ancaster** (SK 9843), and the course of the Roman road between the two is followed by modern highways. For the first 12 miles north of Great Casterton, Ermine Street is represented by the dual carriageway of the A1, but then you should turn off along the B6403, and keep straight on for Ancaster. For the last six miles the road is very straight: it is a fine piece of highway, with the B-road running on top of an *agger* about four feet high.

At Ancaster, Ermine Street is crossed by the A153 (Grantham–Sleaford). Beyond this crossroads, in the field on the right of the B-road, is the SE corner of the defences of the Roman town, here represented by a mound and a broad ditch, less impressive than at Great Casterton. A stone wall $7\frac{1}{2}$ feet thick and backed by a contemporary earth rampart was built to enclose an area of about nine acres sometime between AD 200 and 225. It was defended by one or more ditches, but the visible broad ditch (which was accompanied by a slighter, outer one) is certainly fourth-century. Two fan-shaped bastions, paralleled on the Danube but elsewhere only once in Britain (at Godmanchester), have been discovered at Ancaster at the NW and NE corners. Probably built in the fourth century, they are not now visible.

The line of the western defences can be gauged by going into the churchyard on the other side of Ermine Street. Beyond the tower there is a drop in ground-level and the path cuts through the site of the rampart. The change in levels is also clear in the garden adjoining the churchyard on the south. Little is known of buildings within the town, which was preceded, as so often, by a military fort in the middle of the first century. Some finds from Ancaster, including a representation of the Mother Goddesses and other sculpture, are in Grantham Museum.

The last two towns to be mentioned in this chapter, Caistor and Horncastle, lie in NE Lincolnshire. The status of both is uncertain, but the presence of defensive stone walls, which constitute the visible remains at both places, implies that the places were of some importance in the late Empire. Earlier they doubtless served as market centres, but their late Roman military character is suggested by their strong walls and their proximity to an exposed coastline: geological survey, for example, has shown that Horncastle stood on an estuary in Roman times. Recent excavation here (1984/5) has now confirmed a late third- or early fourth-century date for the defences, and those of Caistor must be contemporary. The bastions were probably part of the original scheme. At Horncastle the wall was backed as well by a contemporary earth rampart.

The remains of the walls at Caistor are insignificant (see App. I for the details), but those of Roman **Horncastle** (TF 2569) have left more numerous and more interesting fragments. The walk round these only takes about 20 minutes, as the area enclosed by the defences is very small (five acres, about three less than at Caistor). There does seem, however, to have been Roman settlement outside the walled area, especially to the south. A convenient starting-point is Market Place, where a plan of the modern town marking the Roman remains can be studied. Now walk down nearly to the end of Church Lane; on the left, at the back of a car-park opposite the churchyard steps, is a piece of wall-core forming the base of a modern brick wall. Turn left along Wharf Road. A fine stretch, 20 feet long and four feet high, including part of the inner face, is displayed in the vestibule of the Branch Library on the left. Go up Bull Ring, turn left into High Street and so back to Market Place. Turn right down St Lawrence Street. On the right, immediately beyond a public toilet, is a yard (in front of the garage) from which the fine north corner bastion can be seen. It is about 10 feet high, and the lowest courses of an adjoining stretch of wall are also visible. The remains are situated in the back garden of a private house. Now return to Market Square and walk over to Woolworths. Two shops further to the right, underneath the plaque announcing Bridge Street, a pair of doors gives access to a derelict yard where a low overgrown stretch of wall-core exists. Now return to Woolworths, go down Manor House Street, and turn right along a private gated road. In a field on the left a fenced-off area encloses a fine stretch of the inner face of the wall at the west angle, some 6 feet high, with part of the core visible too. Continue on down to the end of Manor House Street, where another stretch of wall, six feet high, can be seen at the entrance to the health centre. Now return along this street and go into the churchyard, keeping straight along the path to the other side. On the right, next to house no. 12, is a side-gate giving access to the longest and highest stretch of wall at Horncastle, though once again only core is visible. At present (1979) the door has collapsed and so the wall is visible from the street. With the permission of the respective owners, it is possible to follow this piece of wall, past a short brick interruption and through another gate into another back-yard, and see the wall rounding the south corner. The lowest course of the Roman wall is also visible on the left of the road, before disappearing under the houses.

Chapter 6

Wales

including Cheshire

Wales was something of a problem for the Roman
administration: the area was too hostile to be left alone, as it
provided a threat to the security of the towns and villas of the
peaceful lowlands. It had therefore to be conquered and
garrisoned, and the cost of this can hardly have been offset by
the minerals, especially gold and copper, which the Romans
exploited. Even after its final pacification, Wales remained a
garrisoned zone, and although romanization in the form of

villas and a couple of towns reached the extreme south and
south-west, life for the natives in most places must have been
little changed by the Roman conquest.

We know a fair amount about the military campaigns
against the Welsh tribes from the pages of the historian
Tacitus, but he gives no place-names and few geographical
details, and it is therefore impossible to reconstruct each
campaign with precision. The first attempts were made by
Ostorius Scapula, governor between AD 47 and 52, with
further advances under Veranius in 57 and Suetonius Paulinus
in 58–9 until the latter was halted by the rebellion of Boudicca
in East Anglia. We do not hear of any further campaigns until
AD 74, when Julius Frontinus finally subdued the Silures, the
tribe occupying most of South Wales except the SW corner;
and the Ordovices of North Wales were not quelled until 78
by Frontinus' successor, Julius Agricola.

The archaeological record for these campaigns is sparse.
Until quite recently only three marching-camps had been
known in Wales, but many more have now been discovered
by aerial photography and fieldwork. Most or perhaps all of
those mentioned later in this chapter, or listed in Appendix I,
belong to this early period. So too does the 48-acre campaign
base at Rhyn Park, Chirk (Shropshire), discovered from the
air in 1975 (nothing visible on the ground), and another base,
a vexillation fortress of 26 acres, at Clyro near Hay-on-Wye
(App. I). The strategic importance of the latter site, and the
finds of pottery, which indicate that occupation had ceased
before c. 75, make it clear that this was a base for large
expeditionary forces in their attacks on the Silures.

With the final pacification of Wales in 78, our literary
sources dry up, and the rest of its history under the Roman
occupation has to come from archaeology. The whole area
was controlled by a carefully-designed network of forts,
fortlets and roads. Much work remains to be done both in the
discovery of new sites and in the elucidation of their history,
so that many of the dates given below may have to be revised
in the light of future research.

The two corner-stones for the garrison of Wales were the
legionary fortresses at Caerleon and Chester, which, together
with York, formed the three permanent bases of the legions in
Roman Britain. **Caerleon*** (ST 3490) was ISCA, the home of

the Second Augustan Legion, situated 3m NE of Newport, or 1½m from intersection 24 or 25 on the M4. The fortress was established by Frontinus in AD 74 or 75 with an earth rampart and timber buildings. Refurbishing of the defences in stone began in the late 80s and probably continued at least until 100, on the basis of the inscription from near the SW gate (fig 51). The barracks were gradually given stone footings from *c.* 100/ 120, but the superstructure of these and many other fortress buildings remained half-timbered throughout the life of the fortress. There was some repair in the third century, but by about 290 the fortress was no longer garrisoned: part of the legion either now or later was transferred to Richborough in Kent. Regular excavations since 1926 have provided many details of the lay-out of the 50-acre fortress, but only two important portions remain visible today.

The first, part of the legionary bath-house, can be reached from the car-park of the Bull Inn, which is on the right of the main road soon after entering the village [SSM]. Although the bath-house was normally situated outside the defences to

48   Caerleon, reconstruction-drawing of a corner of the fortress

minimize fire-risk, in a stone-built legionary fortress this was not so. Only part of the baths has been conserved under the modern cover building (opened in 1985); what there is impresses by sheer size and solidity, and the monument is a major addition to the accessible remains of Roman Britain. Excavations between 1957 and 1981 have revealed a detailed structural sequence between its original construction *c*. 75 and its final disuse *c*. 230, curiously some 60 or so years before the garrison left ISCA (by that time, especially if the legion was well below full strength, soldiers may have turned to the smaller extramural bath-house recorded in the nineteenth century near the Castle mound). On leaving the ticket-desk you first see on your right the great swimming-bath (*natatio*), added soon after the original construction (probably in the 80s). In a major renovation of the baths *c*. 150, the pool was shortened by the building of the buttressed wall, also visible; access to this pool was via the steps in the corner to your left. Description ** continues on p. 384.

The second visible portion of the fortress, its west corner [AM; A], can be reached by continuing along the main road and forking left at the church. You are now following the line of the *via principalis* and soon pass through the site of the SW gateway. You are now outside the fortress, with the amphitheatre on your left. Ignore that for the moment, and take the path on your right which runs adjacent to the fortress-ditch, its V-profile now obscured by silt, and passes the site of the parade-ground and civil settlement under the playing-fields on the left. After 150 yards, cross the ditch by the path and you find yourself in the west corner of ISCA. What you first see as you walk down to the far end are the circular oven-bases which back on to the rampart. These were once domed structures of tiles and masonry, probably covered by wooden sheds. They belong to the original fortress of AD 75 but were superseded about 150 by more substantial square stone structures, with furnaces and built-in flues. Two of these cookhouses are visible, built up against already existing stone turrets which are also visible; one is half-way along the fortress-bank here, the other is at the corner. Also at the corner, adjoining the cookhouse and contemporary with it, is a latrine. The most prominent feature is its stone-built sewer running below floor-level on three sides; it would have been surmounted by a row of wooden seats.

The interior of the fortress at this corner was occupied by rows of barrack-blocks arranged in pairs facing each other (fig 48). Only one is visible now, the plans of three others being misleadingly laid out at a higher level in modern materials. This is only a fraction of the total: to get some idea of the fortress' size, you have to imagine 24 of them stretching in a row from here to the north corner; then there were 24 more at the other end, and a further 16 in the centre, flanking the headquarters building: Caerleon church, the tower of which is visible from here, overlies part of the HQ and thus roughly marks the central point of ISCA. As can be seen from the plan before you (fig 49), a barrack-block consists of spacious quarters at one end of the building (that nearer you) for the officer, a centurion, and perhaps his junior staff, and twelve pairs of rooms for the rest of his company, fronted by a verandah. The larger room of each pair providing the living- and sleeping-quarters for about six men, while the smaller was used for storing their arms and equipment; each barrack was thus designed to hold a *centuria* of 80 men. The barracks here were built around the middle of the second century to replace earlier ones of timber, but various modifications were made in the third century to the centurion's quarters; not all the dividing walls visible today belong to one period. The reconstruction drawing (fig 48) shows the barracks built entirely of stone; more probably, as noted above, the

49 Caerleon, a legionary barrack-block

50 Caerleon, the amphithe

superstructure was only half-timbered resting on stone
dwarf-walls.

Another outstanding Roman monument at Caerleon is the
amphitheatre [AM; SSM], dug by Sir Mortimer Wheeler in
1926-7 and still the only completely excavated example in
Britain. It was constructed about AD 90 and so is nearly
contemporary with the most famous amphitheatre of all, the
Colosseum. But whereas the latter was designed purely for the
gratification and enjoyment of the Roman masses, its
comparatively humble counterpart in distant Caerleon was
primarily used for military exercises and displays, though no
doubt blood-sports and gladiatorial combat were also staged
here. There were various modifications in the middle of the
second and at the beginning of the third century, until its final
abandonment on the departure of the garrison.

On passing the custodian's hut and moving round anti-
clockwise, you can see that the amphitheatre has been
hollowed out to create the arena, the upcast earth being used
to form banks on which timber seating was erected. These
banks were encased in masonry both internally and externally,
where buttresses give added support. The stoke-hole for
heating a small bath-building is visible close to the outer wall
on this west side: it preceded the amphitheatre by a few years
but was not used after *c*. AD 125. From here you can use the
broad flight of steps in the adjoining entrance (fig 50) to reach
the arena, passing through a small room where competitors
waited their turn. Over it was suspended a 'royal box' for top-
ranking officers, access to which (as well as to adjoining seats)
was provided by the stairs on either side of the little room:
those on the right, reached through a perfect brick arch, are
still substantially complete. The companies which built the
amphitheatre inscribed their names on some stones in the
arena wall, even though the latter was soon to be covered with
mortar. Four casts are still in position, but they are difficult to
locate and still more difficult to decipher. The two easiest to
find are a short distance on either side of the entrance you
have just passed through, that on your right being six courses
above ground-level, and that on your left seven. Continuing
anti-clockwise, you will follow the arena wall round to the
south entrance. This, and its better-preserved counterpart on
the north, were the principal entrances to the arena and were

originally vaulted to carry an upper tier of seats. Continue round the arena, past one of the four narrow stairways giving access to the seating, until you reach another of the competitors' 'waiting-rooms', this time complete with stone benches. There is also a domed recess here, perhaps for a statuette of Nemesis, the goddess of Fate. From here you can complete your tour of the amphitheatre with a visit to the north entrance, which displays massive external piers of masonry with sockets for the bars barricading the arena. The arena wall near here still bears some traces of its mortar facing. Beyond, a long fine stretch of the fortress' stone defences, still about seven feet high, has recently been consolidated. It is mostly the core of the wall as only a few rows of facing-stones near the base have survived stone-robbing, but at the SE corner it stands 12 feet (3.60 m.) high, only two to three feet lower than the probable level of the sentry walk. An arched sewer-outlet can be seen at the foot of the wall after rounding the corner. Now retrace your steps to the tree and mount the rampart; skirting an interval tower you

51   Caerleon, a building-inscription

come to the south angle tower, excavated in 1982. Note how
the whole of this south corner of the wall bows outward from
the original line, which is represented by the demolished
remains visible in the bottom of the corner tower: this sector
of defensive wall collapsed at some stage in the second century
and was rebuilt on a slightly different line. A mint coin of 86
in the foundation trench of the corner tower showed that
rebuilding of the defences in stone started earlier than was
hitherto thought. The finishing touches are probably
represented by the splendid slab of AD 100 dedicated to Trajan
(fig 51) now in the Museum, which is situated on the main road
close to the church. The classical-style portico belongs to the
original museum of 1850, but a new building behind this facade
was opened in 1987 (15 March–15 Oct.: 10–6, Sun. 2–6;
** 16 Oct.–14 March: 10–4.30, Sun. 2–4.30). See p. 386.

   Caerleon's sister fortress at **Chester*** (SJ 4066), the Roman
DEVA, is even more built over. With the exception of the
amphitheatre, its surviving remains are isolated fragments
which require a good deal of patience to track down. This is
hardly surprising in a city like Chester; its strategic position,
first recognized by the Romans, has ensured its continued
importance to this day. Excavation in the 1970's and 1980's
has added many fresh details of the fortress' development and
history. It is now known that there was a military base here in
the late 50's, not as large as the later fortress, but larger than
a conventional fort. It was replaced by a 60-acre earth and
timber legionary fortress c. AD 76–8, and two lead water-pipes
bearing the name of Agricola show that the finishing touches
had been put by 79. Excavations at Abbey Green in 1975–7
found the turf rampart still standing to walk-way level, which
was, rather surprisingly, only about seven feet above the
foundations. If this was normal elsewhere, it is possible that
the reconstruction at Baginton (p. 162) gives a misleading
impression of height. The initial garrison, as we know from
tombstones, was the Second Adiutrix Legion, but this was
replaced, in 87 or a little later, by the Twentieth Valeria
Victrix, which then remained at Chester throughout.
Rebuilding in stone, first of the defences and of the internal
buildings immediately afterwards, started before the beginning
of the second century. Chester apparently escaped destruction
in c. 196, but there was extensive rebuilding and refurbishing

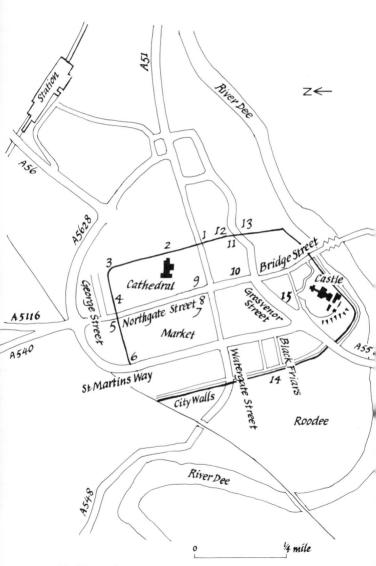

52   Chester, plan

of the defences in the first two decades of the third century, when extensive repairs were also carried out to interior buildings. Many barracks seem to have been in 'mothballs' from *c.* 250 to 300 (presumably because legionary detachments were widely redeployed elsewhere), but they were reoccupied in altered form from *c.* 300, when further alterations to the defences were made.

Rescue excavation, especially during the past two decades, has recovered much of the plan of the fortress' buildings, but little is now to be seen. Many of the surviving fragments are on private property, and prior permission is needed to visit them. Only the most interesting have been included here, while the rest are listed in Appendix I.

The best place to start your tour is to ascend the walls at the Eastgate (1 on fig 52), which lies on the site of a Roman predecessor. Immediately north of this, a fine portion of what is certainly the Roman fortress wall can be seen by descending the staircase to the car-park in Mercia Square (2). Returning to the wall-walk and continuing northwards, you can see the lowest four courses of another stretch of Roman wall just in front of the medieval alignment by leaning forward from the wall-parapet. Descend once more from the walls by another wooden staircase a little further on and walk back to the south end of the car-park to study another well-preserved stretch, incorporated in the bottom of the medieval walls but once more on a slightly altered alignment. Excavation here in 1983 showed that the standing wall was no earlier than *c.* 150 (it probably belongs *c.* 200), but sandstone fragments belonging to a different structure suggested that the visible wall was a replacement for the first stone defences of the early second century. After turning the north-east corner (King Charles' Tower, 3), you can follow the Roman walls, here in a superb state of preservation, to Northgate. Shortly before the latter, excavations in the late 1970s revealed a Roman internal tower and a battery of six ovens inserted in the third century into an earlier rampart building (4), but these have now been backfilled. The tower still stood to rampart-walk height, preserved beneath the earth bank behind the defences which was altered and widened in the early fourth century, rendering the tower and bread ovens obsolete.

Come off the walls at Northgate (5) to view this same stretch on the outside from the canal bridge. The wall here, $16\frac{1}{2}$ feet high to the moulded cornice (the walkway at the top is modern), is one of the more impressive stretches of Roman defensive work in Britain. The slope inwards towards the cornice is due to partial post-Roman collapse and was not a feature of the Roman defences, which would have been vertical. The visible masonry very probably dates to a large-scale Severan reconstruction of the walled circuit in the early third century; but there were further alterations *c*. 300, when the bank behind was lowered and widened and part of the rear face of the wall made freestanding. Tombstones robbed from the nearby cemeteries were used as building material in these alterations; many found in this stretch between 1883 and 1892 are now in the museum. West of Northgate some further stretches of Roman masonry are just visible when leaning over the wall-parapet. At the NW corner (6), Roman and medieval walls part company, and the Roman NW tower was found in 1964–5 standing fifteen feet high. Unfortunately it had to give way to the inner ring road, but its plan is outlined on the pavement below St Martin's Gate. From here the Roman west wall followed the line of the inner ring-road, while the medieval circuit embraced a wider area to the west and south.

** Return to Northgate and enter the street of the same name, which was the Roman *via decumana*. Between the Town Hall and the central cross of the Rows lies the site of the *Principia*, the HQ of the fortress, of which two fragments are accessible. One, excavated in 1970 and visible from Hamilton Place (7: turn right beyond 'The Forum'), is part of the row of offices along the north range of the building, including the shrine where the legionary standards were kept (*sacellum*), and, below it, the rock-cut strong-room (*aerarium*). The other is a massive base for one of the columns of the cross-hall, together with two ends of column shafts projecting out of the cellar walls, in the basement of The Flying Machine, at 23 Northgate Row (8). At no. 14, Miss Selfridge (9), the uninspiring remains of an isolated hypocaust may be viewed (ask an assistant). The area around St Michael's Row was occupied by a large internal bath-building, of which a very well-preserved hypocaust is on show in 'Spud-U-Like' at 39 Bridge Street (ask manageress): part of the floor and its supporting *pilae* are visible (10). From here, turn left along Pepper Street in order to reach Newgate, from which the SE angle tower of the fortress can be seen (11), and, opposite, a public garden containing some re-erected Roman columns and a hypocaust from the bath-building mentioned above. Just north of the angle tower, in an inspection-chamber which is in the backyard of what is currently (1986) AVA Reproduction Furniture, 12 St John Street, is another stretch of the fortress-wall (12). The Roman date of the wall here is not in doubt, as the medieval circuit takes a slightly different line.

The most interesting monument of Roman Chester is undoubtedly the amphitheatre, on display since 1972 (13) [AM; A]. Only the north half is so far visible, but excavation of the rest was due to start in 1987; it cannot therefore yet rival the Caerleon example, even though Chester's is substantially larger – the largest, in fact, known in Roman Britain. Its site, just outside Newgate, has been known since 1929 but proper excavation began only in 1960. This showed that a timber amphitheatre, with an arena the same size but only half the seating capacity, was replaced in stone after a few years, perhaps c. AD 86. Its outer wall, supported by massive buttresses, has been robbed, but the arena wall is well preserved. One major and one minor entrance to the arena are visible, on the north and the east. That on the north was closed by large wooden doors hung on the stone gateposts which are visible on either side, next to the arena wall; behind were flights of steps leading up to the seats, but only those on the right survive. Adjoining this entrance on the west is a small room which was clearly used as a shrine of Nemesis, the goddess of Fate: an altar to her (replaced on the site by a replica), and two column-bases, perhaps once supporting dedications, were placed here at the end of the first century. The east entrance consists of a level passage and then a few steps down to a room at arena-level. Stairs on either side of it led to the seats and also to an officers' box raised above this room; those on one side, much worn, are still visible. The superbly-preserved door-jambs leading to the arena will also be noticed. The position of the subsidiary staircases giving access to the seating (which was wooden, supported on banks of sand) has been marked out on the grass, together with the plan of the outer, buttressed wall. The arena floor showed traces of repair in about AD 300 after a long period of disuse

(which ties in with what is now known about reoccupation of
the fortress barracks about this time). There was also a curious
timber platform in the centre of the arena, carefully avoided
by a drain which ran from the north entrance right through
the centre of the arena, but which is not now visible.

Two other extra-mural monuments complete this survey of
Roman Chester. Part of the Roman quay wall is situated
behind a toilet on the Roodee racecourse (14). It can be seen
from a distance at the foot of the steps which go down to the
course a few yards south of Black Friars, but a closer look
can only be obtained with the permission of the course
manager. The other is a Roman quarry-face and a much-
weathered figure of Minerva visible in a public garden called
Edgar's Field, on the south side of the river, on the right
immediately after crossing Dee bridge. Finally, no visit to
Chester is complete without seeing the Grosvenor Museum in
Grosvenor Street (15), with one of the finest displays of Roman
military and sculptural material in the country (10.30–5; Sun.
2–5). A newly refurbished Roman gallery opened in 1987.

These two fortresses of ISCA and DEVA were, as I have said,
the cornerstones for the control of Wales, though the Chester
command no doubt had responsibilities too in northern
England. Wales itself was studded with carefully-sited forts,
and to some of these I will now turn.

In the south the fort at **Brecon Gaer*** (SO 0029) [AM; A]
was one of the largest and most important, as it lay at the
junction of several roads. It is best reached by following the
A40 west of Brecon for four miles and taking the first road on
the right, to Aberbran. Turn right at the T-junction in this
village, and continue straight on for two miles. Immediately
after the second turning to the left, after crossing a stream,
you will come to an unsignposted cross-roads. (This point can
also be reached by taking a minor road from Brecon to Battle
and turning left in Cradoc, signposted Aberbran and
Aberyscir.) Here you must turn back hard on your right,
along a metalled track which leads to Y Gaer farm. Follow
the track round to the barns, leaving the farmhouse to your
left. Go through the gate between the old and new barn, turn
right, and you will then see a fine stretch of the defences away
to your left. The fort was built *c.* AD 80 with earth ramparts
(clay revetted in turf) and timber buildings. Its garrison at the

turn of the century was a Spanish cavalry regiment of
Vettones, 500 strong. A stone wall was added to the defences
some time between 140 and 160, and the principal internal
buildings were also rebuilt in stone at about the same time.
The gates seem to have been rebuilt at the end of the second
century, perhaps after destruction, but the fort was evacuated
soon afterwards. There was a brief reoccupation at the end of
the third century when the south gate was repaired. A trickle
of finds goes on into the fourth century, and the fort was
probably held by a caretaker garrison of just a few men
during this period. It was excavated by Sir Mortimer Wheeler
in 1924–5, but only three gateways, two angle turrets, and
part of the fort-wall remain visible today.

Turning left and following the walls clockwise, you will
pass an angle tower and then arrive at the east gate. Just one
guardroom with its entrance is now visible; the carriageway
and the other guardroom have gone. Move on now to the fine
south gate (fig 53): both guard-chambers are excellently
preserved, together with the two carriageways separated by a
central pier which is pierced by a doorway. Two of the pivot-
holes for hanging the gates can be seen, as well as a drain

53   Brecon Gaer, the south gate

under one of the carriageways. The stone sill across the front of the western carriageway was inserted later when the road-level was raised. Finally, you will come to the west gate, which is less well preserved but unusual in having projecting rectangular guard-chambers. Once again there are two carriageways, the central pier, and the pivot-holes for the gates. It should in theory have been the fort's main gate as the *principia* faces it, but the steepness of the slope outside probably meant that it was used less than the more accessible north gate.

At least five Roman roads centred on Brecon Gaer: (i) followed the river Usk SE to Caerleon with intermediate forts at Pen-y-Gaer (App. I), Abergavenny, and Usk (App. I); (ii) ran south to Cardiff via Pen-y-Darren (Merthyr Tydfil), Gelligaer and Caerphilly; (iii) ran SW to Neath through a fort at Coelbren (App. I); (iv) went north to Castell Collen; and (v) ran west to Llandovery and beyond. I will now describe the forts in this network where there is still something worth seeing, though the remains are hardly spectacular at any of them.

The fort at **Gelligaer** (ST 1397), on road (ii) above, lies just west of the church on the north side of the B4254. The mounds of the ramparts, interrupted by depressions which mark the site of gateways, are mostly followed by field boundaries, except on the side nearest the road which is the most conspicuous. If you want to examine the banks in detail, ask permission at Gelligaer House (first house on the right). The fort was built in stone early in the second century (as we know from an inscription), was evacuated at the end of the century, but reoccupied from the late third to fourth centuries. The entire plan of its buildings was recovered by excavations at the close of the nineteenth century, but no stonework is visible today. On its east (right-hand side when looking from the B4254) was an annexe, also defended, which contained the regimental bath-house. The annexe stretched as far as the churchyard, but hardly any trace is visible now. This stone fort was not, however, the earliest at Gelligaer: a larger fort, with earth ramparts and timber buildings, lay on a completely different, though adjacent, site to the west, on the other side of Rectory Road. Virtually nothing is traceable of this fort on the ground today. Further north, on Gelligaer Common, five practice camps are known; two of these can be traced quite easily with the help of a 1:50,000 OS Map (sheet 171 (old series 154), ST 1399).

The fort at **Neath** (SS 7497), the terminal point of Roman road (iii) from Brecon, was not identified until 1949, although it had long been known that the Roman NIDVM must have been at or close to the present town. The strategic importance of its position, accessible by sea, guarding an important river-crossing on the east-west coastal road, and controlling a valley which penetrates far inland, was obvious. Yet the occupation seems to have been brief: from about AD 75 for a few years, then a stone rebuilding *c.* 120 after a short gap, and then a final abandonment apparently about 140. Two gates (south and east) of the stone reconstruction, both with double carriageways and guardrooms, have been preserved in a housing-estate served by a road appropriately called Roman Way. To reach this from the centre of Neath, take the road to Swansea (A465) across the river, go straight across at the first roundabout, and then right at the second (A474, Pontardawe). Roman Way is a turning on the right after ¼m, opposite the school.

The road running due north from Brecon Gaer (iv above) aimed for **Castell Collen** (SO 0562), which overlooks a large bend in the river Ithon just north of Llandrindod Wells. The fort-platform is reached by a road which leaves the A4081 (Llandrindod to Rhayader) on the right, immediately after crossing the river ('no through road' sign). Follow this road as far as the red-brick farmhouse, where you should ask for permission to visit. The Roman fort lies in the field behind and to the left of the farm (through wicket-gate and over stile). The banks and ditches of a square fort are impressively visible in their entire circuit, with an apparently isolated bank and ditch lying to the west of it (nearest the farmhouse). In fact the latter was part of the defences of an original large fort, holding an infantry garrison about 1,000 strong, which was built in turf and timber *c.* 75–8 and faced in stone about 140. But in the early third century the area of the fort was reduced by the building of a cross-wall, and the outer defences (the now isolated bank and ditch) were no longer used. There were further repairs to the defences in the late third century and occupation continued into the fourth, though these

periods were separated by spells when the fort was empty.
Some traces of the stone buildings in the centre of the fort,
excavated in 1911–13, still remain, though in a very
dilapidated condition. They comprise an HQ building in the
centre, a granary to the north (nearest the farm) and a
commandant's house to the south.

Llandrindod Wells also has the distinction of having the
largest known group of military practice camps in the whole
Roman Empire. The troops stationed at Castell Collen were
responsible for digging, presumably at various times, no less
than 18 of these small camps, roughly 100 feet square. Very
little of them is left, but if you have the time or the
enthusiasm, you can trace some of them on Llandrindod
Common, south of the town to the west of the A483 (see
Bibliography). The one I found easiest to locate is reached by
a lane leaving the A-road on the right, 600 yards south of a
filling-station; the camp is situated on the crest of the field to
the right, opposite the entrance to 'Castalia'.

The course of the Roman road running west from Brecon
Gaer (v above, p. 202) is not clear until the village of Trecastle
on the A40. Here you can take the minor road to the left and
then after ½m branch along a modern track which roughly
follows the Roman alignment. After three miles it passes the

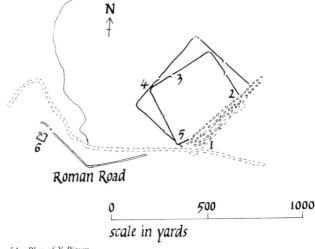

54   Plan of Y Pigwn

fine Roman marching-camps of **Y Pigwn** (SN 8231), in a wild
and desolate position 1,350 feet high. A less arduous
approach for the motorist is from the west. Continue along
the A40 for four miles beyond Trecastle and take the narrow
unsignposted road on the left immediately before Halfway.
Keep along this for two miles, through a metal gate, past a
farmhouse on the left, and up a steep twisting hill, until you
reach a T-junction. Turn left here (signposted 'No Through
Road') and leave your car by the farm after ½m. It is then 20
minutes' walk to the camps.

The camps are temporary ones belonging to the early years
of the Roman conquest and occupied at the most for a few
campaigns. There are two camps here, one inside the other
(plan, fig 54); the inner one, as will be seen, is later in date,
but only by a few years, as both must fall within the period
AD 47–78. Keep walking, bearing left wherever the track
forks, until you see on the left the large series of lead-working
mounds which have destroyed the south ramparts of both
camps. Leave the track at this point (1 on fig 54) and follow
the north edge of the workings for about 350 yards, looking
out on the left for the rampart of the inner camp. This can be
easily spotted by the coarser, browner grass which grows in its
accompanying ditch (2). From here, with the help of the plan,
you should be able to trace the ramparts of both camps. Their
north sides are particularly fine (over the crest and down the
slope beyond), with the north gate of the smaller camp (3) in
an excellent state of preservation, its *clavicula* boldly visible
(fig 55). Note also how the ramparts come very close to

55   *Y Pigwn, the north gate, inner camp*

touching at the NW corner (4). By now your eye should be in and you will be able to see that at the SW corner (5) the inner rampart actually projects over the line of the outer as the former rounds the corner, and this proves that the smaller camp was constructed after the larger one. Furthermore the ditch of the inner camp can be clearly seen cutting through the rampart of the outer. The camps were superseded by a permanent fortlet 500 yards to the west on the other side of the track (6), with a superb view down towards Llandovery, where there was a fort (App. I). The fortlet is about 120 feet square and its north corner is obscured by a low medieval *motte*, but it is extremely hard to trace on the ground today.

The Roman road running NW from Llandovery passed the site of the only known gold mine in Roman Britain, at **Dolaucothi** (SN 6640). I mention it more for its uniqueness than for the spectacular nature of the surviving remains, and if you want to trace these in detail, you should read the works cited in the Bibliography. To reach the site, which is owned by the National Trust, take the first turning to the left after crossing the bridge at Pumpsaint on the Lampeter-Llandovery road (A482), and then turn left again at the crossroads. The main opencast area lies almost immediately on the right,

56   Dolaucothi, entrances to mining tunnels

where a car-park is available. The primary interest lies in the complexity of the Roman activity. Gold-bearing pyrites were extracted by means of opencast workings and underground galleries, traced to a depth of 145 feet at one point and drained by a timber water-wheel (a fragment found here is in the National Museum at Cardiff). Water was brought to the site by means of three aqueducts, one of them seven miles long; these were simple channels cut into the hillside. The water was used partly for washing the ore after crushing, and partly for breaking down soft beds of pyrites. Of the settlement associated with these mines little is at present known, but a bath-house west of the main workings is probably best interpreted as a pit-head establishment rather than as a military baths associated with a fort 300 yards to the north: the fort, discovered under Pumpsaint village in 1972–3, was abandoned in the mid second century, probably just before the baths were built. Most of the visible features at Dolaucothi are probably of Roman date, though it is not yet clear to what extent nineteenth-century workings and even a brief probe in the 1930's have left their marks. From the car-park follow the tarred path to the opencast area, with the ruined mining buildings (modern) on your right, and a mining adit, probably also recent, on your left. A short distance to the left of the latter a path leads up the hillside, passing a fenced track en route (wooden steps and a stile are provided to cross it). Following the arrows you will soon come to some further mining entrances (fig 56), which are certainly Roman in date. To the right of the spot where the photograph was taken is the earth supporting-bank of a water-tank (wooden post with red and blue arrows), the water here being used to wash the ore over a series of stepped washing-tables down the hillside. From this point, follow the direction of the red arrow and walk straight across the open field along the site of an aqueduct-channel which is now completely invisible. Cross the fence at the other side by the wooden steps, and you will come at once to a large depression in the hillside (wooden marker at far end). This is the tank which formed the terminal reservoir of the main aqueduct. These and other remains, which can be traced most easily in winter or early spring before they are obscured by bracken growth, give us an interesting insight into Roman industrial activity in Britain.

Our knowledge of the road-system and its accompanying forts is less complete for North Wales than it is for the south; in particular there is a wide area to the west and south of Chester where there is almost a complete gap. There was a road running west to the coast along the Upper Severn from the town at Wroxeter, and fort-platforms are visible along this route at Forden Gaer and Caersws (both App. I). There are also two fortlets in this part of Wales: one on a deserted hilltop at Pen-y-crogbren and another, seven miles due south, in an isolated position at Cae Gaer (both App. I). The earth ramparts of the latter are impressively preserved, but as the site lies in Forestry Commission property, prior permission to visit must be obtained.

Moving further into the NW corner of Wales, we come to an important fort at **Tomen-y-Mur** (SH 7038), near Trawsfynydd in Gwynedd. Even if there was nothing to see, the site would be worth visiting for the wild beauty of its natural setting, with superb command of the surrounding countryside in nearly every direction. The wind usually blows here, so exposed is the position, and we can sympathize with

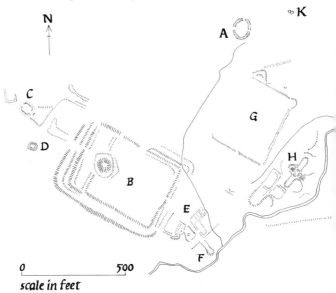

57 Plan of Tomen-y-Mur

the soldiers whose lot it was to serve in this remote spot. Yet its very remoteness has ensured the good state of preservation of the surviving earthworks, and there is much of interest.

Tomen-y-Mur is reached by an unsignposted minor road on the east side of the A470 immediately south of its junction with the Porthmadog road (A487) about 2½m north of Trawsfynydd village. Follow this road until you cross a cattle-grid and you will see on your right (A on fig 57) a unique monument: it is the only known amphitheatre attached to an auxiliary fort in Roman Britain. The arena is now marshy and the surrounding banks are much depleted, but its character is clear. Its primary purpose was surely to provide amusements for the garrison of this remote outpost, though it may have been used in military training as well. Beyond the amphitheatre, on your right, is a wall heavily defended with barbed wire and a clutter of corrugated iron sheeting. The gate here gives a warning to trespassers, so ask for permission if there is a shepherd about. Visitors are clearly not welcome, which is a pity, as there is little to disturb but the sheep. Keep the wall to your right and follow the wire fence which runs away to the left (SE) of the gate, but do not cross its line. Following it you will pass across the NE corner of the parade-ground (G), and immediately above it is a small bluff with an excellent overall view of the parade-ground, the fort and the Trawsfynydd lake beyond. The parade-ground appears to have been unfinished. Banks were made round three sides, increasing in height down the slope so that the top was level throughout. The intention was then to excavate earth just north of the area and cart it down the slope until the ground was level with the banks, but this was only half completed and so the delimiting banks and the excavation-pits are still visible. Hillock (H), with flanking terraces, and earthwork (J) are both of unknown purpose.

Continue following the line of the fence to the far end, where there is a gate. Go through this and then make back towards the path which leads to the ruined farm buildings. Just near these the track stops at the gap marking the NE gate of the fort. The most conspicuous feature at the fort is the large circular Norman *motte* which, as the plan shows (B), sits on the middle of the Roman rampart belonging to the second phase of the site. For here, as at Castell Collen, the original

earth-and-timber fort, built by Agricola in about 78, was
reduced in size at a later date. In this instance it probably
occurred early in Hadrian's reign, c. 110, when the new,
reduced fort was given a stone wall. No stonework is visible
now, most of it having been robbed to build the many
confusing field-walls here which crown the earth banks on all
sides except the NW. Occupation at Tomen-y-Mur seems to
have ceased about 140.

Now follow the fort perimeter in a clockwise direction. In
the middle of the SE side another field-wall, running at right-
angles to your left, should be followed. It aims for, but
finishes short of, the grass mounds about one foot high
marked as E on fig 57. These cover the remains of stone
buildings, comprising the civilian settlement and the bath-
house, which were partly explored in the nineteenth century.
A little beyond (F), is an embankment eight feet high, which
formed the abutment for a wooden bridge carrying the
Roman road from here to Caer Gai; the corresponding
abutment on the other side has presumably been completely
eroded by the stream. Now return to the fort and follow the
rampart round to the NW side, which is especially prominent
and free of field-walls. About 100 yards beyond the NW gate,
if you can surmount the fence in your way, can be found a
small earthwork (C) with two gates and a *titulum*: it is a
practice camp built by the troops as part of their training.
Another earthwork to the south (D) may be another example.
Two mounds (K), close to the amphitheatre and the start of
this tour, are probably small tombs.

This, however, by no means exhausts the list of Roman
earthworks in the vicinity of Tomen-y-Mur, and visitors with
plenty of time may like to explore further by crossing the
stream and proceeding SE on the alignment of the Roman
road (set by the SE gate to the bridge abutment, F): some
more disfigured mounds, probably tombs, lie 500 yards SE
of the SE gate, midway between the two streams. An OS map
will be needed if you want to find two practice camps further
afield. Llwyn-Crwn (SH 713382) measures about 122 by 112
feet and is two feet high in parts; Braich-ddu (SH 717383),
near a disused slate-quarry, is about 75 feet square with four
gates and internal *claviculae* almost touching. Another group
of five practice camps is known further east at Doldinnas

(SH 734378), but their remains are so slight that they are almost invisible except to a trained eye.

The Roman road which passes all these earthworks was heading over the mountains for the fort at the SW corner of Bala Lake, known as **Caer Gai** (SH 8731). The farm of that name which obscures the fort's northern corner is signposted on the north side of A494 ¾m north of Llanuwchllyn. After the track bends sharply to the right, you will see the field-wall, which incorporates part of the Roman stone core, crowning the full length of the SE defences of the fort. Continue on and park to the right of the farmhouse itself (enquire here for permission). Go through the iron gate on the right of the garden wall and keep straight. After passing through the next field-gate you come out to the SW side of the fort, its ditch and rampart (with modern wall on top) very conspicuous. The post was occupied in the period c. 78–125, the original turf rampart being revetted in stone presumably at the beginning of the second century. The garrison at this time was the First Cohort of Nervii from Belgium, as we know from an inscription found in 1885 and now at Cardiff. Two practice camps are known nearby, one of them still visible (Pont Rhyd Sarn, App. I). Another, larger, fort was discovered in 1975 only 5½ miles away at the east end of Bala Lake (Llanfor, nothing visible).

The road north from Tomen-y-Mur led to **Caerhun** (SH 7770) in the Conwy valley, after an intermediate station near Betws-y-Coed (Bryn-y-gefeiliau, App. I). The fort at Caerhun, KANOVIVM as we can read on a milestone in the British Museum, is situated 4½m due south of Conwy and is reached by a lane on the left (east) of the B5106 immediately after its junction with the more southerly turning to Rowen. The lane is signposted 'St Mary's Church'. The history of the place holds some puzzles: the usual earth-and-timber fort of c. 78 is usually thought to have been replaced in stone c. 140, but the odd treatment of the gates, two of them with single guardrooms only, is more characteristic of the third century. Certainly coins, pottery and the milestone mentioned above indicate that occupation lasted into the fourth century, although no structures of this date were apparently detected by the excavators of 1926–9, who uncovered the entire plan of the fort except for the NE

corner underlying the church and churchyard. All the
excavations have been filled in, and only the mound of the
rampart, very well-preserved on the south where the lane
bisects it, can be seen on the site today, with occasionally a bit
of stonework peeping through the turf. If you want to leave
the lane and explore further, permission should be obtained
from the farm on the opposite side of the B-road.

** A road running west from Çaerhun, and another striking
NW from Tomen-y-Mur, met at **Caernarfon*** (SH 4862)

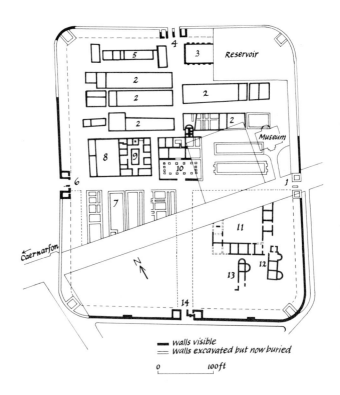

58 Caernarfon, plan of Roman fort

** [AM], a place of the utmost strategic importance not only in Roman times but later too, as the famous Edwardian castle at the river mouth demonstrates. The Roman name, SEGONTIVM, means 'the forceful river'. The remains of the fort lie in the outskirts of the town on the A4085 to Beddgelert: follow first A487 (Portmadog) and then fork left up the hill. The main phases of its history were revealed in excavations of 1920–3 by Sir Mortimer Wheeler, but the precise dating of these phases is still not certain. It started life, as usual, in earth-and-timber form *c.* 78, probably for a part-mounted cohort 1000 strong. Stone rebuilding took place in stages during the second century, from *c.* 140 onwards. The NW gate was replaced *c.* 155, the other gates somewhat later, but it now appears that part if not all of the stone curtain wall was added to the earth defences only in the fourth century. The Twentieth Legion from Chester helped in reconstructing the internal buildings, bringing with it the red Cheshire sandstone. The fort needed repair early in the third century, and an inscription in the museum refers to the rebuilding of an aqueduct 'collapsed through age'. The inscription also tells us that the garrison at this time was the First Cohort of Sunici from Germany. Occupation seems to have continued throughout the third and fourth centuries, with a final reconstruction after a fire, possibly connected with the disaster which brought the emperor Constans to Britain in 343, or else that of 367. The garrison was probably removed in 383 by Magnus Maximus in his attempt to become emperor, although later coins have been found.

The entrance to the site (1 on fig 58) is close to the SE gate (underneath the road) and an adjoining section of fort-wall. First the excellent little museum should be visited, where the main finds from the fort are exhibited; everything is carefully labelled and a description here is unnecessary. Leaving the museum, and keeping close to the boundary-wall skirting the reservoir, you will see the foundations of several barrack-buildings (2) which fill up the whole of the rear portion of the fort: these consist of quarters for officers at one end and a long section, originally divided by partitions, for the men. Most of the visible masonry belongs to the fourth-century rebuilding, except for the buttressed construction half-covered by the reservoir, which is a second-century granary (3). Next to this are the paltry remains of the NE gate with twin roadways and guard-chambers (4). The building on your left as you follow the rampart-bank from here (5) may have provided accommodation for two cavalry troops and their commanders, in contrast to the quite different infantry barracks elsewhere. Rounding the north corner (traces of a turret) you arrive at the NW gate, which is a little confusing as it displays masonry of several periods (6). It started with the normal twin passages and guard-chambers, but in the fourth century the gate was reduced to a single carriageway and the other (on the left) was converted into a new guardroom; the original guardroom here was then filled up, but it has been cleared out again now. Walking in a straight line from here to the modern houses, you are on the line of the *via principalis*. The area of barracks on your right between here and the road has been excavated but is not now visible (7). On the left, first of all, is a long shed with a large adjoining yard – the fort's *fabrica*, or workshop (8). Beyond the yard is the commandant's house, as it appeared in its final fourth-century form of four ranges of rooms around a central

59   Caernarfon, the strong-room

courtyard (9); the far right-hand corner, however, has a few blocks of red sandstone used in the first stone building of the second century. An isolated masonry plinth in a room at the far end was perhaps the base for an altar or household shrine. Finally, you come to the central building of the fort and the most interesting of all, the *principia*, or HQ (10). The front part consists of a courtyard, of which the well and some paving-flags are visible; the central part was a roofed assembly-hall later subdivided for office use; and the rear range consisted of five rooms (two under the modern house) of which the central one was the chapel where the military standard was kept; under it, originally vaulted, a strong-room was built in the third century with steps leading down to it (fig 59). At the same time a heated room was tacked on rather crudely at the rear. It is sometimes claimed, on the strength of an inscription (cast in museum), to be the record-office of the quartermaster. The channels for hot air to circulate below floor-level can be seen.

The rest of SEGONTIVM lies on the other side of the A4085 and part of it was re-excavated in 1975–9; this has been consolidated and left exposed. The largest structure, badly robbed, was a spacious courtyard building with three and presumably once four ranges round a central court (11). Built c. AD 140, its purpose is uncertain: it seems too large to have been the hospital, yet it is clearly not the commandant's house which is in the central range (9) where it ought to be. In the late third or early fourth century, after its demolition, a small but substantially built bath-house (12) was erected, still up to six courses high: it comprised (from N to S) furnace, hot, tepid and cold rooms with an apsed cold plunge-bath. It appears not to have been finished (hypocausts were never installed). Bath-houses normally appear inside the walls of Roman forts only in the late Roman period, and imply that the earlier pressures on space had been relaxed by the presence of smaller garrisons. However an even smaller bath-house further west (13), of which only one corner has survived later demolition, is believed to have been built as early as the mid second century. The SW gate is also visible, at present rather overgrown (14). It originally consisted of a double carriageway flanked by a solid tower on one side and a guardroom and tower on the other, but one of the carriageways was later blocked by a rough wall still in position. The outside of the fort-wall (core only) on the south-east and south sides, masked at first by modern refacing, can be studied by taking the path opposite the entrance to the Museum.

Building operations around the fort have revealed traces of a large civilian settlement, including a temple to Mithras. None of this is now visible. There is, however, an impressive enclosure-wall known as Hen Waliau situated 150 yards west of the fort. To reach it from the Museum, walk westwards along A4085, turn left (Segontium Road South) and then right down the hill (Hendre Street, avoiding Celert Street). Turn right on reaching the main road at the bottom and you come almost at once to a fine stretch of walling, still 19 feet above Roman ground-level, in the grounds of a private house, 'Bron Hendre'. A gateway, blocked up with modern material, is also visible here, but as there is no sign of gate-towers or other bastions it is best to regard this as a stores-compound (it was probably built in the late second century). The provision of such massive walls reflects an insecurity which grew even greater in the later Roman period, as emphasized by two important additions to the Welsh defences at Holyhead and Cardiff. The forts so far described all belong to the detailed Roman plan, worked out in the first century, of garrisoning Wales by means of regularly-placed forts. The new forts, however, at Holyhead and Cardiff belong to the late third or fourth century and were clearly designed, like the Saxon Shore forts of SE England, to combat an enemy expected from the sea, not from the Welsh mountains.

The fort at Holyhead, known as **Caer Gybi*** (SH 2482), owes its preservation to the church of St Gybi which stands inside its walls. Fork left for the town-centre by the war-memorial and you will see the rebuilt south gate on your right, by the telephone-boxes at the top of the hill. The small cliff on which the fort stands was originally much less steep (it was chopped back in the nineteenth century) and the walls continued down to the beach, with the shore-side left open: it is, therefore, a defended beaching-point for the navy using Holyhead harbour. The walls are 5½ feet thick, built of small stones partly laid in herringbone pattern, and still 13–15 feet high where best preserved, on the north and west sides. Even details of the rampart-walk are clearly visible, especially on the north when viewed from the churchyard. Three round towers can be seen, but only that at the NW corner is substantially Roman: the others have suffered in various degrees from medieval and modern rebuilding. The original entrance, on the south, is now much obscured by later work; the gap in the north wall is not of Roman origin. The date of Caer Gybi is not precisely known, but it probably belongs to the late fourth century. Why other similar structures are not known on the Welsh coasts is something of a mystery: perhaps the copper mines of Anglesey were believed to merit special protection.

The fort at **Cardiff Castle*** (ST 1876) is a much more

60   Cardiff, reconstructed north gate

massive affair, closely similar to the Saxon Shore forts of SE England. It was built on or near a succession of earlier forts in the late third or early fourth century, with semi-octagonal bastions and two single-arched gates each protected by guard-towers. It was occupied until at least 367. The fort is particularly striking for the reconstruction of the north, east and part of the south walls, carried out at the turn of the century: the north gate is especially fine (fig 60). We can thus gain a clear idea of what a Saxon Shore fort may have looked like in the fourth century, although the walls were probably rather less high. The original Roman facing is visible at the foot of the walls, especially on the south; it is separated from the reconstruction above by a row of pink stones. On the north stretch, five openings near ground-level give a glimpse of the Roman core which lies behind. The National Museum of Wales, which has an archaeological section, is nearby: it is open weekdays 10 am–5 pm (closed on Mondays) and on Sundays 2.30–5 pm.

Cardiff cannot have stood alone and must have been linked with a series of signal-posts to give warnings of imminent pirate raids. It was designed especially to protect the civilian population of the Glamorgan plain and the Severn estuary. Only in this part of Wales was there the spread of romanization in the form of towns and villas so familiar in the English lowlands. Or rather not quite. Until 1968, Caerwent (between Newport and Chepstow) was the only known Roman town in our area, but a totally new light has been shed on the romanization of SW Wales by the discovery that **Carmarthen** (SN 4120) was a walled town and not a fort. Presumably the Demetae, the tribe which occupied this corner, were rewarded for a lack of resistance to Roman arms by the creation of a tribal capital. Excavations in 1968 and following years suggested that the town was properly laid out in the second century, probably developing from a civilian sprawl around an earlier fort. It was given clay-bank defences at this time, revetted in stone at some later date, and these enclosed an area of some 31 acres. Inside were found buildings of timber and stone (including tessellated floors and hypocausts) which continued in use to the end of the fourth century at least. The only feature of Roman date visible today, however, is part of the amphitheatre, clearly signposted on the north side of the A40 on the east side of the town, adjacent to Priory Close. The south bank is much eroded, but that on the north, which was hollowed out of the hillside, stands to its original height. Excavations in 1971 found traces of the timber beams which supported the seating, as well as a complex drainage-system, but the arena wall had been totally robbed and this has been replaced by modern stonework. This amphitheatre, probably built in the late second century, is a remarkable witness to the extent of the penetration of Roman influence in this far corner of the province, itself so far from the heart of the Roman Empire. The Carmarthenshire Museum, splendidly displayed in the former Bishop's Palace, lies on the A40 on the eastern outskirts of the town, one mile east of the amphitheatre (Mon.–Sat. 10–4.30).

The other town at **Caerwent*** (ST 4690) [AM; A] is one of the most impressive sites not only in this chapter but in the whole of Roman Britain. It was VENTA SILVRVM, the market-town of the Silures tribe which proved so hostile to successive Roman armies in the first century. It was only a small place of 44 acres, hardly more than what we would call a village, but it had all the usual buildings – forum, basilica, temples and baths – that we expect of a tribal capital. It was founded at the close of the first century and given an earth rampart and

61   Caerwent, Roman town-wall and bastion

ditch not earlier than 130, and probably at the end of the second century. The visible stone wall was built in the third century, and polygonal bastions to provide extra cover were added to the north and south walls sometime not much later than 350.

Your tour of the defences can conveniently begin at the 'Coach and Horses' close to the east gate. This, like its counterpart on the west, probably had a double carriageway and flanking towers, a fragment of which can be seen on the south of the road. It is not bonded with the rest of the wall and so is earlier in date – perhaps contemporary with the earth rampart. The wall that stretches southwards from here is on average 10 feet high, though only the core is visible as most of the facing-stones have been robbed. Now go through a wicket gate and round the SE corner (the mound is a Norman *motte*); after a short while you cross a farm track. Some stone steps on the other side of this give access to the top of the wall, and here, where the earth bank makes a detour, are the remains of the south gate, a single arched passageway in a fine state of preservation. The piers on either

62   Caerwent, inscription in the church

side are still complete, together with the springers and even
some voussoirs of the arch. Some time in the fourth century –
a reflection of the growing troubles which had caused the new
fort at Cardiff to be built – the gate was entirely blocked up
(except for openings left for drainage at the bottom), and this
blocking-wall remains in position. From here you can either
walk along the wall or return to ground-level to admire the
superb stretch of walling and bastion which are in their best-
preserved state at this point (fig 61). The putlog holes which
held scaffolding during construction are clearly visible, and
note also how the bastion sits up against the wall without
being bonded into it. Going on you pass other bastions in
varying stages of completeness; the last before the SW angle
has a (blocked) postern door for defenders to slip out. Then,
rounding the angle and following the west wall, you reach the
modern road again and the footings of part of the west gate.

Next, walk along the road to Pound Lane (on the left),
where are the foundations of a couple of VENTA's houses.
The patch of gravel nearest the wall marks the site of the
Roman street, which was much wider than its modern
counterpart. Its side gutter and part of the drain into which it
discharged are visible. The house nearest the road started life
in about AD 100 as two long buildings with shops facing the
street and living-quarters behind; then in the second century
the east one was demolished and the survivor was given two
more wings, on the north and later on the east, to enclose a
courtyard (now buried under the adjacent garden).
Occupation continued into the fourth century when part of it
was used for iron-working. The masonry of the other house
belongs to the second quarter of the second century, but only
part of one wing, and the fragment of another peeping out
from the grass, are visible. At the end of the fourth century
both houses were taken over by squatters, who built stone
hearths over the ruined walls and dug pits into the floors.

A little further on is the war-memorial which marks the
centre of the Roman town. It stands at the SW corner of the
site of the forum and basilica, and on the other side of the
street, adjacent to the church, the public baths lie buried. The
church porch contains two Roman inscribed stones (if locked,
ask at the cottage facing the war-memorial). The larger
(fig 62) is a record of a dedication to a certain Paulinus who,

having commanded the Second Augustan Legion at Caerleon, went on to become the governor of two of the Roman provinces of what is now France, Narbonensis (capital at Narbonne) and Lugdunensis (Lyon). The end of the inscription reads EX DECRETO ORDINIS RES PVBL CIVIT SILVRVM, 'by decree of the local senate (*ordo*) the Community of the Silures (set this up)'. It is an interesting illustration of the machinery of self-government accorded to the tribal system in Britain, a system which Rome allowed to continue in a new romanized form. The other stone is a dedication to Mars Ocelus, a war-god. A plan of the early twentieth century excavations which revealed many details of Caerwent's buildings is displayed beside the entrance to the churchyard.

Apart from the houses mentioned above, the only other Roman building at present exposed within the walls is the little temple of the normal Romano–Celtic type with the central shrine (here with an apse) and surrounding ambulatory. It lies, overlooked by caravans, on the left of the modern road as you return towards the 'Coach and Horses', and is reached through a large iron gate opposite the bus-stop; it is currently (1987) the subject of fresh investigation.

Visitors may now like to return to their cars and take the lane which leads from the east gate back towards the bypass. The core of the east wall is visible to start with. Before joining the bypass bear round to the left and make towards the Northgate Inn. The foundations of two more bastions can be seen peeping from the grass, but the walls are better preserved further on. On the other side of the inn the north gate is visible, in part obscured by flowerpots. It is very similar to the better preserved south gate, with late blocking wall and some voussoirs of the right-hand arch still in position. Other parts of the north wall can be seen running along the back gardens of private houses, but more accessible is a well-preserved bastion near the NW corner, excavated in 1972, which is reached from a private car-park off A48 next to the road coming from the village. The walls can be followed from here round the NW corner and down part of the west side. Finds from Caerwent are in the Newport Museum (Mon.–Thurs. 9.30–5, Fri. 9.30–4.30, Sat. 9.30–4).

Apart from a few farms around Caerwent and a scattering of villas on the Glamorgan plain, civilian life continued in

Wales in much the same way as it had before the Roman conquest. There is, therefore, a whole host of native sites built or adapted in the Roman period which could be mentioned. In contrast to southern Britain, many pre-Roman hill-forts continued to be occupied and even re-fortified. The most famous and impressive is **Tre'r Ceiri** (SH 3744) in the Lleyn peninsula. It is approached by a public footpath signposted on the right of the B4417, 1m SW of Llanaelhaearn (on the A499). It is an exhausting climb, 900 feet or so above the road. The path enters the enclosure by its SW entrance, which has traces of external bastions on each side. The whole girdle of its dry-stone walls is still in an amazing state of preservation, 13 feet high on the outer face. The wall-walk is still visible in the best-preserved stretches on the north and west. There are traces too of an additional wall built further down the slope on the north and west sides where the approach is the least difficult. Inside are about 150 huts of various shapes and sizes, some circular, some D-shaped, some rectangular, many with subdivisions. Undivided circular huts are probably the earliest and some may be pre-Roman. The few objects found indicate that the main occupation was from about AD 150–400. The walls clearly owe something to the Roman model of defences, but they were not as strong: they could have kept brigands out, but not the Roman army, should they have been turned to such a use. Two Anglesey hill-forts also have stone ramparts erected during the Roman period: Caer Y Twr on Holyhead Mountain (SH 218830) [AM; A], and Din Sylwy in the NE corner of the island (SH 5881). You will need an OS map if you wish to find them.

But not all the native inhabitants lived on hill-tops during the Roman period: open villages of circular or rectangular huts also occur, often in large groups. Again there are many of these, and three Anglesey examples [all AM; A] will have to suffice. Twenty huts are still visible of a settlement occupied from the second to fourth century on the SW slope of **Holyhead Mountain** (SH 212820). A rectangular and a circular hut inhabited in the third century were found at **Caer Leb** (SH 4767) in 1866. The double banks which surrounded them are still very prominent: take the first road on the right of A4080 (unsignposted) west of Bryn-Siencyn, and watch out on the left-hand side after ½m. The third site is **Din Lligwy**

(SH 4986), which is signposted from the Llanallgo roundabout (junction of the A5025 with the A5018 to Moelfre). This charming site is the fortified residence of (probably) a native chieftain, and consists of two circular and four rectangular huts enclosed by stone walls in the shape of a pentagon. The buildings still stand to a maximum height of six feet, and appear to have been built in the late fourth century. It is a far cry from the civilized luxury of the villas of southern Britain.

Chapter 7

The Pennines and the Lakes

Cumbria, Durham, Greater Manchester, Humberside, Lancashire, Northumberland (south of Hadrian's Wall) and North and West Yorkshire

(Appendix One only: South Yorkshire)

1 Brough
2 Maiden Castle
3 Rey Cross
4 Bowes Moor
5 Bowes

Nearly the whole of the large area covered by this chapter was inhabited by the Brigantes before the Roman conquest. Their queen, Cartimandua, was friendly towards the new invaders, but she ruled uneasily and civil war broke out on a number of occasions. This resulted in the first official Roman contact with the north of England, for in 48, *c.* 57 and 69, Roman arms came to the help of the queen. The last of these interventions was only moderately successful, and Tacitus pithily comments: 'the throne was left to Venutius, the war to us.' Venutius was the divorced husband of Cartimandua. In

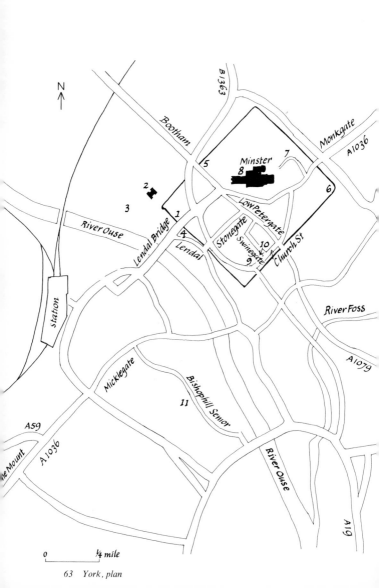

63 York, plan

AD 71, therefore, the new governor of Britain, Petillius Cerialis, took the Ninth Legion from Lincoln and advanced northwards, bent on final conquest. It was in this year or the next that Venutius made his last stand. A small section of stone wall and ditch of the native fortress of Stanwick (either his or Cartimandua's) has been restored [AM; A], part of a circuit which in its final phase enclosed some 600 acres. The site lies close to the hamlet of Forcett, 2m SW of Piercebridge and about 5m NW of Scotch Corner on the A66.

The founding of the legionary fortress for the Ninth at **York*** (SE 6052) is usually attributed to Cerialis in 71. Other large sites, however, suitable for at least half a legion, are known at Malton and at Rossington near Doncaster, and so it is unlikely that the Ninth was brought together in the full legionary fortress at York before the governorship of Agricola (AD 78–85). There was, however, almost certainly a smaller fort on the site under Cerialis or even earlier, but its dimensions are unknown.

From the end of the first century onwards, York was the military capital of Britain and the hub of the northern fort-system. The Agricolan fortress had a rampart of clay and turf with timber breastwork and towers and timber internal buildings, but these began to be replaced in stone at the end of the first century, and at least part of the defences were rebuilt in stone in AD 107–8. This we know from an inscription which also records the last appearance in Britain of *Legio* IX *Hispana*. Soon afterwards it was transferred to the East where it was disbanded after a disaster sometime before AD 165. Its place at York was taken by the Sixth Legion Victrix, which came to Britain in 122.

The next rebuilding of the defences occurred in the early third century. The weak foundations of the wall of 107–8 had caused partial collapse, and total rebuilding on a more imposing scale was necessary. This work was carried out either by the emperor Severus, who died in York in 211, or by his son Caracalla (emperor 211–7). Further reconstruction was done by Constantius I in the early years of the fourth century. The east corner of the fortress remained untouched, but the whole of the river front was given a grandiose series of polygonal towers. This was clearly designed to impress, and the elaboration may be connected with the new commander of

land forces in Britain, the *Dux Britanniarum*, whose
headquarters it was. Constantius died in York in 306, and his
son, the famous Constantine the Great, was proclaimed
emperor here. The Constantian rebuilding remained the basis
of York's defences until the Danes built an earth bank and
stockade in the late ninth century. Various repairs and
additions were made in the interim period, including the so-
called 'Anglian' Tower (see below).

Of the buildings inside this great legionary fortress of
EBVRACVM, little is known except for an internal bath-house
and the headquarters building, both described below, but
current work is gradually adding further details. York,
however, was more than a military centre in Roman times.
The civil settlement which grew up and flourished on the
south bank of the Ouse was given walls of its own, and
acquired the honorary status of *colonia* in the third century.
From 208–11 it was the seat of the Imperial Court while
Severus and Caracalla were engaged on their Scottish
campaigns, and in 213, when Britain was divided into two
provinces, it became the capital of *Britannia Inferior*.
Unfortunately, little is known at present about the town's
buildings, but objects found there are displayed in the
Museum.

This Museum, and the most spectacular portion of the
fortress' defences, are to be found in the public gardens on the
north side of the river. To the right of the main entrance (1 on
fig 63), under a stone archway, are several Roman coffins,
and the conduit-head of a public water-supply found in the
colonia. Nearby, the foundations of a polygonal bastion
emerge from the grass: it was one of the series added to the
fortress on this side *c*. AD 300. From here onwards, shrouded
by trees, is a superb stretch of the fourth-century fortress-wall,
standing virtually to wall-walk height with all its facing stones
and a row of bonding-bricks intact (fig 65). The stretch ends
at the west corner of the 50-acre fortress, known as the
Multangular Tower and one of the best-preserved Roman
structures in Britain. Parts of the exterior have been patched
with later material, but the join between the Roman work and
the top 11 feet of medieval masonry is obvious. Before going
inside the walls it is convenient to visit the archaeological
Museum which lies in the gardens nearby (2). This collection

is one of the richest in the country, and it must be hoped that a new building can be raised soon to give the material the presentation it deserves.

The main museum (10–5, Sun. 1–5) contains the most important finds. In the entrance-hall is a statue of Mars and two reconstructed panels of wall-plaster from Catterick. In the chief Roman room the important items to notice are: the stone head of Constantine the Great, twice life-size (right-hand long wall); the King's Square inscription in the middle of the left-hand long wall, which dates the first stone fortress to 107–8 (note the fine quality of the lettering); below this inscription is a dedication recording a temple of the Egyptian god Serapis (the temple itself has not been found); and finally, the tombstones on one of the short walls. The most interesting (fig 64) portrays the Augustinus family – mother and father and two children, all wearing cloaks. The inscription records that both children died before the age of two; the carving

64   York, tombstone of Augustinus
and his family

65 *York, fortress-wall near Multangular Tower*

represents them a little too old. Other, equally interesting,
exhibits, which used to be housed in the museum annexe, the
'Hospitium', situated nearer the river (3), include some mosaics
and smaller finds (one is the rare and fascinating survival of
a young girl's hair, found in a lead coffin under the Station in
1875); most of these have now been transferred to the main
museum.

Now you should return to the Multangular Tower, pass
through the narrow gate beside it and so enter the Roman
legionary fortress. The interior of the bastion can be seen to
be in a fine state of preservation, 19 feet high. Scaffolding
holes, an internal partition-wall, Roman coffins and the
medieval apertures above are all very clear. On the left of the
Tower is an oven-base, excavated in 1925 under the Public
Library and reset here. Its floor contained one tile stamped
Leg. IX Hisp., and so it is presumably of first-century date.
Beyond is the inside face of wall noted earlier. To the right of
the Multangular Tower is another fine stretch of fourth-
century curtain-wall, excavated in 1969–70. First, walk along
by the rough inside face which would have been covered by an
earth bank. (The wall on the right is of thirteenth-century
date.) Half-way along are the fragmentary remains of an
interval-tower, which is believed from the different quality of
the masonry to belong to an earlier phase of the defences, of
either the second or third century. Then comes the peculiar
'Anglian' tower, a barrel-vaulted structure built of roughly-
dressed stones to fill a breach in the Roman wall. It is unique
in Britain and probably in Europe, and it cannot be dated
more closely than AD 400–870. Some believe that it is late-
Roman, others that it was part of the reorganization of the
defences in the seventh century. Beyond, the fine sequence of
rampart-banks behind the wall has been carefully displayed –
four successive levels from Roman to medieval. Finally, you
can go through the Anglian Tower to examine the outer face
of the fourth-century wall. Not all of it has been exposed:
more lies beneath the path.

Leave the gardens at the main entrance and go into Lendal
opposite. Another of the fourth-century polygonal bastions
here (4), excavated in 1970, was visible until 1979, but when
the site was re-developed in 1980–1 it proved impossible for the
bastion to be preserved. Return to Museum Street, turn right,

and then left at the traffic-lights. Another fragment of fourth-century wall lies near the bus-shelter on the left. Once again only the top portion is visible, and excavation in 1835 and 1928 showed that another 11 feet lie buried below ground-level. It is worth climbing the mound here for a splendid view of the long stretch of Roman wall already described, from the Anglian to the Multangular Towers. Now cross the road and climb the steps to the top of Bootham Bar, which sits on the site of the Roman NW gate (5: a fragment of it, preserved in a room below the public lavatory, is visible on application to the Museum). Turn left and walk along the walls as far as Monk Bar, following the line of the Roman defences all the way, and passing over the site of the NE gate. Descend to street-level at Monk Bar and cross to the yard opposite to see a long stretch of Roman defences, including an interval-tower and the east angle tower (6). These are a century earlier than the remains so far described, as they belong to the early third-century rebuilding which was untouched in the Constantian reorganization. This corner tower is on a much smaller scale and does not project from the wall. The clay lump in the bottom is part of the bank of the first-century legionary fortress and is thus the oldest portion of EBVRACVM still on show. The foundations of the first stone tower, on a slightly different alignment, were also found during excavations in 1926. In front, the Roman curtain-wall still stands to a spectacular height of 16 feet, and even the moulded slab on which the parapet rested survives. The masonry is similar to the fourth-century work, but there are no brick bonding-courses, and the inner side is properly faced even where it would have been covered by rampart-mound. One of the stones on the outer face of the wall at the corner tower, just above head-height, still bears an inscription COH X recording that the tenth cohort (of the Sixth Legion) built this section of wall.

Now retrace your steps to Monk Bar. Turn left and then right down Ogleforth. Past a corner the Treasurer's House will be seen on the right (daily Apr.–Oct., 10.30–5). Here an isolated Roman column-base is preserved, together with part of a Roman street-surface (7). You have now arrived at the Minster and the site of the *Principia*, the Headquarters Building (8). Until 1966, when it was announced that the

Minster was in serious danger of collapse, virtually nothing
was known about the Roman building, but excavations
carried out during the strengthening of the Minster's fabric
have revealed a great deal, and some Roman walling has been
preserved *in situ* in the magnificently-displayed Undercroft,
opened in 1972. Most of the excavated remains are of fourth-
century date, including several column-bases belonging to the
great cross-hall. One of these, 22 feet long and three feet in
diameter, was found virtually complete, and it has been re-
erected opposite the south door of the Minster. What is
particularly interesting is the date at which it fell: pottery
sealed beneath the destruction rubble of the Roman cross-hall
indicates that these columns were still standing in the ninth
century, 400 years after the Sixth Legion had left York.
Detailed description of the remains displayed in the
Undercroft is unnecessary, as labels indicate how the various
walls fit into the plan of the HQ. One special exhibit, however,
must be mentioned. An administrative room added at the
back of the building in the fourth century had decorated
walls, and the surviving fragments have now been reassembled
to form one of the best and largest examples of Roman
painted plaster in Britain. High up on the left is a superb
theatrical mask, in centre-left birds are depicted; at top right
even a window-light survives, and further to the right is a
male human figure. The rest is filled up with architectural
details and abstract panels in brilliant colour.

Before this museum was opened, only a solitary Roman
column-base was visible inside the Minster. This can still be
seen in the Old Crypt, on application to a verger. It must
belong to a building north of the HQ.

The only other Roman structure visible within the fortress
is the bath-house in St Sampson's Square (9). Leave the
Minster by the south door and go down Minster Gates
opposite (this and Stonegate follow the line of a Roman
street). Turn left at Low Petergate and right at the traffic-
lights along Church Street. The remains are preserved beneath
'Roman Bath Inn', and the main feature, the *pilae*-bases of a
large apse forming part of the *caldarium*, is now visible
through a glass panel in the Saloon Bar. If the landlord is not
busy you may be allowed to see the remains at close quarters.
Part of the tiled cold plunge-bath belonging to the *frigidarium*

has also been preserved (far right-hand corner). Excavations in 1930–1 established a fourth-century date for the bath-house, but what earlier building occupied the site is unknown.

In November 1972, part of the sewer-system which served the fortress was discovered on a building-site at the corner of Swinegate and Church Street (10). This structure, some 4–5 feet high and excellently preserved, was traced for over 150 feet, together with six side channels. The sewer was in use from early in the second century to late in the fourth and produced various finds, including a rare piece of silk woven in the west from imported Chinese raw material, and fascinating environmental evidence for latrine sediments, grain pests (indicating a granary nearby), and insects tolerant of the foul sewer conditions. Access to this splendid monument of Roman hygiene is through a manhole in the street, but visits will only be permitted if prior arrangements have been made, in writing, with the Museum.

Apart from a fragment of wall-core visible in the cellar of the Yorkshire Insurance Company's building in Lendal, no other remains of the fortress are now visible. Of the town across the river, nothing has been preserved *in situ*, except for an uninteresting stone wall probably of Roman date incorporated in the base of a modern wall in Carrs Lane (11: off Bishophill Senior opposite Victor Street). Of scraps not *in situ* a column-base kept at the back of Holy Trinity Church, Micklegate, a tombstone in St Martin's Church (also Micklegate), and the tombstone of Baebius Crescens, a soldier of the Sixth, in the Mount School (off The Mount), may be mentioned. A unique burial-vault with coffin and skeleton still in position exists under 104, The Mount, but it can only be visited by prior written appointment with the Accountants who own the building.

The legionary soldiers based at York were responsible for digging, as part of their training, a couple of practice camps on Bootham Stray 1½m north of the fortress, which have been largely obliterated. They may also have been responsible for the remarkable earthworks at **Cawthorn** (SE 7890), the significance of which is still disputed. You are urged, however, to visit the site in winter or early spring, as all the camps except D (plan, fig 66) were totally obscured by luxuriant bracken growth when I was there in August 1972 and September 1978.

The path I followed then through the bracken is marked by the
dotted line on the plan. Turn off the A170 at Wrelton, 2m
west of Pickering, signposted Cropton, Hartoft and Rosedale.
Then turn right in Cropton village, signposted Cawthorne
1½m, and keep going, ignoring all turns to left and right
(including another signed 'Cawthorne') until you pass the
turning to Keldy. Just beyond this, watch out for a track on
the left; it is a well-defined one between a break in the trees
(no signpost). The point where it enters a thick conifer wood
marks the position of the south gate of D, the best-preserved
of the four earthworks. The south rampart and double ditches
separated by a flat mound are especially fine. The path follows
the south rampart of D, over the ditch system and across
camp A. The polygonal shape of the latter is unusual. The
rampart is slight and interrupted by three gates on the east
side, two with external *claviculae*. Just before the main path
reaches the rampart of B, in a slight clearing among the trees,
follow the lesser path to your left, and you soon come out to
the superb view which the camps commanded of the North
York Moors. The rampart of B here is still 10 feet above the
bottom of the ditch outside. Finally comes camp C, which was
tacked on to B but had ramparts of only half the scale.
Excavation has revealed that the camps are of two different
periods. Finds were scarce and the precise date uncertain, but the
camps probably belong to the late first or early second century.

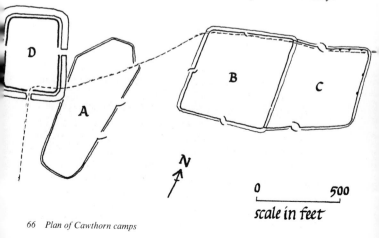

In the first phase camp A was erected to protect tents and
baggage while troops were engaged on constructing B. The
substantial nature of the latter's defences has caused it to be
interpreted as a fort, but neither its irregular layout nor the use
of *titula* at the gates are normal in forts of the late first century,
and no buildings have been located within. Its purpose
therefore remains enigmatic. In the second phase, the east
defences of B were levelled, the remaining gates were modified
with combined internal and external *claviculae*, and the camp
was enlarged by tacking on to the east further defences of less
substantial dimensions. The troops bivouacked there may have
been engaged on building earthwork D, which has every
appearance of being a permanent fort, but excavation has been
too limited to determine whether it had the normal range of
internal buildings or was never finished. Its ditches cut through
the rampart of A at one point and clearly prove that D is later
than A.

The site at Cawthorn lies on a Roman road known as
Wade's Causeway, which ran from Malton to Whitby. Wade
is a giant in local legends and he is alleged to have built the
causeway for his wife who kept cattle on the moor. A $1\frac{1}{4}$-mile
stretch of this road has been excavated and preserved on
Wheeldale Moor* (SE 8097) [AM; A] and is the most
impressive piece of original Roman highway in Britain (fig
67). From Goathland, a village west of the A169

67   Wheeldale Moor, Roman road

(Pickering–Whitby), take the road leading southwards and then follow the AM signs: you have the choice of walking to one end of the exposed sector, or taking your car by a very roundabout route to the other end. The present uneven appearance of the road is misleading: the large slabs which form the most impressive part of the remains were only intended to act as the foundation layer for a final surface of gravel or small stones, long since washed away. In places kerb-stones still remain, and there are several drainage-culverts with large cover-stones, particularly near the eastern end of the exposed stretch.

The road on Wheeldale Moor headed southwards for the fort at **Malton** (SE 7971), DERVENTIO. This was a very large fort ($8\frac{1}{2}$ acres), but little of it remains. From the centre of Malton take the Scarborough road, and where it makes a 90° turn to the right, keep straight on (signposted 'No Through Road'). The fort lies in the field on the left where this road ends. Take the right-hand footpath, which passes the east corner of the fort. The NE rampart-mound is well preserved, the SE one less so. The fort was occupied from *c*. AD 79 (Agricolan) to the end of the fourth century, with rebuilding in stone *c*. 108 and 280. Excavation has also revealed a very large semi-permanent fortress of at least 22 acres beneath and beyond the fort, and this was probably the base for half the Ninth Legion in the campaigns of Petillius Cerialis *c*. 71–2 or of his predecessor Bolanus *c*. 69. Outside the fort was a substantial civilian settlement, with stone buildings, partly excavated in 1949–52 and 1968–70. It was defended by a rampart from the late second century, visible as a low swelling to the right of the path at the east corner of the fort. Finds from the area are displayed in the Roman Malton Museum (Mon.–Sat. 10–4 and Sun. 2–4, from May to the end of September; October to April, Sat. only, 1–3), which lies in the town-centre opposite the church, to the left of the Milton Rooms.

Several Roman roads radiated from York. The east-coast road via Malton and Wheeldale Moor has been mentioned. South-westwards a road ran across the Pennines to Manchester (p. 394); en route the fort-platform at Castleshaw ** (see p. 391) is still visible. From Tadcaster, 10m SW of York, another road headed towards Ribchester on the

western trunk-road, passing through forts at Ilkley and
Elslack (App. I). **Ilkley** (SE 1148), probably the Roman
VERBEIA , has a small museum, and a section of stone fort-wall
is also visible. The Manor House Museum (daily, except Mon.,
Christmas Day and Good Friday, 10–5; May–Sept., 10–6), is
situated on the north side of the A65 (Skipton Road), next to
the church by the traffic-lights in the centre of the town.
Among the exhibits are two interesting tombstones, one
showing a seated woman with long tresses, the other
(uninscribed) portraying a man, his wife and their little boy.
Behind the museum, and always accessible, is part of the fort's
west wall, four feet high, including the NW corner. The fort
was founded by Agricola *c.* 80, evacuated peacefully *c.* 120,
reoccupied in the middle of the second century, and destroyed
in 197. The first stone wall and stone internal buildings were
then erected, in the early third century. At first the stone wall
had a clay bank behind it, but in fourth-century alterations it
was made free-standing as it is today. The second-century
garrison was part-mounted, probably the second cohort of
Lingones from east France.

A branch-road joined Ilkley with Manchester, and part of
what has been assumed to be it, on Blackstone Edge near
Rochdale (SD 9616), is remarkable for being paved with
large stone setts. 1m east of Littleborough the A58 makes a
large U-bend. At the bottom of the U, as the road swings due
north, a public footpath is signposted to the right (east) of
the road and a lighter strip of grass can be seen going
straight up the moorland to the top of the hill. This is $\frac{1}{4}$m
beyond a house marked 'Blackstone Edge Old Road'. It is near
the top of the hill that the stone paving becomes visible,
16 feet wide, with a central groove. This is much worn,
presumably by the brake-pole of carts as they tried to descend
the hill without going out of control. At the top, where
the road becomes level, the central slab flattens out. Earlier
editions of this book treated this road without question as
of Roman date, but the uniqueness of the monument in a
Romano–British context, and the difficulty of finding Roman
parallels anywhere for the central grooved channel, emphasize
the need to question its long accepted Roman date; it
may well rather be part of an eighteenth-century coach
road.

As mentioned above, the east-west road on which Ilkley stood was heading for **Ribchester** (SD 6535), the BREMETENACVM of the Romans and now a village on the B6245 6m north of Blackburn. The main item of interest here at present is the little museum near the church (Mar.–Oct., 2–5; June–Aug. 11.30–5.30; Nov.–Feb., Sundays only, 2–4). This has a collection of inscriptions, reliefs and other smaller material. Outstanding is the pedestal in the centre, which bears reliefs of Apollo and two female figures and an inscription to the god recording both the name of the fort (BREMETENN) and its garrison, a regiment of Sarmatian horsemen from the Danube. The inscription also mentions the emperor Gordian, thus dating the stone to AD 238–44. Nearby is a late first- or early second-century tombstone with a cavalryman riding down his barbarian foe. On the right wall of the room are some more inscriptions, including one with fine lettering in honour of Caracalla and his mother Julia Domna. His brother Geta was murdered in 212 and that name has been erased at the bottom of the stone. The most beautiful find from Ribchester is now one of the treasures of the British Museum: it is the decorated cavalry parade-helmet, of which there is a replica at the site.

In the garden at the back of the museum are the front ends of two of the fort's granaries, probably of third-century date in their present form. They are buttressed, as usual, and both have loading-platforms outside (on the right). The granary nearer the path is the smaller of the two and its floor was supported by the large blocks visible in the middle. That beyond is divided into two parts by a middle wall. Under the flowerbed further away is the site of the north gate. The rest of the fort still lies buried, or rather the part spared by the river Ribble, which has removed the whole of the SE corner and the south and east gates. The earliest fort of turf and timber was founded by Agricola c. AD 78. It extended further north and was differently orientated from its early-second-century successor, which had defences and a central range of stone, at least twice repaired. Occupation continued to the end of the fourth century, but at least part of the interior was empty of buildings then. The first garrison, recorded on an altar in the museum, was a cavalry regiment of Asturians from Spain. The third-century garrison of Sarmatians has already been mentioned. An extensive civilian settlement, largely of timber buildings, lies under the modern village.

Leave the museum and turn right along the river bank. On the right is a long holly bush, and adjoining this at the far end, almost hidden by shrubbery, is a Roman well *in situ*. This was in the courtyard of the CO's house. More substantial are the remains of the bath-house situated outside the fort, which was excavated between 1978 and 1980, and has been on

** permanent display since 1984. See p. 392. The NE corner tower of the fort has been exposed in the custodian's garden; it may be possible to view this (weekends only) on application to the custodian.

The Roman trunk-road to the north from York is still largely followed by the A1, which passes by or through the Roman towns at Aldborough (see below) and Catterick (App. I). At Scotch Corner, then as now, the road splits. The left fork heads over the Stainmore Pass and is described below, while the right-hand fork made for Corbridge and Hadrian's Wall via forts at Piercebridge, Binchester, Lanchester and Ebchester, all in County Durham. At each of these forts stone remains are visible today.

Piercebridge* (NZ 2115) lies 7m N of Scotch Corner on

68   *Piercebridge, fort-wall and pits on the berm*

B6275. The modern road follows the alignment of its Roman predecessor, straight as a die, for the entire distance between the two (and again for some 5 miles north of Piercebridge), until it swings to the left just before crossing the bridge into the village. Park on the right after the bend and walk back to the HMBC notice and the path leading to a Roman bridge over the Tees, discovered and excavated in 1972 [AM; A]. You first reach the tumbled remains of large stone blocks comprising both the bridge-piers and the flagstones on the river bottom, which have been left as found. The remains become more intelligible at the far end, where the paving, designed to prevent river-scouring, is excellently preserved, and first a pier and then the sturdy bridge abutment are reached. The latter is still intact, with its two courses of huge close-fitting blocks, complete with iron tie-bars and lead fixings *in situ* on the upper surface, and the cuttings to take the timber superstructure: for this was not an arched bridge but a wooden one on a stone base. You will appreciate from the position of this abutment, which stood on the south bank, how far the river has shifted since Roman times. But the problem was already acute soon after the bridge was first built (probably in the mid-second century), for it was soon found necessary to carry the road on a causeway, its sides revetted in limestone, which covered the abutment and the first two piers. Part of this causeway has been reconstituted in the form of a grass mound on the site today. But this was only a short-term solution, for the river was shifting too quickly, and the remains were plundered for their stone even in antiquity: it seems to have been this as much as the scouring action of the river which accounts for the tumbled remains at the north end. Presumably erosion was also responsible for the abandonment of the earlier Roman bridge, $\frac{1}{4}$m further west on the line of the main Roman road.

Now follow the road into the village, and take the lane between the cottages nearest the south side of the church. Here an extensive area, excavated between 1975 and 1981, is now laid out on permanent display. It is part of an exceptionally large fort of nearly 11 acres which was a totally new foundation *c*. AD 270, fully garrisoned for only forty or so years, and then reoccupied with a reduced force *c*. 350. But it is inconceivable that such an important site was not defended

in earlier centuries, and the preceding fort, presumably an
Agricolan foundation, probably lies to the east under the later
civilian settlement, on the line of the Roman road which
bypasses the visible fort. You first reach the heavily robbed
remains of the east gate, with two solid gatetowers which
projected behind the line of the wall, and a double
carriageway. Beyond is a long stretch of the fort-wall, also
poorly preserved, but an impressive 10 feet wide (fig 68). On
the berm separating it from the ditch have been cut two rows
of neat rectangular pits. These are clearly deliberate and seem
best interpreted as *lilia*: they would have been filled with
pointed stakes and covered with bracken to deceive an attacker
into thinking he was on solid ground. The device, described
by Julius Caesar, has also been found in Scotland (p. 335),
and it is interesting to find it still in vogue some 350 years
after Caesar. Ends of *vicus* buildings project from the grass
beyond.

Backing the massive stone wall was a road (but no earth
rampart) below which ran a well preserved drain or sewer. It
curves across the line of the *via principalis* at the east gate,
where it was joined by another. One large cover-slab here is a
re-used stone from an earlier building. Parallel with the drain
for most of its course is part of a large, substantial stone
structure, built on footings of river pebbles. Interpreted by the
excavator as a luxury barracks (the rooms had painted wall-
plaster, and two have channelled hypocausts), it seems more
likely to have been one wing of the commandant's house
(*praetorium*). Part of its bath-suite has been excavated in the
yard of an adjacent house and can be seen by looking over the
wall at the far end.

One other, smaller, portion of the fort has been left exposed
since 1934. Walk to the north end of the village, turn right at
the Wheatsheaf, and you will see a public footpath signposted
on your right. Follow this to the first field-gate: the site lies in
the field on your right. Here the NE corner of the fort-wall
can be seen turning the corner, its superbly-cut plinth and
facing blocks better preserved than in the stretch near the east
gate. The sewer is also in a fine state here, one side of it over
seven feet high. The building erected over it, of which
foundations and a doorway are visible, was clearly the fort's
latrine. The circular structure built into the rampart on the

east side is a medieval kiln.

The next fort to the north is **Binchester** (NZ 2131), the
Roman VINOVIA or VINOVIVM, of uncertain meaning. From the
centre of Bishop Auckland, take the Teesside road (A689) and
then turn immediately left by 'The Sportsman', signposted
'Newfield' and 'Roman fort'. Follow this for about a mile, and
then take the access road to the Binchester Hall Hotel. The site,
which lies beyond the hotel car-park, is open (Apr.–Sept. only)
10.30–6, daily except Tuesday and Wednesday. The shed
covers one of the best-preserved and most instructive examples
of a hypocaust in Britain. The concrete floor of one room is
still in position, and the wall-flues for the rising heat can be
seen round the edges (fig 69). Underneath this floor, in perfect
condition, are 88 *pilae* of Roman tiles partially blackened by
the heat. Some of the larger tiles supporting the floor are
stamped N CON, for *N(umerus) Con(cangiensium)*, the name of
the unit which made them. Three fine arches, two perfectly
preserved, allowed the heat to circulate in the adjoining room.
The centre arch and the floor of this adjoining room appear
still intact in a drawing made when the building was first found
in the early nineteenth century. The destruction was reputedly
caused by later explorers who expected to find buried treasure

69 Binchester, hypocaust flue-tiles

underneath and ripped down the centre arch in their desire for
quicker access. Further digging was done in 1878–80 and 1964,
and the hut was put up in 1969, but since 1976 work has been
resumed and is still continuing. The third heated room
(*caldarium*) in its final phase had two plunge baths. That
straight ahead of you stands over the flue arch to the main
furnace beyond, but remains of an earlier flue channel, as well
as the straight joints of the recess with the masonry on either
side, indicate that the plunge-bath here was a later addition to
the main heated block. That is now known to have belonged
to the commandant's house (*praetorium*) in its final form in the
second half of the fourth century (*c.* 360?), when the heated
block visible today was built; but the relationship between it
and the other rooms immediately outside the shed entrance is
by no means clear. The most conspicuous feature here is the
flagged 'courtyard' and pretentious triple-arched entrance
(represented by the moulded blocks) belonging to the
praetorium of a slightly earlier phase (*c.* 270–90). When the
heated block was added this courtyard must have been roofed
over (although the supporting walls look rather insubstantial
for such a wide span), to provide a *frigidarium* which the baths
otherwise appear to lack; two rooms under cover here are
interpreted, somewhat uncertainly, as cold plunge baths. Turn
right on leaving the shed and right again along its east side.
Note at the far end, one course from ground-level, a quoin
sculpted with a now headless dog (or fox), and a small detached
furnace for an unknown structure straight ahead; a second
furnace for the bath-block's *tepidarium* lies to the right.

** Description continues on p. 393.

The next fort, **Lanchester** (NZ 1546), was built under
Lollius Urbicus *c.* AD 140 at a period when both Ebchester to
the north and Binchester to the south were empty. It was
designed to hold a nominal garrison of 1,000 men. Towards
the end of the second century this was a Spanish cohort of
Vardulli, who had the exceptional honour of being Roman
citizens. Evacuated from about 196, it was reoccupied under
Gordian (emperor 238–44), as two fine building-inscriptions
now in the Durham Cathedral collection attest. Its garrison at
this time was a cohort of Lingones 500 strong, reinforced by a
unit of Suebians, who dedicated an altar to their Germanic
goddess Garmangabis. This now stands in the south porch of

Lanchester church. To reach the site of the fort, which lies 8m NW of Durham, leave the A691 in Lanchester and take the B6296 for Wolsingham. At the top of the hill, bordering the left-hand side of the road, you will see a long stretch of stone core belonging to the north wall of LONGOVICIVM. No facing-stones survive, but the stone core of the walls is visible round nearly the entire circuit. In places it still stands six feet high. Inside the fort the only feature is a nettle-filled hollow showing some pieces of stonework, possibly part of the commandant's house. Virtually no trace remains of the three aqueduct-channels which brought water up to 4 miles from the north-west (for the details see article cited in the Bibliography). As so often with Roman forts, the superb position, commanding land in all directions, cannot fail to be noticed.

Between here and Corbridge there was a small fort on the Derwent at **Ebchester** (NZ 1055), the Roman VINDOMORA and now a village on the A694 12m SW of Newcastle. A clay-and-timber fort of Agricolan date (*c.* AD 80) was in occupation until *c.* 120, and then rebuilt in stone and reoccupied from about 163 to the close of the fourth century, with at least two major rebuildings, probably at the beginning and the end of the third century. The main visible relic at the site is a hypocaust in an apse-shaped room, probably part of the bath-suite in the commandant's house. The stone *pilae* and walls of this are still three feet high. We owe their preservation to the generous action of Mr Dodds of Mains Farm, who found the remains in 1962 when digging near his barn. Subsequent excavation showed that the hypocaust went out of use and was filled with debris at the end of the third century. A fragmentary tombstone found during demolition work in 1985 is displayed in the newly refurbished private museum maintained by the Dodds family in a shed nearby. To reach the spot, turn off the main road by the bus-shelter near the church. Mains Farm is the first house on the left after the corner bungalow. There is also a Roman altar in the church porch.

The Roman road which swung west at Scotch Corner headed over the Stainmore Pass for the Eden Valley. Closely followed by the A66, it still forms one of the major east-west highways in North Britain. The route is littered with Roman earthworks, and I will describe them in the order in which they occur when approached from the east, and not in strict chronological sequence. For the first eleven miles the A66 is dead straight and follows the Roman alignment. The first change in direction occurs at **Greta Bridge** (NZ 0813), where a fort was situated. Avoid the bypass of A66 and enter the village of Greta Bridge itself; then turn along the road to Brignall just past the Morritt Arms Hotel, which sits on the north defences of the fort. The conspicuous remains of the earth rampart-mound and double ditches of the southern defences are visible in the first field on the left. Its Roman name is uncertain. Little excavation has been done in the fort here, and the length of occupation is unknown, but rescue work during 1973–4 in the civilian settlement now partly covered by the bypass found timber buildings of c. AD 100/125 overlying late first-century occupation, and renewed activity in the third century lasting not much later than c. 275/300.

Only 5½ miles further west is the fort at **Bowes** (NY 9913), the Roman LAVATRIS. This guarded the eastern end of the Stainmore Pass, as did the Norman castle which obliterates the NW angle of the fort. Follow signs for Bowes village (now bypassed by A66) and then for Bowes Castle. The churchyard occupies the NE corner, and a cemetery the eastern half, but the rampart-mound of its south and west sides (in the field south of the castle) are still well preserved. Note in particular the drop in the cemetery wall where it crosses the south rampart. Excavations here in 1966–7 revealed that the original rampart raised by Agricola c. AD 78 consisted of huge river-boulders set in clay with a rear revetment of turf and a front revetment of timber. In the second century a subsequent clay rampart was cut back to receive a stone wall, later replaced by a second wall nearly eight feet thick which was crudely repaired in the fourth century. Near the cemetery wall, outside the fort, a large hollow showing odd pieces of stonework marks the site of the bath-house, plundered in the nineteenth century. An inscription now at Cambridge records that this building, *vi ignis exustum*, 'burnt by the violence of fire', was restored in the governorship of Virius Lupus (AD 197–202), when a cavalry regiment of Spanish Vettones was the garrison at Bowes. By 208 this had been replaced by the first cohort of Thracians from Bulgaria, who erected a dedication-slab to the emperor Severus and his sons Caracalla and Geta. This can be

seen, poorly lit and nearly illegible, in the north transept of
Bowes church. The name of Geta, as usual, had been erased
after his murder. Some traces of the aqueduct-channel which
brought water to the fort from the NW can be located with
the help of a detailed map (see article cited in the
Bibliography).

One of the few spare-time pursuits open to an officer
serving in such a distant outpost of the Empire must have
been hunting, and it was no doubt to appease the local
moorland god that two rustic shrines were built in a wild and
desolate spot, a couple of miles south of the fort, on the west
bank of the East Black Sike near its confluence with the Eller
Beck. One was rectangular and the other, 25 yards to the
south, was circular. In them were found altars dedicated to
the god Vinotonus, equated with the Roman god of hunting
and woodland, Silvanus. The best-preserved, erected by the
commander of the First Thracian Cohort, Caesius Frontinus,
who came from Parma in North Italy, is now part of the
collection housed in the Bowes Museum at Barnard Castle
(10–4, 5 or 5.30; Sun. 2–4 or 5). Very little can be seen
at the site today, and I have therefore listed it in Appendix I;
but the walk across Scargill Moor to find it is a splendid one,
and a feeling of the past will not be difficult to capture on this
high and windy moor where little has changed since Roman
times.

The next fort west of Bowes was at Brough, 13 miles away
on the other side of the Stainmore Pass. In between was a
series of signal-towers designed to transmit messages by
semaphore over rugged and inhospitable terrain. Six have so
far been identified with certainty, but their detailed layout and
date remain obscure. The idea, advanced 35 years ago, that
they formed part of a much longer system has not been
substantiated by more recent discoveries. The most accessible
of these signal-posts is on **Bowes Moor** (NY 9212), 4m west of
Bowes and a short distance east of Bowes Moor Hotel. Look
out for a P-sign and parking-place just before the hotel on the
south side of the A66: the signal-station is situated on the *other*
side of the road opposite the P-sign, 25 yards north of the
fence. The remains consist of a turf rampart, 10 feet thick, and
a V-shaped ditch outside it. The upcast from the latter formed
a lesser mound on the outer lip of the ditch and this is clearly

visible on the north, the best-preserved side of the signal-
station. There is an entrance on the side facing the road.
Inside the enclosure there would have been a timber tower. To
the west the outlook is very fine, and you may be able to spot
a slight pimple on the skyline. This is the signal-station of
Roper Castle, very similar to that on Bowes Moor. It can be
found with the help of a 1:50,000 OS map, after a long climb
over boggy ground (App. I). Eastwards from the Bowes Moor
post the view to LAVATRIS is blocked by a low spur, from
which another signal-station, not now visible on the ground,
relayed messages to the fort.

Nearly 2m further west is the summit of the Stainmore Pass
(1,468 feet), and the remains of the best-preserved marching
camp in Britain, at **Rey Cross** (NY 9012). Stop in the parking-
place on the left (south) of the road, where the Cross is railed
off and labelled with an AM sign (this is immediately east of
the 'Dual Carriageway Ahead' road-sign). Go back to the
P-sign, where there is a gate in the fence, and then walk
due south to the edge of the ravine. In doing so you will pass
through the more westerly of the two south gates, and from
here, with the help of the plan (fig 70), you will be able to
trace the entire outline of this magnificent earthwork.
Limestone quarrying has removed the southern half of the
western defences, and this accounts for the confusing
unevenness of the terrain here, while part of the northern
rampart has slipped into the bog. Elsewhere it is traceable by
the lighter colour of the grass and the boldness of the
rampart, 20 feet wide and often over six feet high. No less
than nine *titula* survive, each defending a gate. Two more
have probably been obliterated by the road. Rock lying just
beneath the surface made it impractical to dig a ditch, which
only appears near the NE angle. Rey Cross is big enough to
hold a legion, and since the course of the road, which itself
must have been built in the first century, bends slightly in
order to pass through two gates of the camp, the earthwork
belongs to the earliest Roman campaigns in the area. It
probably held the tents of part of the Ninth Legion under
Petillius Cerialis during his campaigns against the Brigantes in
AD 72 and 73.

One mile west of Rey Cross the A66 leaves the Roman
alignment and soon afterwards a minor road goes off to

the left, signposted 'Kaber, South Stainmore and Barras'. Park
where convenient near here and cross over to the north side of
the A66, which is dual-carriageway at this point; opposite the
turning to Kaber is a sign reading 'Public Bridleway, Maiden
Way'. Ten minutes' walk away, and clearly visible on the bluff
to your right overlooking the road, is the Roman fortlet of
Maiden Castle (NY 8713). This small post, probably only
holding about 50 men, was a link in the signalling system
between Brough and Bowes and also a convenient stopping-
place for convoys after the long haul up from Brough. It
commands a magnificent view over the Eden Valley, with
Brough Castle visible in the middle distance. Westwards its
view is blocked by the Stainmore Pass, but it is in sight of the
Roper Castle signal-station (see above) and thence messages
could be relayed to Bowes. It is unlikely to be earlier than the
middle of the second century, which in itself dates the other
signal-stations on the Stainmore route. The remains now
consist of four stony banks about six feet high, representing
the original stone defences. There are two gates. A single ditch
appears on the north, marked by the inner set of reeds. The
outer row of reeds indicates the line of a cart-track which
probably follows a Roman road by-passing the fortlet.

The fort at **Brough** (NY 7914) lies ½m south of the A66,

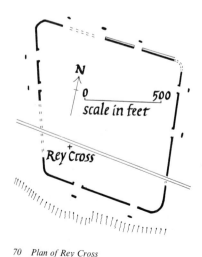

70   *Plan of Rey Cross*

under the Castle. (Avoid Brough village and follow signs to Church Brough). The Castle [AM; S] has obliterated its northern half and it is not clear how much of the impressive rampart and ditch of its southern half is the work of Roman soldiers or Norman castle-builders. A dedication-slab of AD 197, now virtually illegible, is in the church porch. The fort was occupied from its foundation *c*. 79 to about 120, and then again from about 160 onwards. A cremation cemetery was found in 1971 under what is now the A66 500 yards E of the fort, and a civilian settlement identified between the two. The Roman name was VERTERAE.

Westward from Brough the land becomes cultivable again and the Roman earthworks are consequently more damaged. The next fort of which anything is visible is **Brougham** (NY 5328), and once again, significantly of course, Romans and Normans agreed in their choice of a strategic position. Brougham Castle [AM; SSM] lies 2m SE of Penrith, just off the A66. It has removed the northern quarter of BROCAVVM, but the rest of the Roman fort can be traced as a slight bank and ditch in the field south of the castle, especially near the crossroads with the B6262. A first-century date is unproven, as all the finds date from the second century to the close of the fourth. More interesting than the remains of the fort itself are the ten inscriptions preserved at the Castle, formerly displayed in the Inner and Outer Gatehouses but now housed in a site museum next to the ticket office. One is a well-carved tombstone of Crescentinus, who died aged 18 (fig 72). It was set up by his father Vidaris, possibly a Germanic name. Note the pine cone in the pediment, a common funerary symbol. Next to it is the relief of a boy in a cloak with the inscription: 'Annamoris, his father, and Ressona, his mother, had this put up.' Also displayed here are three stones found during excavation in the fort's cemetery in 1966–7, when over 200 burials, mostly cremations, were uncovered (now under A66). A fragment of another tombstone is built into the ceiling of a short passage in the second floor of the Keep. The deceased in this case is Tittus . . ., who lived 32 years 'more or less' (*plu*]*s minus* in penultimate line). This form of words is sometimes used on Christian tombstones.

Between Brougham and Brough there was an intermediate fort at Kirkby Thore, but nothing is visible on the ground

today. An unusual Roman relic does, however, exist nearby,
½m SE of **Temple Sowerby** (NY 6226). Apart from the better
example at Chesterholm, this is the only undoubted Roman
milestone in Britain which occupies its original position. It
stands about 4½ feet high, looking a little sorry for itself in its
iron cage. It is situated on the verge of a lay-by on the north
side of the A66.

From Kirkby Thore a Roman road, known as the Maiden
Way, ran straight to Hadrian's Wall near Greenhead, and en
route is the fort of **Whitley Castle*** (NY 6948). There is no
stonework visible here today, but the remarkable system of
ditches protecting the fort on the SW, where the command of
ground is weakest, makes it an outstanding site comparable
only with Ardoch in Scotland. From Alston take the
Brampton road (A689) for two miles until it descends to cross
a narrow bridge over a stream. Immediately after this there is
a track on the left which leads sharply back to Whitlow Farm.
Ask here for permission to visit the fort, which lies five
minutes' walk north of the farm, beyond the furthermost

71 Whitley Castle, aerial view

outbuilding. The magnificent SW side displays a conspicuous rampart-mound and as many as seven ditches (fig 71). Parts of the NW and SE sides are also very impressive. One of the highest forts in Britain (1,050 feet), it departs from the normal playing-card shape, forming a rhomboid to take full advantage of the hillock on which it lies. The site of the HQ is marked by uneven ground adjoining the field-wall in the centre of the fort. Of Whitley Castle's history little is known. It was built in the second century, and all the spectacular ditches seem to have been part of the original scheme. A couple of dedication-slabs indicate building activity in the period 213–9, perhaps after the fort had been destroyed. The stone wall may have been added to the rampart at this time. One of the inscriptions tells us its garrison, the Second Cohort of Nervii from the lower Rhine, but the Roman name of Whitley Castle is unknown. One of its functions was probably to control nearby lead-mines.

Brougham lay on the major western artery to Carlisle and Scotland. The platform of the next fort to the north, VOREDA, is clearly visible beside the A6 (Old Penrith, App. I). From Carlisle a road ran direct to the Cumberland coast at Moresby near Whitehaven (App. I), and both the forts which

72 Brougham, tombstone

73 Maryport, altar

line this route, and a third slightly off it, have left traces on the ground. Of these by far the most prominent is that at **Old Carlisle** (NY 2546) (for Papcastle and Caermote see Appendix I). Take the A595 for 10 miles out of Carlisle and watch out for B5305 to Wigton. Do not take that, but turn first right after it (minor road signposted 'Wigton 1½'), and stop at the farm on the left. The fort lies two fields behind the farm; alternatively, it can be viewed from afar from the main road a short distance west of the junction. No stonework is visible, but the fort ditches and the mound covering the stone walls and earth rampart are superbly preserved on the west and the west part of the south sides, and the causeways leading to the east and south gates are also very bold, but there has been much disturbance on the north. An extensive area of ridges and mounds in the pasture between the fort and A595 belong to the civilian settlement, and these showed up with sufficient clarity in the parched conditions of 1974–5 for them to be planned with reasonable accuracy. But no excavation has taken place in either fort or settlement and the length of occupation is unknown. Most of our information is derived from the 26 inscriptions ploughed up in the fort or its vicinity: from these we learn, for example, that the garrison of MAGLONA in the late second and early third century was the Ala Augusta, a cavalry regiment 500 strong, and that the inhabitants of the civilian settlement (*vicus*), who call themselves *vik(ani) Mag(lonenses)*, set up an altar to Jupiter and Vulcan in the mid third century.

Other coastal forts apart from Moresby were at Burrow Walls near Workington, Maryport and Beckfoot. These were designed to protect the Solway coast and the western approaches to Hadrian's Wall, and the system of milefortlets and towers continues along the coast from Bowness, where the Wall ends, to beyond Maryport, and probably as far as St Bee's Head. Of all these fortifications, however, only that at **Maryport** (NY 0337), the Roman ALAVNA, has left any visible trace, and even here there is nothing to see except the prominent fort-platform and faint traces of the ditches. Turn right off A596 in the town (signposted 'Maryport town centre'), and then take the first turning on the right. Keep going straight as far as possible, and then turn left and first right (Camp Street). The site lies at the very end of this street

on the left. An Agricolan fort is highly probable but no sign
of it was found during excavation in 1966, which revealed
four building-periods in stone beginning in the early second
century, probably a decade or so before Hadrian's Wall was
built. Occupation continued, but probably with some gaps, to
the end of the fourth century. In 1870, a remarkable find was
made of 17 altars buried in pits 350 yards NE of the fort.
They are unweathered and clearly have been ceremonially
buried soon after erection: the reason for this was the regular
renewal of vows for the emperor's safety on January 3rd or on
the anniversary of the emperor's accession, when new altars
were erected. The one illustrated (fig 73) is dedicated to the
personification of the emperor's Victory by Titus Attius
Tutor, commander of the first cohort of Baetasians from the
Rhine who had the honour of Roman citizenship (as indicated
by the letters C.R. in the inscription). This garrison was at
Maryport in the later second century before being transferred
to Reculver in Kent. Other stones inform us of earlier
garrisons – the first cohort of Spaniards under Hadrian and
the first cohort of Dalmatians from Yugoslavia under
Antoninus Pius. The position of the pits indicates that the
parade-ground, on which the altars were erected, first lay NE
of the fort. This area was later developed as a civilian suburb,
and the parade-ground was then moved to a plot 100 yards
south of the fort, where its *tribunal* was later known as
Pudding Pie Hill. A new inscription, found in 1966, refers to a
third cohort, possibly of Nervii, and these were probably at
Maryport in the fourth century. All these fine inscriptions, the
largest private collection of Roman inscriptions in Britain,
together with other finds from the fort and nearby, are due to
be rehoused by 1991 in a coastal battery alongside the fort,
provided sufficient funds are forthcoming. Donations and
enquiries (enclose S.A.E.) should be directed to Lt. Cdr. B.G.
Ashmore, Camp Hill, Maryport.

Further south in the Lake District is the fort of **Ravenglass**
(SD 0895), the Roman GLANNOVENTA. Turn off the A595 17m
south of Whitehaven for the village of Ravenglass. Park when
the road bends sharply to the right and take the lane
signposted 'Public Footpath, Walls Castle'. After ten minutes
you will come to 'Walls Castle', the Roman bath-house still
standing to a miraculous height of $12\frac{1}{2}$ feet, making it the

best-preserved Roman structure in the north of England.
The first room, possibly for undressing, has a niche in
one wall and three doorways. These have shallow relieving-
arches, but the lintels beneath have disappeared; they may
have been of wood. Go through the doorway on the left into
another room, where the lower part of a splayed window and
a long stretch of pink cement-rendering are excellently
preserved. Traces of windows can also be seen in some of the
other rooms. Excavation in 1881 revealed more of the
building extending under the field to the east, but the bathing
arrangements and the identity of the various rooms are in
doubt. The baths stand at the NE corner of a $3\frac{1}{2}$-acre fort,
now bisected by the railway and covered by a dense
plantation. Excavation in 1976 on the cliff edge where marine
erosion is taking place indicated that the fort was built c. 130
to replace an earlier fortlet, and was occupied until c. 400
with periods in the mid-second and in the third century when
it lay idle. The barracks remained of timber throughout, and
the turf rampart of the defences was provided with a stone
wall only in the third century.

   Nine miles NE of Ravenglass, and half-way down the west
side of the notorious Hardknott Pass, is the Roman fort of
MEDIOBOGDVM, 'the fort in the middle of the bend' in the river
Esk. This is **Hardknott Castle*** (NY 2101) [AM; A], one of the
outstanding sites of Roman Britain. The fact that this is the
best-preserved Roman fort in Britain outside Hadrian's Wall
matters less than its spectacular position: it is a veritable
British Mycenae, with magnificent views of Eskdale to the
west, the Pass to the east, and the Scafell range to the north.
The visitor approaching from the east cannot miss the fort, so
commanding is its situation; from the west its position is
indicated by the signpost: it lies a short distance left (north) of
the road. From the time of Camden, who wrote about it in
1607, it has made a strong impression on its many visitors. It
has been called 'an enchanting fortress in the air', and it needs
little imagination to visualize the fort in its heyday.
Excavation was carried out between 1890 and 1894, and again
as part of DOE consolidation during the 1960's. In 1964 a
fragmentary inscription, now displayed in Carlisle museum,
revealed that the fort was built in the reign of Hadrian and
garrisoned by the fourth cohort of Dalmatians from

Yugoslavia. It does not seem to have been occupied beyond the end of the second century, except for a possible caretaker force.

The track up to the fort passes the shell of the external bath-house, its rooms neatly labelled. Hypocausts found here in the nineteenth century have now disappeared, and only the lowest courses of the brick-built stoke-hole survive. A circular hot-room with flue is detached from the main building. You then arrive at the south gate, which has twin passageways but no guardrooms. The other gates are similar (in no case does

74 *Hardknott, the fort-wall* (top)   75 *Hardknott, the HQ building* (bottom)

the central pier remain), but that on the north has only a
single portal. The entire circuit of the fort-wall and all four
corner turrets stand to a superb height of 8–10 feet (fig 74).
Note how the DOE departed from its usual practice and
partly rebuilt the walls with fallen stones: a slate course
separates original masonry from rebuilt work. In the centre of
the fort is the headquarters building (fig 75). It contains L-
shaped store-rooms flanking the courtyard, the cross-hall with
a *tribunal* at one end, and three administrative rooms at the
back. The middle one would have been the chapel of the
standards. To the west (left) of the HQ is the commandant's
house, but only the north wing and one wall of the east wing
were completed. To the east is a pair of buttressed granaries,
originally a single building, but later re-roofed as two when an
extra dividing wall was built (that on the east). The internal
floor-supports and remains of loading-platforms will also be
noticed. The rest of the fort would have been filled up with
wooden barrack-blocks, and it is very likely that the
superstructure of the central range was also of timber. Finally,
you should round off your visit to the site by walking up to
the parade-ground, an artificially levelled area 200 yards east
of the east gate. It is the finest example in Britain: note in
particular the careful embanking on the south side (nearest
the road).

After Hardknott, the fort at **Ambleside** (NY 3703) is a grave
disappointment. It was excavated in 1913–15 and 1920, after
which two gates, two angle towers and the central range of
buildings of the stone fort were fenced off and kept open. The
stonework was rarely well-preserved, and as the tops of the
walls have been turfed and not consolidated one gets the
impression that the site is very overgrown. The National
Trust, who own it, ought to be able to do better. In the
central range the building on the left is the commandant's
house, and on the right are the buttressed granaries with long
internal sleeper walls to support the floors. The HQ in the
centre is similar in plan to Hardknott's, with L-shaped rooms,
tribunal in the cross-hall and three rear rooms. Here, however,
the central one was later given an underground strong-room,
approached by steps. The visible stone fort was built in the
second century, probably *c.* AD 120/30, and continued in use
well into the fourth. Preceding it, on a slightly different site,

was a clay-and-timber fort, now invisible. Its excavator claimed an Agricolan date for it, but no pottery is earlier than AD 90. These remains of GALAVA lie in Borrans Field (NT sign), on the south side of the short A-road which links the A593 at Rothay Manor with the A591 at Waterhead Hotel, by-passing Ambleside. The finds are kept in the National Park Centre at Brockhole, which is 2m south on the A591.

The next fort to the east, Low Borrow Bridge near Tebay (App. I), lay on the main western trunk-road from Carlisle to Manchester. On this road is a Roman milestone at **Middleton** (SD 624859). It now stands near the top of a slope in the second field south of Middleton Church, which is situated midway between Sedbergh and Kirkby Lonsdale on the west side of the A683. The Roman inscription on it reads simply MP LIII, 53 miles (from Carlisle), but its discoverer re-erected it 200 yards from its find-spot and carved another inscription lower down on the stone. This records that the milestone was dug out of the ground and set up again by William Moore in the year 1836.

Nine miles south of Middleton a road branched off the

76   Lancaster, bath-building cut by later fort ditch

Carlisle to Manchester trunk route along the valley of the
Lune to **Lancaster** (SD 4762). The history of the succession of
Roman forts which crowned the hill overlooking the river at
the highest point of the modern town is very complex, and
excavation has not been made easy by the presence of the
Castle and St Mary's Church on top of the Roman site. A
late-first-century fort with turf rampart and timber buildings
saw some stone rebuilding, possibly of the defences, in the
early second century (the evidence is a Trajanic inscription).
This was then levelled and the site cleared for a new fort, not
later than AD 160, with some stone and some timber buildings.
It was outside the defences of this fort that a bath-building
was excavated in 1973–7 and subsequently consolidated and
left exposed. The main feature here is a well-preserved
hypocausted room with solid stone *pilae*, some preserved to
their full height, and the recesses in the walls through which
the hot air was drawn upwards (fig 76). The furnace flue which
heated this room shows clear signs of rebuilding; it also heated
the other room with a hypocaust here. A drain can also be
seen curving round through the furnace area. The bath
structure dates from *c.* 120/30 but was disused by *c.* 160; later
it formed part of an adjacent courtyard building (not visible)
occupied *c.* 250–300. It was totally demolished in the fourth
century when the last of the forts on the site was built. This had
massive stone walls (and at least one bastion) like some of the
Saxon Shore forts of southern England, and was presumably
designed, like them, to strengthen the coastal defences against
raiders from across the sea. It does, however, belong to a
rather later period, as a slightly worn coin of *c.* AD 326 in the
construction layer suggests a date of *c.* 330/350 for it. It is to
this fort that the large and rather shapeless chunk of masonry
core known as the Wery Wall belongs, standing about 8 feet
high. It was accompanied by a ditch which slices through the
earlier bath-building, as the V-profile cut in the side walls of
the main heated room vividly demonstrates (fig 76). To reach
the site, park in front of the castle and go up the steps
between it and Priory Church, and then turn right behind the
church. As the path descends, a gap in the hedge leads you
into the field on the right, at the far end of which is a railed-in
enclosure with the remains. The footpath is also signposted
from St George's Quay, off Bridge Lane.

The long catalogue of forts in the Pennines and the Lakes
** has now come to an end (but see pp. 391–4), and we can turn
aside from the military to consider the civilian aspects of life
in northern Britain under Roman rule. Nearly all the forts
had villages (*vici*) clustered around them, but no stonework is
visible at any of them today. On the larger scale, the *colonia* at
York has been mentioned, and there were three other towns in
Yorkshire, at Aldborough, Catterick (App. I) and Brough-on-
Humber (nothing visible). **Aldborough** (SE 4066) [AM; S], a
village near Boroughbridge off the B6265, was ISVRIVM, the
tribal capital of the Brigantes. A small town grew up here at
the end of the first century, probably on the site of a fort. 55
acres were enclosed by an earth bank and ditch in the second
half of the second century, and this defence was given a stone
wall in the middle of the third century. One hundred years
later bastions were added but none are now visible. Very little
remains of the town-wall in the section kept by HMBC,
which was excavated in the early nineteenth century. First a
portion of the back of the wall is visible, originally obscured
by an earth rampart-bank. Then comes an internal tower.
Further on is a second stretch of wall, and part of another
tower, which have been largely rebuilt. The position of the
wall elsewhere is marked by a pair of concrete strips, and at
the end of the path fragments of an angle tower are visible. To
the left, under the trees, is a quarry worked by the Romans.

Of the interior of ISVRIVM little is known in detail, but the
large number of polychrome mosaics recorded from the
eighteenth century onwards reveal its wealth during the fourth
century. Two of these are still visible and a third was
re-excavated in 1979; they are reached by a footpath from the
town-wall. One, found in 1848, is in perfect condition: it is
entirely geometric and features an eight-pointed star in the
centre. The second, which is badly damaged, was discovered
in 1832. Its main panel depicted a lion under a tree, but only
the tree, a paw and part of the mane survive. The third
mosaic, which probably was the floor of a dining-room in the
same house as the other two, was first uncovered in 1846 and
consolidated in 1979; it has, however, now been backfilled.
Much of it was geometric, but in the apse a figured panel was
clearly intended to represent the Muses, as the scene is
labelled, rather unusually (for Britain) in Greek, as Helikon,

their mountain home. Another illustration of classical learning at Aldborough may be a cruder pavement illustrating the myth of Romulus and Remus being suckled by the she-wolf, now in Leeds City Museum (Tues.–Fri. 9.30–5.30; Sat. 10–4), although some think it is a nineteenth-century forgery. Some of the smaller finds from Aldborough are displayed in the site-museum. Otherwise, a figure of Mercury in the church, and an earthwork which may or may not be the amphitheatre, a short distance outside the south angle of the defences (Studforth Hill), are all that can be seen of ISVRIVM outside the HMBC enclosure.

The mosaics at Aldborough suggest a considerable degree of romanization, and this is apparent also in the large number of villa-sites now known in the East Riding of Yorkshire. At the height of their prosperity, in the fourth century, many seem to have been fitted with mosaics, painted plaster and hypocausts. The most remarkable mosaics of all, uncovered in 1933, come from a villa at Rudston near Bridlington, and are now displayed in the **Hull** Museum of Transport and Archaeology (10–5, Sun. 1.30–4.30). One of these, a simple geometric mosaic, is competent enough: it shows what a local craftsman could achieve when he kept to conventional patterns. The second, much damaged, portrays a lively aquatic scene. The fish are not brilliantly drawn, but the artist has achieved a moderate degree of success. But when he tried his hand at a more ambitious subject (identical borders prove that the same craftsman was working on both mosaics), the result was ludicrously bad. This third pavement has a central roundel depicting Venus, the goddess of love and beauty, but there is nothing beautiful about this wild creature (fig 77). Her face is hard, her body lacks any sense of proportion, her stance is ungainly. Wearing nothing but armlets, her hair streaming behind her, she has dropped her mirror while a merman holds up what looks like a primitive back-scratcher (probably a torch). The surrounding panels are equally childish: three shaggy huntsmen and four crude animals, two of them labelled in misspelt Latin, surround the central figure. You can view the piece as amusing or just downright bad, but it remains a fascinating illustration of the level to which a local craftsman could sink in his attempt to copy ambitious classical subjects beyond his technical ability.

Enlargement of the museum, which was completed in 1979, has enabled a number of other figured mosaics from Humberside to be displayed, the whole ensemble forming a striking testimony of the popularity of this medium on the northern fringes of the Roman world, as well as of the tastes of the owners who commissioned them and the varying competence of the craftsmen who executed them. Moving left from the Venus mosaic and past the aquatic panel already mentioned, you enter the Horkstow gallery where parts of a vast mosaic originally measuring 50 feet by 20 feet can be seen. The panel in the centre is a much less skilled representation of the theme of Orpheus charming the beasts which the Cirencester school attempted with greater success (cf. pp. 115 and 127), while on the wall is a chariot race simplified to its bare essentials. It would be wrong to think from this that the circus was a familiar part of the Romano–British scene, as this mosaic, unique in the province, is more likely to have been drawn from a copybook of stock themes than provide an accurate reflection of a regular pastime of the villa-owner. Next comes a mosaic depicting a charioteer with the four seasons in the corners and birds in the oblong panels. It comes, like the first three floors, from Rudston, but these were found only in

77   *Hull Museum, Venus mosaic*

1971. You will immediately be struck by the more competent level of workmanship, and this must have been laid at a different time, although also during the fourth century. The bust of Spring (top right) is an especially delicate rendering which compares favourably even with examples from the more romanized parts of Britain (eg Lullingstone, p. 62). Note too how the bottom left-hand corner has been repaired in antiquity, not exquisitely, but not disastrously either. Evident traces of burning, especially above the charioteer, suggest that the villa perished in a fire. The final floor is part of a much larger mosaic from Brantingham, near Brough-on-Humber, which was discovered in 1962. The central circle contains the bust of a crowned goddess (upside down) while water-nymphs recline in the surrounding lunettes.

A number of other villas are known in this area of NE England, but none has left any substantial visible traces on the ground with the exception of **Beadlam** (SE 634842), where part has been consolidated as an Ancient Monument. The field containing the villa, which adjoins the south side of the A170 1½m east of Helmsley and 200 yds W of the turning to Pockley, had long been known to contain 'old buildings', but only excavations in 1966 revealed their Roman date. Since 1969 the site has been more thoroughly explored, and two wings of the villa have been excavated down to the latest fourth-century levels. The north building is in fine condition, with walls standing several courses high. One room contained a geometric mosaic, which had partially collapsed into the hypocaust below. The west block, which was more badly robbed, had projecting rooms and a corridor along the front, and a small bath-suite at one end. The east range was of two main periods, the original rectangular building being replaced by a single, shorter room with an apse. The east and west wings have been temporarily backfilled, but the north building has been consolidated and is accessible at any time. Plans to return the mosaic to the site and to erect a cover building have for the present unfortunately been shelved.

Most of the Yorkshire villas are concentrated in the East Riding around the Vale of York, but isolated examples have been found away to the north, near Piercebridge and Durham, and also to the west at Gargrave near Skipton. Elsewhere, agricultural communities continued to live in

native farmsteads and villages, and numerous examples of
these can be seen. Just two will be included here. They are
quite well preserved, but consist of nothing more than a series
of grass ridges, and so they are unlikely to prove of any great
interest. At **Grassington** (SE 0065) the settlement itself has not
been securely located, but there is a large area of ancient fields
to be seen. Each cultivation-strip measures about 375 feet by
75 feet, and is defined by well-preserved banks. Pottery makes
it certain that the fields were farmed in the Roman period.
Grassington lies about 7m north of Skipton on the B6265.
Turn off this road along Main Street and fork left along
Chapel Street. After 200 yards a track goes off to the right
near a telegraph-pole and two houses called Oak Bank and
Wood View. Follow this until a gate bars the way,
immediately after the track makes a sharp bend to their right.
The first gate in the wall on the right of the track beyond this
point leads into the field where the ancient banks lie.

The other native site is at **Ewe Close** (NY 6113) in
Cumbria. It is near the village of Crosby Ravensworth,
which is signposted from the B6260 (Appleby to Tebay). Turn
right by the telephone-booth in Crosby (signposted 'Shap 3½')
and immediately left by the post office. Bear left when the
track forks and then follow this for 1½m, through one farm,
until it peters out at another. Go through the farmyard,
keeping the hayloft to your right, and pass through the gate

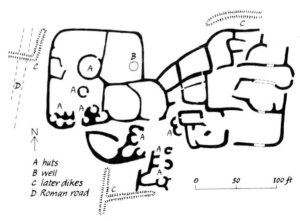

A huts
B well
C later dikes
D Roman road

0   50   100 ft

78   Ewe Close, plan of earthworks

on your left, at the end near the stream. Cross the stream and take the path wheeling up to the right. Go through the gate at the end of this, bear left up to the field wall, and then turn right until you reach the metal gate which leads into the field beyond, where the settlement of Ewe Close lies. A lot of ridges and a few hut-circles are all that can be made out of these confusing and complicated earthworks (see fig 78). There are probably several farmsteads grouped together here, lining the Roman north-south trunk-road which you cross 20 yards before the complex.

In the closing years of the Roman occupation, when the province of Britain was being threatened both by barbarian incursions from the north and by Saxon pirates from across the North Sea, a series of signal-towers was built along the Yorkshire coast. They were solid stone structures, perhaps 80 feet high, each set in a courtyard surrounded by a wall and an outer ditch. Five of them are known, from Huntcliff (near Saltburn) in the north to Filey in the south, and more undoubtedly existed. They were designed to give early warning of impending naval raids, and the news was then transferred by beacon-fire and messenger to military units stationed at Malton and beyond, which then tried to co-ordinate resistance to the attack. Today, only at the **Scarborough** example (TA 0589) [AM; SSM] can the plan of one of these signal-towers be made out. It lies on the edge of the cliff east of the castle, but the site was later occupied by a series of medieval chapels and no Roman masonry is now exposed. The outline of the signal-station has, however, been marked out in concrete, and the surrounding ditch has been dug out on the south and partly on the west. The east side of the remains has slipped into the sea. This chain of signal-stations represents the last desperate attempt to maintain peace and security in Roman Britain. Excavation has shown that they had a short life of only 20 or so years after their erection c. AD 380. Then came the end, at some of them dramatically. At Goldsborough (App. I) the skeleton of a short man lay face down across a hearth fire. His hand was twisted behind him, perhaps because he had been stabbed in the back. Another man lay at his feet, sprawled on top of the skeleton of a powerful dog. The days of Roman rule in Britain were numbered.

Chapter 8

Hadrian's Wall

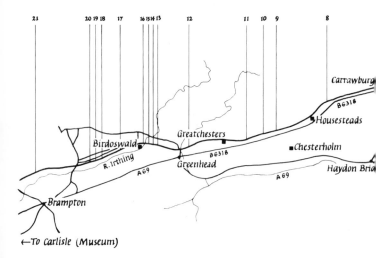

Unlike some of the sites in this book, Hadrian's Wall cannot fail to stir the imagination. It has fascinated countless people, scholars and ordinary visitors alike, from the time of Bede (AD 731) to the present day. The remains are, in parts, strikingly well preserved, and they are situated amid some of the most spectacular scenery in the British Isles. But the deepest impression on a visitor to the Wall is made by the sheer magnitude of the undertaking, which expresses so well the essential flavour of Roman civilization: here was a regime that not only had the confidence to make the bold decision of building a wall from sea to sea, but also had the vast resources of manpower and money, as well as the tremendous

1 Denton Hall
2 Heddon
3 Planetrees
4 Brunton
5 Chesters Bridge Abutment
6 Black Carts
7 Limestone Corner
8 Coesike
9 Peel Crag
10 Winshields
11 Cawfields

12 Walltown
13 Poltross Burn
14 Gilsland
15 Willowford
16 Harrow's Scar
17 High House
18 Piper Sike
19 Leahill
20 Banks East
21 Walton

Visible *forts* are marked on the map
with a square; also some roads, rivers
and modern towns.

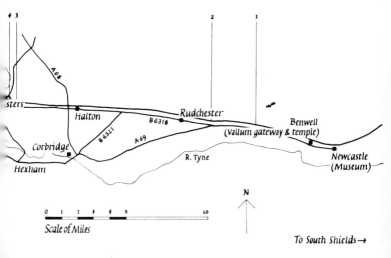

organizational ability, that were required to build it and
manage it for close on 300 years. From the engineering point
of view especially, the achievement is staggering: over a
million cubic yards of stone needed to be quarried, carried to
the spot and set in place. All the right ingredients are there:
the great Wall of Hadrian is not just the most exciting relic of
the Roman occupation of Britain, but perhaps the largest and
most remarkable building-programme ever undertaken in
these islands at any time.

Hadrian's barrier, however, is much more than a single wall
running across the Tyne–Solway isthmus: it is an immensely
complicated group of works, and the problem of their precise

relation, function and date has only been finally resolved, through careful excavation, in the last 50 years. Many, perhaps most, of the people who wander among the ruins of the Wall each year go away without really understanding either its complexity or purpose. Some background information is essential to a proper understanding and enjoyment of its remains.

About AD 105, Agricola's conquests in Scotland were finally given up and a frontier was fixed along the Stanegate. This is the name by which the Roman road from Carlisle to Corbridge is known. It was built by Agricola *c.* AD 80 and some of the forts on its route were his foundations. More were then built, and the road was probably extended westwards and eastwards, though less is known about these parts than about its central sector. In 118, soon after Hadrian became emperor on the death of Trajan, there was a rebellion in Britain and the 'Britons could no longer be held under control.' We have no details beyond these words of Hadrian's biographer, but it is a safe guess that the tribes involved were the Brigantes of northern England and the Selgovae and Novantae of southern Scotland. In 122, after order had been restored, the emperor came to Britain to assess the situation for himself. As a consequence of this famous visit, Hadrian's Wall was constructed: in the absence of any suitable natural frontier (once the decision had been taken not to overrun the whole island), an artificial one had to be created.

The original plan was relatively uncomplicated. The existing Stanegate forts were to hold the main fighting garrison, but the actual frontier was to be marked by a ditch and a wall on the commanding ground a few miles to the north. The **Ditch**, on average about 27 feet wide and 9 feet deep, accompanies the wall on its north side, except where cliffs make it unnecessary. The **Wall** was to run from Newcastle to Bowness on the Solway. From Newcastle to the river Irthing, over half its length, it was to be built of stone, 10 feet thick and perhaps 20 feet high, including the parapet. West of the river Irthing, where limestone was difficult to obtain, the Wall was to be of turf, 20 feet wide at base and probably about 17 feet high, including a timber breastwork. At intervals of one Roman mile (1,620 yards) fortlets, known as **milecastles**, were constructed, each having two gateways (one through the Wall) and barrack accommodation for no more than 32 men, often fewer. These milecastles were built of timber west of the Irthing, of stone elsewhere. Between each were two **turrets**, everywhere built of stone and about 14 feet square internally. The ground floor often contains hearths and was no doubt used as a mess-room and resting-place for soldiers off-duty. A timber ladder to the upper floor rested on a low stone foundation. The top was perhaps normally flat with crenellated parapet, as in the Vindolanda reconstruction (p. 300), but there is evidence that some turrets had tiled roofs, presumably with a wooden observation platform erected around the top. Each turret, perhaps 30 feet high, was to be used primarily for watching enemy movements north of the Wall, and signalling back to the Stanegate if the trouble was more than the local milecastles could cope with. (Milecastles are numbered from the east, and the same number, followed by *a* or *b*, is given to the two turrets on the west side of each milecastle.)

The Wall and its associated turrets and milecastles were built by detachments from all three of the British legions. Differing construction styles, especially in the gateways of milecastles, together with the evidence of inscriptions, make it possible to assign individual structures to individual legions (as is sometimes indicated below). The construction parties were divided up into various groups, some working on the foundation of the Wall, some on the turrets and milecastles, others on the Wall-superstructure, and others, perhaps not legionaries, on digging the Ditch.

Some time after work had started, probably in AD 124, an important alteration was made to the original scheme. This was the decision to move the main fighting force forward from the Stanegate on to the Wall itself, where it was housed in a number of **forts**, originally 12 in number (including an already existing fort at Newcastle), but eventually 16. At the same time, or shortly afterwards, other decisions were taken: to narrow the Wall from 10 feet to 8 feet in width, to extend the Wall from Newcastle eastwards to Wallsend, and to replace the Turf Wall in stone for a stretch of five miles west of the Irthing (as far as the natural fault, after which limestone is absent). Up to this time, many of the turrets and milecastles had been built to the broad gauge, in expectation that the forthcoming curtain-wall would be of the same width. But the building of the actual curtain-wall was lagging far behind: it was nearly finished as far as the North Tyne, and work was also in hand in the sector east of the river Irthing in Cumbria. All this results in a complicated sequence: (i) from Wallsend to Newcastle, the Wall is narrow (eight feet) on a narrow foundation; (ii) from Newcastle to the North Tyne (Chesters), the Wall is broad (10 feet) on a broad foundation, though the final portion had not been given the finishing touches; (iii) from the North Tyne to the Irthing the Wall is narrow on a foundation sometimes narrow, sometimes broad; (iv) for five miles west of the Irthing the Wall is narrow on a narrow foundation; (v) for the rest of its course the Turf Wall was not rebuilt in stone until later, possibly not until *c*. 200; it had an 'intermediate' width of 9 feet.

Very soon after the forts had been built, or as soon as they had been planned, an earthwork known as the **Vallum** was constructed a short distance south of the Wall. It consisted of a flat-bottomed ditch, about 20 feet wide at the top and 8 feet wide at the bottom, and some 10 feet deep; on either side was a berm of 30 feet flanked by two turf mounds 20 feet wide and originally 6 feet high. The whole Vallum was thus about 120 feet across. This earthwork in some ways is the most remarkable of all the components of Hadrian's frontier. It is a formidable obstacle, evidentally designed not to be crossed, but its form shows that it is not a proper military defence. Its purpose was to delineate the area under strict military control, above all to prevent civilians or other unauthorized persons from wandering too close to the military zone: this they were allowed to enter only through the large Vallum gateways opposite every fort.

These two additions of forts and Vallum to the original scheme give us some indication of the hostility with which the whole idea of a frontier-wall was received by the local peoples. Hadrian's biographer says that the Wall divided the Romans from the barbarians, but it would be more exact to say that its purpose was to separate the Brigantes of north England from the tribes of south Scotland, to prevent collusion between them, and so, it was hoped, to lessen the scale of any future uprising. The placing of the striking force on the Wall-line shows that pressure from the north needed to be dealt with more speedily and effectively than was possible when the main body of troops was on the Stanegate; and the building of the Vallum shows that the tribesmen behind the Wall were sufficiently restless to warrant an additional deterrent to their contacting friends in the north.

The main purpose of the Wall, then, was to provide a fixed frontier to the Roman province of Britain, and to separate two sets of potential trouble-makers. This was its political role. In military terms, it acted as a superb cover for movements against an enemy unable to predict from which point troops might emerge. The Wall itself was never meant to be used as a fighting-platform; indeed some even think there was no patrol walk along the top (no other frontier has one), but the Wall's width would in that case have been unjustifiable (the Raetian wall in Germany, for example, is a mere 4 feet wide). The garrison, probably some 11,000 when all posts were fully manned, was provided by auxiliary units of the Roman army; legionaries built the Wall but never patrolled it, except as a temporary measure.

A few words must now be said about the history of Hadrian's Wall. It was begun in 122 (120 according to an alternative suggestion) under the supervision of the governor Aulus Platorius Nepos, then a close friend of Hadrian. Most of it was finished by about 128. In 139–40, when the Antonine Wall was built, Hadrian's Wall was evacuated. The mounds of the Vallum were breached in places and its ditch filled in. Milecastle gates were removed. The forts were given caretaker garrisons, possibly skeleton detachments of legionaries. In 155 the Brigantes revolted and the Antonine Wall was evacuated, and a year or two later Hadrian's Wall was fully recommissioned: the milecastle gates were rehung and the Vallum was restored in most places to its former state. By 159–60 the Antonine Wall was reoccupied and caretaker garrisons were on Hadrian's frontier. By about 163, however, as shown by B R Hartley's detailed study of the samian pottery, Hadrian's Wall had again been fully regarrisoned. It was either at this time, or else about 200, that the rest of the Turf Wall was rebuilt in stone. More controversial is the date of the first destruction of Hadrian's frontier. The historian Dio records that in 180 the British tribes crossed 'the Wall' and inflicted much damage. This presumably refers to

Hadrian's Wall rather than a barrier out of commission, and archaeological evidence is now mounting for destruction at this date at Corbridge and at two of its neighbours on the Wall, Rudchester and Halton: if so, it looks as though the tribes burst through the centre and left the rest of the Wall unharmed. But the great destruction is usually believed to have happened in 196–7, when Clodius Albinus stripped Britain of troops in an attempt to become emperor. Virius Lupus, sent by Severus to recover the province, had to buy off the Maeatae of south Scotland, and this has been taken to mean that they had already destroyed the Wall and its works. If so, it is very odd that the Wall lay in ruins for 10 years or more, for it was not until the governorship of Alfenus Senecio (205–8) that restoration was begun. Most scholars, however, now believe that the Wall was not destroyed in the troubles of 196–7 and that the work of *c*. 205–8 was merely a massive refurbishment of the aging frontier. In this reconstruction (Severan), some of the turrets were demolished, others not reoccupied (only a quarter of the 45 turrets so far examined show evidence for later use); the gateways of the milecastles were narrowed, and the Vallum was not restored: a few of the forts' civilian suburbs were allowed to grow over its filled-in course.

The expeditions of Severus to Scotland in 209–11 gave peace to the Hadrianic frontier for a long time. Apathy set in and certainly some of the forts were in a state of neglect and disrepair by the end of the third century. A thorough rebuilding and reorganization was set in motion by Constantius, who came to Britain in 296 to regain the province from the usurper Allectus. While units were no doubt withdrawn from the Wall to serve in Allectus' army, it is far from certain that the Wall was destroyed at this time: signs of burning may be due to demolition-work by army construction-gangs rather than to enemy action. Similarly, the extensive repairs carried out by Theodosius in 369–70 may have been necessitated by frontier neglect and decay rather than enemy destruction in the 'barbarian conspiracy' of 367–8. Obviously the amount of reconstruction necessary on each occasion (Severan, Constantian, Theodosian) must have varied, but the Wall of Hadrian was certainly rebuilt in places from its foundations, as reused 'centurial stones' show.

Destruction in 383, when another pretender, Magnus Maximus, tried for the throne, is equally uncertain. Some forts were certainly occupied after this date, and by now soldiers had their families with them inside the protection of the walls: the undefended *vici* outside were abandoned. By 400 the final garrison had gone, and the work of the Wall was finished. The slow process of decay and destruction began, only to be halted in the present century.

Very substantial remains of Hadrian's great frontier still survive, and I can hope to do no more than indicate here which are the best-preserved or most instructive portions. For those who wish for more, the first two works listed in the bibliography for this chapter are indispensable; in particular, the OS Map of Hadrian's Wall will be found most useful even for the briefest of visits. A taste of the Wall can be had in a day (Chesters, Vindolanda and Housesteads should be seen), and a fair sample can be taken in two days (visit all sites with an asterisk). All the places mentioned below can be visited, with the aid of a car, in 3–4 days. The best way to see the Wall is to walk its full length, which can be done in a fortnight. The standard direction is from east to west, and that has been adopted in the description below.

Hadrian's Wall itself ran from Wallsend to Bowness, a distance of 73½ miles. But its flanks needed protection. On the west, the system of milefortlets and towers (none now visible) continued for another 40 miles down the Cumbria coast, the sea here providing a sufficient barrier. On the east the

** extension of the Wall to **Wallsend** was made to prevent an enemy slipping across the river, and there may have been one or more posts on the south bank between Wallsend and the Tyne mouth. The latter was guarded by a fort at **South Shields*** (NZ 3667), and part of it, found in the late nineteenth century, has for long been visible (Easter–Sept., Mon.–Fri. 10–5.30, Sat. 10–4.30, Sun. 2–5; Oct.–Apr., Mon.–Thurs. 10–4, Fri. 10–3, Sat. 10–12). Recent work, first in the late 1960's and then since 1978, has added a great deal to our knowledge of the fort, and, thanks to the enlightened attitude of Tyne and Wear County Council, much of the fort is now consolidated and exposed. It is important to remember, however, that much of what is at present visible is not typical of a Roman fort. The stone second-century fort was indeed regular, but in the early third century virtually the whole area inside the walls was converted into a store-base for Severus' campaigns in Scotland. No fewer than 23 granaries are now known, and parts of 11 are visible.

The fort is not at present (1987) well signposted, but follow directions for the city centre and then watch out for a sign to the fort from the main shopping street; the site lies at the top of the hill on a prominent plateau overlooking the Tyne. The recently refurbished site museum at the entrance should be visited first. The room on the right has some splendidly displayed small finds (note especially the helmet cheek-guard decorated with a figure of one of the Dioscuri (Castor or Pollux) and a replica of an elaborate shield-boss, the original of which is in the British Museum). The room on the left contains the principal inscriptions and other stones from the site, three of which are especially important. That near the entrance gives the name of the fort's third-century garrison, the Fifth Cohort of Gauls, who dedicated an aqueduct in AD 222, while the pair of magnificent tombstones at the far end belongs to the later second century. That on the right commemorates Regina, an

79 *South Shields, fort-wall at S.E. corner*

ex-slave who gives her origin as CATVALLAVNA, that is, a member of the Catuvellauni tribe whose capital was at Verulamium (St Albans). She became the wife of her former master Barates, who hailed from Palmyra in Syria, and by chance part of his tombstone has also survived (it is on display in the Corbridge Museum). The wicker chair in which Regina sits and the wool-basket on her left give us a rare glimpse of the kind of furniture in use in Roman Britain. Even better preserved is the fine tombstone of Victor, who came from Mauretania (roughly the equivalent of modern Morocco). He is shown reclining on a couch at the heavenly banquet, while a tiny slave holds up a wine jar filled from the bowl on the floor. A stylized tree is engraved behind Victor. Both tombstones, recording an African and the wife of a Syrian, reflect the cosmopolitanism of life on the northern frontier (as indeed in many other parts of Britain). Furthermore, stylistic comparisons suggest not only that both tombstones were carved by the same man but that he himself also came from Palmyra, a suggestion further reinforced by the assured use of Aramaic at the foot of Regina's tombstone.

On leaving the museum cross the scanty remains of the fort wall and turn left to the splendid west gate, reconstructed in 1986. This and the one at Manchester (p. 394), built in 1984, are the first examples in Britain of reconstructed fort gateways in stone, an exercise first tried in Germany nearly a century ago. The decision to reconstruct on the same site as the original gateway rather than elsewhere was controversial, but the loss was minimal (only footings survived, and they of course were comprehensively recorded before destruction), by comparison with the very considerable gain of being able to visualize the approximate original appearance of such structures. Many details of the superstructure, as well as its exact height (it may well have been rebuilt higher than the original), are of course guesswork. In particular it is by no means certain that gate towers (or interval towers for that matter) were roofed rather than provided with open flat tops and crenellation (cf. fig 2, p. 12). The Romans probably used both types of construction, perhaps in different regions and at different times, but the archaeological evidence for superstructure is generally too exiguous for clear conclusions to emerge. A splendid view of the fort may be obtained from here; plans are afoot to use the gatetowers also for supplementary museum display.

From the west gate you can follow what remains of the stone rampart round past the NW angle-tower to the north gate, the fort's principal gate until the radical transformation of the third century. It too had twin portals and guard chambers, but the west passageway was subsequently blocked with a wall still partly in position, and the other arch, apparently in danger of collapse, had to be propped up with the massive pier of blocks visible in the middle of the eastern portal. The squared masonry of the gate towers and the central pier is very fine, and the drains below both carriageways will also be noted.

The date of these defences still requires clarification. Until very recently the first stone fort was reckoned to be of Hadrianic date, but the current excavator has now (1986) suggested that both the west gate and the first stone headquarters building are no earlier than the Antonine period in the middle of the second century. Such a dating in particular makes better sense for the form of the gatetowers which project forward from the line of the walls, a feature unparalleled in

80   South Shields, the latrine

Hadrianic work in Britain, but known elsewhere (at Brecon,
Castell Collen and Dover, for example) in Antonine forts.
Fragmentary traces of a turf-and-timber fort have been
detected below, presumably no later than *c*. 105, as a turf-and-
timber fort here of Hadrianic date when contemporary work
elsewhere on the northern frontier was in stone seems very
unlikely. But equally unlikely is the complete absence of a
Hadrianic fort at South Shields, a vital prerequisite for
securing the east flank of Hadrian's Wall. If the earliest stone
fort on the site is Antonine, as seems likely, a Hadrianic post
may lie undetected somewhere else on the same hill.

** Description continues on p. 396.

A visit to Hadrian's Wall is best preceded by a study of the
exhibits in the Museum of Antiquities in the University of
Newcastle (weekdays 10–5). This is one of the outstanding
Roman collections in the country. The many inscriptions
displayed here form the basis of our knowledge of the Wall's
history. The one illustrated (fig 81) comes from a milecastle
and simply records the emperor (Hadrian, lines 1–2), the
governor (A. Platorius Nepos, line 4), and the builders (men
from the Second Augustan Legion, line 3). Some of the stones
from forts north of the Wall are mentioned in Chapter 9
(figs 102–3), and various other exhibits are noted, in passing,
below. Especially important are the scale-models of the Wall
and its structures as they may once have appeared (fig 2),
and with these in mind the visitor to the Wall can better
appreciate the original appearance of the ruins before him.
There is also an impressive full-scale reconstruction of the
Carrawburgh Mithraeum.

After Wallsend (p. 395) the first visible site on the Wall-line
is in **Benwell** (NZ 2164), 2m west of Newcastle. Nothing can be
seen of the fort of CONDERCVM, but two structures which lay
outside its walls have been preserved. One is the tiny temple of
a native god, Anociticus or Antenociticus [AM; A], on the
left-hand side of Broomridge Avenue (signposted from the
A69). Of three altars known from the temple, two use the
latter form of the god's name, one the former. All are now in
the museum at Newcastle, but two have been replaced by
casts (now nearly illegible) at the site. Also in Newcastle is the
head of the god himself. It is a powerful rendering, and well
displays, like other pieces of Romano–British art (cf.

especially the Bath pediment), the strong influence of Celtic traditions, here represented by the large baggy eyes and the deeply-grooved, snake-like hair.

Return from the temple to the A69, turn left and then first left (Denhill Park). At the bottom of this road is the sole visible example of one of the Vallum gateways which existed opposite every Wall-fort [AM; S]. The ditch of the Vallum was not dug in the centre, and the sides of the resulting causeway have been revetted in stone with an opening left for drainage. The roadway over it (note several periods of metalling, displayed in step-fashion) was closed by a large doorway, of which one pier and a pivot-hole survive. These gateways ensured a strict control over movements into and out of the military zone.

One mile further west along the A69, immediately after the roundabout (keep straight on: left is signposted Ring Road South), the first extant fragment of Hadrian's Wall may be seen on the left-hand side of the road. About 300 yards further on, also on the left, is the much longer stretch at **Denton Hall** (NZ 1965) [AM; A]. This is a good example of the broad Wall, and bonded into it is turret 7b, the work of Legion XX. The pivot-hole of the door and the base for the stairway will be noted. Excavation in 1929 revealed that the

81   Newcastle Museum, milecastle inscription

turret was still in use in the fourth century. Another fragment of Wall-foundation can be seen on the left of the road at West Denton [AM; A], another 200 yards further west. At the roundabout immediately after, take B6528 for Walbottle.

Very little is visible of the Wall or its attendant works for nearly two miles, until you approach Heddon, where the Vallum is well preserved on your left. Just before the village of **Heddon** (NZ 1366), 110 yards of the broad Wall have been consolidated [AM; A] (turn left along the lane signposted 'Heddon $\frac{1}{4}$' if you wish to stop). The structure built into the west end of this stretch is a post-Roman kiln.

At Heddon, turn left along A69 and then immediately right along the B6318. This is the Military Way, built in 1751. For many miles the Wall is invisible, as it was ripped down at that date to provide a foundation for the road. $1\frac{1}{2}$m beyond Heddon is a crossroads (Horsley and Wylam, left; Stamfordham and Ponteland, right), and immediately west of it the fort of VINDOBALA, **Rudchester** (NZ 1167), straddles the B-road. The earth mound which covers its stone defences is not impressive; it is best viewed at the SE corner (turn left at the crossroads and look over the first field-gate on your right). 4m west of Rudchester, $1\frac{1}{2}$m past the reservoirs, both Vallum on the left and Wall-Ditch on the right become conspicuous. Take the road signposted Stelling Hall and Stocksfield on the left immediately before the notice announcing the Corbridge road (B6321), and stop at the gap in the hedge on the left. The Vallum is not very impressive here, but the gaps in the flanking mounds and the causeways across its ditch are clearly visible. This is one of the few places along the course of the Vallum where the breaches made about AD 140 were not later repaired. It is worth walking back to the B-road to look at the picturesque, tree-grown stretch of Wall-Ditch, which is in good condition at this point. 2m further west is the fort of ONNVM, **Halton** (NY 9968): turn left (gate-piers) over the cattle-grid after the bend-sign, just after Halton Red House. The road passes through the southern part of the fort, but only the mounds of its ramparts and uneven ground marking the sites of interior buildings can be seen today.

After another $\frac{1}{2}$m comes a roundabout where the A68 crosses the B6318. There was a gateway through the Wall at this point (Portgate), taking Dere Street into Scotland: its route is described on p 314. Here it is convenient to make the 2m detour to **Corbridge*** (NY 9864), and visit the remains of CORIOSOPITVM [AM; S], ½m west of the modern town. Most of the structures in the exposed portion belong to the third and fourth centuries, when Corbridge was a flourishing town and a military supply-depot for the Wall. Below them lies a succession of earlier forts. The earliest was for long thought to have been an Agricolan foundation of *c*. AD 79, but the Agricolan site is now known to lie ¾m to the W, where part of a very large stores-base was excavated in 1974 on the line of the bypass, and the contemporary structure uncovered nearby in 1955–7 now falls into place as the bath-building of this early fort. It was, however, demolished on the withdrawal from Scotland *c*. 87, and the first turf-and-timber fort on the main Corbridge site erected. Its garrison was probably a cavalry regiment, the *Ala Petriana*, then 500 strong but later doubled in size. To it belonged a certain Flavinus, whose tombstone, depicting him riding down his barbarian foe, is now in the south transept of Hexham church (other stones are

82 *Corbridge, the granaries*

displayed at the north end). The fort was burnt and rebuilt *c.*
105 and abandoned *c.* 124 when forts were moved to the line
of the Wall. It was then rebuilt in stone *c.* 139 with the
Antonine advance into Scotland, and it probably remained in
use for about thirty years.

The present site, which represents only a small part of the
final settlement, is bisected by the Stanegate. The first portion
of this road, still lined by its side gutters, represents the final
fourth-century level, which is many feet higher than the
original first-century surface. On the left, immediately below
the road and half-buried by it, are the lower parts of some
columns. These supported a porch in front of the two large
third-century granaries beyond, the best-preserved examples in
Roman Britain (fig 82). For once, substantial portions of the
floor remain in position. The ventilation-openings between the
buttresses are also clear, and one in the right-hand wall of the
second granary is still in perfect condition. Immediately next
to it is an elaborate fountain consisting of three elements: an
aqueduct-channel, originally covered with stone slabs; a
fountain-house, of which only a few blocks remain; and a basin
into which water was discharged. Its sides became so worn
down by the sharpening of knives that the fountain can hardly
have worked properly in its final years. The third structure on
this side of the Stanegate is a vast building, perhaps a
storehouse, consisting of four wings enclosing a courtyard. The
fine quality of the massive masonry blocks, which would have
been dressed off flush when finished, will be noted. The
archaeological evidence for dating this building has been
scanty. It now seems possible that construction was under way
in the late 160's or during the 170's, but it was never completed,
except on the side facing the Stanegate. Possibly it was a
casualty in the upheavals which followed the enemy destruction
of Corbridge in 180. Fragments of two other buildings are
visible within the courtyard. The rooms nearer the granaries
formed part of the rear range of the HQ building of the second-
century stone fort, including the *sacellum*; this alone had not
been demolished during the erection of the grand storehouse,
and it was then converted to other uses, probably domestic.
The other building exposed within the courtyard is part of the
commandant's house of the same fort.

At the far end, you should mount the steps and survey the

jumble of fragmentary remains on the south side of the
Stanegate. Subsidence has contributed to the crazy effect. It is
well to have a good look at the helpful reconstruction-
drawing which is displayed here. From this you will see that
the area consisted of two military compounds, surrounded by
enclosure-walls. These take an irregular course to avoid
temples and other buildings fronting the Stanegate. The
compound-walls can be recognized by their more massive
construction (five feet wide), and the projecting plinth at their
bottom. At the beginning of the fourth century the
compounds were united by building a wall, broken by an
entrance, along the Stanegate. The buildings inside these
compounds – officers' houses, stores, workshops, clubs – can
be understood with the help of the excellent information
panels. A small administrative building in the west compound,
adjoining the path near the museum, has an underground
strongroom approached by steps.

The superb museum, opened in 1983, contains a replica of
the Flavinus tombstone (p. 280), an important hoard from an
armourer's workshop, some informative inscriptions, two
partly recoloured to give an idea of their original polychrome
effect, and many fascinating sculptures. One is a rugged,
unrealistic portrayal of a lion devouring a stag (a tomb
monument), another is part of a frieze representing the
crowned Sun-god riding on a winged horse towards a pedimented
building, in which stands Castor or Pollux. Along with other
sculptures it came from a temple dedicated to Dolichenus, an
eastern deity equated with Jupiter, and he is named on an altar
also in the museum. At the far end are two large tombstones
of children, striking for the perfunctory nature of their reliefs.
Other fragmentary sculptures testify to the remarkable
diversity and elaboration of the buildings that must once have
graced this distant settlement of the Roman Empire.

Return now to the B6318. For three miles west of Portgate
the Ditch on the north of the road and the Vallum on the
south are in an outstanding state of preservation. The Wall
itself is buried beneath the road, but when eventually the two
part company, after descending the first part of a 1:8 hill one
mile before Chollerford, some stone steps over the wall on the
left lead you to the interesting stretch at **Planetrees** (NY 9269)
[AM; A] (no parking-place, or signpost). It preserves the

junction between the broad wall and a portion only six feet
thick, standing on broad foundation. The reason for this is
uncertain, but there may have been a desire to finish this
stretch of curtain wall quickly at less than normal width, even
for Narrow Wall, or else this is a stretch totally rebuilt later,
perhaps *c*. 205. A drainage-culvert is also visible here.

You are now approaching the North Tyne and the central
sector of Hadrian's Wall, where the scenery becomes more
beautiful and the Roman remains better preserved. A long
stretch of the Wall, seven feet high and incorporating a well-
preserved turret (26b), is only a short distance from
Planetrees. Turn left along the A6079 at the bottom of the hill
and you will see **Brunton** turret (NY 9269) [AM; A]
signposted on the left (parking place). It is the most westerly
section of broad Wall on a broad foundation, for it was when
the curtain-builders had got this far that the order came to
change the width from 10 to 8 feet. They had, however, only
finished work west of the turret; to the east of it the Wall was
completed only six feet wide, as at Planetrees. The turret, built
by men from Legion XX, preserves its door-sill and pivot-
hole, and an uninscribed altar and the lower part of a corn-
mill can be seen inside.

Return to the crossroads and turn left for Chollerford.
Most visitors now go on to Chesters, but if you have half an
hour to spare you will not regret parking immediately before
the river-bridge and taking the path on the left which leads to
Chesters bridge abutment (NY 9169) [AM; A]. The Wall, here
on its Broad Foundation, ends in a tower adjacent to the
massive masonry apron forming the abutment. Consolidation
work in 1982–3, which included removal of the stones formerly
on the abutment (fig 83) to a display area under the trees, has
demonstrated that the visible work belongs to a rebuilding of
c. 220 and that the Hadrianic bridge abutment lay further east.
Part of the river-bed paving of that date is visible in the base
of the third-century tower, and the outline of a pier of the
Hadrianic bridge, with cutwater to the south, can be made out
in the apron immediately west of the tower, where it was
incorporated in the later masonry. The Hadrianic bridge may
have had stone arches, the third-century one a timber
superstructure on stone piers. Three other piers and the west
abutment have been detected in the river, which has shifted

some yards to the west since antiquity. The channel (a later addition) running through the tower, once covered by the huge slabs which lie shattered on its south side, was a water-race for turning a millstone in the tower (part of the apparatus is in
** Chesters Museum). See further p. 399.

Turning left in Chollerford, you will soon see the entrance to the Roman fort of **Chesters*** (NY 9170) [AM; SSM], a charming spot, set in a lush estate beside the North Tyne. The remains of CILVRNVM, mainly excavated in the nineteenth century, are well preserved. The path first leads to the north gate: of its two portals, the west has been cleared down to the original Hadrianic level, the other preserves a sill of a later date. In the next enclosure is part of a double barrack-building. The rooms originally would each have been divided into two by a timber partition. As usual there are more spacious quarters for officers at the far end. The pieces of column lying around supported the verandah along each side of the street, which has a gutter to collect water from the eaves. As you make your way to the east gate, in the same enclosure, you

83   Chesters, the bridge abutment

pass a partially-exposed stable (flagging): Chesters was a cavalry fort; the *Ala Augusta* (Hadrianic) and the Second *Ala* of Asturians are recorded. The east gate, entirely Hadrianic in form as all later masonry was removed in 1867, is very well preserved: the cap from which the rear arch sprang is still in position on the south side. Now leave the fort and walk down to the river, passing a fragment of the Wall on your way. You will soon reach the bath-house, one side of which still stands to a height of 10 feet. A porch, added later, gives access to the large changing-room (fig 84). The seven niches probably held wooden lockers for clothes, and no doubt there was once a second row above. On the river side is a heavily-buttressed latrine. All that remains of it are the foundations and the lower part of the sewer: the floor level and the supports for the wooden seats have gone. From the changing-room the bather would cross the worn threshold, and turn left into the cold room with its cold plunge-bath. Then he had a choice of hot rooms, though not all belong to the original building. Returning to the lobby he could either keep straight ahead

84 *Chesters, bath-house, undressing-room*

and then turn right for the hot-dry room, or turn left for the long room of moist heat. This was originally divided into two parts, the *tepidarium* and the *caldarium*. Its floor and hypocaust have completely disappeared, but the stoke-hole survives at the far end, together with part of the supports on either side for the hot-water boilers. On the right, the imposing wall of the hot plunge-bath still has the lower part of a window. Another set of warm rooms runs parallel on the river side.

From the bath-house you may like to wander down to the river. If the water is low a bridge abutment and two piers may be visible; the eastern abutment can be seen on the far side (see above). Returning to the fort, you first reach the hypocaust of the commandant's private bath-suite. Its floor is supported by a mixture of brick and stone pillars: the irregularity is due to partial reconstruction, probably in the fourth century. The hypocausts in the living-rooms are also additions to the visible building, the original plan of which is not clear. Some fragments of wall-foundation detectable here

85 Chesters, inside the HQ

and there at a lower level presumably belong to an earlier
commandant's house. Next comes a long narrow structure of
unknown purpose. In the centre of the fort is the headquarters
building, the clearest example visible in Britain. The entrance
led to a courtyard surrounded by a covered colonnade on
three sides. The gutters and part of the courtyard paving are
visible, and on one of the flags near the well a phallus has
been carved for good luck. The courtyard led to the covered
cross-hall, with a *tribunal* on the right from which the officer
could address his assembled troops. Beyond are five
administrative buildings, the central one of which contained
the statue of the emperor and the regimental standards (fig 85).
In the third century, a strong-room, still covered by its
roof, was inserted below the floor (fig 86): it now appears to
stick up above ground, but the floor-level elsewhere was much
higher at this period than it is now, as the excavators removed
the later floors to expose the Hadrianic masonry. Finally, you
should visit the rest of the defences: a single-portalled gate on
the east side (near the commandant's house), an angle tower,
two interval-towers, and the south and west gates all remain
exposed. Of the south gate, one portal was blocked up soon
after being built, but its blocking-wall has been removed to
reveal the Hadrianic masonry; the other remained in use,
resulting in a build-up of road-levels and the raising of the
east portal. Its rear threshold, much worn, is built of reused
gutter-stones. The west gate was entirely blocked up, but once
again the blocking-walls have now been removed. A water-
tank with a leat bringing water from the west can be seen in
one guardroom, and beyond it an oven. A portion of
Hadrian's Wall is also visible, adjoining the south guardroom:
the fort lay astride the Wall, and three of its gateways,
therefore, opened into enemy territory. A tour of the Chesters
Museum, crammed full of important sculptured and inscribed
stones, will complete your visit to the site.

Now continue westwards along the B6318. At the top of the
hill, after the turning to Wark, you will see a fine piece of
Wall and a turret at **Black Carts** (NY 8871) [AM; A]; they
deserve closer inspection. Turn off, therefore, along the next
lane on the right. The back wall of the turret is still eleven feet
high, but the front has been reduced to ground-level. The
adjacent Wall is built to the narrow width, and so this is the

first visible turret with wing-walls of the broad gauge on both sides. Two 'centurial stones', recording the erection of stretches of Wall by working-parties of legionary *centuriae*, are also visible here. One on the bottom course of the south face, 12 blocks west of the end of the turret's wing-wall, is now illegible: it read 'from the sixth cohort the century of Gellius P(h)ilippus (built this)'. The other, on the bottom

86 (top) *Chesters, the headquarters building*   87 (above) *Carrawburgh, the val*

course of the north face midway between the turret and the wooden gate, reads COH I|NAS BA ('from the first cohort, the century of Nas . . . Ba(ssus built this)'). As these stones were normally placed on the south side when the Wall was originally raised, it looks as though this portion was entirely rebuilt in a later reconstruction, and the centurial stone was incorporated into the outer face as if it were a normal building-stone. The Ditch is conspicuous here, but is even more striking on the other side of the lane, where another long stretch of the Wall has been consolidated.

After Black Carts, the road climbs again. On the downward slope there is a lay-by on the right near an iron gate. This leads at once to the stretch of Ditch on **Limestone Corner** (NY 8771), here unfinished because of the hardness of the rock. It is an imposing sight, and a sobering reminder of what Roman engineers were capable of achieving without the use of explosives. A mile further on, after passing a superb stretch of the Vallum (fig 87), you will come to the car-park adjoining the fort of BROCOLITIA, **Carrawburgh** (NY 8571), of which only a lofty earth rampart-mound is visible. It was added later than the main series of forts, about AD 130–3, covering the Vallum in the process. Outside is the fine little temple of Mithras, excavated in 1950 [AM; A]. Founded soon after AD 205, it was extended a decade or so later and had three further major repairs or rebuildings before its final desecration in the early fourth century, presumably by Christians. The visible remains represent the building in its final form (fig 88). An ante-chapel containing the statuette of a mother-goddess is separated from the nave by a screen (some concrete posts, representing wooden uprights, remain). Low benches, revetted with a wooden interlace, flank the nave, where stand smashed representations of the torch-bearers and four tiny altars. The stone walls visible half-way along the benches mark the limits of the first Mithraeum, which was only half the size of the present building. At the end are three magnificent altars, and in the shelf behind them would have stood the bull-slaying relief. A few words about Mithraism and a reconstruction-drawing of a ceremony in progress will be found on p. 355. The originals of the inscriptions and sculptures are now in the Newcastle museum, together with a full-scale reconstruction of the building. The shrine of Coventina, a nymph to whom

88 *Carrawburgh, Temple of Mithras* (top)   89   *Coesike, turret 33* (bottom)

numerous offerings of all kinds were thrown, is now
represented by the marshy well 150 yards to the north,
adjoining the field-wall and surrounded by wooden rails.

Go on from Carrawburgh for 2½m and park on the verge,
just before the road swings to the left and crosses the Vallum
at the start of a wood. Take the field-gate here (signposted
Sewingshields, Public Footpath), and strike across the field
until you reach the Wall Ditch. Walking westwards you soon
come to turret 33b, **Coesike** (NY 8270), which furnishes an
excellent illustration of the fate which befell many of the
turrets at the beginning of the third century. The original
structure has wing walls of the broad gauge as well as the
usual ladder-platform and doorway. Excavation in 1968 and
1970 found very little pottery of the second half of the second
century, suggesting that it went out of use soon after the
recommissioning of the Wall in the 160's, and its doorway
was blocked up. Then in the Severan reorganization it was
decided that this turret was no longer required and it was
demolished. Hadrian's Wall was then partly reconstructed
over the wing-walls and in the north end of the recess, where
it has bulged and sagged (right of pole in fig 89). Those with
time to spare may like to continue walking westwards. No
Wall is exposed in this sector, but the Ditch is very striking,
especially where it stops abruptly opposite the site of
milecastle 34 (clump of trees). From here onwards as far as
Greenhead, the cliffs rendered it unnnecessary except for a few
stretches. Turret 34a, demolished to foundations, has been
** consolidated immediately beyond the next field-wall.

Now press on for another 1½m and visit the most famous
and popular of all the Wall-forts, **Housesteads*** (NY 7968)
[AM; SSM]: if it is high summer and you want to visit the site
in comparative peace, be sure to arrive early. Its Roman name
was VERCOVICIVM (the meaning is uncertain), but it is widely
known by the incorrect form Borcovicus. The third-century
garrison was an infantry cohort of Tungrians (from Belgium),
1,000 strong. The fame of Housesteads is mainly due to its
dramatic setting, on the edge of a craggy precipice in a lonely
part of Northumberland. The little museum has a few items,
notably a relief of three hooded deities, and an uninscribed
slab flanked by cupids. A few buildings of the large civilian
settlement are exposed near the south gate, by which the fort

is entered (1 on fig 90). Now walk up the slope, along the line of the *via principalis*. The first building on the left, entered through the room in the middle of the east wing, is the commandant's house (2). In its visible, third-century form it consists of four wings around a courtyard, but only the north and west wings are of Hadrianic origin. The kitchen in the NE corner, with an oven, served the adjacent dining-room, and the next room along, originally part of a small bath-suite, was provided with a hypocaust in the fourth century: its stone *pilae*, some of them broken columns probably robbed from demolished verandahs, are well preserved, and part of the floor is in position (fig 91). A paved passage at the west end of the courtyard-corridor leads to a small toilet, made in the third century when the larger latrine immediately beyond (on the south side) was filled in and its doorway blocked up. The sewer in this latrine is very fine; note especially the massive slab covering it where it leaves the west side of the building. At the SW corner are two further rooms, heated from the

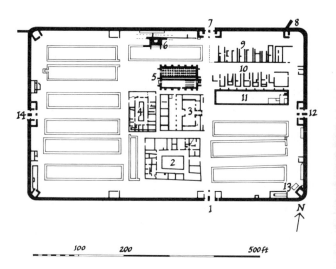

100   200   500 ft

90   Housesteads, plan of Roman fort

beginning, with fragmentary remains of hypocausts. It is
worth looking at the outside wall of the house here, where the
junction between the Hadrianic masonry and the later
addition of the south wing is very clear. The large flagged area
at the SE corner with drainage-channels (to ease mucking-out)
and a water-tank in one corner, was used as stables, and had
separate access from the street; no doubt the commandant's
servants lived above. The stone flagging in the courtyard (note
the decorated slab in the centre) and in the two rooms at the
NW corner is partly made up of reused material brought
from other buildings and belongs to the final period of the
house, when the comfortable life-style of the commandant
was no longer relevant to the changing military situation, and
the building was split into at least two separate flatlets.

Now return to the *via principalis* and visit the headquarters
building, which also dates mainly from the third century (3).
It contains the usual courtyard, cross-hall (with *tribunal* to the
right and statue-base to the left) and five administrative

91 Housesteads, the commandant's house

rooms, but it is not well preserved. Behind it is the hospital, the only visible example of its kind in Britain (4). This too was a courtyard building, originally with a verandah which was later demolished when the flagging was laid in the whole central area. The hospital was entered on the west side with the operating theatre occupying the north end. The east wing contains small wards alternating with corridors, but the building is not well preserved here and the doorway arrangements uncertain. The room at the SW corner with a deep stone-lined pit and accompanying drains was apparently for ablutions, and that next to it was a small latrine. Next to the headquarters is a pair of granaries (5), probably third-century in their visible form. One has been marred by the insertion of a post-medieval kiln, but elsewhere the pillars that supported the now-vanished floor may be seen. After the granaries you reach the north wall of the fort. Built up against the back of this is a long base for a staircase up to the rampart-walk and, immediately in front of it and partly buried under it, are the footings of a small square structure (6)

92 Housesteads, fourth-century barrack-block

with a hearth-base. This is turret 36b, demolished about AD
124 when the order came to place forts on the Wall itself. It
will be seen from the position of the turret that Hadrian's
Wall was originally designed to run a little behind its present
course. Now turn right to the north gate (7). Originally a
roadway sloped up to it from outside, but this was removed in
1853 to expose the massive foundations. A water-tank rests
against one of the well-preserved guardrooms. From the NE
corner (8) the Wall can be seen running down to the Knag
Burn, where a customs-gateway, flanked by a pair of
guardrooms, was inserted in the fourth century.

In the NE portion of the fort three buildings are visible, all
of them in their final, fourth-century, state. Nos. 9 and 10 are
barrack-blocks, excavated in 1974–7 (fig 92) and 1959–60
respectively. Both were conventional barracks during the
second and third centuries, with the more spacious officers'
blocks at the east end, but no masonry of these buildings is
exposed. The structures which replaced them in the final phase
were very different, consisting of individual one- or two-

93   Housesteads, the latrine

roomed chalets, most built as free-standing units, although
the more westerly group in no. 9 have party walls. All are
north-facing, but their lengths vary considerably. Many have
flagged floors and benches, and the most easterly
compartment of 9 has an oven, of 10 a hearth. Some were
rebuilt and modified in the second half of the fourth century.
The structure to the south (11) is a long store-building with a
bath-suite inserted at one end. At the east gate (12), note the
deeply-rutted threshold of the north portal; that on the south
was blocked up in the third century and became a guard-
chamber, while the original guardroom became a coal-store.
At the SE corner is one of the most fascinating buildings at
Housesteads, the best-preserved latrine in Roman Britain (13:
fig 93). The soldiers would have sat on wooden seats erected
over the deep sewers on either side, and washed their sponges
– the Roman equivalent of toilet-paper – in the water running
along the gutter in front of them. Two basins were provided
for rinsing their hands. It is a remarkable monument to
Roman hygiene, the level of which was not equalled until the
present century. Continue following the fort-wall clockwise.
The earth rampart originally backing this was partly removed
in the third century to make room for new buildings; at the
same time the fort wall was widened and faced with stone on
the inside too. After passing the south gate and rounding the
SW angle (one oven and part of a second are visible in a
building here), you reach the west gate, still standing to a
spectacular height (14).

The walk along Hadrian's Wall westwards from here is
always a popular one, though other stretches equally fine but
less well known exist elsewhere (especially on Peel Crag and at
Walltown). This stretch is owned by the National Trust,
whose policy is to leave a turf capping on the Wall for the
convenience of visitors. The tremendous views over a vast
tract of the Northumbrian fells make the walk particularly
memorable, but structurally there is not a great deal to note.
After emerging from a picturesque coppice, you will notice a
few offsets on the inside face of the Wall, marking the
junction between different portions of slightly differing widths.
Presumably each building-gang had a different idea about
what was meant to be the exact width of the Wall, and
discrepancies had to be rectified in this manner. Milecastle 37

is soon reached, the work of the Second Legion. The visible stone barrack was matched by another of timber. The north gateway is very fine. The massive masonry of the gate-piers, together with the two springers *in situ* and more voussoirs of the arch lying on the ground, are of Hadrianic date. On the outer side you can see clearly that the gate-jambs have been levered out of the perpendicular. This is usually thought to have been the work of barbarian destruction at the end of the second or the beginning of the third century; but it seems hard to believe that a crowbar-wielding attacker would have paused to be so thorough, nor equally that a Roman demolition-gang would have found it necessary to remove the gateway in this fashion. In position, too, is the Severan stonework which reduced the gateway to a narrow postern. Thereafter, the Wall can be followed over Cuddy's Crag with its famous view to the east, and on over Hotbank Crags (1,074 feet), where Crag Lough comes into view, before it drops down to Milking Gap and milecastle 38 (whence the stone in fig 81 came). No turrets are visible on this stretch. Visitors with cars, of course, will have to retrace their steps to Housesteads.

2½m W of Housesteads on B6318 is the Steel Rigg crossroads where you should turn left. As the road descends, the outlines of two temporary camps can be made out in the field facing you on the other side of the stream. Several examples are known in the Wall region: some were used in training, but these two would have sheltered troops engaged in building or possibly reconstructing the Wall. Next turn left along the Stanegate Roman road (note the stump of a Roman milestone midway between the first and second passing-places on the left) to visit the fort at Chesterholm, now usually known by its Roman name of **Vindolanda*** (NY 7764). The site is open daily from 10 am, closing at 4 (Nov.–Feb.), 5 (March–Oct.), 5.30 (Apr.), 6 (May, June and Sept.), or 6.30 (July and Aug.). Here an ambitious programme of excavation, begun in 1968, has uncovered a substantial part of the civilian settlement (*vicus*) attached to the fort, the only visible example (apart from a few buildings at Housesteads) of a type of village which sprang up round nearly every fort soon after its foundation. The *vicus* at Vindolanda was apparently built as early as *c.* 160, and continued in use to the end of the

third century with at least one break and a major repair in
the second quarter of the third century. Much of the visible
masonry would appear to belong to the second century, but if
so the standard of living here was remarkably high at a time
when the major towns of the province were only just
beginning to have houses built of stone, and many other *vici*
(at least at the forts in the hinterland) remained as a collection
of timber shacks until the late third century.

After passing a well and a water-tank (1 on fig 94), where
the fine upright slabs are deeply scored by knife-sharpening,
aim to the left towards the military bath-house (2). This
stands within a fenced enclosure and is not therefore
accessible, so it is best to observe it from the north side, near
the steps. Its walls are in part extraordinarily well preserved,
standing up to eight feet high. In front of you is the main
furnace-chamber with a stoke-hole which heated the adjacent
hot moist room (*caldarium*). The *tepidarium* lies beyond, with
most of its *pilae* intact, and you can also see the top of the
apsed hot-plunge with its cement lining. A covered drain runs

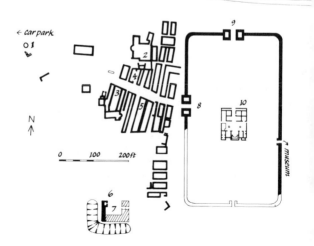

94 *Vindolanda, plan of fort, and civilian settlement*

through the hot room, under the flue, and then curves away. To the left of the hot room is another heated room, with a separate stoke-hole and part of its floor *in situ*; it may have been a hot dry room (*laconicum*). Beyond it is the cold room (*frigidarium*) and a cold plunge-bath. Moving now to your left down the slope you come to a latrine, flushed by the drain already mentioned; it is joined here by another that brought waste water from the cold plunge and passed under a long rectangular room. The latter is interpreted as a changing-room, and, like the latrine, is secondary to the main block of *c.* 160; in the original baths the *frigidarium* no doubt doubled as the changing-room.

Now make towards the paved street which divides the *vicus* into two halves. The first building to the right of the road, labelled 3, is the *mansio*, a hotel for travelling officials and presumably anyone else who could afford it. Before you enter it, note on the right what may have been a small brewery, with two semicircular vats and interconnecting flue heated from a pair of stoke-holes in front. The *mansio* has a paved

95 Vindolanda, the 'corridor-house'

room in the right-hand wing, interpreted as a dining-room because of the adjacent kitchen (with hearth), but it is surely too small for that purpose. A bath-suite at the far end has blackened flue-arches and floors partly *in situ*. The latrine in the middle of the east wing had wooden seats over the sewer surrounding the central block (the floor), but this one was not flushed with running water.

Now cross the road to the house with a central corridor (4), originally one large dwelling, split into two in the late-third-century alterations (fig 95). The triple drains in one room have been interpreted as serving a butcher's shop or something similar. Crossing the road once again you come to the remains of two long strip-buildings (labelled 5), but their interpretation as official married-quarters blocks is not universally accepted: if they belong to the second century they are too early, for soldiers were not allowed to marry legally until the third century. A corn-drying oven in one of them belongs to later houses and workshops now removed. The rest of the structures between here and the west gate contain nothing of interest, so turn southwards to the stone turret, stretch of turf wall, and timber milecastle-gateway which have

96   *Vindolanda, the headquarters building*

been built here (in 1972–4) to give visitors a three-dimensional idea of what the Wall and its works may once have looked like (7). Just before them are two stone-built tombs within walled enclosures (6).

The visible fort at Vindolanda is the product of a complete rebuilding c. AD 223/5, but there is an earlier stone fort below, of Hadrianic date repaired c. 163, and it is to that fort that the attendant *vicus* originally belonged. The earliest forts at the site, however, which went through several phases between c. 85 and 125, lay further west below the visible settlement. Of the third-century fort, the west and north gates (8 and 9 on fig 94), with towers projecting beyond the line of the fort-wall, were excavated and conserved in the 1930's. Go through

** the north gate to examine the outside face of the fort-wall. A crude sculptured tombstone of a young woman, now in the Museum, was found reused in it during consolidation work in 1978. At the NW corner a fine drain-outlet with central dividing upright is visible, and at the NE corner, where the wall stands 7 feet high, two outlets at the bottom discharged from the latrine, located in 1972 but now back-filled. The headquarters building in the centre (10) is excellently preserved, and has many interesting features not visible in the Chesters example (fig 96). A few foundations of the second-century *principia*, which faced in the opposite direction, can be seen here and there, but the visible layout belongs entirely to the third century. Several rooms round a small courtyard in the front half of the building were turned into store-rooms in a major reorganization in the fourth century: parts of their ventilated floors remain, built of stone flags resting on sleeper walls. Beyond is the usual cross-hall with its *tribunal* on the right; the latter still preserves its moulded edge, and the steps leading up to it. Of the administrative rooms at the back, two features are outstanding: the unusual — -shaped pit for storing pay-chests and other valuables; and the ornamental stone screens flanking rooms on either side.

From here you descend to the stream and the charming house which now contains the Vindolanda Museum. The main gallery, the last you come to, has a staggering collection of wood and leather finds which survived in exceptional, waterlogged conditions in the pre-Hadrianic levels below the *vicus*. The leatherware includes a perfect apron-pouch for tools, large fragments of clothing, part of a tent-piece, and above all the huge collection of Roman shoes, including a superb lady's slipper in the centre, complete with maker's name. Note also the rare survival of woven textiles, and the ox-head skulls punctured by holes in target-practice. The woodwork includes pieces of doors, but above all the astonishing writing tablets which have been the most sensational find of the 1973–5 excavations; over 100 bear texts. Some of them are letters of recommendation; some are private letters, one mentioning the dispatch of sandals, woollen socks and two pairs of underpants; others are official accounts, including lists of foodstuffs such as barley, goats' meat, young pig, ham and venison, washed down by wine (both good-quality and 'plonk') and beer. It is hard to overestimate the importance of the information these tablets have so far yielded (which are now all in the British Museum) – about Roman army organization, about clothing and diet, about the private, everyday concerns of the ordinary soldier – quite apart from the light they shed on handwriting and the nuances of grammar and syntax. Since 1985 many more have been found: one refers to *Britiunculi* ('little Brits'), another is a birthday-party invitation from one CO's wife to another. On leaving the museum, walk up to the farm track and turn left: just before the stream is a Roman milestone standing complete and *in situ*, but uninscribed.

   Now return to the B-road and go straight across it and up to Steel Rigg Roman Wall car-park. You then have the choice of going west or east. Westwards, a 15-minute walk takes you up to **Winshields** (NY 7467), the highest point on the Wall (trig-point, 1,230 feet), with spectacular views as far as the Solway on a clear day. At the start the Ditch is rarely better preserved, and the overgrown remains of milecastle 40 are detectable just after the field-gate, but no Wall is visible until a long stretch just before the summit [AM; A]. Eastwards, on **Peel Crag** (NY 7567), there is much more of the Wall to see: it is just as spectacular, and the scenery as fine, as the more famous Housesteads sector. Three offsets will be noted on the inner face of the Wall on the superb level stretch (see p. 296 for an explanation). After 25 minutes you drop down to Castle Nick milecastle (no. 39), the work of the Twentieth Legion. Its gateways are made of small stones, as the usual massive

blocks were probably too awkward to transport to this remote
spot. In the Severan period the gateways were reduced in
width, and this later stonework remains in position at the
south gate.

From Steel Rigg, turn right on to the B-road and then
second right (signposted Whiteside). On the left, between road
and stream, the rampart-mounds of the fortlet of Haltwhistle
Burn are visible, built under Hadrian but only briefly
occupied. On its north side, at the point where the road
swings to the left, is a small temporary camp, right by the
road. Park here, and walk along the track leading straight on.
Immediately on the right, the low defences of another tiny
camp can be made out. Both are too small to have served
other than as training-exercises in camp-building. Next you
cross the Vallum, which is most striking as it stretches away to
the right in a near-perfect state of preservation. Then the
Military Way is clearly visible, laid in the later second century
to link forts and milecastles. Finally you reach the Wall at
Cawfields* (NY 7166) [AM;A]. (If you prefer not to walk the
whole way, follow the road round to Cawfields car-park and
then take the path to the Wall.) Here is milecastle 42, built by
the Second Legion (fig 97). The massive masonry of its south

97   *Cawfields milecastle*

gate stands six feet high, thus preserving the bolt-hole. It is
worth walking eastwards at least as far as the gap at Thorny
Doors, where you should go through the iron gate to admire a
magnificent piece nearly ten feet high, and nowhere higher on
the whole Wall. So steep is the slope here that the foundation
of the Wall must be stepped, for the courses are laid nearly at
right-angles to the lie of the ground. In places such as this,
you can fully appreciate just how tremendous an engineering
achievement Hadrian's Wall is. There is much of interest too
in the stretch from here all the way to the minor road $\frac{1}{2}$m
away. First follow the inside of the Wall, noting the offsets
which mark varying thicknesses of Wall in different stretches
(cf. p. 296). Then cross to the north side at the second stile
after Thorny Doors, and you soon come to a remarkable
stretch where the wall is stepped to ensure great stability (cf.
p. 305). Just before the minor road the foundations of
turret 41a will be reached. This was demolished and the Wall
rebuilt over it in the third century: the line of both the inside
face of the original north wall of the turret and the third-
century masonry filling can be seen, as elsewhere on the Wall
(cf. Coesike, p. 291). This point can also be reached by taking
the turning to Cawburn off B6318.

Return from Cawfields once more to the B-road, turn right
and first right (unsignposted). Keep straight on at the fork,
and after the fifth gate across the road you come to the south
gate of AESICA, **Greatchesters** (NY 7066). A good deal is visible
here – most of the south and west ramparts and their gates,
some barracks and the arch of the underground strongroom
in the *principia* – but the ruins are in a sorry state, overgrown
and neglected. The place is perhaps worth a visit to show how
exposed masonry deteriorates when it is not treated, and to
enable us to admire even more the consolidation work of the
men from the HMBC. Greatchesters would look very different
with a little help from them. The fort was a later addition to
the Wall than most, as it was not built before AD 128. The
main item of interest is its west gate, which alone of all the
gates visible on the Wall still has blocking-walls across both
portals. Excavators at other forts removed such masonry to
expose the thresholds beneath. A six-mile leet brought water
to the fort from the north: parts of it can be traced with the
help of the OS Map of Hadrian's Wall.

Follow the B6318 for another three miles until a signpost to
Walltown* (NY 6766) [AM; A] appears on the right, $\frac{1}{2}$m east
of Greenhead. Follow the HMBC signs. The path leads to a
hollow between the trees, but it is better to climb up the slope
on your right, until you reach turret 45a. This was built as an
independent signalling-tower, probably early in Hadrian's
reign when the Stanegate was still the frontier, and was later
incorporated into the Wall. From here westwards for some
400 yards the Wall is at its very best. First comes a
magnificent dive into one of the Nine Nicks of Thirlwall, and
the effortless climb up the far side (figs 98 and 99). A
'centurial stone' reading COH III can be seen built upside down
into the north face of the Wall, although now nearly illegible:
it is on the bottom course 25 blocks west of a point level with
the HMBC notice (for the implication, see p. 289). Then, still
standing to a stately height of 7–8 feet, the Wall weaves a
sinuous course round whinstone outcrops (fig 100). At one
point where it has to change direction suddenly on a steep
slope, the inner face is 'stepped' slightly to ensure stability.
Finally, this exciting sector is abruptly ended on the edge of a
quarry, which has sadly removed the Wall for $\frac{1}{4}$ mile. If you
have time you may like to follow the Wall eastwards from
turret 45a. Most of it is visible, unconsolidated, all the way to
Greatchesters, but it lacks the grandeur of the Walltown stretch.
Turret 44b, above Walltown Farm, still nine courses high, stands
** unusually in an angle, as the Wall changes direction here.

After Walltown, the dramatic parts of Hadrian's Wall are
past, and you leave the crags for the gentler slopes of
Cumbria. Turn right in Greenhead, and follow the signs for
Gilsland, right along the B6318. Just before the railway-
bridge at the beginning of Gilsland, turn left to the hotel car-
park and visit milecastle 48 at **Poltross Burn** (NY 6366)
[AM; A], the most instructive on the Wall. Both gates were
narrowed in the Severan reconstruction, and the blocking-wall
and pivot-hole are clearly visible at the north gate. There is an
oven at the NW corner and, in the NE, a staircase to the
rampart-walk. The outlines of the two stone barracks survive.
The milecastle was built by the Sixth Legion with broad gauge
wing-walls on either side; one of these can be seen, together
with a fragment of narrow Wall on broad foundation. The
latter feature continues as far as the Irthing.

Go under the railway-bridge, turn left at the junction and stop on the brow of the hill. On your left an HMBC board advertises the sector of Wall in the former vicarage garden of **Gilsland** (NY 6366) [AM; A]. Here it only stands 3–4 feet high, but there is no better place to study the narrow Wall on a broad foundation. The stretch near the railway has some superb drainage-culverts, because of the proximity of a stream, and the first of these (the most westerly) is the culvert through which the stream itself originally passed. Here too it

98   Hadrian's Wall on Walltown Crags, looking west

can be seen most clearly that the narrow Wall does not merely
rest on broad foundation, but on three courses of broad Wall.
It seems that construction of the curtain-wall was actually in
progress here when the order came, in 124 or 5, to reduce the
width of the wall, and rather than demolish what was already
constructed, the builders merely carried the Wall on upwards
at its new width.

On the other side of the road, the Wall is impressively
visible on its broad foundation all the way to **Willowford***
(NY 6266) [AM; A] and the bridge over the Irthing. First
comes an excellent example of a turret (48a) with wing-walls
built to the broad gauge. Nearer the farm a cart-
track runs in the Ditch, and turret 48b is visible. Then comes
the final slope down to the Irthing. The bridge-abutment here
is a very complicated structure displaying work of three
periods. It is less impressive than the example at Chesters.
Starting from the wicket-gate on the north side of the Wall,
you will first see a large masonry embankment which
protected the ground here from erosion by the river. The
latter has now shifted far away. Then come two culverts

99   *The same stretch as it may have appeared, looking east*

which belong to phase II and were probably flood channels for
a river in spate. The recesses for the timbers of the bridge
superstructure, as well as the cramp-holes to bind the stones
together, can be seen in the pier here: they also belong to the
phase-II bridge, after the stone arches of the phase-I bridge had
been removed. Now round the bridge pier and a paved section
of the river-bed. The pier and the parallel abutment, which
blocks one of the culverts, belong to the phase-III bridge of the
third century, which carried the Military Way: the cobbles are
part of its approach ramp, which extended east of (and buried)
the tower. This (built of reused blocks) belongs to the phase-II
bridge of *c*. 140, and the edge of its abutment is represented
by the diagonal line incorporated in the later ramp. A slight
recess in the Wall-face here may represent a staircase-
emplacement of the Hadrianic bridge; the Wall later extended
across it.

Walkers should be able to cross the Irthing and climb up
the bank opposite, now much steeper than in Roman times.
Motorists must return to Gilsland, turn left and left again
after the bridge; then follow the B6318 for about 1¼m until
Birdoswald is signposted on the left. From the car-park ½m
later you can walk along a fine stretch of the Wall to the

100 Another view of the Wall on Walltown Crags

poorly-preserved **Harrow's Scar** milecastle (NY 6266)
[AM; A]. Parts of its walls and one blocked gate are visible,
but most of the stonework inside belongs to a post-Roman
farmstead. The Wall here is narrow on a narrow foundation,
for it was not built in stone until late in Hadrian's reign. It has
an above-average frequency of drainage culverts, and six
examples of centurial stones still in their original positions on
the inside face of the Wall (cf. p. 289). The whereabouts of
each of these, and of two stones with phallic emblems, has
been indicated by a small metal strip near the base of the
Wall. The earlier Turf Wall, which for two miles west of the
Irthing takes a slightly different course to that of the Stone
Wall, is not now visible except for a short sector mentioned
below.

Fifty yards from the car-park is the farm-drive leading to
the fort of **Birdoswald*** (NY 6166) [AM; A]. Its defences are
more interesting and better preserved than those of any other
Wall-fort. On the left of the drive is the NW corner, still
standing over six feet high. Clamber up the bank to have a
look at the angle tower. Its doorway has been blocked,
probably in the fourth century. Some second-century ovens,
often rebuilt, are visible within. After a short break comes an
interval-tower with a flagged floor of Severan date and
blocked doorway. The main west gate still lies buried. Beyond
major excavations (1987–90) are uncovering two well-
preserved granaries and other structures near the centre of the
fort. Continuing along the west rampart you pass the lesser
west gate (single portal) and reach the SW angle. Here is visible
some vivid evidence of the reconstruction sometimes necessary
on Hadrian's Wall due to destruction or decay: the bottom two
courses are probably Hadrianic, the next three (set back a
little, giving a step-like appearance) are Severan, and the top
two are Constantian (or possibly post-Roman). Next comes
the south gate. Both thresholds of the Hadrianic gate,
together with pivot-holes, are visible; the later blocking-walls
have been removed. The irregular masonry of the wall on the
left belongs to a fourth-century rebuilding. Both the flanking
guardrooms have kilns and ovens. Next, it is worth walking to
the edge of the promontory for the view over the Irthing. The
name of the fort, BANNA, which means the 'horn' or 'spur',
must refer to its dominant position overlooking the river.

Now follow the fort-wall round the SE angle. Just after the
gap are more signs of Roman rebuilding: a 20-foot stretch,
with a thin stone bonding-course, is not quite flush with the
rest of the masonry and is built of larger stones. The east gate
is excellently preserved. In both portals remains of
two successive pivot-holes can be seen, probably Hadrianic
and (above) Severan. The massive jamb of the right-hand
(north) portal still stands to its full height and the springer of
the arch is in position. In the fourth century, this portal
became a guardroom, and part of its back wall is still visible.
The door of the original, adjacent guard-chamber was then
blocked up and a new door opened in its south wall, giving
access to the portal now used as a guardroom. At the same
time masonry was inserted between the back and front central
piers. Two rounded window-stones lie on the grass near the
south guardroom, which lies over the site of Hadrian's Turf
Wall. Until the Stone Wall was built on a new alignment,
then, Birdoswald fort projected north of the barrier. Finally, a
stile at the north end of the east rampart, near a post-Roman
kiln, gives access to an interval-tower.

   Westwards from Birdoswald you will get your last view of a
substantial length of Hadrian's Wall. Turret 49b is also
exposed here. Then, ½m later, look out for the first track on
the left (metal gate), with a sign **High House** (NY 6085). Just
after passing through a fence on this track you will see a low
broad mound and accompanying Ditch stretching for a short
distance on the left. This is the only visible fragment of the
Turf Wall. Do not confuse it with the high mounds and ditch
of the Vallum which lie immediately beyond and are a striking
sight in both directions. Return to the minor road and stop
after the slight bend ¾m further on, at the gate on the right at
the top of a slope. The Wall Ditch is boldly preserved here on
your right, but so also is the Turf Wall Ditch which can be
seen over the stone field-wall on the left of the road. The lines
of the Turf and Stone Walls converge a few yards further on
and remain identical, with one short exception, all the way to
Bowness. Soon afterwards, three Turf-Wall turrets will be
passed. These were built of stone from the beginning and the
Turf Wall came right up to either side: when the latter was
replaced in stone, it too stood up against the existing turrets,
and its masonry is never bonded with that of the turrets. First

comes turret 51a, **Piper Sike** (NY 5865) [AM; A], excavated in
1970 and the least well preserved. A flagged platform, usually
thought to have been a clean and dry 'living area' where meals
were eaten, can be seen inside. Turret 51b, **Leahill** (NY 5865)
[AM; A], like Piper Sike, seems not to have been used after
the second century. Finally $\frac{2}{3}$m further west, comes the
imposing turret of **Banks East** (NY 5764) [AM; A]. Unlike the
other two this was occupied into the third century. Here the
plinth that was a characteristic of Turf-Wall turrets is
perfectly preserved on the north, and the stone Wall of
Hadrian abuts on each side. Two hearths and a living-area
platform can be seen within the turret, and a fallen piece of
superstructure lies nearby. The view to the south is very fine.
A path leads eastwards for 100 yards to the single surviving
corner of the tower on Pike Hill which, like the one at
Walltown (p. 305), seems to have been built early in Hadrian's
reign before the Wall was conceived. Despite being so close to
turret 52a, it appears to have continued in use, right into the
fourth century.

Further west, all the way to Bowness, Hadrian's Wall has
little of interest for the visitor. Short stretches of Ditch or
Vallum appear here and there, but the Wall itself has
disappeared completely except for the smallest fragments. One
final stretch may, however, be mentioned. Westwards from
milecastle 54 ($1\frac{1}{2}$m W of Banks East), the Wall remained in
turf until reconstructed in stone perhaps *c.* 200, when the gauge
was neither 10 feet (Broad) nor 8 feet (Narrow) but 9 feet. One
20-yard portion of this Intermediate Wall has been preserved
$\frac{1}{4}$m E of **Walton** (NY 5264) [AM; A], but the friable nature of
the deep red Cumberland sandstone in which it was built
demands a covering of straw and tarpaulins during the winter
months. After Banks East go on to Lanercost Priory (2m),
then turn right (Burtholme) and left at Gathside $1\frac{1}{2}$m later.
The Wall is at Dovecote bridge 1m from this last junction.
The five remaining forts have left little visible trace. That at
Stanwix (NY 4057), now a suburb of Carlisle, was the largest
fort on the Wall. Here was stationed the commander-in-chief
of the Wall garrison and a cavalry regiment 1,000 strong, the
Ala Petriana. The position of this headquarters so near the
western end may seem surprising, but when the 40 miles of
Solway posts, which were an integral part of the Hadrianic

frontier, are included, Stanwix is near the centre of the system.
It is also in this part that the Wall's command of ground
to the north is weakest. In 1984 the footings of the north wall
of the fort were found further north than expected, making the
fort over 9¾ acres in size. A length of 80 feet (24 m.) was
uncovered, including an interval tower; the date was
apparently Antonine, when the fort must have been expanded.
Two short lengths of this curtain wall have been consolidated
and left on display, in the rear of the Cumbria Park Hotel on
Scotland Road, a little to the north of St Michael's Church.
Permission to view should be obtained from the hotel
management. Part of the mound representing the fort's south
rampart is just visible in St Michael's churchyard.

Across the river, at **Carlisle** (NY 3955), lay the flourishing
70-acre town of LVGVVALLIVM, preceded by and incorporating
a series of military structures of which much has been learnt
in excavations prior to redevelopment over the last ten years.
Particularly striking were the timber remains of the south gate
of the earliest, Agricolan fort, which were excellently preserved
in waterlogged conditions. The fort was demolished *c.* 105, but
the finds from a succession of second-century timber buildings
with industrial workings, and from the stone barrack-type
structures put up in their place in the third century, suggest a
continued military presence; Carlisle, like Corbridge, must
have been always a 'garrison town' in the modern sense,
perhaps with separate military compounds as at Corbridge. All
that can be seen, however, of Roman Carlisle today is the
single building exposed in the garden of the Tullie House
Museum. The latter [weekdays Apr.–Sept. 9–6.45, Oct.–Mar.
9–5; Sat., 9–5 (all year); Sun., Jun.–Aug. only, 2.30–5] contains
another impressive display of sculptured and inscribed stones
and of small objects.

Note: this map does *not* mark all the
sites between Risingham and Chew
Green (described pp 315–322) or on
the Antonine Wall (heavy black line
between Forth and Clyde, described
pp 329–340).

Chapter 9

Scotland

and England beyond Hadrian's Wall

1: Between the Walls

Driving into Scotland along Dere Street (A68) is an exhilarating experience. For many miles the modern road sticks resolutely to the Roman alignment, rising and falling dramatically over the hilly terrain. Agricola came this way on his first campaign into Scotland, in AD 80, and Dere Street was constructed in the wake of his advance, probably in 81. Thereafter the route was used by many Roman armies marching into Scotland, and numerous earthworks which they constructed can still be traced today. Apart from the permanent posts, the remains of no less than 14 Roman marching camps are visible on an 18-mile stretch south of the Scottish border, and there is no better place anywhere in the Roman Empire to study this particular class of military antiquity. Unfortunately their dates are less well known than those of the camps further north in Scotland. Some of them are no doubt Agricolan, though only two are proved as such.

For the first seven miles from Corbridge, the A68 does not swerve from the Roman alignment. Then they part company for one mile, taking different routes to cross a stream, before joining forces again for another four-mile stretch. ½m beyond a crossroads signposted Bellingham (left) and Knowesgate (right), the A68 bends sharply to the right and a track marked 'Private Property, Vickers PLC' leaves it on the left. A gate in the field-wall on the left here leads to the temporary camp of **Swine Hill** (NY 9082), which lies immediately in front of you on the other side of a rivulet. Its prominent NE corner is marked by a concrete post, as are all the other corners and the three gateways with their internal *claviculae*: it is therefore easy to trace the outline of this small and well-preserved camp. The west rampart is confused by modern ridges and the south side is rather low, but the north gate is in excellent condition. The camp would have been large enough for about three cohorts, roughly 1,500 men.

Continue along the A68 for another 3m as far as West Woodburn. Within the village, as you descend the hill, you will see a lane on the right signposted 'E. Woodburn 1, Monkridge 4½'. Take the farm-track opposite it, on the left of the A68, and after ½m you will have a good view of the prominent grass mounds which cover the stone ramparts of

HABITANCVM, **Risingham** (NY 8986). Odd pieces of stonework
are still visible, mostly at the west gate and the NE angle, and
there are faint traces of multiple ditches on the south and
west. If you wish to inspect the site more closely, ask for
permission at the farm. Risingham was a permanent fort,
founded not by Agricola but by Lollius Urbicus in the mid-
second century. Little is known of this earliest structure, when
a part-mounted cohort of Gauls was its garrison. The visible
fort, which served as an outpost for Hadrian's Wall, dates
from the early third century. At this time the original fort was
entirely rebuilt with massive defences, including polygonal
projecting towers flanking the south gate. Two fine building-
inscriptions, now in Newcastle, record this work. One of them
is enormously long and fills the whole of the back wall of the
museum. It is dated to AD 213 and records the new garrison as
the First Cohort of Vangiones, brigaded with 'Raetian
Spearmen and the Scouts of Habitancum'. Further alterations
and repairs occurred in the fourth century.

After crossing the Rede, the modern road joins the line of
Dere Street again and follows it, with the occasional
deviation, as far as the next Roman earthwork. This is a
temporary camp called **The Dargues** (NY 8693). One mile
after the A68 is crossed by the B6320, a minor road is
signposted 'Highgreen 4'. Carry on down the slope and over
the burn and you will see two houses facing each other across
the road. Walk northwards along the A68 to the next field-
gate, and from it you will see the east rampart of the Roman
camp clearly visible 20 yards away. Bigger than Swine Hill,
this camp is nearly large enough to hold a legion, but it is in
much worse condition. The east rampart survives only in
short stretches. That on the north is clear but much eroded,
just beyond the line of the wire fence. The west side is low, but
the line of its ditch, marked by dark rushes, is very clear, and
the *clavicula* of a gate can just be seen near the stone wall
dividing this field from the next. The rest of the west rampart
is visible from here, but the whole of the south rampart is
virtually invisible, though the ditch (dark rushes) is clear. The
farm has obliterated the whole of the SE corner.

½m after Dargues the A68 again leaves Dere Street,
swinging away sharply to the right. There is a parking-place
on the left of the road at the bend. Cross the road and look

over the stone wall. You are now at the NW corner of the
Roman fort of **Blakehope** (NY 8594), but very little of it is
visible. Excavation in 1955 showed that its turf rampart had
been burnt down before the reign of Hadrian and never
rebuilt. It may therefore be an Agricolan fort, one of the
praesidia (fortifications) that Tacitus says were built in AD 81
as part of the consolidation of southern Scotland. The dark
reeds clearly mark the position of its single ditch for the whole
of the west and north ramparts, and the causeway leading to
the north gate is marked by a break in the line of reeds. The
turf rampart accompanying this ditch now only survives as a
low broad mound. Do not, incidentally, be confused by the
higher 'ramparts' visible to the left near the telegraph-poles;
these are modern banks connected with drainage ditches.

½m later the Newcastle road (A696) joins the A68. Turn left
and go on for another mile. Shortly after the road passes through
a wooded area, a driveway on the left is closed by a gate
labelled 'Bagraw'; 350 yards after it is a slight lay-by on the
right (metal gate; take care parking). Cross the road, walk back
10 paces and look towards the gap in the stone wall on the far
side of the field. You are now looking along part of the west
rampart of the temporary camp of **Bagraw** (NY 8496), here
visible as a prominent ridge. Most of the rest of its circuit has
been obliterated. The Bagraw camp is rectangular, but
elongated to make it fit on to a narrow shelf of ground. It was
originally big enough to accommodate a full legion, but at
some later stage it was divided into two.

There is not much to see at Bagraw and it is best to press
on soon for another 1½m and visit the fort of **High Rochester***
(NY 8398). This was BREMENIVM or 'the place of the roaring
stream'. There are stone remains visible here, more substantial
than at any other site in Britain north of Hadrian's Wall; and
after the final withdrawal from Scotland, this little post bore
the distinction, if such it was, of being the most northerly
occupied fort of the Roman Empire. It was founded by
Agricola, rebuilt in stone by Lollius Urbicus *c.* 139, and
rebuilt again at the beginning of the third and the fourth
centuries. It was finally abandoned sometime before 325/50.

Just after you have passed the sign announcing the village
of Rochester, turn off to the right by the war-memorial. The
house opposite it has two catapult-balls and several Roman

gutter-stones built into its porch. The road leads up to the
hamlet of High Rochester and the site of the fort. This is
entered by the south gate, of which a few blocks are visible in
the right-hand verge. The rampart-mound is prominent along
the whole of this side, but the stone wall crowning it is
modern. A little to the left of the road, however, the huge
stone blocks of an interval-tower, still six feet high, are clearly
visible. The front side, where the fort-wall originally stood,
has been robbed, and the rear door is blocked. The tower
dates from the last, fourth-century, rebuilding. Park inside the
fort and go through a gate on the left: the track cuts through
the Roman rampart. Turn right and you come almost
immediately to the rather overgrown west gate. The flanking
towers of massive masonry, flush with the fort-wall, make an
impressive sight, and the moulded cap of one of the gate-
jambs as well as a springer of the arch survive. The visible
masonry belongs to the fourth century. Continue walking to
the NW angle of the fort, where more Roman work is visible.
Excavation here in 1935 revealed the foundations of three
superimposed fort-walls, thought to date to AD 139, 205–8, and
297, and two different sizes of stonework are still
distinguishable. Emplacements behind the ramparts were
provided to take artillery, for *ballistaria* are mentioned on two
third-century inscriptions, and these supported the catapults
that hurled the stone balls which you saw built into the porch
by the main road. Now return to the far side of the hamlet,

101 *High Rochester, Roman tomb*

pass through the metal gate across the road (the site of the east
gate), and follow the defences on your left round the NE corner
to the north gate; some blocks of its east jamb are visible. You
can admire the command of terrain from here, and you should
also be able to pick out the entire outline of the Roman
temporary camp of Birdhope (see below). It lies on rough
ground to your left, on the other side of the stream but before
the modern army-huts. In front of you traces of the multiple
ditch-system are still visible. A plan of two-thirds of the fort's
interior was made during excavations in the 1850's, but fresh
work is needed to clarify problems of interpretation and
chronology.

Dere Street, the Roman road you have been following from
Corbridge, skirted BREMENIVM to the east, and lining it 750
yards south of the fort were some monumental tombs. One of
them, known locally as the Roman Well, is still visible. It is
circular and now consists of two courses of large blocks on a
rubble base (fig 101). Originally it must have been an
impressive structure some 15 feet high, probably the resting-
place of an important officer. One of the stones of the lower

102   High Rochester, an inscription (in Newcastle)

course is decorated with the head of an animal, perhaps a fox
and a reminder of the hunting pastimes of the deceased. Two
adjacent tombs are now entirely robbed of their masonry. To
find the spot (which is not easy) go down the road from the
hamlet until you reach the third field-gate on your left. Make
first for the house on the skyline and then continue straight on
for another farm set in front of some trees. Watch out for a
third farm away to your left and the start of a long, low
outcrop of rock away to your right. When you are level with
these two landmarks, turn right and you will find yourself
walking along Dere Street, visible as a low, broad *agger*,
although at first not easy to detect amid the confusion of
modern drainage-ditches and bumpy terrain. Just before
reaching the rocky outcrop, on the right (west) side of Dere
Street, you will see the Roman tomb.

High Rochester, like Risingham, has produced a wealth of
Roman inscriptions. Most of them are in Newcastle, but there
are some in the Durham Cathedral collection, and another is
in Cambridge. One of them, found about 1744, is a well-
preserved and well-executed example of a dedication-stone
(fig 102). Similar inscriptions would have appeared on every
major building, civilian and military, in Roman Britain, and a

103 High Rochester, Venus and nymphs (in Newcastle)

full translation of it will not be out of place: 'For the emperor
Caesar Marcus Aurelius Severus Antoninus Pius Felix
Augustus, Most Great Conqueror of Parthia, Most Great
Conqueror of Britain, Most Great Conqueror of Germany,
high priest, in the nineteenth year of his tribunician power,
twice acclaimed Imperator, four times consul, proconsul,
father of his country, the loyal first cohort of Vardulli,
Roman citizens (CR), part-mounted (EQ), one thousand
strong (∞), styled Antoniniana, built this under the charge of
. . ., the emperor's propraetorian legate.' The building it
adorned is unknown. The date of the stone is AD 216, as we
know the year of the magistracies held by the emperor, who is
here given his full official titles. He is better known as
Caracalla. The inscription also gives the name of the garrison,
and another stone from the site, also in Newcastle, tells us
that they were brigaded with a unit of scouts (*exploratores*):
the Spanish Vardulli cannot have been at anything near their
full strength, for 1,000+ is far too many men to fit into such a
small fort. Yet another inscription, also in Newcastle, came
from the east gate and declares that a *vexillatio* of the
Twentieth Legion (from Chester) built it. Crude figures of
Mars and Hercules flank the inscribed panel. Finally, a
poorly-executed but ambitiously-conceived stone may be
mentioned. It represents Venus and two water-nymphs
disporting themselves in their bath; they seem a little offended
by our presence (fig 103).

On regaining the A68 from BREMENIVM, turn right. If you
want to see a Roman altar (itself well preserved but the
inscription is illegible), take the first track on the right: the
altar is built into the wall near the front door of the last house
on the left of this track. Return once more to the main road
and continue to the end of the village, where you should take
another track, involving a sharp right turn off the A68.
Continue straight along this, avoiding the modern camp, and
park at the metal gate. Keep walking until you see a white-
star marker-post on your left. This is at the SE corner of
Birdhope (NY 8298) temporary camp. The camp is in a fine
state of preservation, its entire circuit being easily traceable by
the lighter colour of the grass growing on the ramparts and by
the white posts which mark its corners. There were three gates
(one on each side except the north) defended by *titula*, but the

latter have nearly disappeared into the bog. The substantial rampart suggests that the troops encamped here were staying for some time. The camp lies within a much larger, earlier enclosure, of which few traces now survive.

The rest of the Roman earthworks along the Northumberland sector of Dere Street lie within the Redesdale army camp, and as the area is used as a firing-range, permission to proceed must be sought from the camp supervisor on arrival (or phone Otterburn 20658 ext. 29 to check in advance). The entrance lies ¾m beyond the turning to Birdhope. Two roads lead north from the centre of the camp (look at the map in the officer's hut if you have no 1:50,000 map of your own). The more westerly passes through the Roman marching camp of Bellshiel (App. I); but it is better to take the eastern road, which winds a little on leaving Redesdale Camp and then joins Dere Street. This it follows, dead straight, for nearly three miles. Soon after joining the alignment, when you are level with the half-way point of the pinewoods on the hill away to the right, you will see four star-markers, at present silver-grey, which stand at the corners of **Sill Burn South** camp (NY 826996). It is small, rectangular and unusually narrow. There are *claviculae* at the north and south gates. Also on Dere Street, a few yards further on (about level with the end of the pinewoods just mentioned), another marker indicates the corner of **Sill Burn North** camp (NY 826999). Like its neighbour it is in good condition, though ploughing has removed the east rampart.

Shortly after this a road goes off to the right to Silloans farmhouse. The point of intersection marks the position of the south gate of **Silloans** camp (NT 823005), but it is the least conspicuous of all the earthworks on this route. As Dere Street passes straight through the north and south gates of the camp and destroys the *titula* which once defended them, and as Dere Street was constructed c. AD 81, Silloans must be one of Agricola's marching camps in his Scottish campaign of AD 80.

Two miles further on, the road bends near a farmhouse. Turn left at the fork just after this. At the next junction, ¾m later, a road goes off on the right to Ridleeshope. A few yards along this is the west rampart of **Featherwood East** camp (NT 8205), the SW corner of which is marked by a rusty star-post to the right of the road. This earthwork measures about 1320 by 1350 feet, and has a gate and *titulum* in each side, but it is now less conspicuous than the Sill Burn camps. Return to Dere Street. After a further ½m, this time on the left of the road, is **Featherwood West** camp (NT 8105). Now difficult to locate, it was slightly larger and less regular than its neighbour, and had five gates.

Soon after the road turns sharply to the left, there is another junction. Turn right here and keep climbing for about 1¼m. When you come over the pass (1,674 feet) you will have a dramatic view of the **Chew Green*** (NT 7808) earthworks on the other side of the valley. They are perhaps more impressive from afar than from closer quarters, for they are extremely complex (see plan, fig 104). As their excavator Sir Ian Richmond wrote, the group 'rewards the connoisseur in such sites rather than someone visiting Roman earthworks for the first time, striking though the first impression can hardly fail to be'. Further complications are added by the much slighter enclosure-banks of post-Roman date: they have also been indicated on fig 104. The sequence of earthworks, established by Richmond in 1936, is as follows. Camp I occupies the best ground and is the earliest construction here. It is an Agricolan marching camp of *c.* AD 80, big enough for a full legion. A few years later a small permanent convoy-post was

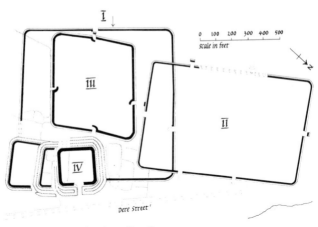

104   Plan of the earthworks on Chew Green

built on the site occupied by the later fortlet (IV), but it is not now visible. The second main phase of activity belongs to the mid-second century. The troops on arrival at the site first built a temporary camp (II) to the north of the main earthworks. They then constructed III, a strong semi-permanent labour-camp. The nature of its occupation is suggested by the more substantial size of its ramparts, still over three feet high, and by the pits and metalled streets which were found inside. The men living in III were engaged on erecting IV, a small permanent fortlet surrounded by triple ditches except on the south. These form the most conspicuous remains at Chew Green. On its south side are two annexes used as waggon-parks, with entrances on Dere Street. This route must have seen heavy traffic during the occupation of Scotland, and the fortlet was clearly designed to house a small force assisting and protecting convoys over the remote moorland.

From Chew Green walkers will be able to follow Dere Street into Scotland to the next site, Woden Law, about three miles to the north. On the way they will pass a Roman signal-station on the summit of Brownhart Law (App. I). The motorist, however, has to make nearly a complete circle to reach Woden Law. Return the way you have come as far as the junction, turn right, and you will eventually reach the A68. Follow this over the Scottish border and ignore the A6088 on the left. You need the first turning on the right three miles further on, signposted Edgerston Tofts and Hownam. At the crossroads four miles later, take the road labelled Hownam and Hindhope. After another mile comes the junction (cattle-grid and wooden building) at the bottom-left corner of the sketch-map (fig 105). Here is another group of Roman temporary camps, the best preserved in Scotland: **Pennymuir** (NT 7514). The largest, camp A, encloses 42 acres and could have accommodated two legions. Its rampart is in an excellent state, 15 feet wide and up to four feet high. The east half of the north side, near the road, is outstanding, and the whole of the west side, with two *titula*, is impressively visible as a light strip of grass contrasting with the dark colour of the surrounding moorland. Most of the south and east sides have been destroyed. Camp B is smaller and later than A. Its west rampart is also well preserved. The defences of C were on a less massive scale and the surviving portion is no

more than one foot high. Camp D has been almost
obliterated.

At Pennymuir you can rejoin Dere Street and motor along
it, through the ford of the Kale Water, to the road-junction
on the other side. From here a 20-minute walk takes you to
the native fort and Roman siege-lines of **Woden Law***
(NT 768125). Go past a mountain-hut until you are level with
the trees away to the left; a steep climb up the hill to your
right will then bring you to the site. The summit of the Law is
crowned with a pre-Roman hill-fort. Its defences were first
built in the early first century AD and were strengthened
before Agricola's invasion (P on inset in fig 105). Surrounding
this fort on all sides except the west is a remarkable, well-
preserved earthwork consisting of two banks and three ditches
(Z). It is at a uniform distance of 70 feet away from the native
ramparts, and excavation has shown that the outer bank of Z
was flat-topped and built on a stone ballast: it has been
interpreted as a support for heavy Roman catapult-machines.
Thus in theory the besiegers would be out of the range of a

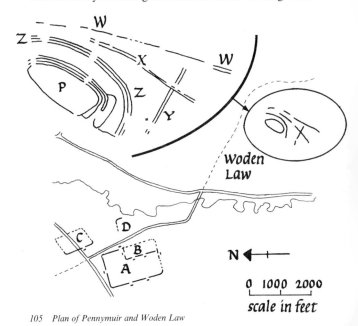

105   Plan of Pennymuir and Woden Law

hand-thrown missile from the native fort, but could themselves bombard the natives. Elsewhere on the hillside are three independent 'siege-lines', W, X and Y. All have been erected in short stretches only, by separate working-parties, and are clearly unfinished. The banks of Z too are not entirely even. Their unfinished nature, the insignificance of the hill-fort and the tactical uselessness of W, X and Y suggested to the excavator that Roman troops, bivouacked at Pennymuir, erected these earthworks at various periods as part of their peacetime training. That may be so, but it is only fair to point out that no Roman pottery has been found and that the 'Roman' ditches lack the usual crisp V-shaped military profile.

We have followed Dere Street into Scotland and seen the many forts and camps that line its route. Its destination was Inveresk on the Forth (App. I), but apart from another marching-camp (Channelkirk, App. I) no further visible remains lie beside it north of Pennymuir. The reason, quite simply, is that Scotland becomes more cultivable, and Roman earthworks have suffered as a result. Brief mention must be made, however, of the site at Newstead on the Tweed. The succession of large and very strongly-defended forts discovered here make it clear that TRIMONTIVM was a major stronghold, the king-pin of the occupation network of southern Scotland. Founded by Agricola _c._ AD 81, it was finally abandoned about 100 years later. Excavations have yielded a remarkable haul of metal tools and weapons, which now fill several cases in the National Museum of Antiquities in Edinburgh. One is a fine late-first-century cavalry parade-helmet (fig 106). There is nothing whatever to see at Newstead today, except for a commemorative stone erected in 1928 beside the B6381, 1¾m east of Melrose. But the beautiful back-drop of the triple Eildon Hills which gave the fort its Roman name makes a visit to the site worth while. The most northerly hill (1,327 feet) is crowned by a native hill-fort, in the centre of which is a Roman signal-station (App. I).

Two other sites in the eastern half of southern Scotland are worth a brief mention, Lyne and Castle Greg. The fort at **Lyne** (NT 1840), near the upper reaches of the Tweed, lay on an east-west road linking Newstead with the western trunk route. 5m west of Peebles on the Glasgow road (A72) is the junction with the B712 to Broughton. Half a mile beyond this,

watch out for the houses lining the road on the right (Hallyne
Cottage); you want the track immediately before these, to
Lyne Church. Park where the track ends, facing the church.
The fort lies behind you, 200 yards beyond (west of) the trees.
There is not a great deal to see here. The rampart has been
nearly levelled by agriculture, but survives as a bold mound at
the NE, NW and SW corners and as a ridge along the west
side. Of the ditch-system only the outer ditch on the east and
south sides is visible today. This was originally V-shaped but
is now flat-bottomed. Its edges are lined by two surprisingly
well-preserved mounds, formed by piling up the earth
excavated from the ditch. The causeway leading to the site of
the east gate is also notable. The central buildings of this fort
were of stone, but the rampart was of turf only. Excavations
in 1901 and 1959–63 revealed that it was built c. AD 158 and
occupied for only a few years. It is, however, only one of a
series of Roman works in the vicinity. There was a tiny fortlet
160 yards to the north, two temporary camps to the east, and
an Agricolan fort of c. AD 81 on a bold eminence at Easter
Happrew, ½m east-south-east on the other side of Lyne Water.
All these are normally invisible from the ground, but a crop-
mark of the north rampart of the Agricolan fort can
sometimes be seen from the second-century site in especially
dry summers.

Castle Greg (NT 0459) in Midlothian is among the best-
preserved examples of a Roman fortlet in Britain. It probably
dates from the later first century. Measuring just 150 feet by
180 feet, the single earth rampart and double ditches of this
convoy-post are in perfect condition. The only entrance is in
the east side. It lies 3m SE of West Calder, on the east side of
the B7008, ⅜m north of its junction with the A70. Watch out
for a conspicuous hollow about 10 feet deep bordering the
east side of the B-road, and a wide firebreak in the forest on
the west of the road about 75 yards further south. The Roman
earthworks lie on the skyline to the east between these two
points, about five minutes trek away through long grass and
bog.

Roman earthworks in the western part of southern
Scotland fall into two distinct categories. The most accessible
sites, such as the camps at Cleghorn and Little Clyde and the
fort at Castledykes, are so poorly preserved that they do not

** warrant detailed description, and are therefore listed in
Appendix I. On the other hand, three earthworks in superb
condition lie in very remote areas, and 1:50,000 OS maps and
a deal of patience are needed to track them down. These are
Redshaw Burn in Strathclyde, and Durisdeer and
Raeburnfoot in Dumfries and Galloway (all in App. I). The
first two are Antonine fortlets like Castle Greg, their single
gates defended by *titula*. Raeburnfoot consists of a fortlet
inside a larger enclosure, both apparently Antonine. NE of
here, on high moor between Eskdale and Borthwick Water, a
remarkable stretch of Roman road can be followed for about
6½m. In places the Roman engineers cut through the peat to
the natural rock and used that as the road-surface. On Craik
Cross Hill it passes the site of a possible signal-station (App. I).

106 Newstead, a parade-helmet (in Edinburgh)

Two sites near Hadrian's Wall can conveniently close this section on southern Scotland. Just as the eastern half of the Wall had outlying forts at Risingham and High Rochester (though a later addition to the original Hadrianic scheme), the western end was also protected by a series of advance-posts of which Bewcastle in Cumbria (App. I) was one and **Birrens** (NY 2175) in Dumfries and Galloway another. The latter, BLATOBVLGIVM, was founded by Agricola and also occupied under Hadrian. The visible fort was first constructed about 142, when the garrison was the first cohort of Nervii from the Rhine, but it was burnt down and rebuilt in 157/8. This we know from an inscription, now in Edinburgh's Museum of Antiquities, which also records a different Rhenish regiment, the second cohort of Tungrians, as its garrison. It was finally given up in the 180's. There is not much to see at Birrens today, but the rampart survives as a bold mound on all sides except the south, where the stream has eroded it, and there are faint traces of a system of ditches on the north. Turn northwards for Eaglesfield off the A74 at its junction with the B722, 7m NW of Gretna Green, and then immediately left for Middlebie. After one mile the minor road crosses a river-bridge and the fort lies on the left just beyond it.

Much more interesting than Birrens are the nearby practice siege-camps of **Burnswark*** (NY 1878). Continue on into Middlebie, turn left and keep going for $1\frac{1}{4}$m, over the stream, until the road makes a 90° turn to the left, $\frac{1}{2}$m before Ecclefechan. Turn right here (not signposted) and keep straight on for two miles. When the metalling ceases, take the right fork and park when the wood on your left ends. A field-gate here leads immediately to the SW corner of the first (south) Roman camp. This is in an excellent state of preservation. The entire, roughly rectangular, circuit can be traced with ease. The gates in the middle of the south, east and west sides are protected by normal-sized *titula*, but the three entrances on the north are shielded by enormous mounds, known locally as The Three Brethren. They were built to support the Roman catapult machines which were used in assaulting the native hill-fort on the prominent summit ahead. Excavations here at the turn of the century found 67 Roman lead sling-bolts, and it was then believed that a real attack did indeed take place. More recent work,

however, in 1967–70, has shown that the native ramparts
(now largely invisible) were not standing when the bullets
were fired, and it is clear that the 'attack' was only a training-
exercise. In the NE corner of the Roman camp is a small
fortlet, of mid-second-century date, and excavation has shown
that the camp was built after it. From the native fort at the
top you can see the outline of another Roman camp on the
north side of the hill. This is unfinished and it too must have
been built for practice, as it is too far below the native fort to
have served any useful purpose in its bombardment. From the
top too you can admire the spectacular views in all directions,
and on a clear day Hadrian's Wall is visible.

2: The Antonine Wall

While the great Wall of Hadrian is a familiar monument,
especially to the many thousands who trek its course each
year, it is not so well known that the Romans built another
frontier-barrier in these islands, nor that substantial stretches of
it still survive. Almost immediately after the death of Hadrian
in 138, the new emperor Antoninus Pius ordered a fresh
advance in Britain and the building of another wall, this time
entirely of turf. The literary evidence is confined to a single
sentence: 'he (the emperor) conquered the Britons through
Lollius Urbicus the governor and after driving back the
barbarians built another wall, of turf (*muro caespiticio*).'
Archaeological evidence shows that the campaign was already
planned in 139 and completed by 142/3, when a coin depicting
Britannia, much as she appears on our own coinage, was
minted (fig 107). The reason for building another wall, apart

107 Britannia on a coin of AD 142/3

from the emperor's desire to win military prestige, was
apparently trouble in southern Scotland, but of the details we
know nothing. At any rate Hadrian's Wall was evacuated,
and the whole of southern Scotland refortified and
regarrisoned.

The Antonine Wall is a much simpler structure than the
Hadrianic frontier. It ran for 37 miles from Bridgeness on the
Forth to Old Kilpatrick on the Clyde. The Wall had a stone
foundation 14 feet wide, on which rows of cut turves were laid
to a height of nine feet. The sides of the turf Wall sloped
inwards, so that it was only about six feet wide at the top, on
which was built a timber patrol-walk about five feet high. On
the north the Wall was accompanied by a massive ditch 40
feet wide and at least 12 feet deep. On the south ran a military
service-road.

The frontier was manned, like Hadrian's Wall, by men from
the auxiliary cohorts of the Roman army, though small
numbers of legionaries also seem to have been stationed on it.
They were housed in 19 forts (15 identified) attached to the
south side of the Wall at roughly two-mile intervals. These
were defended by turf ramparts, except for two examples
which had stone walls. Barracks were of timber, but the
central range of buildings usually had stone foundations. It
used to be thought that these forts were all part of a single
plan, and that their close spacing made a complete system of
milecastles and turrets as on Hadrian's Wall most unlikely,
but in 1975 John Gillam suggested that the original scheme
was to have only half a dozen forts about 8 miles apart and a
system of fortlets between each. Nine milecastle-type
structures, five of them found only in 1977–80, are now known,
and two of them were replaced by forts at a later date: so some
of the forts at least are secondary to the original Antonine Wall
plan. But it may be too early to talk of a complete 'milecastle
scheme' for the northern Wall, and although signalling towers
formed an integral part of most frontier-systems elsewhere in
Europe, only six signalling-platforms ('beacon-stances') about
18 feet square have been recognized on the ground and two or
three more are suspected from aerial photographs.

The Wall itself, and some at least of the forts, were built by
detachments from all three of the British legions. Their work
is attested by 18 stone tablets or 'distance-slabs'. Each

construction party would have set up one of these at the beginning and the end of its allotted stretch. A particularly fine example was ploughed up in 1969 (fig 108). The inscription, spread out over different portions of the stone, reads: 'For the emperor Caesar Titus Aelius Hadrianus Antoninus Augustus Pius, father of his country, a detachment of the Twentieth Legion Valeria Victrix built 3,000 feet.' In the centre is a Roman standard-bearer bowing in respect to the personification of the province of Britain, who is putting what may be a victory-wreath into the beak of the eagle on the standard. On either side is a grotesque portrayal of an ancient Briton, as seen through Roman eyes. Each kneels in captivity, his hands tied behind his back. Below is the running boar, the symbol of the legion. This splendid stone is now in the Hunterian Museum of the University of Glasgow, along with many other finds from the Wall and all but two of the distance-slabs (Mon.–Fri. 9.30–5, Sat. 9.30–1). The Bridgeness stone, which marked the eastern end of the Wall, is housed in

108   Antonine Wall, a distance-slab (in Glasgow)

the Royal Museum in Queen Street, Edinburgh, where the
Newstead collection (see p. 325), a Roman silver hoard from
Traprain Law, and many other important finds from Roman
Scotland are also displayed (Mon.–Sat. 10–5, Sun. 2–5).

A few words must be said about the fortunes of the new
frontier. It has long been known that there were certainly two
separate occupations of the Antonine Wall, but the precise
dating of these has been a subject of constant dispute. The
length of the first occupation was about 13 years, for a serious
crisis in north Britain in 155 caused the frontier to be
temporarily abandoned, and its forts were dismantled before
withdrawal. By about 159 the situation was calm enough to
allow reoccupation, but about 163 the Antonine Wall was
again abandoned, probably after enemy destruction, and
Hadrian's Wall was fully recommissioned. This dating, based
largely on a study of samian pottery, means that Antoninus'
massive engineering work had an active life of less than 20
years. Previously the second occupation was thought to have
ended *c*. 185, but in either case the Antonine Wall and the
attendant reoccupation of Scotland must be regarded as a
failure. There are traces at a few of the Wall-forts of a
mysterious third occupation, and it may have been the
intention of the emperor Severus, who campaigned in north
Scotland in 208/9, to reoccupy the Antonine Wall; if so, the
plan came to nothing.

Though the more northerly frontier was less than half the
length of Hadrian's Wall, it was flanked by deep estuaries
which had to be guarded. Little is known at present about
posts at the western end, but on the east there were forts at
** Carriden, very close to Bridgeness, and at Cramond and
Inveresk (App. I). **Cramond** (NT 1977) is now a delightful
village about 6m west of the centre of Edinburgh and 1½m
north of the A90. The fort built here about 142 shows the
same history of an evacuation and a later destruction as the
Antonine Wall. This is not surprising, for its harbour
provided a good anchorage for transport-ships and Cramond
no doubt became a supply-depot for the Wall, much as South
Shields served Hadrian's Wall. Unlike forts on the barrier, it
was thoroughly repaired and reorganized at the beginning of
the third century, when it was a base for Severus' Scottish
campaigns. Even after his withdrawal, the fort and civilian

settlement were still inhabited. One stretch of wall, which belongs to a workshop built under Severus, is still visible, and the outlines of many other buildings within the fort have been marked out and labelled. The site, excavated in 1956–61, lies on the north side of the church and is reached by the driveway to Cramond House, on the right of the road before it descends steeply to the harbour. Beside the car-park near the Cramond Inn the fort's bath-house, part of it standing over 6 feet high, was excavated in 1975–6, but has been back-filled through lack of funds for consolidation and display. A civilian settlement east of the fort has also recently been located. At the harbour a pedestrian ferry (daily except Friday) and a 10-minute walk along the seashore on the other side will bring you to Eagle Rock [AM; A], which juts out on to the beach. On its east face, now protected by a grille, a figure standing in a niche has been cut out of the natural rock. It is now very worn, and all details have been obliterated. When first discovered the carving was thought to represent an eagle, but it is more likely to be a figure of Mercury, protector of travellers. It was probably cut by Roman soldiers to bring good luck to ships entering and leaving Cramond harbour.

Whereas the Antonine Wall itself has suffered badly over the centuries from cultivation and now only remains in a very few places, the great Ditch is a more formidable obstacle to the plough and it often survives impressively in places where the Wall has completely disappeared. A substantial portion of the Ditch near the eastern end of its length is visible in

** **Callendar Park** (NS 8979), beyond the greensward on the south side of the A803, $\frac{1}{2}$m east of the centre of Falkirk. It is about six feet deep and can be traced here for $\frac{1}{3}$m. Far more impressive is the stretch at **Watling Lodge*** (NS 8679) [AM; A], one of the outstanding remains of the Antonine frontier (fig 109). Here the Ditch survives in something like its original dimensions, some 40 feet wide and 15 feet deep, and gives a magnificent impression of the formidable nature of this man-made obstacle. To reach it, turn off the A803 in Camelon, 1m west of Falkirk, along the B816 to High Bonnybridge (Union Road). Go left over the canal, then right at the T-junction and first right along Lime Road. The Ditch lies behind trees on the left of this road.

Now continue along the B-road, which twists to the left and

so crosses the line of the Wall. Turn right at the next crossroads. On your left, by a sign reading 'Ancient Monumet (*sic*): No Dumping of Rubbish', there begins the picturesque stretch running through **Tentfield Plantation** (NS 8579). Here both Wall and Ditch survive in fine condition and they can easily be followed, though much overgrown with bracken and trees, as far as the railway-line one mile away. Two beacon-stances survive in this portion, but they are difficult to spot. They consist of slightly raised mounds projecting from the back of the Wall. One lies opposite the entrance to Rowan Crescent, the other 50 yards east of the railway. Beyond, the Roman frontier can be traced all the way to Rough Castle, but it is more convenient to approach the latter from the west. Continue, therefore, along the B816 to High Bonnybridge, and turn right towards Bonnybridge. Immediately before crossing the Forth-Clyde canal, you should take a lane on the right, signposted Rough Castle. (If you are coming from the north, leave the A803 in Bonnybridge, cross the canal and turn first left.) Soon after

109   Antonine Wall-Ditch at Watling Lodge

crossing the railway, the road, now untarred, bends to the left. Stop at the mesh-work gate on the left and walk back 18 paces. The large mound which you will see projecting from the back of the Antonine Wall almost as far as the stone wall is a beacon-stance.

From here onwards both Wall and Ditch survive in superb condition all the way to Rough Castle. Just before the track turns left to the AM car-park, opposite the third iron gate on the right (counting from the last stop), is the most conspicuous of all the beacon-stances on the Antonine frontier. Excavation revealed its stone foundation, 18 feet square, and heavy burning indicated the use of beacon-fires for long-distance signalling. All four stances near Rough Castle have good command of the only known Roman road running beyond the Wall to outpost forts in the far north, and they probably received and transmitted messages from and to this road.

At the car-park there is a spectacular view of the Ditch and the Wall, which is here five feet high and nowhere in a better state of preservation (fig 110). Then a short walk, down to the stream and up the other side, leads to the fort of **Rough Castle*** (NS 8479) [AM; A]. It is a very tiny post, occupying only about one acre, but the earth rampart and ditches are very well preserved on all three sides, and so are the Antonine Wall and Ditch which form its north front. A few overgrown traces of the stone buildings excavated in 1902–3 can be seen in the middle of the fort; they include a small office-building and a granary. The post was garrisoned by men from the sixth cohort of Nervii (from the Lower Rhine) under the command, unusually, of a centurion from the Twentieth Legion, one Flavius Betto. To the east was an annexe, also defended by rampart and ditches, and one of the buildings here was the fort bath-house. North of the fort, 20 yards beyond the Ditch, a remarkable find was made of ten rows of small defensive pits. These, described as *lilia*, or lilies, by Roman military writers, were given pointed stakes and then covered with brushwood and leaves. The idea was to deceive an approaching enemy into thinking the ground was solid, and to capitalize on the resulting confusion. A few rows of these pits have been left open.

Return now to Bonnybridge and turn left along the south

side of the Forth-Clyde canal (B816). After ⅓m, soon after the houses stop, a blue board announces the **Seabegs Wood** stretch (NS 8179) [AM; A]. Both Wall and Ditch are well preserved here, though somewhat overgrown. Another 1½m will bring you to the complicated road-junction at Castlecary. Where B816 crosses the A80, turn left along the road signposted Walton, and then immediately left. Park by the school where an AM notice and plan help you to locate what little remains of **Castlecary** fort (NS 7978) [AM; A]. Part of the west and east ramparts survive as low ridges, and a hollow near the fence with a few stone blocks represents the site of the north gate. This was one of only two forts on the Wall equipped with stone defences. Avoid the dual-carriageway of the A80 and continue along the B816 for another ¾m. Then turn right (signposted Wardpark North) and stop when the road bends. Here it crosses the line of the Antonine frontier at **Tollpark** (NS 7777) [AM; A], as announced by two AM sign-boards. The Wall is not visible here, but the Ditch survives on both sides of the road. Westwards it is in very good condition and can be followed for two miles to Westerwood fort (App. I) and beyond, until it is interrupted by the railway-line. Further west, on both sides of Croy Hill, the Ditch again becomes visible, but this portion is best approached from the west.

From Tollpark continue northwards, cross the canal and

110 Antonine Wall and Ditch near Rough Castle

turn left along the A803. In Kilsyth take the B802 for Airdrie. After crossing the canal again and climbing the hill, turn left for Croy village and then first left and first right. Park by the disused quarry and you come at once to the beginning of the Ditch on **Croy Hill** (NS 7276) [AM; A], which continues to remain impressively visible for nearly $1\frac{1}{2}$m. Here too is a particularly good position from which to admire the fine command of the Wall over ground to the north, since the view, for once, is not obstructed by trees, electricity pylons or factory chimneys. The line chosen was on the northern slope of an almost continuous range of hills. This enabled the Wall to dominate completely the broad depression now drained by the Forth-Clyde canal, and still to be at a safe distance from the loftier hills on the horizon. The path follows the line of the Wall, here almost entirely denuded, but two closely-spaced signalling-platforms are visible 150 yards from the start of this stretch. The first is crossed by the path half way up the first ascent (in 1978 it was an oasis of grass amid the dense surrounding bracken), and the second lies on the flat ground where the path levels off before climbing again. Then the Ditch, here hewn resolutely from the solid rock, swings down and away to the left (don't be misled by the natural, wider, crevice which goes straight on), and it can be followed, round the projecting crags, as far as the point where tumbled remains of rock interrupt its course. Then comes an 80-foot stretch where the Ditch-diggers gave up in despair at the hardness of the rock. On the summit of Croy Hill, 470 feet above sea-level, and one of the highest points of its course (cf. Winshields on Hadrian's Wall, 1,230 feet), a fortlet was located in 1977 (see p. 330), and 50 yards to the east a fort-site has long been known, but nothing can be seen of either on the ground. Thereafter the Ditch is excellently preserved, 40 feet wide and 8 feet deep, as far as Dullatur station.

   Now return to B802 and turn right. The next stretch, on Bar Hill, is signposted at the first lane on the left, but for motorists a western approach is more convenient. Cross the canal again and turn left for Twechar. At the beginning of the village turn left again over the canal; Bar Hill is signposted 200 yards further on, on the left. Park here and walk along the rough road which leads up to the fort at **Bar Hill***
(NS 7075) [AM; A] (follow the direction-arrow). First

excavated in 1902–5, the fort has received fresh examination in recent years, and the re-excavation and consolidation of the bath-house (1978) and the headquarters building (1979–82) now make this the most instructive fort-site visible on the Antonine Wall. An information board here gives salient details of the fort's history and layout. The HQ follows the usual tripartite division into courtyard, cross-hall with *tribunal* and rear rooms (here three in number), of which the central one as usual was the regimental chapel, with stone-lined strong-box below. The well in the courtyard caused much excitement when excavated in 1902: it contained coins, arrowheads, a wooden bucket and pulley-wheel, two inscriptions and column-shafts together with their capitals and bases – vivid evidence of the systematic demolition of the fort, presumably on the final withdrawal of the garrison in the 160's. The stone granaries and workshop (?) in the central range, and the timber barracks elsewhere, have not been re-excavated, but over the slope are the fragmentary remains of an elongated, rectangular bath-house which lay in the NW corner of the fort. The Antonine Wall is exceptional in having several examples of bath-houses built within the fort defences, a feature normally found in Britain only in the fourth century (cf. Caernarfon, p. 215). Unlike the other known forts, Bar Hill is detached from the Antonine Wall, whose Ditch is clearly visible 60 yards to the north. The turf ramparts of the fort, less impressive than at Rough Castle, are clearest on the west and east sides, and were broken by four timber gateways. There were double ditches on all sides except the north, and the causeways at the east and south gates were protected by *titula*, not usually found in permanent structures (cf. p. 9). Two garrisons are known, the First Cohort of Baetasians (later at Reculver) and the First Cohort of Hamii from Syria, indicating that a change of garrison occurred in the second occupation of the Wall. Both were infantry units 500-strong.

Further west Wall and Ditch have left no substantial remains for the rest of their course, except for four short sections of the stone Wall-base which have been preserved near its western end. The two longest can be seen in **New Kilpatrick Cemetery** (NS 5572), which lies on the north side of the B8049 (Boclair Road), ½m east of its junction with the A81 in Bearsden. Each has a drainage-culvert

running across it, and one has a 'step' in it to ensure stability
for the turf superstructure. From New Kilpatrick Cemetery,
go straight across the A81 at the traffic-lights, then turn left at
a junction and go on up the slope. Almost at the top, on the
right just after Grange Road, is a Roman bath-house excavated
in 1973–5, which has been on permanent display since May
1982 [AM; A]. This lay in a separately defended annexe
immediately east of the fort at **Bearsden** (NS 5472), now under
a housing-estate. The bath-building is a much more intelligible
and better-preserved structure than the one inside the fort at
Bar Hill; in places it stands 8 courses high and substantial
portions of stone flagging and cement floors survive. Very
unusually both the central cold room (*frigidarium*) and the
changing-room were built of timber (presumably to
economize), but the heated rooms were stone-built as the
steam would soon have warped wood. The bather entering the
frigidarium had the semicircular cold plunge-bath on his right
and a hot-dry room (*laconicum*) with channelled hypocaust on
his left. Straight ahead were three small heated chambers
(*tepidaria* and *caldarium*, with *pilae* supporting the floors) and
** a hot-water bath attached to the last. The 2¾-acre fort had
buildings entirely of timber except for two buttressed
granaries, but it appears not to have had an HQ or quarters
for a full garrison. Like the bath-house it seems to have been
used only in the first occupation of the Antonine Wall
(*c.* 142–158) and not later. Now continue westwards and turn
right at the traffic-lights. Just after A809 branches off to the
right (Drymen), go first left (Whitehurst), second right, first
left and first right (Iain Road). The steps near the end of this
road on the left, lead up to a small piece of stone base at **West
Bearsden** (NS 5372), exposed in 1964 with an accompanying
Ditch-section (now backfilled). Finally, the tiny fragment
exposed on the western slope of Golden Hill, **Duntocher**
(NS 4972), may be mentioned, as it is the most westerly piece
of the Antonine frontier still visible. Turn south off the A810
at the roundabout in the eastern outskirts of Duntocher,
along A8014. After the right-hand bend, as the road twists to
the left, turn right at the filling-station (Milton Douglas
Road) and follow this (it becomes Roman Road) until just
after a church on the right. A gate here leads to Golden Hill
and a railed-off portion of Wall-base, including a culvert.

Excavations on top of the hill in 1948–51 revealed that an
Antonine fortlet preceded a very small fort here. In view of
recent speculation about the planning of the Antonine frontier
(p. 330), the fortlet's stone foundations, which served to
stabilize the turf rampart above, were re-exposed in 1978;
they have however been backfilled, no trace of fort or fortlet
being now visible. The fortlet had been demolished and
replaced by the fort even before the actual Wall was built in
this sector, and it may be presumed that the latter was built
from east to west. The same conclusion was reached when the
terminal fort at Old Kilpatrick, now built over, was excavated
in 1923–4 and 1931.

3: Romans in the far north

Though Scotland north of the Antonine Wall never strictly
became part of the Roman Empire, military campaigns were
carried out here on a number of occasions, and these have left
their traces in the form of marching-camps, forts, fortlets and
signal-towers. Our knowledge of Roman operations in the
area has been vastly increased since the last war by excavation
and by the aerial discoveries of Professor Kenneth St Joseph
of Cambridge University. The majority of the earthworks
seem to be the work of either Agricola (AD 83–5) or the
emperor Severus (AD 208–11). Other generals campaigned
north of the Forth-Clyde isthmus, including Lollius Urbicus
in 142/3 and Constantius Chlorus in 306 (and possibly Ulpius
Marcellus *c*. 186), but their camps have not been located. It is
not, however, the shadowy records of these invasions, or even
Severus' punitive expeditions, which capture our imagination,
but the great campaigns of Julius Agricola in AD 83 and 84.
Here is a man who still lives for us in the pages of Tacitus,
and at last archaeology is starting to clothe with specific forts
and camps the bare narrative handed down to us. As a result
we can begin to understand Agricolan strategy a little better.
He had no intention of entering the Highland mass; the
valleys leading from this were carefully blocked by forts at
Drumquhassle, found only in 1977 (Loch Lomond), Malling
(Lake of Menteith), Bochastle (pass of Leny), Dealgin Ross
(Strathearn), Fendoch (Sma Glen) and Inchtuthil (Dunkeld
Gorge). The idea was to prevent the Highland tribes from

breaking into Strathmore and using that as the base for
inevitable attacks further south. Strathmore and Strathearn
were themselves carefully protected by a line of forts, no
doubt linked with harbour installations on the east coast
which still await discovery. But this grand plan was never
allowed to be brought to fruition. Agricola was recalled in
84/5 and the emperor Domitian soon ordered withdrawal,
though this was only partial at first. Tacitus bitterly comments
that 'Britain was thoroughly subdued and then immediately
let slip' (*perdomita Britannia et statim omissa*).

   Not a great deal survives on the ground of the Agricolan
and later earthworks, as they lie in a fertile part of Scotland
which has been intensively cultivated, and most of our
knowledge is derived from aerial reconnaissance and
excavation. The outstanding visible site is the fort at **Ardoch***
(NN 8309), which was founded by Agricola, but the visible
remains date from 142/3 when it became an outpost fort for
the Antonine Wall. And what remains there are! Ardoch is
one of the most spectacular sights of Roman Britain, but not
in the way that Chedworth or Pevensey are. There is not a
scrap of stonework to be seen at Ardoch today: instead it is
the system of multiple ditches, surviving on the north and east
sides of the fort, which bears vivid witness to the presence of
Romans in the far north, and shows above all the steps they

111   Ardoch, fort-ditches on the east side

were prepared to take in order to provide a defensible position in an area known to be hostile.

To reach Ardoch, turn off the A9 11m north of Stirling, along the A822 for Crieff. After 1½m you reach the village of Braco, where the road bends to cross the river Knaik. Park on the right immediately after crossing the river and climb over the fence near the gatepost at the beginning of the track. Walk northwards and you will soon come to the NW corner of the fort. From here you can see the whole of the north rampart of the fort and the five ditches defending it. Not all of these are of the same date, as the fort was originally slightly longer on this north side and its rampart was protected by just three ditches, now the outermost. In fact the north rampart of this earlier fort, and especially its NW and NE corners, are still prominently visible between the second and third ditches (counting outwards). When the fort was reduced in size, two further ditches were dug in the deserted end of the larger enclosure. The date of this alteration is not certain, but all the **ditches probably belong to the Antonine period. Nothing can be seen of the Agricolan fort which lies below, but pottery belonging to it was found in the excavations of 1896–7. A tombstone now in Glasgow (Hunterian Museum) informs us that at some stage the First Cohort of Spaniards was the garrison here.

From the north gate you can either follow the ditches round to the east side or else cut across the interior of the fort to the break in the east rampart. Here the defences are even more staggeringly well preserved than those on the north (fig 111). The fort rampart is high and bold, and the causeway striding magnificently up to the east gate is the only break in the superb quintuple ditches. Here it is the outermost two which have been added later.

Ardoch provided an admirable camping-ground, and it is not surprising that five different temporary camps are known immediately north of the fort. A 13-acre camp and a subsequent enlargement to one of 30 acres were the work of Agricola. Both were overlapped by a 63-acre camp, to which a small annexe was added. Then a camp of 130 acres was constructed, overlapping all the other works on the site. The 130-acre earthwork is probably Severan (AD 208/9), and possibly also the 63-acre one, although it would be surprising if there was no Antonine activity here while the adjacent fort was being built and occupied. The only substantial visible fragment of all these encampments belongs to the west side of the 130-acre enclosure. Continue northwards along the A822 for ½m and take the B827 to Comrie. After 220 yards, just before the electricity sub-station, the road cuts through the camp, and 300 yards of overgrown rampart, with a gate and *titulum* at the far end, can be seen running away to the right. Parts of the east side of this camp can be traced with the help of a large-scale map (see Bibliography).

Six miles NE of Ardoch lay another fort, Strageath, which was also an Agricolan foundation reused as an outpost fort of the Antonine Wall (not visible). Between the two lies a smaller post, the fortlet known as **Kaims Castle** (NN 8612). The A822 is straight for 1m north of Ardoch. 1¼m after it swings to the right, and just before a minor road leaves it on the left, you will see two houses facing each other across the road (that on the right is named Kaimes Lodge). The impressively preserved earthworks of the Roman fortlet lie behind the house on the left and are reached through the adjacent field-gate. The enclosure is about 80 feet square and surrounded by a circular ditch. A single entrance faces the road. Excavation in 1900 produced no secure evidence of date, but the fortlet probably belongs to the Antonine period. It probably succeeded an Agricolan post, however, and the site is now known to have been linked to the fort at Ardoch by means of three signal stations, also first-century; another N of Kaims suggests a link also with Strageath, which guarded the western end of a remarkable group of Roman signal-stations on the **Gask Ridge** (NN 9118 to 0220). No less than 11 are known on an 8-mile stretch of Roman road, followed by the modern minor road which leaves A9 5m west of Perth (signposted Kinkell Bridge 8). Most of them are now ploughed-out or totally obscured by undergrowth, but three are relatively easy to locate. After leaving A9 continue westwards for 1¾m until, after a bend to the left and then one to the right, a track goes off on the left at the top of the hill. The first signal-station (no. 1 in the series) lies on the right of the road, opposite this: it is the more westerly of the two knolls, but although not much survives of its earthworks the fine view will be appreciated. Each signal-station consisted of a circular

platform between 35 and 50 feet across, surrounded by a
circular ditch and an outer bank of upcast material. There
was a single entrance on the side facing the road. In the centre
of the platform was a timber tower about 10 feet square and
presumably two storeys high. In three examples, nos. 1, 7
and 9 (counting from the west), the tower was surrounded
by a rampart as well as the usual ditch and upcast mound.
Continue on for another ½m, over the crossroads, and stop
at the first house on the left (gate-piers with finials). Go
down the track opposite. Signal-station no. 3 lies on your
right amid the trees and can just be made out by the
discerning eye. By far the most rewarding is signal-station no.
10, 7m further west. Continue along the minor road to
Kinkell Bridge, where you should turn right along B8062.
After nearly two miles the B-road bends sharply up to the left
near a group of cottages, and a wood begins on your right.
Take the track at the top (Forestry Commission notice) and
after a few yards you will see the prominent earthworks in a
clearing on the right. The close spacing of these signal
stations, very similar to those on the German frontier, makes
it very likely that they formed part of a temporary frontier,
perhaps *c*. 85/90 when the forts further north were abandoned;
but only two scraps of pottery have come from excavations of
the signal stations, and more dating evidence is needed.

Both the chief Roman operators in northern Scotland
needed bases. Severus built a 24-acre fort on the south bank
of the Tay at Carpow, a few miles east of Perth (nothing
visible), and Agricola's legionary fortress lay on the same river
much further upstream, at **Inchtuthil*** (NO 1239). From Perth
follow the Blairgowrie road (A93) for 12 miles until the A984
crosses it near Meikleour. Turn left here and continue for three
miles until the B947 to Blairgowrie goes off to the right. At
this point, take the track leaving the left-hand side of the
A984 and keep straight along it wherever possible. One mile
later, after bending to the right at the edge of the Tay, you
should fork right at the houses until the track peters out at a
field-gate. Follow the wire fence on your right, from which
you can see the rampart and ditch defending the so-called
Redoubt (5 on fig 112), probably a stores-compound. When
the fence turns a corner keep straight on and you soon come
to the site of the east gate and the conspicuous hollow

marking the ditch on this side of the legionary fortress (7 is a post-Roman burial-mound). Rather more impressive is the massive rampart of the south defences, reached by going over to the far side of the pasture and through the field-gate at its SW corner, and then turning left to another gate near the trees. The southern defences are crossed immediately after the second gate. Of other earthworks, the north end of the 'Western Vallum' (2) is still prominent (this was built to enclose the tents of soldiers building the fortress), but nothing is now visible of the compound on the SE (3) which contained offices, stores, a barrack-block and a spacious residential building for the officers supervising construction-work. The temporary bath-house was also here (4); a permanent one was due for construction within the fortress. The native fort (6) is post-Roman.

The surviving earthworks at Inchtuthil are not striking, but this is one of the very few places in Britain where one can look at remains and associate them with the great governor of Britain made famous by the biography of Tacitus – Gnaeus Julius Agricola. This was the spot he chose to be the hub of his proposed operations to secure a stranglehold on the Scottish tribes, and the base fortress of the legion he had

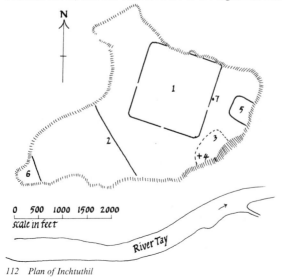

112 Plan of Inchtuthil

commanded earlier in his career, the Twentieth Valeria
Victrix. In the 53 acres enclosed by the defences of the fortress
nothing is now visible. But excavation between 1952 and 1965
by Sir Ian Richmond and Professor St Joseph has revealed the
complete plan of the timber buildings erected there.
Construction was started *c*. AD 83 and was still in full swing
when the order to abandon the site came about four years
later, after Agricola had left Britain. 64 barracks, four houses
for junior officers, six granaries, a large hospital, a drill-hall, a
workshop and a headquarters building had all been finished,
but no baths or CO's house had been erected. There were four
timber gateways and a single ditch, and the original turf rampart
had already been modified by the addition of a stone facing-
wall – one of the first forts in Britain to be so defended. Then
came withdrawal: not a mere abondonment, but a thorough
destruction in order to let nothing of value fall into enemy
hands. Foundation trenches were filled with nails bent by
extraction from timber posts. The hospital drain was jammed
with gravel. Unused pottery and glassware were deliberately
pounded into tiny fragments in a gutter of the main street.
The stone from the circuit-wall was systematically dismantled.
The unfired stone bath-house outside the walls was stripped
and demolished. Most dramatic of all was the discovery of a
hoard of one million unused nails of all sizes which had been
buried in a pit in the workshop. They have now been
distributed round the world. Agricola was of course not there
to watch: he was left to an embittered retirement in Rome.

A short distance NE of Inchtuthil lies an earthwork called
the **Cleaven Dyke** (NO 1640). Its purpose, date and original
length are not certain, but if the earthwork really is Roman,
its non-defensive character suggests that it was probably meant
to delineate part of the area near the fortress under strict
military control. It is now about 30 feet wide and 5 feet
high, and was originally flanked by ditches 16 feet wide and 2
feet deep. The whole earthwork measured 150 feet overall.
The surviving stretch, about one mile long, lies in the middle
of a plantation and is not easily accessible. From Inchtuthil
return via the A984 to the A93, and turn left. The road
crosses the line of the earthwork after exactly $\frac{1}{2}$m. Its
southern end was guarded by a signal-station on Black Hill
(App. I).

North of Inchtuthil over twenty marching camps have been identified from the air, but at only three of them are there substantial traces still visible on the ground. The camps are distinguishable, mainly on grounds of size, as belonging to five main classes varying from 30 to 130 acres. Each group presumably represents a different campaign, and all have been associated with one or other of the two great generals who are known for certain to have pushed Roman arms this far north into Scotland. One was Agricola, the other the emperor Septimius Severus, who campaigned here in AD 208–9. Unfortunately our literary evidence is too scanty to tell us if Lollius Urbicus (142/3), Ulpius Marcellus (186) or Constantius Chlorus (306) ever ventured into these parts, and on archaeological grounds marching camps are notoriously difficult to date. The largest camps, of 130 acres, represent the movements of a vast army, fitting for an imperial show of force, and they are plausibly linked with the campaigns of Severus. The one at Ardoch, the only visible example (p. 343), overlies a camp belonging to the 63-acre series, and was apparently constructed before silt had collected in the latter's ditch: if so, the 63-acre camps are probably also Severan, perhaps marking the line of the first expedition, in 208. The only 63-acre camp still partly visible is at **Kirkbuddo** (NO 4944). Take B961 from Dundee for 3m, then go along B978 (Kellas) for 7m and left again for 1m along B9127 (Inverarity). When the road enters a wood, after passing a house, park at the first gate leading into the plantation on the left. Walk along the road for 40 paces and you will see on your left a stretch of rampart in what is at present a slight clearing. It is visible also on the other side of the road, although totally covered with trees. Walk on to the next gate on the left and follow the track through the wood until it makes an obvious dip. Here, at the south corner of Kirkbuddo camp, the rampart is bold and clear, curving away to the right, and the accompanying ditch has been partly recut as a drainage channel. Return to the road and continue walking along to the next gate on the left, at the beginning of a slight bend. Just before it, on your right, is another fine stretch of rampart and ditch, the top of the surviving bank a full six feet above ditch-bottom. The camp has been known from at least the eighteenth century, when it was in perfect condition, but the portion outside the wood has now been totally ploughed away.

The other two camps of which substantial remnants survive, Normandykes and Raedykes, have been assigned to the 110-acre series, although the size of Raedykes (93 acres) is considerably less than the others and not closely matched elsewhere. Of **Normandykes** (NO 8399), only the east part of the north rampart survives impressively; the remainder has been ploughed away. In the western outskirts of Peterculter (8m SW of Aberdeen) take the minor road on the left (south) side of A93, opposite the B979 turning to Elrick. After crossing the stream fork left and then keep straight, under the railway bridge, until, ½m later, you reach Oldtown Farm. Ask here for permission to visit and directions: the earthwork lies in the northern edge of a wood a ten-minute walk away (to the NW) across three fields, and access to it depends on the nature and state of the crop. The rampart-mound is still sharp and clear, and the ditch too lacks the silt which so often obscures its true profile elsewhere. **Raedykes*** (NO 8490), however, is a much more impressive site, an outstanding witness to the energies and determination of a Roman army campaigning on the fringes of the then known world. The camp has an irregular plan to suit the terrain, but it is basically rectangular with a change of direction in the middle of the north rampart. There were six gates with *titula*, two in each of the long sides and one in each short side. It lies 3½m NW of Stonehaven and is reached by taking a minor road to the north off A957, signposted Stonehaven Riding School. Fork right immediately and keep going until the road swings sharply to the right. Keep straight on here, along a track leading to Broomhill cottage. Park at the corner where the track turns into the farmyard and keep walking straight. After crossing the first wire fence you come to a fine stretch of the camp's rampart and ditch, and this can be followed all the way up to the NE corner. A gap for an entrance is very clear just after the first telegraph pole. After the second wire-fence the earthworks are densely covered with bracken in summer and the rampart is much less conspicuous, but it is worth following the line of the ditch right up to the group of trees on the skyline. Here you will be rewarded with the magnificent sight of the rampart and ditch curving to the left at the north-east corner of the camp, the rampart-top ten feet or so above ditch-bottom. The north rampart can then be followed for its entire length, very impressive as far as the first field-gate, then crowned by a fence as far as the second gate, where the line changes direction and swings to the right. Excavation in 1914 demonstrated that the east rampart and part of the north had been deliberately made more massive than elsewhere because the ground was less steep and the camp more prone to attack on those sides. The slighter west rampart is now largely covered with gorse.

The 110-acre camps continue northwards almost as far as the mouth of the Spey, but apart from Glenmailen near Ythan Wells, where part of the south rampart survives along a field boundary (App. I), no trace of any is visible on the gound. This is not the only camp-size found in this part of Scotland: that at Glenmailen overlies a 35-acre camp with distinctive gateways, which is certainly Agricolan, another similar example lies 15 miles further north-west (Auchinhove), and what may possibly be another Roman camp of Agricolan date has been detected at the mouth of the Spey (Bellie). But the most exciting find of recent years is the discovery in 1975 of a camp at Durno, 20 miles NW of Aberdeen, which covers about 144 acres, the largest yet located north of the Antonine Wall. Is it just mathematical chance that its size represents the sum total of the two known camp-series in the area, one of 110 acres, the other, certainly Agricolan, of about 35? Could it be the camp where Agricola reassembled his forces before the final battle of his long Scottish campaigns? This intriguing possibility has been suggested by Professor St Joseph and, if accepted, then Normandykes and Raedykes may be Agricolan. Problems remain, however, and not all scholars accept the identification; more evidence is required before it can be substantiated. Certainly Mount Bennachie near Durno is a worthy candidate for the location of Mons Graupius, and it was probably in this region that the historic confrontation of AD 84 took place, when Agricola defeated the Caledonian tribes under the leadership of Calgacus. 10,000 barbarians were killed, with only 360 losses on the Roman side. Then indeed, as Tacitus made Calgacus say in his speech before the battle, the end of Britain lay revealed (*nunc terminus Britanniae patet*).

Chapter 10

London

The vast urban conglomeration known today as London owes
its origin to the Romans. There is no evidence to suggest that
in pre-Roman times there was any permanent settlement in
the area now occupied by the City of London, for the Bronze
Age sherds found in 1975, apparently all from one pot, do not
amount to evidence for habitation at that period (1500–1200
BC). But from AD 43, when the first buildings were planted

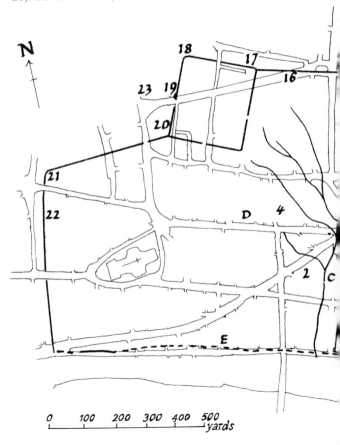

here, the city has expanded and flourished, and the almost
continuous succession of occupation-layers from that day to
this has resulted in a steady rise in the level of the ground.
Yet, between 10 and 20 feet below the modern pavement,
some traces of Roman London still remain, and it is not
perhaps commonly realized just how much has been preserved
of this earliest phase in the city's history.

A bridge across the Thames was essential to the Romans
from the earliest stages of their occupation, and the first
London Bridge, 60 yards downstream from its present

Both letters (site) and numbers (remains) are referred to in text. The outline of
the Walbrook stream and the fort and city walls is also shown.

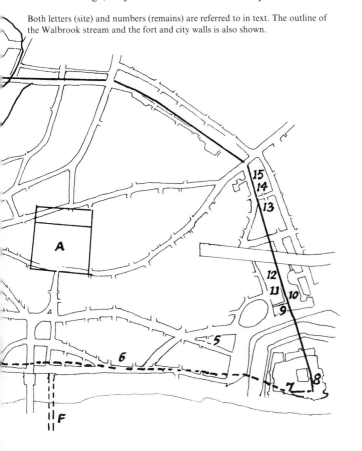

successor, was no doubt constructed in the year of the
** invasion (AD 43). Its position (F on the map on pp. 350–1)
was dictated by what was then the tidal limit of the Thames,
and also by the solid gravel banks on either side of the river at
this point. The bridge would undoubtedly have been
accompanied by a military post, and the first indication of
military activity came in 1972 with the discovery of a V-
shaped ditch at Aldgate and of pre-Boudiccan timber
buildings, possibly military, both there and below the later
Roman palace (B). But it was the trading, not the military,
potential of the site that was fully realized from the beginning,
and the early fort soon gave way to the first city. Streets were
laid out and substantial timber buildings, some with wall-
plaster and roofing-tiles, were constructed. Docks were built,
and the very large amount of Claudian material found in the
City suggests London's immediate importance, no doubt as
the principal supply-base for the armies campaigning further
north. Rapid communication with these was ensured by the
great trunk roads, which fanned out from London from the
earliest years of the occupation. Though Claudius had
intended Colchester to be the capital of the new province,
close to the site of the most important pre-Roman settlement,
it is likely that London soon usurped this position, probably
after AD 60–1. Even before that, the financial headquarters
may already have been in London, and, as at St Albans, earth
defences may have been erected.

In AD 60 or 61, the first city came to an end, destroyed by
Boudicca and her followers. The historian Tacitus, who gives
us the first literary reference to LONDINIVM, says that it was
already packed with traders and a hive of commerce, though
not graced with the title of *colonia*. (Later it was probably
given this status as a mark of honour, but we have no record
of it.) London soon rose from the ashes, and it is extremely
likely that at this time, and certainly before the end of the first
century, the city became the official capital of the province.
The first forum was built *c.* AD 80 and then replaced *c.* 100 by
one five times the size (360 feet by 200 feet), investigated prior
to redevelopment in 1985–7; and by about AD 85, a large
residence identified as the Governor's Palace had already been
erected. The state cult of emperor-worship was also
transferred to London from Colchester before the end of the

first century, possibly in AD 61. Finally, at the beginning of
the second century, a fort was established, smaller than a
legionary fortress but, at 11 acres, three times the size of most
normal forts. Its garrison, which included men from all three
of the regular British legions, would have fulfilled a variety of
functions, supervising the transference of military supplies
and acting as the governor's bodyguard. London had become
the political, financial and commercial capital of Britain, and
the Roman genius in selecting its site is attested by its
continuing role today.

Another fire swept London c. 125–130, this time probably
accidental. About the middle of the century serious flooding,
caused by subsidence, troubled some low-lying parts of the
city. But expansion was not greatly interrupted, and when
walls were built at the end of the second century they enclosed
an area of 330 acres, by far the largest city in Britain and the
fourth largest north of the Alps. The other dates known in the
history of Roman London may be briefly noted. In 197, when
Britain was divided into two provinces, LONDINIVM became
the capital of *Britannia Superior* (Upper Britain). About 286,
the rebel emperor Carausius established the first mint in
London. In 296 the city was looted by Allectus' troops after
he had been defeated by Constantius. The mint closed down
c. AD 326, but about the middle of the century London was
given the honorary name of AVGVSTA. Of the end little is
known, but recent evidence from Lower Thames Street
suggests that life continued well into the fifth and possibly the
sixth centuries. Then came the Dark Ages, and the only lapse
in the predominance that the city has enjoyed from Roman
times to the present day.

Of the buildings belonging to the Roman city not a great
deal is known. Continuous occupation has allowed
archaeologists little opportunity for large-scale excavation,
and even when areas of a reasonable size are available,
Roman levels have usually been partially or completely
removed by medieval and Victorian cellars and pits. This
continuous occupation has largely obliterated the topography
of the Roman city: originally London fell into two distinct
halves, consisting of two gravel plateaus separated by a
stream known as the Walbrook. On the top of the eastern
plateau stood the most important public building, the **Forum**

and **Basilica** (A on map, p. 350). This vast structure lay in the area which is now bounded on the north by Cornhill and Leadenhall, on the south by Lombard Street and Fenchurch Street, and is roughly bisected by Gracechurch Street. Some parts of it have been observed in the nineteenth century and again in 1985–7, and we know that the basilica was at least 500 feet long, far bigger than any other example in Britain. The first stone forum was built *c.* AD 80, probably during Agricola's governorship, but this was replaced by the much larger final version about 20 years later. Nothing can be seen of either forum or basilica, for the few walls of the latter preserved beneath Banks (App. I) are inaccessible to the public at all times.

The second remarkable public building is the **Governor's Palace** (B), situated between Cannon Street and Upper Thames Street. Various massive foundations had been reported in this area, partly after the Great Fire of 1666, partly during sewer construction in Bush Lane in 1840–1, and partly during the building of Cannon Street station in 1868, which overlies the western portion of the palace. The function of the building was only recognized during recent excavation, mainly in 1964–5, in advance of office development. A large reception-hall, 82 feet by 42 feet internally, lay in the centre of the complex, and on its south side was a garden with an ornamental pool over 100 feet long. The floor of the pool lay on a massive concrete raft six feet thick. Rooms round two sides of this courtyard have been excavated; those on the east were probably offices, and the residential quarters no doubt faced the river. The official nature of this great complex is not in doubt, and the conclusion that it is indeed the headquarters of the Provincial Governor seems inescapable. It was built in the last quarter of the first century, and so is contemporary with the Fishbourne Palace, but it seems to have been abandoned *c.* AD 300. By then York had effectively become the political capital of Britain, because of its close contact with the crucial northern frontier.

No remains of the Palace can now be seen, though one relic nearby ought to be mentioned. This is the **London Stone** (1), a shapeless lump of Clipsham limestone now built into the wall of the Bank of China, on the north side of Cannon Street next to St Swithin's Lane. It was first recorded in 1189 and is of

either Roman or Saxon date. Sir Christopher Wren saw its
foundation and believed that it was part of an elaborate
monument connected with a large complex further south.
That complex we now know to be the Governor's Palace, and
the original position of the stone, in the middle of Cannon
Street a few yards from its present site, seems to be exactly on
the north-south axis of the Palace. If so, its Roman origin
seems very likely, and one suggestion, that it is part of a great
milestone from which distances in Britain were measured, may
not be far wide of the mark. It is unlikely that we shall ever
know for certain.

Another important class of public buildings were the
temples, but only one has securely been identified in London.
This is the notorious **Temple of Mithras** (C; 2). The discovery
of this shrine in September 1954 caused a sensation. Intense
public interest demanded a temporary suspension of work on
the modern building (Bucklersbury House) while 80,000
people flocked to see the remains. Questions were asked in the
Commons about the possibility of preserving it, but to have

113   Walbrook Temple of Mithras, a ceremony in progress

kept it *in situ* would have cost too much money. A compromise was reached, and the building was dismantled and eventually reassembled in its present position in Temple Court, 11 Queen Victoria Street (2). This is about 60 yards NW of its original site on the east bank of the Walbrook stream (C). The reconstruction does give a good idea of the outline of the temple, with its nave, two aisles and an apse for the main statue-group. In addition, the entrance threshold, much worn by the tread of Roman devotees, and the bases of the pillars that supported the roof can be seen. But there are many misleading features about the 'new' temple of Mithras: the nave was originally much lower in relation to the side-aisles, and was reached from the doorway by two wooden steps; the earth floor of the nave and the wooden floor of the aisles have both been replaced by crazy paving; a wooden water-tank in one corner has been rebuilt in stone. Also the present position of the remains on a lofty platform is quite the opposite of the original low-lying site. The temple, built towards the end of the second century, was graced with a beautiful set of sculptures, displayed in the Museum of London (p. 366) together with a Mithraic relief found here in the nineteenth century. The reconstruction-drawing shows a Mithraic ceremony in progress in the temple (fig 113). Mithraism was a secret religion popular with soldiers, merchants and officials. It has some affinities to freemasonry and some to Christianity: like the former there were different grades of initiates, like the latter it promised salvation and joy in the world to come. Another temple of Mithras is visible on Hadrian's Wall at Carrawburgh.

Parts of Roman bath-houses have come to light in the city, but it is not always clear whether they were for public or private use: an example is the small building found but not preserved in **Cheapside** in 1956 (D). A much larger complex on **Huggin Hill**, Upper Thames Street, however, is certainly a public establishment (E). Excavation in 1964 and 1969 revealed that in the original late-first-century building there were three unheated rooms here, before two were given hypocausts and a large apsed *caldarium* was added. The whole building was demolished before the end of the second century and some poorly-constructed private dwellings were erected on the levelled remains. Part of this bath still survives, buried beneath the courtyard east of Dominant House, 205 Upper Thames Street, but nothing can be seen of it at present except for a stretch of Roman retaining-wall, with a double course of bonding-tiles, incorporated as a feature in the landscaped garden on the north side of the building's service bay.

About the middle of the second century the Walbrook stream silted up, its revetting-banks collapsed, and the area was redeveloped to become one of the high-class residential districts of the city. One beautifully-preserved geometric mosaic, found in Bucklersbury in 1869, aroused as much public interest as the Temple of Mithras: 33,000 people visited it in three days. 17 feet long and of third-century date, it is now displayed in the Museum of London. Two much smaller geometric mosaics were found in 1933–4 during building work at the **Bank of England** (3). Both have been lifted from their original positions: one has been reset in the Bank's private museum, which contains other Roman material, and can only be visited by special appointment; the other, much restored, now lies at the foot of the main staircase and may be viewed (from a distance) during normal hours, on enquiry at the entrance-hall. A dull and dusty portion of third-century mosaic, which does remain *in situ*, exists on the premises of 11 **Ironmonger Lane** (4), currently occupied by the Bank of Argentina (but a change of tenancy was due in January 1988). Written permission to view should be obtained in advance. Finally, a red tessellated floor, originally bisected by a wooden partition, can be seen *in situ* in the crypt of **All Hallows Church** (5), near the Tower of London. Another patch of red *tesserae* can be seen nearby, but this has been relaid. Several Roman finds are also displayed in the crypt, including a model of Roman London. The tombstone with a Greek inscription has almost certainly been brought to this country in recent times and is not a genuine relic of the city's past.

Much more interesting than these isolated mosaics are the remains of a Roman house and attached bath-suite in an inspection-chamber below 100, **Lower Thames Street*** (6). In order to visit this outstanding site, enquiries should be made in advance by letter or telephone with the Museum of London (p. 365). They will then make arrangements for you to view the Roman site with an employee from the office building situated above the archaeological basement; note that a visit is only possible between Mondays and Fridays during normal working hours. With the exception of some stretches of city-wall, the surviving fragments of Roman London are isolated relics, looking rather pathetic in their modern surroundings. Here, however, is a more substantial building, and its appeal is therefore the greater. It is also, of course, the earliest dwelling-place of a Londoner that can be seen today, and was indeed the only Roman house in London that had until recently been explored. Parts had been discovered in 1848 and 1859, and even a small portion preserved beneath the Coal Exchange. Excavation in 1969–70, and again in 1975–6, has now revealed that these earlier discoveries belonged to the bath-house of an L-shaped private residence. Pottery suggests that the whole building was constructed about AD 200, but more interesting is the evidence of its end. A group of 246 bronze coins points to occupation after AD 395, possibly up to the mid fifth century, and an early Anglo-Saxon brooch found in the rubble of the collapsed roof implies that the house did not become ruined until *c.* AD 500. This is the first evidence that life went on in London well after the withdrawal of the official Roman government, and it confirms evidence from St Albans and elsewhere that Romano–British towns did *not* end in flames kindled by Saxon raiders. Of the house itself parts of two corridors serving the north and east wings, and some of the rooms of these wings, have been explored, but the main feature of the preserved remains is the fine bath-suite, situated in the angle between the two wings. A worn door-sill leads from a corridor of the house to a small undressing-room with a red tessellated floor. On either side are two heated rooms with apses. On the bather's right (west side) was the *tepidarium*, with a brick seat still visible in one of its walls; this is the part that was preserved beneath the Coal Exchange. On his left was the *caldarium*, which is in excellent shape. 29 *pilae* bases for supporting the floor can be seen, as well as the stoke-hole and flue-tiles for the hot air to escape. The walls of the room are still about three feet high. On the south side of these heated chambers was a large *frigidarium*, probably vaulted. Its original floor of red *tesserae* was later covered after heavy wear with a layer of pink cement, probably in the fourth century. At one end is a small plunge-bath.

The great defences of Roman London, which have left

more numerous and more substantial fragments than the buildings they eventually enclosed, fall into three separate phases. Early in the second century, before the construction of the city-wall, a large fort was erected NW of the built-up area (p. 353). This fort was the most important discovery of the post-war excavations: though the peculiar course taken by the city-wall in the Cripplegate area had been noted before, the reason for it was only revealed in 1949.

When the city-wall was constructed, the existing north and west walls of the fort were incorporated into its circuit. This was done at the very end of the second century. At a time when most other towns in Britain were receiving only an earth bank and ditch, the capital was given a great girdle of stone walls, backed by a (contemporary) rampart of earth. The wall, some eight feet thick at base and 15–20 feet high, was made of courses of Kentish ragstone separated at intervals by tile bonding-courses. The fort-wall, however, was only four feet thick, and so fresh masonry was tacked on to its inside face (on the north and west sides) to make the defences the same width here as they were elsewhere. London's appearance at

114 *London c. AD 200*

this time is suggested in fig 114: the fort is prominent in the foreground, and the forum and bridge can be seen in the background.

The third phase in the fortification of Roman London came sometime in the fourth century, probably *c*. 350, when projecting bastions were added to the existing wall. This seems to have been completed only on the eastern side of the city, where the bastions are solid and firmly dated to the Roman period. The western bastions, in the Cripplegate area, are all hollow and are now known to belong to the early medieval period. Curiously enough, they do not appear to have had Roman predecessors.

The final phase in the city's defences came about the same time (*c*. 350/70), when new walls were built along the Thames. There was, however, even later work *c*. 390 near the SE corner (Tower of London: see below), but this represents a late rebuilding of only a short sector, just north of the earlier alignment (note abrupt turn to meet it). The Thames-side defences, long suspected, were only finally located in 1974, when a stretch of 125 feet was excavated in advance of destruction at the western end, near the Mermaid Theatre. The wall, erected on oak-pile foundations, was about 8 feet wide and had a clay bank piled behind it. Like the bastions a great deal of reused material was built into it, including an astonishing haul of 52 sculptured blocks and inscriptions which are now in the Museum of London (p. 368). In 1976–7 another stretch of riverside wall was uncovered and left on permanent display in the grounds of the **Tower of London** (7 on map, p. 350) [AM; weekdays 9.30–4 (Nov.–Feb.), 9.30–5 (Mar.–Oct.); Sundays, Mar.–Oct. only, 2–5)], and this forms a convenient starting-point for a tour of the Roman defences. The 70-foot length of riverside wall, situated near the History Gallery (turn left at the Water Gate), is still over seven feet high. It too was partly constructed of reused stones and had internal timber lacing, detectable as cavities in the masonry which at one point have been filled by modern beams. The date in the 390's was clearly indicated by coins in the material dumped during construction (see also above). Now go up the steps at the far (east) end and turn left up the slope. The ruins of the Wardrobe Tower sit on the site of a Roman bastion, and behind it a low portion of Roman wall, 10 feet long, survives (8). This of course belongs to the landward defences and is 200 years older than the masonry of the riverside wall. The rest of its line in this area, and the site of an internal turret, have been marked out in concrete. Outside the Tower, on the north side of **Tower Hill***(9) [AM; A] is a magnificent stretch of wall, best viewed from the terrace near Tower Hill Underground Station. Near the road only the base of the wall is visible, but to the north the Roman work survives in splendid condition – 15 courses of beautifully squared ragstone blocks, separated at intervals by four sets of bonding-bricks (the bottom two in triple rows, the upper two double). Above, the wall is medieval. Set in the modern wall at the rear is the cast of a Roman inscription; the original is now in the British Museum. Julius Alpinus Classicianus was the financial administrator (*procurator*) of Britain immediately after the Boudican revolt, when he urged policies of restraint in dealing with the offending natives. He died in London, and his tomb was set up outside the perimeter of the city. In the fourth century, it was broken up and incorporated into a bastion very close to where the cast is. The upper portion, including part of his name, was found in 1852, and it was then claimed as part of the tomb of the *procurator* mentioned by Tacitus. This theory was later rejected until the lower part of the inscription was found in 1935, still in position at the bottom of the bastion. This reads PROC.PROVINC.BRIT., '*procurator* of the province of Britain', and the identification was no longer in doubt. It was set up by his wife Julia Pacata I(ndiana): both her name and that of her husband indicate that they were Gauls, probably from the area around Trier in what is now Germany.

Immediately north of here is **Tower Hill Underground Station** (10), where a fragment of wall found in 1967 is preserved high up in the tiled facing opposite platform 1 (westbound). A few yards further north, at 40–1 Trinity Square, is the entrance to **Wakefield House** (11), and a stretch of the outer face of the Roman wall is preserved in its basement. The plinth is visible here, and a triple row of bonding-tiles. This can only be visited provided written permission has been sought in advance. Accessible at any time and much more interesting is a fine stretch a little further north, in the courtyard behind Midland House, 8–10 **Cooper's Row***(12). This was found in 1864 when it was incorporated in a warehouse. The latter was knocked down in 1961, and the wall exposed. It stands 35 feet above ground-level here, but the upper part is medieval. The Roman portion, with considerable parts of the inner face and rows of bonding-tiles still preserved, stands about 13 feet high (fig 115). A plaque indicates clearly what is Roman and what is not. The outer face of the wall, more repaired but still displaying the Roman sandstone plinth, can be seen by going through the modern

** breach to the other side.

Return now to Cooper's Row and go northwards, under the railway, into **Crutched Friars** (13). In what used to be Roman Wall House, 1 Crutched Friars, a substantial piece of the inner face of the wall survives, 40 feet long and 8–9 feet high. This and adjacent properties, however, are undergoing complete redevelopment in 1987–8 ('Crusader House'), and arrangements about further access are currently uncertain. A miserable fragment is preserved in the **Sir John Cass School of Science and Technology** (14), 31 Jewry Street (the porter may have time to

115   Cooper's Row, the Roman city-wall

escort you), and a larger piece exists under **'The Three Tuns'**
public house (15), 36 Jewry Street: the landlord will only show
it to you if business is very slack. Thereafter, no remains of
the city-wall are visible at present until you reach the
Cripplegate area. For those who wish to walk, the line of the
wall is followed by Bevis Marks, Camomile Street,
Wormwood Street and the road called London Wall. There
were Roman gates at Aldgate and Bishopsgate. The next
surviving portion of city-wall above ground is that in **St
Alphage Churchyard** (17), reached from Wood Street, a
turning off London Wall. The brickwork battlements are
Tudor and most of the rest of the facing is medieval, but one
interesting Roman feature is visible here. Go up the stairway
on the east side of the garden and look down at the outer face
of the wall. At the bottom, on the left, there appears to be a
crack in the masonry, but in fact there are two walls of
different periods side by side here. That on the right (outer)
belongs to the Cripplegate Roman fort, and dates to the early
second century; that on the left is the masonry added when
the city-wall was built in the late second century (as explained
above, p. 359).

West of Wood Street, which passes through the site of
Cripplegate, the north gate of the Roman fort, is the new
Barbican development. This impressive mass of steel, concrete
and glass may be reached by turning right out of St Alphage's
Garden and left at 'The Postern'. In the middle, starkly
contrasting with the modern architecture, is the church of St
Giles and a long stretch of city-wall. This stands on Roman
footings and incorporates Roman core, but most of the
masonry visible here is medieval, including the lower part of a
bastion. Excavation in 1966 dated the latter to the thirteenth
century, and this is presumably also the date of the
spectacular **Cripplegate Bastion** (18) a few yards to the west. It
marks the position of the NW corner of the Roman fort and
city-wall. The only Roman work visible in this Barbican
stretch is behind the 1966 bastion, where neatly-built squared
stones and slight traces of a tile-course (not the extensive
brickwork above) can be seen in the lower part of the wall.
The later bastion protected the wall here, so making
unnecessary the repair which has removed the Roman facing
elsewhere.

Return to Wood Street and back to London Wall, then turn right (westwards) until you reach the ramp descending to Bastion House and the underground car-park. The **West Gate*** (19) of the Roman fort is preserved in an inspection-chamber to the right of the car-park entrance, but it is only open on the first Tuesday of every month from 10.30–12, and the third Friday of every month from 2.30–4. A good portion is visible of the original fort-wall standing on its base-plinth, and behind, jutting up against it, is the masonry added when the city-wall was built. Then comes a fine guardroom, originally matched by another which has not been preserved. In between were two carriageways spanned by arches. Some traces of the central dividing wall remain, and one of the carriageways is still blocked with a late Roman or post-Roman wall of crude material.

From the chamber in which the gateway is preserved, access can be gained (through doors saying No Admittance) to the large underground car-park under **London Wall** (16) (7.30–5.30, Mon.–Fri. only). Officially people without cars are not admitted here, but if you ask one of the attendants you may be allowed to see a good fragment of the Roman wall, found in 1957 during clearance for the new road. This portion lies east of the Cripplegate fort and so is of one thickness and build. It can also be reached by another staircase on the south side of London Wall near its junction with Coleman Street.

At the west end of London Wall, on the corner with Aldersgate Street, is the new Museum of London, which should be visited before proceeding further south (below p. 365). On the other side of London Wall, opposite the entrance to the west gate, and next to the Plaisterers' Hall, is **Noble Street** (20). Parts of the outer (fort) wall and the inner (thickening) wall are exposed here for a considerable length, including part of the foundations of an internal turret to the left of the steps leading down to the Hall. At the end of this stretch comes the crucial junction between fort- and city-walls, and it was here in 1949 that the existence of the fort was first confirmed. The fort-wall can be seen curving round, with a conspicuous internal corner turret. Projecting out from it and disappearing under the modern brickwork is a short portion of the Roman city-wall added nearly a century later. The difference in thickness between the two will be noted.

Further west, a small portion of Roman wall, together with a substantial part of one of the hollow medieval bastions, survives below the yard of the **General Post Office**, King Edward Building (21). It can be visited, Mondays to Fridays only, if prior arrangement has been made with the Postmaster Controller, King Edward Buildings, EC1A 1AA. The wall turns southwards at this point, and at Newgate there was a Roman gate. It had two carriageways and large square flanking towers, and the whole structure was about 100 feet wide. Finally, a short section of the bottom of the Roman wall has been preserved under the new extension to the **Central Criminal Court** (22), north of Warwick Square. For obvious security reasons, this can only be seen by prior arrangement, and you should write to the Keeper of the Court at the Old Bailey if you wish to inspect the relic.

Outside the city limits, there is very little of Roman interest. A red tessellated pavement *in situ* is reflected in a mirror in the crypt of **St Bride's Church**, Fleet Street (off map), and the position of a Roman ditch has been marked out on the lino floor nearby. Further west there was a Roman building under Westminster Abbey, and a sarcophagus found there is now in the entrance to the Chapter House. The so-called 'Roman Bath' in the Strand is of sixteenth- or seventeenth-century date. Some of the finds from the Roman suburb in Southwark are in the Cuming Museum, Walworth Road (10–5.30 except Sun.; closes at 7 on Thurs., 5 on Sat.). A tiny fragment of red mosaic has been relaid in the south chancel-aisle of the cathedral. Slight traces of a Roman building in Greenwich Park (App. I) may also be mentioned.

Roman London has yielded a whole host of interesting finds, more than any other single site in Britain. The best are in the British Museum, but the main collections are housed in the **Museum of London** (23), Aldersgate Street, which is undoubtedly one of the most important Roman displays in the country. The whole museum is a masterpiece. An exciting modern building provides the setting for a wide variety of creative and imaginative displays skilfully designed, with moody, evocative lighting (sometimes to the detriment of our appreciation of the objects they illuminate) and full information-panels and labels (occasionally set uncomfortably near floor-level). Space prevents more than a list of some of the outstanding exhibits displayed in the museum, which is open daily, except Monday, from 10 to 6 (Sun. 2–6).

After the initial collection of military equipment (a reminder that London was a garrison town) and other small finds, including evidence for the earliest of the Great Fires of London, a number of inscriptions are displayed, including one found in the riverside wall in 1975 which documents the existence in the city of a temple in honour of the Egyptian goddess Isis. The next section features dockside London in Roman times, an area about which we know much more after the recent discoveries (1973–7) of substantial lengths of well-preserved Roman quayside. In the following room pride of place goes to the amazing haul of sculptures from the Temple of Mithras. Some pieces were found in the nineteenth century, and almost certainly come from the Mithraeum, though the building itself was not found then. The most interesting of these earlier finds is a small but complete slab depicting Mithras slaying the bull. He is accompanied by the torchbearers Cautes and Cautopates, who represent light and darkness, salvation and death. Signs of the zodiac appear in the surrounding circle. But it is the beautiful sculptures found in 1954 which deserve even closer attention. They had deliberately been buried in the floor of the sanctuary early in the fourth century, perhaps through fear of Christian iconoclasts, but the building seems to have continued in use for some years after this. One of the sculptures is a marble head of Mithras in his Phrygian cap, and it was the discovery of this that conclusively proved the identity of the temple. Its late-second-century date makes it roughly contemporary with the building of the shrine, and it is a reasonable guess that it formed part of the main bull-slaying relief in the apse; the rest of the relief may have been of stucco and so have perished. An enormous hand clasping the hilt of a dagger was also found, but this cannot have belonged to a similar group, for its scale would have been too big for the Walbrook temple: it was probably meant to be a symbolic object. Other sculptures found in 1954, all of marble, include a figure of Mercury, a head of Minerva and a small damaged group of Bacchus and his companions. But the most beautiful discovery of all is the head of Serapis, Graeco-Egyptian god of the underworld

116   Museum of London, head of Serapis

(fig 116), the first you come to in the display. Like the head of Mithras it is an imported work, made of Italian marble at the end of the second century AD. On his head is a corn-measure, symbolic of the prosperity which the god will bestow both in this life and the next. The sensitive modelling of the face, the skill in the design and execution of the hair, and the splendour of the burnished finish cannot fail to be admired. The presence of so many other deities within the temple may seem surprising, but all of them are in some way connected with the after-life and are not therefore out of place in a Mithraic sanctuary. Finally, an enigmatic silver box and 'strainer' should not be missed (to the right of Mithras). Very strange scenes of combat between men and animals, including griffins, are represented. The precise significance of these scenes is debated, but they presumably allude to Mithras in his role as a conqueror of death and evil.

On the end wall near the Fire Exit a fine sculptured panel shows four seated female deities, another of the stones recovered from the riverside wall in 1975. The deities are mother-goddesses, normally shown as a triad (as in the stone below) but here accompanied by a unique interloper: the figure on the far right may represent the dedicator. To the left, in a case illustrating religion, the Roman name of the city can be clearly read on a jug inscribed LONDINI AD FANVM ISIDIS, 'in London next to the shrine of Isis'. The jug was found in Southwark, and it is hard to tell if there was another temple there different to the one inferred from the inscription mentioned above, or whether the jug had strayed from its rightful home across the river. London is also named on a famous gold medallion from Arras in France, of which a replica (the original is in Paris) is displayed in the coin-case opposite. It shows a personification of the city kneeling before the emperor Constantius, who is described as the 'restorer of eternal light'. It commemorates the recovery of the city in 296 after the rule of Carausius and Allectus. Behind the kneeling figure is the earliest portrayal of the city, a schematic representation of one of the city-gates. The medallion was minted in Trier (Germany) and so it is unlikely that the designer had ever seen London.

In the corner beside the corridor to the Saxon and Medieval room is a pile of large stones, some of them sculpted. These are a few of the many carved blocks from the riverside wall, pillaged, as careful study has shown, from just two major buildings. One was a decorated monumental arch, the other an ornamental screen featuring at least five deities. The carving is provincial, but in the best classical tradition: it is vigorous, highly competent work, of a quality matched in Britain only by some of the sculpture at Bath, and its subject matter and decorative motifs were directly inspired by the mainstream art of Italy. That such imposing monuments once graced the capital comes as no surprise; but so much has been destroyed by the later history of the city that finds such as this are rare. Too large and too numerous to win the museum presentation they deserve, these sculptures represent a major addition to our knowledge of Romano-British art and architecture.

117   British Museum, head of Christ on a mosaic floor

Finally, a few steps lead up to the spectacular display centred around the Bucklersbury mosaic (p. 357), itself a rare survival of what must have been a common embellishment in the stylish houses of a great commercial city. Some particularly fascinating finds are in the cases on either side of the gangway. One is a graffito scratched on tile, which reads 'Austalis has been wandering off on his own every day for the last fortnight' – usually claimed as the first recorded example of absenteeism by a British workman. Another British worker, presumably female, is implied by the so-called 'bikini' trunks, but whether she was employed in some muddy job near the Walbrook (where the find was made) or as a dancing girl in a Roman-style night-club is left open to the imagination. A more fragmentary example, also displayed, came from a third-century military site at Shadwell, a mile east of the Tower. Perhaps most immediate of all the objects displayed are the simple things of everyday life, the needles and pins, the jewellery and the tools. The last in particular (in the case facing the Cripplegate bastion) are remarkably close to their modern counterparts.

The most important collection of Romano–British

118 British Museum, Chi-Rho from Lullingstone

antiquities, including some finds from London, is the property
of the **British Museum** (10–5, Sun. 2.30–6), Great Russell
Street. There is plenty, of course, to enjoy here, and if you
read all the labels and information-panels that are displayed
with the exhibits you will leave the museum with a very
thorough idea of life in Britain under Roman rule. Once again
only a handful of items can be mentioned here. At the top of
the main staircase is the large fourth-century mosaic from
Hinton St Mary, Dorset, found in 1963. In the central roundel
of the main portion of the pavement is the earliest portrait of
Christ known in Britain. A Chi-Rho monogram appears
behind his head, and pomegranates, symbols of immortality,
are represented on either side (fig 117). The other part of the
floor contains a roundel which depicts Bellerophon slaying the
Chimaera. The same subject, an allegory of the triumph over
death and evil, appears on a mosaic at Lullingstone,
significantly close to the Christian rooms there.

Next comes the main Romano–British room. Immediately to
the right is the important reconstructed fresco showing six
Christians, from the house-chapel of the Lullingstone villa
(p. 60), their hands outstretched in the ancient attitude of prayer.
Then come the two marble portrait-busts from the same villa,
with the Chi-Rho monogram fresco from the chapel displayed
above them. Above that again is the best of the painted panels
to have come from the Verulamium excavations, an ambitious
floral scroll on a pleasing yellow background, with two
handsome peacocks and panther heads in attendance (detail,
fig 119). The remarkable late-fourth-century Thetford treasure
discovered in 1979 is the subject of the first showcase,
comprising a hoard of gold jewellery, a set of 33 silver spoons
and strainers, and a shale jewellery box. All but two of the
spoons are inscribed, a dozen of them in honour of Faunus,
an Italian god of the countryside otherwise unattested in
Roman Britain. Two of the spoons have gilt inlay, the larger
decorated with a spirited rendering of a triton blowing a conch.
The jewellery is unworn and, in part, unfinished; it appears to
have been the collection of a single jeweller, but its connection
with the Faunus spoons, and the reason for the deposition
(votive?; fear of pagan persecution in the 380s or 390s?) are
enigmatic. Note especially the superb rendering of a dancing
satyr on the gold belt-buckle in the centre of the case. The next

contains the finds from Uley (1977–79), an important
Gloucestershire rural shrine with Romano–Celtic temple and
surrounding buildings. Small votive bronzes of the god with his
characteristic wand (*caduceus*) and winged hat (three are on
display here) made it clear that the honorand was Mercury, but
the outstanding discovery is what must have been the head of
the cult statue of the god, crisply carved in local limestone
(probably *c.* 150–200) with somewhat stylized hair, but a
vigorous, competent work, wholly in the classical tradition and
a cut above the average product of most Romano–British
sculptural workshops.

Facing the Uley Mercury is the Water Newton treasure,
found in 1975, another outstanding testimony of early
Christianity in Britain. This fourth-century hoard comprises
nineteen tiny votive plaques bearing the Chi-Rho monogram,
and nine silver vessels, one looking remarkably like some
modern communion chalices. This is the earliest known
collection of church plate from the Roman Empire, and the
votive inscriptions of the dedicators furnish us with the names
of some members of an early Christian congregation in Britain:
Innocentia, Viventia, Publianus. On the other side of this
group of showcases is the Mildenhall Treasure. Familiarity
does not deaden the breathtaking impact on the viewer of this

119   British Museum, wall-plaster from St Albans

120   *British Museum, detail of the Mildenhall dish*

superlatively high quality imported silver tableware, of which
the great circular dish 2 feet in diameter is the showpiece (and
presumably used only for display): the photographic detail (fig
120) shows the central mask of Oceanus surrounded by nereids
and tritons. The dish is a product of a Mediterranean
workshop in the fourth century AD, as is probably also the
rectangular dish from Corbridge displayed alongside. At the
far end of the room is the Classicianus tomb-monument (see
p. 361) and, at the foot of the stairs, a handful of the hundreds
of wooden writing tablets with ink handwriting, miraculously
preserved in a waterlogged deposit at Vindolanda (p. 302). The
ones displayed include quartermasters' lists of food supplies
needed for the garrison, a letter of recommendation, another
letter in which the name Vindolanda itself can be read, and the
famous scrap recording the arrival from a lady called Sattua
of 'two pairs of underpants, two pairs of sandals . . .'

Finally, in the showcases on the upper level illustrating the
Roman army, are finds from more of the places described
earlier in this book: military buckles and arrow-heads from Hod
Hill, for example, and the handsome parade helmet from
Ribchester. Note especially here the elaborate shield-boss
belonging to a member of the 8th legion, a detachment of which
is known to have served in Britain under Hadrian; it comes from
the river Tyne at Newcastle. In the final showcase are two more
river-bed finds: a bronze head of the emperor Claudius from
the river Alde in Suffolk, possibly deposited there by jubilant
supporters of Boudica during the uprising of 61, and a famous
bronze head of the emperor Hadrian, found in the Thames. It
is fitting that I should end a guidebook to Roman remains in
Britain with him, for it was due to the eccentric genius of this
emperor that our most famous and impressive antiquity, the
great Wall of Hadrian, was ever built. But more remains of
Roman Britain than a well-known frontier-barrier and objects
in museum showcases: a tremendous number of monuments,
differing immensely in character, can still be tracked down in
these islands. Some of them may now be tucked away behind
hedgerows or factory chimneys, others are lost on barren
moorland, but all of them bear a living witness to nearly 400
years of Roman rule in Britain.

Third edition: supplementary material

Fishbourne

p. 54 When the Cupid was raised in 1980 for conservation, a first-century palace-phase mosaic was found beneath, inevitably mostly destroyed by the later floor. It had a border depicting a stylized town wall, with towers at the corners and a gateway in the middle of each side, a design common in Italian and other Continental mosaics but rare in Britain. This mosaic has been lifted from its original position and is now displayed in a nearby room.

Excavations east of the main site in 1983–5, in advance of the building of the bypass, found more timber buildings related to the early military storebase (p. 50) as well as timber and stone structures which must represent palace outbuildings. More recently, in 1987, a plot of land including part of the south wing of the palace (the owner's residential suite) has been purchased, and excavations there are planned.

Exeter

p. 74 After excavation the legionary baths, and the excavated portion of the forum and basilica that replaced them, were reburied; they lie under the greensward immediately west of the cathedral. At the time of writing, however (1987), plans are afoot to re-expose these structures and to erect a cover building over them.

Silchester

p. 80 The amphitheatre, not explored by the Victorians, came into guardianship as an AM in 1979, and was subsequently excavated in a series of campaigns between then and 1984. These have shown that it was built sometime between AD 50 and 75, and possibly before 60; its early construction can no doubt be attributed, along with the very early baths (p. 79), to the Romanizing influence of Cogidubnus (cf. pp. 49, 76), within whose client-kingdom Silchester probably lay. The arena wall and entrance passages were of timber at this period, and the exterior wall was revetted with turves. There were various repairs in the second century, including a major rebuilding in timber at the north entrance, but it was only in the third century that the seating banks were cut back slightly and a new arena wall in stone was built, enclosing a slightly larger arena than its timber predecessor. Unlike the military amphitheatres of Chester and Caerleon this stone revetment was never carried round the exterior of the building. Note the tile-lined triangular drainage-holes, particularly prominent in the arena wall east of the south entrance (to the right as you enter), and the two semicircular recesses, one still standing some 7 feet high (2.2 m.), on the short axis of the amphitheatre. Slight evidence of a possible altar was detected in the eastern recess, and Continental analogy would suggest they were both shrines, one perhaps for Nemesis (cf. p. 199). The amphitheatre probably remained in use throughout much of the fourth century.

Littlecote Park

pp. 83–4 Two buildings in the west range have now been consolidated and excavation is proceeding on the south range. On leaving the mosaic room you first come to a workshop with adjacent domestic quarters (for a farm worker or slave?); the visible layout dates from the late third century. Bronzeworking furnaces were found in the largest room here. It is separated by a narrow alley from the main residential block, originally laid out about AD 170 but substantially remodelled in the closing years of the third century. This is a good example of the so-called 'winged corridor' type of villa. A corridor runs along the front of the house giving access to the principal rooms, and is flanked at either end by projecting L-shaped rooms which in the late alterations were converted into square chambers: added masonry can be detected by the straight joints with earlier walls (a plan displayed at the site aids elucidation). The main visible features of this house are the unusual circular hypocaust in the central room (installed *c.* 270), the kitchen behind it with its oven, and the modest bath-suite at the south end. The baths were stoked from the small chamber adjacent to the kitchen and main hypocaust; of its two flues leading into the tiny *caldarium* one was later blocked, the blocking wall being still *in situ*. The channelled hypocaust in the apse of the *caldarium* would have heated water in a now-vanished hot bath above; the box-tile used as its outflow drain can be seen. The next room to the south was the *tepidarium*; the other heated rooms here probably provided alternative dry-heat bathing. Many of the brick *pilae* have for conservation reasons been replaced in modern materials. The cold-water plunge-bath and steps down to it can be seen at the corner of the building; the wall plaster displayed in the temporary site museum (1986) came from here. Curiously the excavations appear to have shown that the bath-suite was entirely demolished in the late alterations of *c.* 290, when the main circular hypocaust was also filled in; the only heating thenceforth seems to have been in the square room at the south end of the front corridor (only its brick flue is visible; the *pilae* have gone), stoked from what had formerly been the *frigidarium*. At least five of the rooms had tessellated or mosaic floors (only scraps survived), including at least one added after demolition of both baths and main hypocaust. The block was certainly a much less comfortable residence then, perhaps for summer occupation only. Final decay did not set in until the late fourth or early fifth century.

A well and part of the enclosure wall are visible nearby. Excavation on the badly-robbed south range has uncovered (1986) part of another bath-suite, apparently unfinished; whether this served a farm manager's cottage or another well-appointed residential block for the villa owner remains to be seen.

Of the heavily restored mosaic in the *triconchos* (p. 83) the portions entirely in modern materials are detectable by the use of cream rather than white background *tesserae*. Elsewhere (loose) Roman *tesserae* were used to repair the extant original parts of the mosaic, but the extent of the repair can only be worked out by studying excavation photographs of 1978. I remain unconvinced by the excavators' belief that this was a meeting hall for an Orphic cult, preferring instead to see it as a summer dining room.

Gloucester

p. 111 Only the medieval work is visible from street level. At the bottom of the stairs inside the inspection-chamber, turn sharply left to reach the fine ashlar masonry of the Roman

gate-tower of *c.* AD 90. The position of one of the wooden posts
of the legionary fortress gate is indicated in the linoleum floor,
and an actual oak post, from an interval tower, is displayed
nearby. The masonry foundation for the late Roman wall of
c. 270–90 is also impressive; note the lewis-holes in many of
the stones, to facilitate lifting. The blocks above this belonged
to the Roman wall erected on this foundation but were reset
in their present position during a medieval repair. The black
line marked in the floor by the custodian's desk indicates the
course of a third-century water-pipe; a black area beyond
marks the position of the wide, shallow Roman defensive ditch
of the fourth century, dug as elsewhere in Roman Britain to
replace the V-shaped ditches of earlier centuries (cf. p. 184).
Bastions apparently belonged to the *c.* 270–90 reconstruction
rather than later as was customary in Romano–British towns
(indicating perhaps a quasi-military role for Gloucester at this
period, approximately contemporary with the building of the
Cardiff fortress: p. 218), but none are now visible.

In addition to the other fragmentary remains of Roman
Gloucester indicated on p. 111, mention may be made of the
massive rusticated blocks on display in the premises of the
National and Provincial Building Society, 45–9 Northgate
Street, last remnants of the gate which stood adjacent to this
site (visible through the window when the office is closed), and
a Roman mosaic excavated in 1978–9, visible through a trap-
door in the nave of St Mary-de-Lode, which lies immediately
outside the west door to the cathedral precinct. Other mosaics,
presumably belonging to the same Roman house (which was
built in the second century and occupied to the fourth) were
found during the earlier repair work on the church, in 1825.
There are small finds from excavations on the respective sites
preserved at three premises in Westgate Street (1 – Royal Bank
of Scotland; 4 – Midland Bank Ltd.; 30 – Alliance and
Leicester Building Society).

A small building inscription has recently (1985) been spotted
built upside down in the outer (south) face of the blocking wall
of the second arch from the west in the triforium of the
cathedral. It refers to the century of Cornelius Crescens of the
XXth. Legion, Valeria Victrix (a title it received for valiant
service against Boudica in 61). The stone, along with the
Aurelius inscription found in 1983 (p. 111), confirms the

presence of this legion at Gloucester (and probably also at Kingsholm), at least until about 70. The inscription must have come from the legionary baths, likely to have been the only stone building in the otherwise timber fortress.

Cirencester

p. 116 Although not *in situ* the following additional Roman antiquities may be of interest to the assiduous student of Roman Cirencester: a Roman column base at the corner of West Way and South Way, just to the left of the Police Station as one faces it (South Way, not marked as such on fig 26, p. 113, is the northward continuation of Tower Street); a fragment of mosaic pavement border in the entrance to the Health Clinic on the west side of Watermoor Road (visible when the Clinic is open); other scraps of mosaic in the entrance to the United Reform Church, Dyer Street, and in the foyer of the Cotswold Sports Centre, Tetbury Road; and a fourth-century Roman coffin from the cemetery excavated prior to the building of the western bypass, exhibited in the forecourt of the premises of Christian Brown Ltd., Phoenix Way (not marked on the map; turn right at the west end of Quern's Lane and first left into Phoenix Way).

Woodchester

p. 127 Immediately west of the site of the Roman villa, in the housing development in Woodchester village known as Lawn Field, a section of stone water-conduit is visible. This is known to have ended very close to the villa itself; it brought water from a spring 600 yards (550 m.) to the west. There is no dating evidence, but the inference that it is Roman and served the villa seems irrefutable; rich villas in Italy and other provinces are also known to have laid on their own water-supply.
Excavations at the villa when the Orpheus mosaic was last exposed (1973) added significantly to our knowledge of the site: as so often the final plan (that recovered in the eighteenth-century excavations) represents only the culmination of a long period of development, beginning perhaps *c.* 100. Thirteen rooms are known to have had mosaics, most of them contemporary with the laying of the Orpheus pavement (probably *c.* 325/50 rather than earlier), but more no doubt await discovery: the main bath-suite, for example, has not yet

been located. Imported marble veneers and statuary (fragments of eleven sculptures are known) further emphasize the impression of a luxury dwelling: indeed no other known fourth-century villa in Britain can match its degree of lavish interior decor.

Littledean

p. 132 A short distance north of Lydney what is claimed to be another Roman temple-site has been excavated and preserved since 1984. It lies in the grounds of Little Dean Hall, just south of the village of **Littledean** (SO 682119) and is reached by an unsignposted turning off the Gloucester–Chepstow road (A48) in the centre of Newnham-on-Severn ('Dean Road'). Little Dean Hall itself is only open between April and October (10.30–6), but the 'temple', near the car-park, is accessible with permission at any reasonable time. Excavations here have revealed a heavily-robbed stone building at two levels. On the lower level is a rectangular '*cella*' with an ambulatory on three sides; at the upper was a structure which has been restored as a square within a square and so superficially similar to the normal Romano–British temple, although the arrangement of two contiguous 'temple' structures in this way is unique in Roman Britain. Some material was found indicating second–third century AD activity at the site, but doubts have been expressed as to whether the visible structures are in fact Roman at all. The plan of the complex as a whole, and certain features discovered during excavation such as the irregular west wall (nearest the car-park) with a series of odd-shaped niches in no particular arrangement, do not find ready parallels in Romano–British temple-building. Many of these irregularities have disappeared in the restoration carried out in 1987, and it is therefore important to point out to visitors that there is no archaeological evidence for the symmetrical arrangement now presented for the west end of the building (no apse was found, for example, at the point where the drain passes through; it has been provided to balance the one at the opposite end of the corridor). More significantly, there is no archaeological justification for the modern water-basin which now occupies much of the '*cella*' of the excavated building. Claims that this was a water-shrine in honour of Sabrina, goddess of the Severn (the river can be glimpsed, but only at a distance, by walking

into the next field) are unsubstantiated. It is with some
misgivings that I include the site in this book at all.

Colchester

p. 136 Construction work on a temple to Claudius would not
have begun until after his death and deification in AD 54, and
was still unfinished at the time of the Boudican revolt in 61.
Although the temple underwent various repairs and
alterations, and although the temple precinct around it was not
formally enclosed by a stone wall and monumentalized until
c. 80–100, the likelihood is that the visible masonry of the
temple substructure is indeed that of the initial building period
of *c.* 55–65. Recent work has, however, demonstrated that
additional concrete was added in the fourth century along the
front (south) of the temple to provide a narthex or entrance
hall (with an apse at least at one end); this may have happened
on the adoption of Christianity in 313, although it is by no
means certain that the temple was converted for use as a
church, either then or later in the fourth century.

p. 138 An important discovery of 1981, that of Colchester's
Roman theatre, has in part been preserved. Leave Upper
Castle Park through the small gate on its west side (near the
temple-precinct wall noted on p. 138), cross Ryegate Road and
go through the narrow alley into Maidenburgh Street.
Immediately opposite is St Helen's Chapel. The north and east
walls of this incorporate Roman foundations (overgrown in
1987) which have now been shown to belong to the north-east
corner of a Roman theatre of classical D-shaped plan, about
70 metres in diameter. The well-preserved curved walls and
passage-floor belonging to the east side of the theatre are
displayed inside a modern building a short distance south of
the Chapel, and are clearly visible through windows even when
the building is locked. In the street between here and St Helen's
Chapel, the line of the outer wall of the theatre, first exposed
in 1891 (when its significance was not understood) and again
in 1984, has now been marked out with the aid of differently
coloured bricks. The dating evidence for the theatre recovered
by the excavations was negligible, but the visible walls probably
belong to a second-century rebuilding, although the early
theatre mentioned by Tacitus, completed before the Boudican

revolt of AD 61 (p. 134), no doubt stood on the same site.

p. 139 The modern office block on your left by the traffic lights (headquarters of the Royal London Mutual Insurance Society) covers the site of the spacious extramural house excavated in 1979. A fine mosaic which came from it is now displayed in the modern building: the central panel depicts wrestling cupids, and there are sea-horses in the surrounding lunates and a running tendril border. The floor, datable to *c.* 150–175, is one of the earliest products of a mosaic workshop responsible for other pavements both at Colchester (e.g. the North Hill geometric mosaics, p. 135) and Verulamium.

Bancroft

p. 156 (upper) One feature of another Roman villa has also been preserved, at **Bancroft**, Bradwell (SP 827403) on the NW edge of Milton Keynes. Turn off A422 ('H3') at the second roundabout E of A5 along V6 (northwards), then left along Millers Way ('H2'), then left into the car park. The villa, partly excavated in the 1970s and then more comprehensively in 1983–6, is a good example of a medium-sized winged corridor villa (see p. 376 for another). Built in the late second century to replace an earlier timber house, it underwent various modifications, most notably around AD 340 when geometric mosaics were added in nearly every room (parts of three were well preserved) and the bath-suite was rebuilt. In front of the villa a formal garden was laid out in the fourth century with an ornamental pool on the main axis. Six outlying farm buildings were also located to the north, three rectangular (one at least probably a barn) and three circular in the pre-Roman tradition; all belonged to the second century. A fourth-century mausoleum 300 metres NW of the villa is also known. At one stage it was hoped that the site would be consolidated and left exposed, but this has not proved possible. The only visible Roman structure is the fourth-century stone-lined pool which stood in the centre of the walled garden, but plans are in hand (1987) to mark out the walls of the villa itself in modern materials and to erect information panels. The mosaics were lifted in 1983 and are now in store.

Harlow

p. 156 (lower) Although ground-plans marked out in modern
materials are not normally included in this volume (p. 3),
an exception may perhaps be made for the temple at **Harlow**
in Essex (TL 468124). The site was already important in
the pre-Roman Iron Age, and the quantity of brooches and
gold and silver British coins testify to its importance before AD
43, although no certain traces of pre-Roman religious
structures were detected during excavation. The first temple, on
stone footings, dates to the last quarter of the first century and
is a good example of the 'Romano–Celtic' type, consisting of
square *cella* and surrounding ambulatory; it was enclosed by
a palisade. Extensive alterations in the third century included
the construction of a precinct wall with ornamental gateway
and other rooms added to the south and west sides of the
temple; there was an altar now in the forecourt, and long
buildings of unknown purpose there too. The sanctuary, to an
unidentified deity, continued in use into the fourth century
before going into decline; it was therefore the focus of
apparently uninterrupted worship for close on half a
millenium. A Roman settlement of uncertain size and
significance is known in the locality. The sanctuary buildings,
first recognized as long ago as 1764, investigated in 1927, and
fully excavated between 1962 and 1971, are marked out
between the river Stort and the railway line immediately west
of Harlow Mill station, on the northern edge of Harlow New
Town; they are approached via a lane from the north side of
the site.

Lincoln

p. 169 (upper) If you want to be even more thorough, there
are also fragments of wall on private property visible
immediately east of the Newport Arch in the garden of
Newport Cottage (52 Bailgate), and another, largely obscured
by ivy, in the grounds of Hilton House at the south end of the
west wall in the upper circuit, immediately south of the Castle
walls.

p. 169 (lower) Near the Roman well-shaft the plan of a simple
but sizeable apsed building has been marked out in modern
materials. Discovered when the Victorian church of St Paul-in-

the-Bail was demolished here in 1971, it stood in the middle of the open space of the Roman forum. There can be no doubt that it is a church, and some of the earliest burials associated with it can be dated at least to the fifth and sixth centuries. Some prefer to push the dating back into the later fourth century and see it as a Roman church, although there is no direct corroboration of this, and its location in the middle of the forum is somewhat irregular if the latter was still operating normally. It is safer to assume that the church is sub-Roman, built in the decaying forum after the latter had ceased to function as such.

Caerleon

p. 191 (the fortress baths) Now turn the corner on the catwalk so that you can see the steps down into the original *natatio*, still partly lined with slabs of Purbeck marble, and the remains of the fountain house, from which the stone dolphin water-spout displayed at catwalk-level came; the whole was demolished in the mid-second-century alterations. From the bridge bisecting the swimming pool half-way along can be seen the bench along the right-hand wall, another set of steps at the far left corner, and the waste-pipe of lead in the centre of the end wall. The original pool was a massive 135 feet (41 m.) long, the shortened version 85 feet (26 m.).

Now turn and face the rest of the baths with the *natatio* behind you. On your right is a rectangular cold plunge-bath, an early-second-century enlargement of the original bath (not now visible); next is the massive vaulted drain, here curving round to your right, an impressive early document (*c.* 75) of Roman water technology in Britain, like the great drain at Bath (p. 106), and the source also of a wealth of finds, some of them mentioned below (p. 386). Above it was later erected the entrance lobby to the baths, one of the alterations, together with the heated changing room you see to your left, of *c.* 150 (the original entrance was at the opposite end of the building). Now go down to the far end to the catwalk parallel to the one you have just left, and turn and face back towards the ticket-counter. You are now in what remains of the *frigidarium* (approximately half of it), with the final second-century floor-level to your left (some slabs are *in situ*, while impressions of others are detectable in the concrete bedding). The two vast holes in front of you (and two more behind) originally contained the massive piers of carefully dressed stone which took the main thrust of the vaulted roof above; the holes are the work of stone robbers who removed the stonework almost in its entirety. Note that, immediately below you, the final flooring has been cut away to reveal an earlier floor, and the corner of a phase-1 wall and associated floor can be detected below that: there were major refloorings of the baths (apparently to combat flooding problems caused by a high water table) c. 100/110 and again c. 150. Both the great circular wash-basin with Medusa head and the circular drain cover displayed here come from the extramural Castle Baths; a smaller but similar cover would have closed the entrance to the great *frigidarium* drain (situated in the modern alcove to your left). To your right are two semicircular plunge baths flanking a rectangular pool (partly covered by the catwalk). Now go down to the furthest point inside the cover building: the Bath stone flags of the last *frigidarium* floor are well preserved here, and you can also detect the conversion of the semicircular alcove of the original baths (*c.* 75), which no doubt contained a freestanding wash-basin, into a plunge bath, a change which occurred *c.* 100/110. The passage to the right of it led to a vast, aisled covered exercise hall (*palaestra*), not now visible, similar to civilian examples at Wroxeter (p. 173) and Leicester (p. 176); this was an afterthought added in the 80s. The mosaic on the wall here, which came from another adjacent room, is apparently primary; if so it ranks among the earliest mosaics from Roman Britain (*c.* 75/80); but the work is heavy-handed (notice especially the poorly drawn guilloche), presumably by an inexperienced legionary craftsman, not a specially imported Continental mosaicist. The dimensions of the *tepidarium* and *caldarium* which lay south of the cover building have been established by trenching and an outline plan of the baths can therefore be ascertained. They are in the mainstream of legionary bath-development at this period (the second half of the first century) and would undoubtedly have been designed by a military architect trained, if not in Rome, then perhaps in Germany or Switzerland where the closest parallels occur. Claims advanced in the display panels, however, that the Caerleon baths and its military fellows may have influenced or inspired the baths of Titus in Rome (*c.* 80) are unfounded. The latter belong to a different and more sophisticated type arranged symmetrically around a central axis, a type which can be traced in Rome back to the baths of Nero in the 60s.

p. 195 The Caerleon Legionary Museum (for opening times see p. 195) houses an outstanding collection of finds now superbly displayed. First turn left to see the material from the Usk fortress (*c.* 55–75), situated upstream on a site subject to flooding which was aborted in favour of Caerleon. Among the many noteworthy exhibits from Caerleon itself in the main room are: on your right, the maze mosaic from the HQ building, one of very few British mosaics from military sites (another is in the Baths, p. 385); the silver tip of a legionary banner (*vexillum*), and, in the same case, a painted inscription naming the Second Augustan legion on a Rhodian wine jar (found in 1986); and the inscriptions in the far corner which are important for piecing together the history of building work in the fortress. The fine inscription to Trajan (TRAIANO in line 2) was dedicated in AD 100, as indicated by his holding a third consulship (COS III in line 5); note how the third stroke was clearly added later, indicating that the stone was prepared in 99, when Trajan was COS II, but not erected until the following year. Along the back wall to the right are funerary monuments, including a cremation burial in a lead canister with pipe protruding from the ground for libations. The cases in the centre of the room include some important glass and outstanding finds from the Baths excavation. The great drain there, for example (p. 384), yielded no fewer than 88 gemstones lost by bathers from their signet-rings (the largest collection from a single findspot in Roman Britain until 117 were found in a pot in Snettisham, Norfolk, in 1985; those are due for display in the British Museum). Also lost in the drain was a superb and very rare bronze strigil (for removing dirt from the body), inlaid in gold and silver with scenes of six of the twelve labours of Hercules. This outstanding find, inscribed in Greek 'it washed you nicely', must have been made in Italy or even in the Greek east, and was presumably the prized possession of some high-ranking officer.

Chester
p. 198 Some Roman bases and a Tuscan column can be seen

(not *in situ*) outside the Coach and Horses pub at the corner of Northgate Street with Princes Street, as well as a Roman gutter-stone and grooved slabs at the rear of the public library, off Princes Street. These are *disiecta membra* of fortress buildings recovered in this area prior to redevelopment, Northgate Street bisecting the site of what was probably the hospital, and a possible stores depot lying between the library and the bus station. Of other fragments listed in Appendix I (p. 412), the column at 35 Watergate Street (possibly from a Tribune's residence) is readily accessible (provided the staff are not busy) at the back of a toyshop called Toycraft. To the list given on p. 412 can be added a Roman mains culvert under the car-park of 3–5 Shipgate Street (off Bridge Street) and a well in the official inn-cum-post-house (*mansio*), in the garden of 5 Castle Place nearby. Both of these, which lay in the civilian settlement outside the fortress walls, are on private property and can only be seen by prior written arrangement.

Prestatyn

p. 212 A road headed eastward from Caerhun in the direction of St Asaph in the vale of Clwyd, where Roman finds have been made and a fort is suspected, probably the Roman VARIS. But our knowledge of the Roman occupation of north-east Wales has been complicated in recent years by the discovery of a further site near **Prestatyn** (SJ 062817), 5 miles NNE of St Asaph. Two successive forts in adjacent positions are in fact thought to have existed here, although little excavation has been carried out at either; however a small bath-house lying outside what is taken to be the south-east corner of a putative eastern fort (the existence of which has yet to be definitely confirmed) has been consolidated and left exposed. The site lies on the west side of the A547 midway between the centre of Prestatyn and the village of Meliden, 2 miles south: take the turning called Melyd Avenue (cul-de-sac), at the bottom of which you will find the tiny three-roomed bath-house. The walls of the cold room, nearest the road, and of its adjacent semicircular plunge-bath, were badly robbed, but the two heated rooms beyond, built of neat coursed rows of white limestone and red Cheshire sandstone, are well preserved. The *pilae* supporting the floors are of brick, some stamped by the XXth Legion and made at the legionary brickworks near

Chester; no stamped examples are visible. The stoke-hole of the *caldarium* at the far end employed an inscribed slab reused from elsewhere: three letters (?COR, the last not certain) survive. First located in 1936, the bath-house was re-excavated in 1984–6, when it was found that the two heated rooms were built earlier (*c.* AD 100) than the *frigidarium* and its cold plunge, added *c.* 150. But two heated rooms alone do not make a bath-house, and the earliest cold room must have been of timber, as at Bearsden (p. 339). An oblique stone-built structure at the higher level in this room is of unknown function, probably post-Roman. Water was brought to the baths on a wooden leat supported on posts; also found nearby were several timber buildings, including a bronze workshop with remains of crucibles, slag, and, unusually, clay moulds for brooch-production. Both the baths and the workshop were abandoned by *c.* 160. The baths were presumably civilian rather than military, as the structure is too small to have served as the garrison bath-house.

Caernarfon

p. 213 The 1987 daily opening hours were: May–Sept., 9.30–6 (Sun. 2–6); Mar., Apr. and Oct., 9.30–5.30 (Sun. 2–5); Nov.–Feb. 9.30–4 (Sun. 2–4).

Holyhead

p. 217 The defence of Caer Gybi is likely to have been assisted by a series of watchtowers from which warning could be signalled of impending attack, and one of these, excavated on the summit of **Holyhead Mountain** (SH 218829) in 1980–1, has been consolidated and left exposed. To reach the site, turn left off the main street in Holyhead opposite the telephone kiosks near the fort's south gate, turn right at the end (one-way system), and then at the church take the Porth-y-Felin road on your left, signposted Holyhead Mountain. After $\frac{2}{3}$ mile watch out for Old School Road on your left; ignore that but continue on for another $\frac{1}{3}$ mile until the other loop of Old School Road joins the main road. Turn right here (unsignposted) and follow the road as far as you can until it begins to peter out near a pillar-box and a group of houses. Walk up the track from this point and keep straight; an eventually well-defined path leads in approximately 15 minutes to the entrance of **Caer Y Twr**

(SH 218830) hill-fort, mentioned on p. 223. The stone ramparts of this 17-acre enclosure, probably built early in the Roman period, are well preserved, up to 10 feet high with remains of the rampart walk in places. Aim now for the OS triangulation pillar clearly visible from here; a further ten-minute walk will bring you to the summit of Holyhead Mountain and to the two remaining walls of the Roman watchtower, next to the OS pillar. Measuring some 18 feet (5.45 m.) square, it has walls 4 feet thick on wider footings; the scanty dating evidence pointed to construction in the late fourth century, in keeping with the assumed chronology of Caer Gybi. Not surprisingly there are fine views of Holyhead harbour, but the view northwards is blocked by Carmel Head, on the summit of which another Roman watchtower, so far unexcavated, is suspected (SH 293924). By leaving the tower behind you and continuing down to the bluff just below, where the mountain falls steeply to flattish moorland, you can make out some of the hut circles mentioned on p. 223, to the left of the track and to the right of the rectangular reservoir.

Barry

p. 218 An enigmatic building at Cold Knap, **Barry**, South Glamorgan (ST 099664), excavated in 1980–81, has been consolidated and is accessible at any time. In the western outskirts of Barry, turn westwards off the A4050 along Salisbury Road, signposted Porthceri and The Knap. Follow signs for the latter into Romilly Park Road, where you should turn right under the railway (Lakeside) and then immediately right (Bron-y-Mor). The Roman building lies at the end of this road behind (i.e. west of) Hotel Water's Edge, above the parking area (Knap Car Terrace). Built throughout of coursed rubble limestone, it consists of 21 rooms and corridors arranged on all four sides of a central rectangular court with walk-way around; there is a cellar at the SE corner. The south range was planned first, and the rest followed; the verandah on the beach side was an afterthought. But the building seems never to have been put into commission. There was no sign of floor levels or rendering on the walls or occupation debris, and one wall had collapsed directly onto builders' levels, but at least part of it had been roofed. This is a substantial building of Mediterranean courtyard type, constructed of stone to roof height, and no doubt intended to be furnished with a colonnade round the central court; yet as to its purpose and the reason why it was abandoned before completion we can only speculate. It is certainly not a villa, indeed not a civilian structure at all; rather it has an air of officialdom about it, and in plan it most resembles the *mansiones* or lodging-houses for government officials of the type visible at Wall (p. 183) and Vindolanda (p. 299). What it is doing here, far from the known main lines of communication in this part of Wales, is harder to explain; but the adjacent small harbour might conceivably have been used as the northern terminal of a ferry service across the Severn estuary. Why the scheme was aborted before completion we shall never know, but the limited dating evidence for the building's brief life points to the later third century, when the increasing insecurity of the area is reflected by the decision to build the massive new fort at Cardiff (pp. 217–18). But conditions must have taken a dramatic, unexpected and very sudden turn for the worse if they really were responsible for the *'mansio'* builders' change of heart.

Caerwent

p. 221 Another Roman house, excavated in 1981–4 and consolidated in 1987, is now visible further north in Pound Lane, on the left. It is an excellent example of the spacious courtyard house, erected in the late third century over the demolished remains of at least two predecessors. The main court has a verandah on three sides and rooms opening off it; that in the middle of the west side had a hypocaust (flue), but few *pilae* survived and none are now visible. The hypocaust of a room in the north wing is better preserved; from here a corridor led northwards to another group of rooms. That at the far end has another hypocaust (stone *pilae*); part of a second garden court lies to the right. Its portico had a geometric mosaic and Tuscan columns, traces of which were found in the excavations (as were fragmentary mosaics in some other rooms) but are not now visible.

p. 222 Excavation at the temple site has demonstrated that the shrine was not built before the late third century: below it lay a street, lined by first timber and then stone buildings, secular rather than religious. In front of the temple a long forehall with apse at one end was added in the fourth century, and other small rooms (priest's rooms, souvenir booths?) were erected on its north side facing the temple. The religious precinct was still maintained in the late fourth century, its presumably pagan ritual continuing despite the advancing strength of Christianity.

Caer Y Twr

p. 223 For directions to this hill-fort, see now p. 388.

Castleshaw

p. 237 Recent work, still continuing (until the end of 1988), has greatly expanded our knowledge of the fort-site at **Castleshaw** (SD 9909). Turn off the A62 (Oldham–Huddersfield road) 2m NE of Delph in Greater Manchester, along the road marked 'Castleshaw Centre' (gate piers inscribed OCWW). Keep straight, leaving the first reservoir to your left, and then take the right fork (leaving the second reservoir also to your left) up to the fort site, which lies at the top of the hill right of the road. When work is completed it is planned to have a car-park near the reservoirs, and visitors will then walk up to the fort along the line of the Roman road. The first fort, of which the earth defences are still partly visible, was an Agricolan foundation, built *c.* 75 and abandoned about fifteen years later. Trial trenching in 1957–64 revealed traces of Agricolan timber buildings within (and a hint of pre-Agricolan structures too). The fort was a small one (about 2½ acres), presumably designed for 500 infantry if a full unit was posted here. About AD 105 a fortlet measuring 49 yards by 60 yards (45m by 50m) was built inside it. It had a turf rampart on a stone base and two timber gateways; the line of the SE defences coincided with that of its predecessor. Thoroughly explored in 1907–8, after which untidy spoilheaps were left all over the place, it is this fortlet which is the focus of the current reinvestigation. The spoilheaps have been removed, and the defensive circuit recreated as a low bank. The purpose of the fortlet, which was occupied until *c.* 150, remains enigmatic. A stone-built room with a hypocaust, now reburied for its own protection, presumably belonged to the commandant/administrator, and a large granary discovered in the earlier excavations (an indication, perhaps, that the fortlet served as a collection-point for the corn-tax levied from the local farmers) are the principal known internal buildings, but there appears to have been no regular barracks of the type usually encountered in fortlets. When excavations are complete some of the principal features and the line of the roadways will be marked out, and an information board erected on the site.

Ilkley

p. 238 A fragmentary Roman inscription, probably Severan, which was found in 1982 reused in the foundations of the west wall of the church, is now displayed in the tower with Saxon stones from the churchyard.

Ribchester

p. 240 The bath-house, identified in 1837, first dug in 1927, and re-excavated between 1978 and 1980, is not a particularly instructive example of its type. Closed between November and Easter, it is accessible at any time during the rest of the year, either from the main road in the centre of the village (turn down Greenside and then take the first turning on the right), or from the path along the river, leaving the main road near the museum (signpost). The architectural development and function of the various rooms of this bath-building are by no means clear. Make first for the square room with remains of hypocaust *pilae* of two different periods, some round, some square. This and the adjacent square room with the flagged floor at a higher level were both part of the earliest bath-house apparently erected *c.* 100, the rest of which now lies under the grass to the south. Both rooms were heated in this first phase, as flues to enable the underfloor circulation of warm air are visible in the party wall between the two. Later (*c.* 160?) these openings were blocked with brickwork, when the room nearer the river became either a *frigidarium* or the *apodyterium* and received the flagged floor still partly visible. On the other side of the remaining heated room, which probably now served as a *tepidarium*, a fresh heated chamber (*caldarium*) was added, covering in the process a well which lay outside the phase-1 building. New flue arches were opened in the party wall between *tepidarium* and *caldarium*, and new furnace stoke-holes were added to the north wall, that serving the *caldarium* showing signs of particularly heavy use. The detached circular sweating-room (*sudatorium*) is thought to have been added *c.* 120. The purpose of the cobbled area is uncertain (a base for a water tank?). The baths were demolished *c.* 200/25, although the furnace area seems to have remained in use later for industrial purposes.

Piercebridge

p. 242 The Roman site can be viewed from afar at the field-gate mentioned on p. 242, but in 1986 the gate was firmly wired up and access made impossible. Alternative access to the Roman site is from the yard of the farm (with permission from the owner) on the north side of the church. At the north end of the village it is also worth turning left at The Wheatsheaf for a fine view (opposite the bus-shelter) of the NW corner of the fort, visible here as a boldly upstanding earthwork.

Binchester

p. 244 Return now to the ticket office and walk down to the fence at the far end, passing a fine stretch of Roman street (the course of Dere Street passing through the fort) with guttering on the far side. Then turn right along the blue-gravelled corridor, at the far end of which (and in the room beyond) are some demolished foundations of third-century structures. The function and layout of the rest of the rooms here, which are of fourth-century date and appear to have also formed part of the *praetorium*, are not easy to interpret. The original arrangement of *c.* 290 has been obscured by the radical changes of the late fourth century, when this part of the building was turned into self-contained flatlets of two or three rooms, and others were used for iron-working and other processes: the room with the single square slab adjacent to the blue-gravelled corridor, for example, is interpreted on the basis of bone finds as a cattle-slaughterhouse. Binchester was a cavalry fort, founded by Agricola, evacuated early in the second century, and apparently reoccupied *c.* 160. Its north and east ramparts are very prominent as earth mounds in the field beyond the farm. To the south lay an extensive civilian settlement.

Ebchester

p. 245 The mound of the south rampart defences can be made out in the graveyard behind the church; the school beyond sits

on the site of an annexe. More striking is the rampart bank at
the NE corner, reached by crossing the main street (Vindomora
Road) and going into the children's playground opposite
Mains Cottage.

Manchester

p. 260 Part of one further fort-site in the north of England,
Manchester (SJ 8397), the Roman MAMVCIVM, has been
extensively excavated over the past fifteen years, and this has
been followed (in 1984–6) by an enlightened programme of
reconstruction, an exercise now tried also at South Shields
(p. 275). Heading north from Deansgate in the centre of
Manchester, turn right along Liverpool Road just before the
railway bridge (signposted A57, Warrington); if you are
approaching from the north follow directions for Deansgate
and then (white signs) Castlefield. The fort's north gate lies in
gardens opposite the Manchester Air and Space Museum.
Three simple buildings in the civilian settlement (*vicus*) north
of the fort are marked out in modern materials. Early
makeshift shacks with signs of iron-working around them were
demolished *c.* 120; buildings on stone footings took their place
c. 200 and were occupied until *c.* 350. Pottery, bone, bronze
and iron objects were all made here. Beyond rises part of the
north defences of the fort together with the reconstructed
gateway. The first fort on the site (4.8 acres) was a turf-and-
timber one built under Agricola *c.* 79 and renovated *c.* 90; it
was demolished in the first quarter of the second century,
probably *c.* 124 when troop movements consequent on the
decision to place forts on Hadrian's Wall involved the
abandonment of many garrison-posts further south. A slightly
larger fort (5 acres) took its place *c.* 160 as part of the
consolidation necessary after the Brigantian uprising of *c.* 155.
This was apparently also of turf and timber and was not
refurbished in stone until the early third century, later than
usual in this part of the province (although Ilkley among visible
forts shares a similar construction history: p. 238). What you
see today, therefore, is the twin-portalled gateway as it may
have appeared in the third century, with flat platform above
but no flanking guard towers. The simulated gateway is
noticeably squatter than its reconstructed counterpart at South
Shields, and may be nearer the original height, although such

conjectures are always problematical in view of the lack of evidence (p. 275). The inscriptions are bogus but plausible. Only the robbed-out foundations of both gate and wall survived. The only Roman masonry visible *in situ* are three slabs of the base plinth on the outer face to the left of the gateway as you approach it (clearly distinguishable from the modern blocks either side). A few facing stones are ancient but the vast majority are modern. For another fragment of MAMVCIVM, see p. 415. Some finds are displayed in the Castlefield visitors' centre at the corner of Liverpool Road and Deansgate.

Wallend

p. 273 The fort at **Wallsend** (SZ 3066), the Roman SEGEDVNVM, was covered by housing in the nineteenth century, and its outline was discovered by careful trenching only in 1929. Nothing, however, was known of the fort's interior layout until excavations commenced in 1975 in advance of proposed redevelopment, and the consequent archaeological work over the following ten years has resulted in the important recovery of the first almost complete fort-plan from Hadrian's Wall excavated under modern conditions. Fresh housing has been built over the northern quarter of the fort. The southern part has been grassed over, as apart from the headquarters building the structures were too extensively robbed to merit permanent consolidation and display. To reach the fort, follow the signs for Wallsend (A187) eastwards out of the centre of Newcastle, and continue straight wherever possible. When signs for Wallsend disappear, follow the directions for Tyne Tunnel (two roundabouts), and watch out for Buddle Industrial Estate on your right. The road bisects the fort immediately beyond this. The line of the fort wall and the east, south, and part of the west gates, all double-portalled, have been marked out in white paving stones; there was also a single-passage postern-gate on the SW side. Interval towers are also marked out. Note how the white paving stones extend westwards from the west gate and south-eastwards from the SE corner, marking the line of Hadrian's Wall (which actually commenced from the river bank below the fort). Excavation in 1929 demonstrated that this was Narrow Wall and of one build with the fort, and so that the extension to Wallsend and the fort itself were

afterthoughts which belong to the second-phase plan for
Hadrian's Wall, *c*. 124 (p. 269). The few blocks of masonry
visible at the east gate are not precisely *in situ*: the gate was
recorded before destruction in 1912 during the erection of a
hotel, and surviving blocks were transferred to Wallsend Park,
whence they have now returned. The HQ (*principia*), which has
been left exposed, is of the usual plan of forecourt (note the
guttering), cross-hall (entered also from the east), and five rear
rooms. As displayed, the *principia* is in its third-century form,
by which time the colonnade had been walled off to form two
L-shaped rooms (with moulded base-piers for the roof
supports), the *tribunal* in the cross-hall had been removed, a
water-tank placed in the courtyard, and a strong-room inserted
under the central regimental shrine in the rear range. A
freestanding second water-tank behind the *principia* is also
visible. The granaries and a hospital lay west of the *principia*
in the central range, the commandant's house to the east; the
rest of the fort had barracks, workshops and stables. The third-
and fourth-century garrison was the Fourth Cohort of
Lingones, 500 strong, a part-mounted unit (hence the stabling).
An unusual secondary addition to the front of the *principia*,
spanning the main east-west road (the *via principalis*), was a
drill-hall (not visible), a feature common on the German
frontier, but only the sixth such example to be identified in
Britain. More details of the fort's layout and history can be
learnt from the display in the Wallsend Heritage Centre, across
the road from the east gate (Tue.–Fri. 10–5.30; Sat, 10–4.30;
Sun. 2–5).

South Shields

p. 277 Some of the structures in the NW corner of the fort were
uncovered in 1966–7 but now lie under the grass. Retrace your
steps past the reconstructed gate and turn left. First on your
left is a double granary which belongs to the original second-
century stone fort (currently labelled 'Hadrianic granary'; for
discussion of the date, see above p. 277). In the fourth century
the floor of one of the granaries was removed and two tile-kilns
were inserted. One, in excellent condition, was re-excavated in
1980 in the hope that it could be consolidated, but it was found
to be too fragile to withstand winter frosts and has been
reburied under a protective earth mound. The plan of the other

has been marked out in modern materials. The bases of the portico designed to give shelter during delivery of supplies are visible in front of the granary. The next building is also a granary (C7), one of many provided when the fort became a supply base for the emperor Severus' northern campaigns *c*. 208. After it comes the headquarters building (*principia*), a structure with a long and complicated history elucidated during re-excavation in 1984–5. You first enter the courtyard of the third-century headquarters building of *c*. AD 220: the two columns belong to the colonnade which once flanked it, and part of its gutter can also be seen. This building replaced a partly demolished second-century *principia* which faced in the opposite direction: its rear range of five rooms, with buttresses along the back wall, are marked out in pebbles in front of you. Beyond this lies the cross-hall, which remained in the same position in both buildings. The *tribunal* of such halls, however, lies on the right of anyone entering from the courtyard, and so when the HQ was turned round a new *tribunal* had to be built. That on your right (confusingly indicated in identical-type pebbles to those used for the second-century rear range) belongs to the *principia* of *c*. 220, that on your left is the masonry of the second-century *tribunal*. Beyond lies the massive third-century strong-room, with double-thickness walls of cramponed blocks (some re-used from the second-century fort), and with a sump in the bottom to keep it dry. Its size, much bigger than in a normal auxiliary fort, emphasizes the continued importance of South Shields even after the conclusion of Severus' campaigns: pay-chests for the garrison of more than one fort were surely stored there, if only on a short-term basis before distribution to their respective HQs. The administrative rooms on either side were given hypocausts (of the channelled variety) in the fourth century; traces are visible. Beyond the back wall of the third-century *principia* lies a well. This was in the courtyard of the second-century HQ but remained in use even after the building switched direction. Some of the square bases which supported the colonnade flanking this early courtyard can be detected beyond, on the north and east sides, as well as the gutters which flanked the entrance to the second-century *principia*. That building was largely demolished *c*. 208 and replaced by two granaries. One was inserted into the shell of the cross-hall (which was left standing), although no walls belonging to the granary phase are indicated there now. The other was inserted into the northern end of the second-century *principia*, using the latter's walls on three sides and having a new (buttressed) wall only on the fourth. The latter has been marked out in pebbles, and part of the sleeper walls and a reconstituted fragment of floor (which originally of course extended the full length of the granary) are also visible. Now that it is known that even the HQ gave way to granaries in Severus' storebase of *c.* 208–11, and that the later HQ postdates his campaigns, there remains the problem of locating the administrative nerve-centre for control and distribution of the campaign supplies.

Facing the granaries and HQ already described, five further granaries (and part of a sixth under what is currently (1987) a spoil heap) are visible, all of them belonging to the period of Severus' supply base. Below them the plans of earlier barracks are marked out. Many of the granaries, understandably, did not retain their original function for long, and when the fort returned to normality *c.* 215/20 some were divided up by internal partition walls to provide barrack accommodation, well seen in granary C13 and to a lesser extent in C12. They remained in use for at least part of the fourth century when the garrison of ARBEIA was the *numerus barcariorum Tigrisiensium*, a detachment of boatmen from the area of the Tigris river in Mesopotamia, who were clearly specialists called in to accompany supplies past the dangerous shoals of an undredged Tyne. The two granaries nearest the museum are good examples of their type: the outer buttressed wall, occasionally broken by ventilation-gaps, and the low sleeper walls which supported the floor, are clear, the later subdividing partitions here having been largely removed.

Now walk over to the far side of the site to examine the eastern defences. First come the bases of two ovens, and then you will see a fragment of curving wall inside the line of the main defences. This, discovered in 1978, represents the SE corner (and part of an angle-tower) of the second-century fort, and shows conclusively that the site was enlarged (from 3.9 to 5.1 acres) when it was converted into the Severan storebase *c.* 208. The stone defences south of this point, including the south gate (of single-passageway type with flanking guardrooms which do not project forward from the line of the wall),

belong therefore to the early third century. Next comes the fort
latrine, with central flagged floor and stone seat-supports
(fig 80, p. 276). The drains which flushed it, their cover slabs
partly *in situ*, can be seen in two parallel branches heading for
it. The fort wall is mostly reduced to foundations, and is
severely robbed on the south side, but the base-plinth at the
SE corner survives (fig 79, p. 274), and the back wall of the SW
angle tower stands a few courses high. The earth rampart
backing the wall has been entirely levelled. Much of the
defences here was first uncovered in the nineteenth century and
then re-exposed in 1977–9. Further Severan storehouse
granaries, as well as a large courtyard building built over them
c. 220, are currently (1987) under investigation in the SE sector,
and more of the fort will be consolidated as work progresses.
Only at Housesteads and Caernarfon is a comparable
proportion of a fort's interior layout in Britain available for
permanent inspection.

Corbridge

p. 281 The pediment in the museum which came from this
fountain house indicates that it was built by men from the
Twentieth Legion, on detachment from Chester probably in
the third century. Note the statue bases on either side of the
fountain, and also, partly destroyed by the criss-crossing
drains, a small square room at the lower level in front of the
fountain. This and a portion of corridor adjacent (a drain
crosses the latter obliquely) belong to a building of the stone
fort of *c.* 140 which underlies the site; part of the HQ and
praetorium belonging to it are visible in the middle of the
courtyard building (p. 282). This fragment infront of the
fountain house is conjecturally interpreted as belonging to the
fort's hospital; both its position within the fort and the
fragmentary plan suit such an interpretation.

Chesters Bridge Abutment

p. 284 Other features to note at the Chesters bridge abutment
are a phallus carved for good luck on the northward face of
the abutment; the massive projecting foundation stones of the
south abutment, set obliquely to the edge of the masonry apron
above; and a cylindrical tapering stone with square base and
rounded raised knob on the top, lying on the apron, one of a

pair of bollards (a more fragmentary one is under the trees)
which are believed to have flanked the approach to the bridge
ramp.

Sewingshields Crags

p. 291 Those with time to spare may like to continue westwards
along the Wall line for another 15 minutes, skirting round the
north side of the farm in the coppice, in order to reach another
length of consolidated Wall on **Sewingshields Crags** (NY 8070),
together with what is left of milecastle 35. The Crags are
spectacular here, 1068 feet above sea level, and there are fine
views in all directions, but the Wall, excavated in 1978–80, is
not preserved to any great height. Reduced in width by one or
two offsets above its Narrow Wall foundation (in turn resting
on Broad Wall footings), the superstructure here is only some
$6\frac{1}{2}$ feet wide, considerably less than the norm for the Hadrianic
narrow gauge: the whole stretch seems to have been rebuilt
more or less from foundations, probably early in the third
century (Severan). The milecastle is much robbed and the
jumble of structures within is at first sight confusing. The
earliest is the small rectangular structure (Hadrianic) at the SE
corner, later overlain by another, also visible (?Severan). The
west building, presumably a barrack, is not before the early
third century; note its small square hearth near the centre with
traces of burning. In the fourth century this was demolished
and other structures, given over entirely to metal-working,
were erected on top. The milecastle had evidently ceased to
have any military function by then; indeed the metalworkers'
principal access was over the demolished remains of the
milecastle's east wall. The oven in the NW corner also belongs
to this fourth-century phase. Note that there is no north gate,
at least in the third century, when rebuilding removed all traces
of the Hadrianic arrangement; but although at times Hadrianic
builders did indeed rigidly stick to their blueprints, and were
blind to the demands of local topography, no building gang at
any period would surely have been idiotic enough to build a
gate here, leading to nowhere except a precipice.

Vindolanda

p. 301 Some enigmatic circular buildings partly visible here
belonged to the second-century stone fort which extended

further north than its successor. Unparalleled inside a military fort, these 'huts' in the native tradition are of unknown purpose.

Peel Crag – Highshield Crags*

p. 302 Excavation and consolidation work since 1982 (still in progress in 1987) has rendered the sector between Peel Crag and Highshields Crags one of the most dramatic and rewarding on the whole Wall-line. East of the level stretch on Peel Crag the Wall drops into a gap, where excavation in 1986 discovered an unexpected supernumerary turret. The distance between milecastles 39 and 40 is the longest on the Wall, and the planners evidently decided to add a third turret in the stretch between the two. But it is situated in a blind gap, with poor visibilty except back to the Stanegate, and it is hardly surprising that it was later demolished and ignored in the third-century reconstruction. Evidence for the various phases of Hadrian's Wall is especially clear here: the Broad Wall foundation, the Narrow Wall foundation on top, three or so courses of regular Narrow Wall standing on it, and then the Severan Wall of the early third century above that. The distinction here between the hard white mortar of the Severan work and the second-century pinkish mortar was strikingly clear prior to consolidation work in 1987. The excavation here and elsewhere on this stretch has in fact dramatically confirmed just how extensive was the early-third-century rebuilding of the Wall, at least in this central section – something suspected from evidence elsewhere (e.g. cf. p. 289), but only fully confirmed by the excavations of the last few years (cf. also Sewingshields, p. 400). After climbing the hill on the far side you soon dip down again into Castle Nick milecastle (see pp. 302–3), still under excavation in 1987. As at Sewingshields the buildings within are all fragmentary, and belong to at least three periods; there is no sign of a pair of regular barracks on either side of the central road, such as occurs at Poltross Burn (p. 305: it may not have been typical). Broad Wall foundations are visible on the inside on the milecastle's north wall. On the crag east of the milecastle are a number of small irregular stone buildings erected in the shelter of the Wall and, beyond them, a short stretch of Wall foundation (Broad gauge) laid out on a quite different alignment to that eventually chosen. Clearly the original plan was to swing the Wall eastwards down into Sycamore Gap on a more gentle curve: as built, the Wall turns abruptly to descend the steep slope. Here is a splendid example of the Wall, on carefully stepped foundations, keeping its horizontal coursing as it takes a dramatic dive down into the gap – steeper and even more impressive than similar examples elsewhere in the consolidated sector (e.g. Thorny Doors, p. 304; Walltown, p. 305). It is worth walking through the modern breach at the foot of the gap to examine the drainage culvert at the lowest point; note also how the very hard basalt whinstone blocks, distinct in colour from the limestone courses above (and much more difficult to quarry), are used at the base of the Wall for extra stability. Also visible (1987), on the outer face as the Wall climbs eastwards out of the gap, are some traces of hard white mortar not just joining but also covering the facing stones. This feature (which the elements may well remove after a few years), also detectable in parts on the inner face, has given rise to the suggestion that the Wall, at any rate at the time of the Severan reconstruction (which employs the distinctive white mortar), was 'whitewashed' throughout its entire length to make it an even more forbidding sight. But it has not certainly been detected elsewhere, and for the present it seems best to interpret this feature as idiosyncratic behaviour on the part of one building gang with excess mortar to spare. Return now to the inner face and climb up on to Highshield Crags where the newly-consolidated sector ends. The Broad Foundation, in places with a single building course present, is clearly visible here as the Wall climbs up to the crags again, with the Narrow Wall foundation cutting into it.

Carvoran

p. 305 After Walltown, before rejoining the B6318 near Greenhead, the Roman Army Museum is worth a brief visit. There are few finds on display here (except for a little 'overflow' material from Vindolanda, a site under the same management), but several life-size mock-ups and reproductions of Roman armour, as well as a Hadrian's Wall video, are informative and entertaining. It is worth walking down the path to the right of the entrance door of the museum, as far as the metal gate, for an excellent view of the north rampart of the fort of **Carvoran** (NY 6665), standing high and bold under its turf capping. Virtually no excavation has ever been carried out at this fort, but there has been a rich haul of inscribed stones and other chance finds, now mainly divided between the museums at Chesters and Newcastle. The garrison attested here in 136/8 and 162 is the First Cohort of Hamian archers, a specialist unit from Syria; not surprisingly dedications to Syrian deities such as the 'Syrian goddess' (*dea Syria*) and Jupiter of Baalbeck are also known. Also from Carvoran and now in Chesters museum is the very rare find of a bronze dry-measure (*modius*), designed to hold, according to its elegant inscription, the equivalent of nearly 17 pints (17½ *sextarii*).

Bothwellhaugh

p. 327 One site in Scotland that is now worth a visit is the 4-acre fort at **Bothwellhaugh** (NS 731577), reached from the M74 by taking either the Motherwell (A723) or the Bothwell (A725) exits and following signs to Strathclyde Country Park. Once inside the park, head for the bridge over a small river, and park in the picnic area south of the river. The car-park sits on the NE angle of the Roman fort, which has been known since the 1790s and was partly dug in 1938–9 and 1967–8. It is not, however, the fort itself which merits a detour (only the SE rampart is easily distinguishable now), but the remains of the garrison bath-house down by the river (the path from the car-park follows the line of the NE rampart, represented by the very slight bank on your right). The baths were discovered in 1973, excavated in 1975–6 in advance of the artificial flooding of the valley bottom, and then dismantled and rebuilt on a higher level in 1979–81. The *frigidarium* is at the east end nearest the fort (note the splendid drain-cover, represented by a replica at the site; the original is in Glasgow's Hunterian Museum), and off it open a semicircular cold plunge-bath and the heated rooms, with a furnace at the far end. Bothwellhaugh is an Antonine fort, perhaps (on the slender basis of size) for a part-mounted unit 500-strong. Limited excavation of the defences revealed more than one phase, as did also work in the baths, but the site as a whole had a short life of not more than 25 years.

Kinneil

p. 332 About 2½ miles from the eastern end of the Antonine
Wall, on the A993 just west of Bo'ness, lies the sixteenth-
century Kinneil House. Cross the stream behind the House,
pass the twelfth-century ruined church which you will see on
your right, and make for the field beyond, where a solitary tree
sits on the northern lip of the Antonine Wall Ditch, visible here
as a hollow. Beyond the small reservoir, on a gentle hilltop, are
the remains of the 'mile'-fortlet of **Kinneil** (NS 977803), the
only exposed example of the nine such fortlets so far identified
on the Wall (see p. 330). Located in 1978 and completely
excavated in 1981, the fortlet was found to measure some 61
feet by 71 feet internally (18.5 m. by 21.5 m.), with timber gates
set in the north and south ramparts. The road through the
former, of rammed pebbles, is flanked by a drain, some
capstones being still in place. Two small wooden buildings
were traced within the fortlet, in addition to a pit in the NW
corner which yielded some well-preserved shoes. Ploughing
was found to have dealt unkindly with the fortlet defences
except at the NE corner, where the stone base on which the
rampart turves were erected still survived. The line of the
ramparts and of the Antonine Wall has been marked out with
modern paving slabs, and the timber gateways and buildings
are represented by wooden posts set in the original post-holes.
The finds are in Kinneil Museum, 10 minutes' walk away, near
the House (Mon.–Sat., 10–12.30, 1.30–5, May–Oct.; Nov.–
Mar., Sat. only, 10–5).

Callendar Park

p. 333 There are two separate places here where the Ditch is
preserved: one is in the grounds of Forth Valley College of
Nursing, and the other is in what was formerly Callendar Park.
The Antonine Wall Ditch in the latter is reached by turning off
the A903 into Callendar Park, and then left (Seaton Place); go
down to the far end, and then walk northwards. The rampart
is detectable here as a low mound, and the Ditch is impressive.
Further west, where the line of the Wall descends to Kemper
Burn, a Roman heated structure, which must be a bath-house,
was partly revealed in 1980 but then backfilled; some kerb-
stones of the Antonine Wall base discovered nearby, as well as
the course of the rampart, are however still visible. Turn off

the A903 at the roundabout (Arnot Street), then take Kemper Avenue; the Wall lies at the far end of the car-park on your left.

Bearsden

p.339 The timber posts marking the outline of *frigidarium* and *apodyterium* stand in the original socket-holes for the uprights of the timber-framed structure. Also visible is the outline of a demolished buttressed room on the north (left) side of the second hot room. This was planned as a heated room (it had provision for a stoke-hole) but the hypocaust was never installed and it was demolished during construction when the bath-builders decided on a change of plan: a different hot room (the dry-heat *laconicum*: see p. 339) was added alongside, incorporating the timber posts of the already completed *frigidarium*. A small latrine, built up against the east rampart of the annexe, has also been preserved (except for its south wall, destroyed by a modern sewer); it was flushed by two overflow channels from the baths. Wheat, barley, coriander and opium poppy (the last two used for seasoning) were identified in sewer-deposits from here.

Ardoch

p. 342 Dr David Breeze, in a bold attempt to explain the somewhat odd final arrangement of the ditch-system, has recently suggested that the two outermost ditches on the north and east belong to the Agricolan fort, but that would give the first-century defences a most peculiar outline not readily paralleled elsewhere. The irregular groundplan of the ditches at the NE corner is probably to be explained by the adding of further ditches in the later Antonine period ('Antonine II') to those of the first Antonine fort; in any case all five ditches on the east side must have been thought necessary in the final phase, as obsolete ditches from an earlier fort or forts would almost certainly have been filled in.

In addition to the marching camp mentioned on p. 343, the defences of the annexe on the north side of the Antonine fort at Ardoch can also be traced on the ground. From the fort's north gate head towards the field-gate near the A822, where the ditch on the west side of the fort annexe is visible, and follow the latter northwards across a fence into the ground beyond. If the bracken cover is low you may be able to detect, as the annexe defence turns a corner at the NW angle, the south rampart of the 130-acre camp (probably of Severan date) cutting through it. The continuation of the north rampart of the annexe can be traced adjacent to, and south of, the minor road to Auchterarder.

London

p. 352 The exact position of the Roman bridge has now been pinpointed by the discovery of two Roman roads on the south bank converging on the same point, and of a box-structure on the north bank interpreted as a bridge-pier support. Somewhat surprisingly the dating evidence points to construction around AD 50 rather than earlier, but the absence of a bridge here for seven or so years from AD 43 is inconceivable: either evidence for the first structure has been obliterated, or the bridge was a temporary affair, perhaps a pontoon. Excavations just north of Lower Thames Street and elsewhere along the Roman waterfront have provided graphic evidence of the commercial life of the city, in the form of massive timber quaysides and accompanying warehouses. In the mid-first century the Thames water-line here was 100 metres north of its present line, but successive rebuilding and land reclamation advanced the line of the quays southwards by some 350 meters before the end of the third century.

p. 362 Go through the breach in the wall at Cooper's Row to the gate at the far end of the yard. Turn left, go under the bridge, and keep straight on until you reach Vine Street. Here on your left is **Emperor House**, in the basement of which has been incorporated the external face of the Roman city wall, some 30 feet (10 m) long and 10 feet (3 m) high, excavated in 1979–80. Also visible is the projecting rectangular foundation for one of the D-shaped external bastions added *c.* 350 (the bastion itself was demolished in medieval times), the only such example of Roman date from the London defences permanently accessible. The wall with its base-plinth and a portion of the bastion footings are visible with difficulty through an inspection window in the yard to the right of the main entrance to Emperor House; this is accessible during normal working hours only, Monday to Friday. Closer inspection (from the staff canteen) is only possible by prior written arrangement with The Secretary, Lloyd's Register of Shipping, 71 Fenchurch Street, London EC3M 4BS.

p. 363 In the subway under Houndsditch (Aldgate end), a cross-section of the Roman wall with its accompanying earth bank, recorded here before destruction during the construction of the subway, is represented in modern tiling near exit 1. The Roman level here was found to be 14 feet (4.2 m) below the present-day one. This is item 6 on the 'London Wall Walk' itinerary, created in 1983 with information panels at the various points of interest: Emperor House (see above), for example, is the subject of panel 4, Cooper's Row panel 3, and so on.

Appendix I

Gazetteer of visible remains not mentioned in the text

For explanation of the symbols, see introduction, p. 5. Places listed here do not appear in the index or on the maps at the beginning of each chapter. A few antiquities which appeared in this Appendix in the First Edition have been omitted, not because they have disappeared, but because their Roman date is now in doubt and they have been omitted from the OS Map of Roman Britain, 4th ed. 1978.

Chapter One

OS Grid ref.	1:50,000 map no.	Name	County	Description	Notes
TQ1133	187	Alfoldean	W Sussex	settlement(e)	1
TQ0317	197	Hardham	W Sussex	settlement(e)	1, 2
SU8426	197	Iping	W Sussex	settlement(e)	1
TQ4054	187	Titsey	Surrey	villa(s)	3
TQ4565	177	Orpington	Gtr London	villa(s)	4
SU8105	197	Bosham	Sussex	building(s)	5
TQ0544	187	Farley Heath	Surrey	temple(s)	6
TR1342	189	Stowting	Kent	barrow(e)	
TR1752	179	Bishopsbourne	Kent	barrow(e)	
SU810402	186	Alice Holt	Hants	pottery kilns(e)	7

Notes

1　Three small road staging-posts, all displaying remains of earth ramparts.
2　Cut through by railway. Only S side and NE corner. Occupied AD 50–150.
3　Small building excavated 1864, but now largely overgrown with nettles. Parts of two rooms clearly visible, one with hypocaust. Ask permission and directions from South Lodge, on B-road.
4　Flint walls and red tessellated pavements project from bank of driveway to Borough Council Depot and Offices, off Crofton Road, immediately SW of, and adjacent to, Orpington Station.

5 W wall of nave of Bosham Church is of Roman masonry with brick bonding-course. Base for Roman arch remains *in situ* below bases of Saxon chancel arch.

6 Foundations of a typical Romano–Celtic temple, dug in nineteenth century in the usual fashion of the day, as this ditty by Martin Tupper *c.* 1848 amply demonstrates:

> Many a day have I whiled away
> Upon hopeful Farley Heath,
> In its antique soil digging for spoil
> Of possible treasure beneath.

7 Series of irregular mounds, mostly in S end of forest, covering sites of Roman kilns.

Chapter Two

OS Grid ref.	1:50,000 map no.	Name	County	Description	Notes
ST4401	193	Waddon Hill	Dorset	fort(*e*)	1, 2
ST0927	181	Wiveliscombe	Somerset	fort(*e*)	1, 3
SX0367	200	Nanstallon	Cornwall	fort(*e*)	1
SX6699	191	North Tawton	Devon	fort(*e*)	1
SS733072	191	Bury Barton	Devon	fort(*e*)	1, 4
ST5222	183	Ilchester	Somerset	town(*e*)	5
SZ0099	195	Wimborne Minster	Dorset	building(*s*)	6
SU7863	175	Finchampstead	Berkshire	milestone(*s*)	7
SU4313	196	Bitterne	Hants	bath-house(*s*)	8

Notes

1 See p. 65 for context.

2 Very slight.

3 Roman date not proven, but virtually certain.

4 Part of larger earthwork (?19 acres) visible on W side and at SW angle (immediately W and SW of farm, next to track). Later fort within, traceable on all sides except SW, where the farm has obliterated it. Fort probably occupied *c.* 55–75. Possibly NEMETOSTATIO.

5 Section of rampart in fields E of village.

6 Tiny piece of tessellated floor is *in situ* on S side of the Minster's nave.

7 Uninscribed. In gardens of 'Banisters', a short distance from place of discovery.

8 Tiny baths (*c.* AD 175), with 4 rooms, converted into two-roomed structure later and demolished *c.* 370 when late Roman fort-wall (overgrown rubble beyond; note change in ground-level) was built. At left-hand end of Bitterne Manor House (flats), reached from Southampton by first turning off A3024 east of river-bridge.

Chapter Three

OS Grid ref.	1:50,000 map no.	Name	County	Description	Notes
SO3974	137	Leintwardine	Hereford and Worcs	fort (*e*)	1
SO4442	161	Kenchester	Hereford and Worcs	town(*e*)	2
SP0425	163	Spoonley Wood	Glos	villa(*s*)	3
SO5708	162	Scowles	Glos	iron mine	4
SP2712	163	Widford	Oxon	mosaic	5
SP3011	164	Worsham Bottom	Oxon	villa(*s*)	6
ST5269	172	Gatcombe	Avon	settlement(?)(*s*)	7

Notes

1 Only on W side of village.
2 Almost totally ploughed out; best on NE near farm.
3 Difficult to find; walls mossy and nettle-grown; one mosaic (Victorian replica) is visible. Permission from E W Bailey, Charlton Abbots Manor.
4 Opencast rocky hollows, much overgrown with foliage.
5 Fragment *in situ* in floor of church.
6 Overgrown walls and one floor of red *tesserae* just visible in a coppice.
7 Short section of late-third-century defensive wall surrounding a small market settlement (rather than a villa). Fork left on farm drive and cross stream; wall is at wooden railings in field on right.

Chapter Four

OS Grid ref.	1:50,000 map no.	Name	County	Description	Notes
TM0308	168	Bradwell-on-Sea	Essex	fort(s)	1
TF7844	132	Brancaster	Norfolk	fort(e)	2
TL3954	154	Barton	Cambs	barrow(e)	
TL4534	154	Langley	Essex	barrow(e)	3
TL3717	166	Youngsbury	Herts	barrow(e)	
TL8961	155	Eastlow Hill	Suffolk	barrow(e)	

Notes

1 Saxon Shore fort of OTHONA. One overgrown fragment of S wall 4 ft long and the same high; near cottage, to right of fine seventh-century chapel largely built of Roman materials.
2 Depression marking ditch on W side is all that remains of Saxon Shore fort of BRANODVNVM.
3 Now largely ploughed away, on SW side of the NW-SE farm-track (not NE side as shown on OS map).

Chapter Five

OS Grid ref.	1:50,000 map no	Name	County	Description	Notes
SP0483	139	Metchley	W Midlands	fort(e)	1, 2
SK1882	110	Brough-on-Noe	Derbys	fort(e)	1, 3
SO8688	139	Greensforge	Staffs	fort(e)	1
SO6978	138	Wall Town	Salop	fort(e)	1
SK7041	129	Castle Hill	Notts	town(e)	4
TA1101	113	Caistor	Lincs	town (s)	5
SP3459	151	Chesterton	Warwicks	town(e)	
SP6948	152	Towcester	Northants	town(e)	6
TL1298	142	Castor	Cambs	building(s)	7
SK9876	121	Riseholme	Lincs	barrow(e)	
TL2174	142	Great Stukeley	Cambs	barrow(e)	8

Notes

1 See p. 164.
2 NW corner of large fort, reconstructed, behind new building of Medical Faculty, University of Birmingham.

3 NAVIO, occupied *c.* 75–120, 155–350.
4 Part of E defences of MARGIDVNVM visible as low mound.
5 Best fragment of late Roman defences (p. 185), 7 ft high, is seen over fence on S side of churchyard; part of a bastion is visible in yard reached between gap in houses next to 6, Chapel Street; other bits in Grammar School grounds (Church Street) and in private cellar on south corner of Bank Lane with Market Square.
6 Earth ramparts at NW corner of LACTODVRVM, in field W of police station; reached by footpath to Greens Norton (signpost).
7 Two lumps of Roman walling project from modern wall on Stocks Hill, opposite church. Relaid mosaic in dairy at Milton Hall. See p. 180.
8 Low and very overgrown. Note rise and fall of fence bordering road.

Chapter Six

Chester:
The following visible fragments of the fortress, all on private property, were not included in the text above: (i) 48 Eastgate St (guard chamber); (ii) 35 Watergate St (column-base); (iii) 104 Watergate St (furnace arch); (iv) 18 St Michael's Row (mosaic panel); (v) 22 St Michael's Row (wall); (vi) 28 Eastgate St (Browns) (column-base). See also p. 387.

OS Grid ref.	1:50,000 map no.	Name	County	Description	Notes
SS7998	170	Blaen-cwm-Bach	West Glam	marching-camp(*e*)	1
ST0098	170	Twyn y Briddallt	Mid Glam	marching-camp(*e*)	2
ST059878	170	Pen-y-Coedcae	Mid Glam	marching-camp(*e*)	3
SO379007	171	Usk	Gwent	fort(*e*)	4
ST379917	171	Coed-y-Caerau	Gwent	fortlet(*e*)	5
SO1621	161	Pen-y-Gaer	Powys	fort(*e*)	6
SS5697	159	Loughor	West Glam	fort(*s*)	7
SS6097	159	Mynydd Carn Goch	West Glam	2 practice camps(*e*)	
SN8510	160	Coelbren Gaer	West Glam	fort(*e*)	8
SN862102	160	Camnant	West Glam	marching-camp(*e*)	9
SN924164	160	Ystradfellte	Powys	marching-camp(*e*)	10

OS Grid ref.	1:50,000 map no.	Name	County	Description	Notes
SN8026	160	Arosfa Gareg	Dyfed	marching-camp(e)	11
SN7735	146	Llandovery	Dyfed	fort(e)	
SN919507	147	Beulah	Powys	marching-camp(e)	12
SN647485	146	Pant-teg-Uchaf	Dyfed	practice camp(e)	13
SN6456	146	Llanio	Dyfed	bath-house(s)	14
SO0292	128	Caersws	Powys	fort(e)	15
SO2098	128	Forden Gaer	Powys	fort(e)	
SH6555	115	Pen-y-Gwrhyd	Gwynedd	marching-camp(e)	16
SO2243	148	Clyro	Powys	fort(e)	17
SN8281	136	Cae Gaer	Powys	fort(e)	18
SN828067	160	Hirfynydd	West Glam	fortlet(e)	
SN856935	136	Pen-y-Crogbren	Powys	fortlet(e)	
SH7457	115	Bryn-y-Gefeiliau	Gwynedd	building(s)	19
SH477454	123	Derwydd-bach	Gwynedd	marching-camp(e)	20
SH860278	124	Pont Rhyd Sarn	Gwynedd	practice camp(e)	
SN927699	136	Esgairperfedd	Powys	marching-camp(e)	21
SN985717	136	St Harmon	Powys	marching-camp(e)	22
SJ4163	117	Heronbridge	Cheshire	settlement(e)	
ST4791	171	Castle Tump	Gwent	building(s)	23
SS9569	170	Llantwit Major	South Glam	villa(e)	24

Notes

1 Best on W side (*titulum* survives) and near NE corner, due N of farm.

2 Most of outline traceable, with *claviculae* on NW and NE sides.

3 Only E end and angles are well preserved.

4 SE side of BVRRIVM, E of Court House.

5 Immediately NE of pre-Roman 'enclosure' marked on OS map.

6 Best preserved on N.

7 Part of fort-wall exposed in S side of castle mound (1979).

8 Whole fort visible as prominent banks, partly marked by field-boundaries.

9 Best on W side, and part of E, about 300 yards S of 8.

10 Only a very low bank, best preserved near SE corner. Fire-breaks in the plantations are so positioned as to leave the ramparts free from trees.

11 Nearly whole circuit can be traced.

12 Most of N and W sides are traceable. $\frac{1}{4}$m S is site of a Roman fort, partly covered by the farm (very prominent platform, but no real remains of ramparts).

13 Unfinished. N side 2 ft high. Another similar camp nearby (SN 641493) is now obscured by trees.

14 Remains of hypocausts, etc., clearly visible, but vandalized. On S side of a fort-site (invisible). Ask permission and directions from farm.

15 Best preserved on SW in road near station and level-crossing.

16 Very fragmentary condition, best seen on S side of A4086 200yds W of junction with A498, as road bends to left (W rampart), and on E side of A498, also 200yds S of junction, immediately beyond road-sign (S rampart).

17 NE and SE sides of vexillation fortress (p. 189) covering 26 acres, not occupied after *c.* AD 75.

18 See p. 208.

19 Prominent mounds with some stonework exposed; in annexe on W side of a fort (invisible).

20 Reed covered, at best 1 ft high: parts of NW and SW sides. A Roman fort and fortlet, now entirely quarried away, existed $\frac{1}{3}$m E.

21 Most of circuit traceable.

22 Only S end, including *clavicula* at S gate, is visible.

23 On Ministry of Defence property and not accessible to the public.

24 Enclosure-banks, and mounds covering walls, of Roman villa.

Chapter Seven

OS Grid ref.	1:50,000 map no	Name	County	Description	Notes
SJ8397	109	Manchester	Gt Manch	fort(s)	1
SD9909	109	Castleshaw	Gt Manch	fort(e)	2
SD9249	103	Elslack	N Yorks	fort(e)	
SD9390	98	Brough-by-Bainbridge	N Yorks	fort(e)	
SE5703	111	Doncaster	S Yorks	fort(s)	3

OS Grid ref.	1:50,000 map no.	Name	County	Description	Notes
NY998104	92	Scargill Moor	Durham	shrines(s)	4
NY8811	92	Roper Castle	Cumbria	signal-station(e)	5
NY829148	91	Punchbowl Inn	Cumbria	signal-station(e)	6
NY818147	91	Augill Bridge	Cumbria	signal-station(e)	7
SD913655	98	Malham Moor	N Yorks	marching-camp(e)	
NY4938	90	Old Penrith	Cumbria	fort(e)	
NX9821	89	Moresby	Cumbria	fort(e)	
NY2036	89	Caermote	Cumbria	fort(e)	8
NY1031	89	Papcastle	Cumbria	fort(e)	9
SD5190	97	Watercrook	Cumbria	fort (e)	9
NY3827	90	Troutbeck	Cumbria	marching-camps(e)	10
NY6001	91	Low Burrowbridge	Cumbria	fort(e)	
SE2299	99	Catterick	N Yorks	town(s)	11
SE1387	99	Middleham	N Yorks	building(s)	
SE6775	100	Hovingham	N Yorks	barrow(e)	12
NZ8315	94	Goldsborough	N Yorks	signal-station(e)	13

Notes

1 Fragment of E fort-wall of MAMVCIVM. Under a blocked railway-arch in a timber-yard at the end of Collier Street, off Liverpool Road. For the N Gate, see p. 394.

2 See p. 391.

3 Part of E wall of DANVM, in Church St, uncovered in 1972, between church and multi-storey car-park 3.

4 See above, p. 247. The best approach is from Spanham farmhouse, $1\frac{1}{8}$m to E. Circular shrine is still very conspicuous, opposite footbridge over stream. Site of northern shrine is marked by a heap of stones.

5 See above, p. 248

6 In pasture on crest of small hill on S side of Inn.

7 Bisected by modern ditch.

8 Smaller fort inside NW corner of larger. Ramparts of both are grassy, rest of area full of reeds.

9 Only very faintly visible.

10 3 camps here: smallest (384274) has two gates with external *claviculae*; second (382273), crossed by road, has two gates with internal *claviculae*. Ramparts of both 2 ft high. Third (largest) camp is very difficult to trace.

11 Stretch of E wall of CATARACTONIVM, excavated and

restored in 19th cent. Overgrown. On S side of A6136,
200 yds E of A1 bridge, adjoining inside of racecourse
track.

12 Very well-preserved, *c.* 10 ft high.

13 Now only a prominent mound; no stonework visible.

Chapter Eight

Numerous other Roman antiquities are visible on the Wall or
in the Wall region, apart from the selection described above.
They can be found with the help of the OS *Map of Hadrian's
Wall* (HMSO, 2nd. ed. 1972), although there is very little to
see at some of the sites marked on it as 'remains of'. The
inscribed Roman quarry-face called Rock of Gelt, near
Brampton, is worth mentioning here, as it does not appear on
the map. It is very difficult to find, and it is wise to look up
beforehand: R G COLLINGWOOD and R P WRIGHT, *Roman
Inscriptions of Britain I* (OUP 1965), nos. 1007–16, where a
large-scale map of its location can be found.

Chapter Nine

OS Grid ref.	1:50,000 map no.	Name	County	Description	Notes
§1					
NT909009	80	Yardhope	N'umberland	marching-camp(e)	1
NY8199	80	Bellshiel	N'umberland	marching-camp(e)	2
NT7909	80	Brownhart Law	Borders	fortlet(e)	3
NZ135885	81	Longshaws	N'umberland	fortlet(e)	4
NT4224	73	Oakwood	Borders	fort(e)	5
NT4754	66	Channelkirk	Borders	marching-camp(e)	6
NT555328	73	North Eildon	Borders	signal-station(e)	7
NT3472	66	Inveresk	Lothian	bath-house(s)	8
NS7357	64	Bothwellhaugh	Strathclyde	fort(e)	9
NS9146	72	Cleghorn	Strathclyde	marching-camp(e)	10
NS9244	72	Castledykes	Strathclyde	fort(e)	11
NS944265	72	Wandel	Strathclyde	marching-camp(e)	12
NS9916	78	Little Clyde	Strathclyde	marching-camp(e)	13
NT0213	78	Redshaw Burn	Strathclyde	fortlet(e)	14
NS9004	78	Durisdeer	Dum & Gall	fortlet(e)	14

OS Grid ref	1:50,000 map no.	Name	County	Description	Notes
NY2599	79	Raeburnfoot	Dum & Gall	fort/fortlet(e)	14
NT303047	79	Craik Cross Hill	Dum & Gall	signal-station(e)	14
NT0901	78	Tassiesholm	Dum & Gall	fort(e)	
NY389792	85	Gilnockie	Dum & Gall	marching-camp(e)	15
NY1281	78	Torwood	Dum & Gall	marching-camp(e)	16
NX9681	78	Carzield	Dum & Gall	fort(e)	17
NY5674	86	Bewcastle	Cumbria	fort(e)	18
NY5771	86	Gillalees	Cumbria	signal-station(e)	19
§2					
NS7677	64	Westerwood	Strathclyde	fort(e)	5
NS6774	64	Auchendavy	Strathclyde	fort(e)	5

(Only additional fort remains are listed here; other visible pieces of Wall and Ditch can be found with the help of the OS *Map of the Antonine Wall*, HMSO 1975.)

§3					
NO1739	53	Black Hill	Tayside	signal-station(e)	20
NN9028	52	Fendoch, Sma' Glen	Tayside	signal-station(e)	21
NO023149	58	Dunning	Tayside	marching-camp(e)	22
NS565998	57	Menteith	Central	marching-camp(e)	23
NJ6538	29	Glenmailen	Grampian	marching-camp(e)	24

Notes

1 Entire outline traceable of nearly square camp, up to 3 ft high, including three *titula*; discovered only in 1976.
2 Much obscured by field-banks.
3 Just north of the border fence.
4 Rampart about 4 ft high over the entire circuit.
5 Very faint.
6 Part of gigantic 165-acre camp, probably third-century.
7 See above, p. 325
8 Four hypocaust *pilae* with a lump of concrete on top, in the private garden of Inveresk House. It is part of the bath-house outside the Antonine fort (under St Michael's Church); an Agricolan fort was on a separate site 3 miles S. (Elginhaugh), totally excavated before destruction in 1986.

  9 SE rampart 5 ft high. Antonine. See now p. 403.

10 Well preserved on NW and NE sides in Camp Wood with two *titula* in NW side, but obscured by conifers and long grass.

11 Faint except on E. Antonine, with Agricolan occupation below.

12 450 ft of E rampart and 100 ft of S rampart visible. A fortlet lay immediately to N but is now denuded and invisible.

13 Best preserved near NW angle in field beyond farm.

14 See above, p. 327.

15 Most of SE side of camp, including two *titula*, is well preserved; partly in a wood.

16 Single surviving side is a field-boundary.

17 SE angle and part of S side only is visible. Antonine.

18 Outpost fort of Hadrian's Wall. First Hadrianic, but totally rebuilt under Severus on a very unusual hexagonal plan. Of latter, only SW rampart survives as a bold mound; lower bank in front of it is post-Roman. Castle sits on NE corner and contains many Roman stones. Famous Bewcastle Cross, eighth century, in churchyard.

19 Connected Bewcastle with Birdoswald on Hadrian's Wall.

20 See above, p. 346.

21 $\frac{3}{4}$m W of site of Agricolan fort, of which the complete plan was recovered in 1936–8.

22 430 ft of bank and ditch, 3–4 ft high, preserved in Kincladie Wood, on W side of B934.

23 Parts of two sides of an Agricolan camp, up to 1 ft high, in rough moorland on S side of Lake Menteith.

24 See p. 349; also faint traces of NE corner in pasture.

Further details of these, and other, Scottish sites, with full details of access, can be found in L. Keppie, *Scotland's Roman Remains*, 1986.

Chapter Ten

All the visible fragments of Roman London which are still *in situ* have been mentioned in the text (as far as I know). The only exceptions are the following, but for security reasons they cannot be visited by members of the public:

Basilica: National Provincial Bank, Cornhill Bank of
          Australia and New Zealand, Cornhill
Wall: basement of GPO Headquarters Building,
          Aldersgate
          Bowyer Tower, Tower of London

In Greater London, a tiny piece of red tessellated floor
belonging to a Roman building in Greenwich Park (TQ 393774)
has been preserved. It is set in an enclosure in the N part of
the Park, 100 yds from the E wall, half-way between
Vanbrugh and Maze Hill Gates. Further excavation took
place here in 1977 and 1979 in advance of treeplanting. The
floor belongs to a third-century building, possibly a hill-top
temple, which replaced a predecessor erected *c*. 100.

Appendix 2

Some museums displaying Romano-British material

The list is not complete, but it gives most of the major Romano-British collections with the exception of those in private hands and those in small site-museums (Richborough, Chedworth, Housesteads, etc.). A museum mentioned in the text is indicated by a page number in brackets; if the mention is more than a passing one, the number appears in bold type. In towns where there are several museums, the full title of the relevant one has been given to avoid confusion. Opening times can be found in *Museums and Galleries in Great Britain and Ireland*, published annually by British Leisure Publications.

Aylesbury
Bangor, Museum of Welsh Antiquities
Barnard Castle (p. 247)
Basingstoke
Bath, Roman Museum (pp. 103 and **104**)
Battle
Bedford, Museum
Birmingham, City Museum and Art Gallery
Bradford, City Art Gallery and Museum
Brecon
Brighton, Museum and Art Gallery
Bristol, City Museum (p. 118)
Bury St Edmunds, Moyse's Hall Museum
Buxton
Caerleon (p. **386**)
Cambridge, University Museum of Archaeology and Ethnology (pp. 158, 246 and 319)
Canterbury, Royal Museum (p. **46**)
Cardiff, National Museum of Wales (pp. 207, 211 and 218)

Carlisle (pp. 255 and 312)
Carmarthen (p. 219)
Castleford
Chelmsford
Cheltenham
Chester, Grosvenor Museum (p. 200)
Chichester (p. 47)
Cirencester (pp. **114**, 127)
Colchester, Castle Museum (p. **135**, 141, 157)
Dartford
Devizes
Doncaster
Dorchester, Dorset County Museum (pp. 70 and **72**)
Dover
Dumfries
Dundee, McManus Galleries
Durham, Cathedral Collection (pp. 244 and 319)
Edinburgh, Royal Museum of Scotland (pp. 325, 328 and 332)
Edinburgh, Huntly House Museum
Evesham
Falkirk
Folkestone

Glasgow, Art Gallery and Museum
Glasgow, Hunterian Museum
(pp. 331 and 342)
Gloucester, City Museum (p. **111**)
Grantham (p. 185)
Guildford, Museum and Muniment
Room
Halifax, Bankfield Museum and Art
Gallery
Harlow
Hereford, City Museum and Art Gal-
lery
Herne Bay
Hertford
Huddersfield, Tolson Memorial
Museum
Hull, Transport and Archaeology
Museum (p. **261**)
Hutton-le-Hole
Ilkley (p. **238**)
Ipswich, Museum
Jedburgh, Abbey Museum
Kettering, Westfield Museum
Kidderminster, Art Gallery and
Museum
Lancaster
Leeds, City Museum (p. 261)
Leicester, Jewry Wall Museum
(p. **177**)
Letchworth
Lewes, Museum of Sussex Archaeology
Lincoln, City and County Museum
(p. 171)
Littlehampton
Llandrindod Wells
Llandudno
London, British Museum (pp. 60, 61,
62, 101, 144, 211, 239, 361 and **371**)
London, Museum of London
(pp. 357, 364 and **365**)
London, Cuming Museum (p. 365)
Ludlow
Luton
Maidstone, Museum and Art Gallery
Malton (p. 237)
Manchester, City Art Gallery
Margate
Middlesborough, Dorman Museum
Newark-on-Trent
Newbury

Newcastle, Museum of Antiquities
(pp. **277**, 291, **315** and **319**)
Newport, IOW, Carisbrooke Castle
Museum
Newport, Gwent (p. 222)
Northampton, Central Museum
Norwich, Castle Museum
Nuneaton
Orpington, Bromley Museum (p. 63)
Ospringe, Maison Dieu (p. 64)
Oxford, Ashmolean Museum
Oxford, Museum of Oxford
Perth
Peterborough
Pontefract
Poole, Museum
Reading, Museum and Art Gallery
(p. **81**)
Ribchester (p. **239**)
Rochester
Rotherham
St Albans, Verulamium Museum
(pp. 142, **143** and 147)
Saffron Walden (p. 159)
Salisbury, Salisbury and South
Wiltshire Museum
Scarborough, Museum
Scunthorpe, Museum and Art Gallery
Sheffield, City Museum
Shepton Mallet
Shrewsbury, Rowley's House
Museum (p. 172)
Skipton
Southampton, God's House Tower
Museum
Stockport, Municipal Museum
Stroud
Sunderland
Taunton (pp. **81** and 101)
Thetford, Ancient House Museum
Tunbridge Wells
Warrington
Warwick, Warwickshire Museum
Whitby
Winchester, City Museum (p. 76)
Worcester, City Museum and Art
Gallery
Worthing
Yeovil
York, Yorkshire Museum (p. **228**)

Appendix 3

Bibliography

This bibliography is intended for the reader who wants more information about a given site than the scope of this book allows. The list is far from comprehensive, but references to other works will be found in many of the books and articles given below. A cross (+) denotes a work suitable for the non-specialist reader.

Abbreviations used

AA:	Archaeologia Aeliana (4th series)
Antiq.:	Antiquaries, Antiquarian, Antiquary
Arch.:	Archaeological, Archaeology
Arch. Camb.:	Archaeologia Cambrensis
Arch. Cant.:	Archaeologia Cantiana
Archit.:	Architectural
BBCS:	Bulletin of Board of Celtic Studies
CA:	Current Archaeology
CW:	Trans. of Cumberland and Westmorland Antiq. and Arch. Soc. (2nd series)
Hist.:	Historical
Inst.:	Institute
J:	Journal
JBAA:	Journal of the British Arch. Association
JRS:	Journal of Roman Studies
N.H.:	Natural History
Proc.:	Proceedings
PSAS:	Proc. of Soc. of Antiq. of Scotland
RCHM	Royal Commission on Historical Monuments
Soc.:	Society
TBGAS:	Trans. Bristol and Gloucestershire Arch. Soc.
Trans.:	Transactions
Univ.:	University
VCH:	Victoria County History

Introduction
Guidebooks to Roman Britain
Since the publication of the Second Edition in 1980, a flood of archaeological guidebooks has poured on to the market, most of them covering a much wider time-span than that attempted by the present book; an example is + P CLAYTON, *A guide to Archaeological Sites*, Batsford 1985. Of those exclusively concerned with Roman Britain, D E JOHNSTON, ed., *Discovering Roman Britain*, Shire 1983, was out-of-date to a significant extent even when published and prone to other error; the best available by far is + P OTTAWAY, *A Traveller's Guide to Roman Britain*, Routledge 1987, which is up to date and contains fine, evocative photographs; it is, however, more a book for armchair reading than a practical handbook to use in the field.

General Works
S FRERE, *Britannia*, Routledge, 3rd ed. 1987
P SALWAY, *Roman Britain*, Clarendon Press 1981
+ M TODD, *Roman Britain (55 BC–AD 400)*, Fontana 1981
+ J WACHER, *Roman Britain*, Dent 1978
+ H H SCULLARD, *Roman Britain, Outpost of Empire*, Thames and Hudson 1979
+ J WACHER, *The Coming of Rome*, Routledge 1979
+ S JOHNSON, *Later Roman Britain*, Routledge 1980

Literary and Epigraphic Source Material
+ S IRELAND, *Roman Britain: a source book*, Croom Helm 1986
R G COLLINGWOOD and R P WRIGHT, *The Roman Inscriptions of Britain* vol. I, Clarendon Press 1965
R GOODBURN and H WAUGH, *The Roman Inscriptions of Britain I: Epigraphic Indexes*, Alan Sutton 1983
A R BIRLEY, *The Fasti of Roman Britain*, Clarendon Press 1981

Topography
Ordnance Survey Map of Roman Britain, HMSO, 4th ed. 1978
Tabula Imperii Romani: Condate–Glevum–Londinium–Lutetia, OUP/British Academy 1983
Tabula Imperii Romani: Britannia Septentrionalis, OUP/British Academy 1987

A L F RIVET and C SMITH, *The Place-Names of Roman Britain*, Batsford 1979

Invasion Period
G WEBSTER, *The Roman Invasion of Britain*, Batsford 1980
id., Rome against Caratacus, Batsford 1981
id., Boudica, Batsford 1978
J PEDDLE, *Invasion: the Roman Conquest of Britain*, Alan Sutton 1987

The Archaeology of Roman Britain
General: R G COLLINGWOOD and I RICHMOND, *The Archaeology of Roman Britain*, Methuen, 2nd ed. 1969
S S FRERE and J K ST JOSEPH, *Roman Britain from the Air*, CUP 1983
Military: G WEBSTER, *The Roman Imperial Army of the First and Second Centuries AD*, Black, 3rd ed. 1985
P A HOLDER, *The Roman Army in Britain*, Batsford 1982
D J BREEZE, *The Northern Frontiers of Roman Britain*, Batsford 1982
+ *id., Roman Forts*, Shire Publications 1983
+ R WILSON, *Roman Forts*, Constable 1980
A JOHNSON, *Roman Forts of the First and Second Centuries AD in Britain and the German Provinces*, Black 1983
C S SOMMER, *The military vici of Roman Britain*, British Arch. Reports 1984
J S JOHNSON, *The Roman Forts of the Saxon Shore*, Elek, 2nd ed. 1979
D A WELSBY, *The Roman military defence of the British province in its later phases*, British Arch. Reports 1982
D B CAMPBELL, 'Ballistaria in first to mid-third century Britain: a re-appraisal', *Britannia* xv (1984), 75–84
Towns: J WACHER, *The Towns of Roman Britain*, Batsford 1974
+ A SORRELL, *Roman Towns in Britain*, Batsford 1976
+ J BENNETT, *Towns in Roman Britain*, Shire Publications, 2nd ed. 1984
J S WACHER, ed., *Civitas Capitals of Roman Britain*, Leicester Univ. Press 1966
F GREW and B HOBLEY, ed., *Roman Urban Topography in Britain and the Western Empire*, Council for British Arch. 1985

J CRICKMORE, *Romano–British Urban Defences*, British Arch. Reports 1984

J MALONEY and B HOBLEY, *Roman Urban defences in the West*, Council for British Arch. 1983

S S FRERE, 'British urban defences in earthwork', *Britannia* xv (1984), 63–74

Villas: A L F RIVET, ed., *The Roman Villa in Britain*, Routledge 1969

M TODD, ed., *Studies in the Romano–British Villa*, Leicester Univ. Press 1978

+ D JOHNSTON, *Roman Villas*, Shire Publications, rev. ed. 1983

Social aspects: J LIVERSIDGE, *Britain in the Roman Empire*, Routledge 1968

A BIRLEY, *Life in Roman Britain*, Batsford 1964

id., The People of Roman Britain, Batsford 1979

Roads: + I D MARGARY, *Roman Roads in Britain*, Baker, rev. ed. 1973

+ D E JOHNSTON, *An Illustrated History of Roman Roads in Britain*, Spurbooks 1979

+ R W BAGSHAWE, *Roman Roads*, Shire Publications 1979

+ C TAYLOR, *Roads and Tracks of Britain*, Dent 1979

Religion: M HENIG, *Religion in Roman Britain*, Batsford 1984

M GREEN, *The Gods of the Celts*, Alan Sutton 1986

G WEBSTER, *The British Celts and their Gods under Rome*, Batsford 1986

W RODWELL, ed., *Temples, churches and religion*, British Arch. Reports 1980

C THOMAS, *Christianity in Roman Britain to AD 500*, Batsford 1981

Art, general: + J M C TOYNBEE, *Art in Roman Britain*, Phaidon 1962

ead., Art in Britain under the Romans, Clarendon Press 1964

Mosaics: + A RAINEY, *Mosaics in Roman Britain, a gazeteer*, David and Charles 1973

D S NEAL, *Roman Mosaics in Britain*, Soc. for Promotion of Roman Studies 1981

N A COOKSON, *Romano–British Mosaics*, British Arch. Reports 1984

R STUPPERICH, 'A reconsideration of some fourth-century British mosaics', *Britannia* xi (1980), 289–301

Painting: +R LING, *Romano–British Wall Painting*, Shire
    Publications 1985
    N DAVEY and R LING, *Wall-Painting in Roman Britain*, Soc.
    for Promotion of Roman Studies 1982

Chapter One

General: +A DETSICAS, *The Cantiaci*, Alan Sutton 1983
    +S JOHNSON, *The Roman Forts of the Saxon Shore*, Elek
    1976, 2nd ed. 1979
Richborough: +DOE *Guide*, HMSO (pamphlet)
    B CUNLIFFE (ed.), *Richborough V*, Soc. of Antiq. 1968
    Britannia i (1970), 240–8
    Britannia ii (1971), 225–31
    A DETSICAS, (ed.), *Collectanea Historica: essays in memory
    of Stuart Rigold*, Maidstone, Kent Arch. Soc. 1981, 23–30
Reculver: +B PHILP, *The Roman Fort at Reculver*, Reculver
    Excavation Group, 8th ed., 1986 (booklet)
Lympne: +S JOHNSON, *op. cit.* (see General), 53–6
    Britannia xi (1980), 227–88; *ib.* xvi (1985), 209–36
Dover: B PHILP, *The Excavation of the Roman Forts of the
    Classis Britannica at Dover 1970–1977*, Kent Arch. Rescue
    Unit, Dover 1981
    Kent Arch. Review 28 (1972), 236–44 (house)
    +B PHILP, *The Roman Painted House at Dover*, Dover n.d.
    (booklet)
    Arch.J. lxxxvi (1929), 29–46 (lighthouse)
Pevensey: +DOE *Guide*, HMSO 1952 (booklet)
    Antiquity xlvii (1973), 138–40 (brick-stamps)
Holtye: +I D MARGARY, *The London–Lewes Roman Road*, n.d.,
    guide pamphlet obtainable from The White Horse, Holtye
Beauport Park: *Arch.J.* cxxxi (1974), 171–99
    Britannia x (1979), 139–56
    CA 77 (May 1981), 177–81
Canterbury: +S S FRERE, *Roman Canterbury*, Canterbury
    Excavation Committee, 4th ed., 1965 (booklet)
    S S FRERE, S STOW and P BENNETT, *Excavations on the
    Roman and Medieval Defences of Canterbury* (Arch. of
    Canterbury vol. II), Maidstone, Canterbury Arch. Trust
    1982
    Britannia i (1970), 83–113; xvii (1986), 426
    JBAA xxviii (1965), 1–15

CA 62 (June 1978), 78–83

Rochester: *Arch. Cant.* lxxxiii (1968), 55–104; *ib.* lxxxv (1970), 95–112; *ib.* lxxxvii (1972), 121–57

Chichester: R A WATSON, (ed.), *The Chichester Excavations I* (by Alec Down & Margaret Rule), Chichester 1971
A DOWN, *The Chichester Excavations II*, Phillimore, Chichester 1974
id., *The Chichester Excavations III*, Phillimore, Chichester 1978, esp. 177–83 (early history)
id., *The Chichester Excavations V*, Phillimore, Chichester 1981
Britannia x (1979), 227–54

Fishbourne: + B CUNLIFFE, *Fishbourne, A Guide to the Site*, Times Newspapers 1971 (booklet)
+ B CUNLIFFE, *Fishbourne, a Roman Palace and its Garden*, Thames & Hudson 1971
B CUNLIFFE, *Excavations at Fishbourne 1961–9*, 2 vols., Soc. of Antiq. 1971
Britannia xii (1981), 364; *ib*, xv (1984), 328; *ib.* xvii (1986), 423–4

Bignor: + *The Roman Villa, Bignor, West Sussex*, illustrated guidebook, Bignor n.d. (booklet)
Britannia xiii (1982), 135–95; *ib* xvii (1986), 421–3
Oxford J. Arch. ii (1983), 93–107
Popular Arch. May 1986, 2–13

Lullingstone: + G W MEATES, *Lullingstone Roman Villa*, HMSO 1962 (guidebook)
id., *The Roman Villa at Lullingstone, Vol I: the site*, Phillimore, Chichester 1979

Orpington: S PALMER, *Excavation of the Roman and Saxon site at Orpington*, Bromley 1984

Keston: *CA* 14 (May 1969), 73–5

Stone-by-Faversham: *Antiq.J.* xlix (1969), 273–94; *ib.* lvii (1977), 67–72; *Arch.J.* cxxxviii (1981), 118–45

Chapter Two

General: + L V GRINSELL, *The Archaeology of Wessex*, Methuen 1958
+ P J FOWLER, *Wessex* (Regional Archaeologies), Heinemann 1967
S M PEARCE, *The Archaeology of South-West Britain*,

Collins 1981, 132–64

M TODD, *The South West to AD 1000*, Longmans 1987, 189–235

+ B PUTNAM, *Roman Dorset*, Dovecote Press, Wimbourne 1984

+ M ASTON and I BURROW, ed., *The Archaeology of Somerset*, Somerset Co. Council 1982, 63–82

C THOMAS, (ed.), *Rural Settlement in Roman Britain*, Council for British Arch. 1966, 43–67 and 74–98

Old Burrow, Martinhoe: *Proc. Devon Arch. Soc.* xxiv (1966), 3–39

Hod Hill: I A RICHMOND, *Hod Hill II*, British Museum 1968
    Arch.J. cxxiii (1966), 209–11 (summary)

Maiden Castle: + DOE *Guide*, HMSO (pamphlet)

Jordon Hill: RCHM *Dorset* II, iii, HMSO 1970, 616–7

Dorchester: *ibid.* 531–92;
    Archaeologia cv (1976), 1–97 (amphitheatre)

Exeter: + P BIDWELL, *Roman Exeter: fortress and town*, Exeter City Council 1980
    P BIDWELL, *The Legionary Bath-house and Basilica and Forum at Exeter*, Exeter 1979

Winchester: *Arch.J.* cxxiii (1966), 182–3
    Proc. Hampshire Field Club xxii (1962), 51–81
    Antiq.J. lv (1975), 109–16, 295–303, 321–6

Silchester: + G C BOON, *Silchester, the Roman town of Calleva*, David and Charles 1974
    M FULFORD *et al.*, *Silchester: excavations on the defences 1974–80* (Britannia Monographs 5), Soc. for Promotion of Roman Studies 1984
    Archaeologia cv (1976), 277–302 (church)
    Antiq.J. lxv (1985), 39–81 (basilica and amphitheatre)

Rockbourne: *Arch.J.* cxl (1983), 129–50

Littlecote Park: + *Littlecote Roman Villa, illustrated guide*, n.d. (booklet)
    CA 80 (Dec. 1981), 264–8
    Britannia xii (1981), 1–5

Bokerley Dyke: *Arch.J.* civ (1974), 62–78; *ib.* cxviii (1961), 65–79

Woodcuts, Rotherley: *Arch.J.* civ (1947), 36–48

Berwick Down: C THOMAS (ed.), *op. cit.* (see General), 46–7

Meriden Down: RCHM *Dorset* III, ii, HMSO 1970, 298

Cerne Giant: +M MARPLES, *White Horses and Other Hill Figures*, Country Life 1949, ch.8
+H L S DEWER, *The Giant of Cerne Abbas*, The Toucan Press, Guernsey, 1968 (booklet)
Antiquité Classique xliv (1975), 570–80

Chysauster: +DOE *Guide*, HMSO (pamphlet)
Arch.J. cxxx (1973), 238–40

Carn Euny: +DOE *Guide*, HMSO 1983 (booklet)
CA 44 (May 1974), 262–8

Scilly Isles: C THOMAS, *Exploration of a drowned landscape: archaeology and history of the Isles of Scilly*, Batsford 1985, ch.6
+S BUTCHER, *Nornour* (Isles of Scilly Museums Publication No. 7), n.d.

Cornish milestones: R G COLLINGWOOD and R P WRIGHT, *The Roman Inscriptions of Britain I*, Oxford Univ. Press 1965, nos. 2230–4

Brading: +D J TOMALIN. *Roman Wight, a Guide Catalogue*, Isle of Wight County Council, Newport 1987, 19–28
J M C TOYNBEE, *Art in Britain under the Romans*, Oxford Univ. Press 1964, 254–8 (mosaics)

Newport: *Antiq.J.* ix (1929), 141–151 and 354–71
TOMALIN, *op. cit.* (see Brading), 13–18
+D J TOMALIN, *Newport Roman Villa*, Isle of Wight County Council, 2nd ed. 1977 (booklet)

Combley: *Proc. Isle of Wight N.H. & Arch. Soc.* vi, 4 (1969), 271–82; *ib.* vi, 6 (1971), 420–30
Britannia vii (1976), 364–6

Carisbrooke: B HARTLEY and J S WACHER, ed., *Rome and her northern provinces: papers presented to Sheppard Frere*, Alan Sutton 1983, 290–301

Portchester: +DOE *Guide*, HMSO (booklet)
B CUNLIFFE, *Excavations at Portchester Castle, vol. I: Roman*, Soc. of Ant. 1975

Chapter Three

General: K BRANIGAN and P H FOWLER, *The Roman West Country*, David and Charles 1976
+K BRANIGAN, *The Roman Villa in South-West England*, Moonraker 1976
RCHM *Gloucestershire I*, HMSO 1976, esp. xxxiv–li

+ A MCWHIRR, *Roman Gloucestershire*, Alan Sutton 1981

+ M HEBDITCH and L GRINSELL, *Roman Sites in the Mendips, Cotswolds, Wye Valley and Bristol Region*, Bristol Arch. Research Group 1968 (booklet)

Charterhouse: + J CAMPBELL, D ELKINGTON, P FOWLER and L GRINSELL, *The Mendip Hills in Prehistoric and Roman Times*, Bristol Arch. Reseach Group 1970 (booklet)

BRANIGAN and FOWLER, *op. cit.* (see General), 183–97

Proc. Univ. Bristol Speleological Soc. xiii (1974), 327–47

Britannia xiii (1982), 113–23

Bath: + B CUNLIFFE, *The Roman Baths and Museum*, 1985 (booklet)

+ B CUNLIFFE, *Roman Bath Discovered*, 2nd ed. Routledge 1984

+ B CUNLIFFE, *The City of Bath*, Alan Sutton 1986, 16–43

B CUNLIFFE, *Roman Bath*, Soc. of Antiq. 1969

B CUNLIFFE and P DAVENPORT, *The Temple of Sulis Minerva at Bath*, 2 vols., Oxford Univ. Committee for Arch. 1985

Britannia vii (1976), 1–32

Britannia x (1979), 101–7 (temple)

Britannia xii (1981), 357 (defences)

Gloucester: BRANIGAN and FOWLER, *op. cit.* (see General), 63–80

+ C HEIGHWAY, *Gloucester: a history and guide*, Alan Sutton 1985, 1–17

ead., *The East and North Gates of Gloucester*, Western Arch. Trust, Bristol 1983

H R HURST, *Kingsholm*, Cambridge 1985

H R HURST, *Gloucester: the Roman and later defences* (Gloucester Arch. Report 2), Gloucester 1986

J F RHODES, *Catalogue of Romano–British Sculptures in Gloucester City Museum*, 1964 (booklet)

TBGAS lxxxvi (1967), 5–15; *ib.* xciii (1974), 15–100

Glevensis xiv (1980), 4–12

Antiq.J. lv (1975), 338–45 (Bon Marché head)

Britannia vi (1975), 272–3; *ib.* xvii (1986), 414, 429

Cirencester: BRANIGAN and FOWLER, *op. cit.* (see General), 81–98

Corinium Museum Cirencester, Exhibition Guide, Cirencester Museum 1980 (booklet)

+ D J VINER, *The Corinium Trail*, Cirencester Museum

1980 (pamphlet)

Britannia i (1970), 227–39

CA 29 (November 1971), 144–52; *ib*. 42 (January 1974), 216–19

Antiq.J. liii (1973), 191–218

Kingscote: RCHM, *Gloucestershire I* (see General), 70–3
+ E J SWAIN, *Kingscote Archaeological Association, The Chessalls Excavations, Kingscote, 1975–8 Seasons*, 1979 (booklet)

CA (Nov. 1979), 294–9

Keynsham & Somerdale: *Archaeologia* lxxv (1924–5), 109–38

King's Weston: + guidebook by G C Boon

TBGAS lxix (1950), 5–58

Wadfield: *JBAA* i (1895), 242–50

TBGAS xc (1971), 124–8

RCHM, *Gloucestershire I* (see General), 121–3

Great Witcombe: *ibid.*, 60–1

TBGAS lxxiii (1954), 5–69

M R APTED, R GILYARD-BEER and A D SAUNDERS, *Ancient Monuments and their Interpretation*, Phillimore 1977, 27–40

Chedworth: + R GOODBURN, *The Roman Villa, Chedworth*, NT 1972 (booklet)

TBGAS lxxviii (1959), 5–23

TBGAS ci (1983), 5–20 ('cult centre')

RCHM, *Gloucestershire I* (see General), 24–8

Britannia x (1979), 318–19; *ib*. xvi (1985), 298

Woodchester: RCHM, *Gloucestershire I* (see General), 132–4

Britannia xiii (1982), 197–228

+ D J SMITH, *The Great Pavement and Roman Villa at Woodchester. Gloucestershire*, Woodchester 1973

North Leigh: + D R WILSON and D SHERLOCK, *North Leigh Roman Villa, Oxfordshire*, HMSO 1980 (booklet)

R G COLLINGWOOD and I RICHMOND. *The Archaeology of Roman Britain*, Methuen 1969, 143 (and plan)

Lydney: T V and R E M WHEELER, *The Prehistoric, Roman and Post-Roman Remains in Lydney Park*, Soc. of Antiq. 1932

Britannia xii (1981), 357; *ib*. xiii (1982), 380

Littledean: *Britannia* xvi (1985), 299–300; *ib*. xvii (1986), 410

Blackpool Bridge: + I D MARGARY, *Roman Roads in Britain*, Baker 1973, 332–3

+ A W TROTTER, *The Dean Road*, Bellows, Gloucester 1936

Chapter Four
General: I A RICHMOND, 'Roman Essex', in VCH *Essex* iii
(1963), 1–23
+ R DUNNETT, *The Trinovantes*, Duckworth 1975
+ K BRANIGAN, *The Catuvellauni*, Alan Sutton 1985
Colchester: + P CRUMMY, *In Search of Colchester's Past*, 2nd
ed., Colchester Arch. Trust 1984 (booklet)
+ *Roman Colchester*, Colchester Borough Council 1980
(booklet)
Britannia viii (1977), 65–106; *ib*. xiii (1982), 299–302
(theatre); *ib*. xv (1984), 7–50 (temple)
VCH *Essex* iii (1963), 90–122
Arch.J. cxxiii (1966), 27–61
Trans. Essex Arch. Soc. iii (1971), 1–115
JRS lii (1962), 178
St Albans: + I ANTHONY, *The Roman City of Verulamium*,
Official Guide 1970
+ K M KENYON and S S FRERE, *The Roman Theatre of
Verulamium and adjacent buildings*, n.d. (guide booklet)
S S FRERE, *Verulamium Excavations* I, Soc. of Antiq. 1972
id., *Verulamium Excavations* II, Soc. of Antiq. 1983
id., *et al.*, *Verulamium Excavations* III, Oxford Univ.
Committee for Arch. 1984
Caistor St Edmund: *Arch.J.* cvi (1949), 62–5
Britannia ii (1971), 1–26
J N L MYRES and B GREEN, *The Anglo-Saxon Cemeteries of
Caistor by Norwich and Markshall, Norfolk*, Soc. of
Antiq. 1973, 12–34
Caister-on-Sea: *JRS* xlii (1952), 96–7; *ib*. xliii (1953), 121–2;
ib. xliv (1954), 97; *ib*. xlv (1955), 136
Norfolk Arch. xxxiii (1962), 94–107; *ib*. xxxiv (1966),
45–73 (correct plan)
Burgh Castle: + DOE *Guide*, HMSO 1978 (booklet)
S JOHNSON, Burgh Castle, *Excavations by Charles Green
1958–61*, Norfolk Arch. Unit, Dereham 1983
Car Dyke: *Antiq.J.* xxix (1948), 145–63
Britannia x (1979), 183–96
Durobrivae vi (1978), 24–5
Welwyn: *CA* 27 (July 1971), 106–9

Bancroft: *Britannia* x (1979), 303–4; *ib.* xv (1984), 303–4; *ib.*
   xvi (1985), 290–3; *ib.* xvii (1986), 399–401
   CA 90 (Jan 1984), 200–3
   Roman Milton Keynes, Bucks. Arch. Soc. 1987
Harlow: N E FRANCE and B M GOBEL, *The Romano–British
   temple at Harlow*, Alan Sutton 1985
Harpenden: *St Albans Archit. and Arch. Soc.* v (1937), 108–14
   JBAA xxii (1959), 22–3
   JRS xxviii (1938), 186 (summary and plan)
Mersea: VCH *Essex* iii (1963), 159–61 (also information sheet
   at site)
Thornborough: *Record of Bucks.* xvi (1953–60), 29–32; *ib.* xx
   (1975), 3–56
Stevenage: *Antiquity* x (1963), 39
Bartlow: VCH *Essex* iii (1963), 39–43

Chapter Five

General: J B WHITWELL, *Roman Lincolnshire*, History of
   Lincolnshire Committee 1970
   M TODD, *The Coritani*, Duckworth 1973
   J B WHITWELL, *The Coritani: some aspects of the Iron Age
   tribe and the Roman civitas*, British Arch. Reports 1982
   G WEBSTER, *The Cornovii*, Duckworth 1975
   Trans. Leicestershire Arch. and Hist. Soc. lviii (1982–83),
   1–5 (for the name Corieltavi rather than Coritani)
Baginton: *Trans. Birmingham Arch. Soc.* lxxxiii (1966–7),
   65–129; *ib.* lxxxv (1973), 7–92; *ib.* lxxxvii (1975), 1–56
   CA 4 (Sept. 1967), 86–9; *ib.* 24 (Jan. 1971), 16–21; *ib.* 28
   (Sept. 1971), 127–30; *ib.* 44 (May 1974), 271–80; *ib.* 63
   (Sept. 1978), 123–5; *Popular Arch.* (May 1985), 25–9
Melandra Castle: *Derbyshire Arch.J.* lxxxiii (1963), 3–9 (fort);
   ib. xci (1971), 57–118 (civilian settlement)
   Britannia v (1974), 420; *ib.* vi (1975), 244; *ib.* vii (1976),
   322–3; *ib.* viii (1977), 387–8; *ib.* ix (1978), 432; *ib.* xvi
   (1985), 283
Lincoln: WHITWELL, *op. cit.* (see General), ch.3
   + C COLYER, *Lincoln, The Archaeology of an historic city*,
   Lincoln Archaeological Trust 1975 (booklet)
   M JONES *et al.*, *The defences of the upper Roman enclosure*
   (Arch. of Lincoln 7/1), London, Council for Brit. Arch.
   1980

CA 26 (May 1971), 67–71; *ib.* 83 (August 1982), 366–71

Antiq.J. lv (1975), 227–45; *ib.* lix (1979), 84–7

Britannia v (1974), 422–4; *ib.* vi (1975), 245; *ib.* xi (1980), 61–72

Wroxeter: + DOE *Guide*, HMSO 3rd ed. 1978 (booklet)

Antiq.J. xlvi (1966), 229–39

Antiquity lviii (1984), 117–20, 224 (city plan)

CA 1 (March 1967), 10; *ib.* 9 (July 1968), 231; *ib.* 14 (May 1969), 82–6; *ib.* 25 (March 1971), 45–9

Britannia vi (1975), 106–17; *ib.* xi (1980), 368; *ib.* xiii (1982), 360; *ib.* xiv (1983), 302–3; *ib.* xvii (1986), 391–3

P BARKER, ed., *Wroxeter Roman City: excavations 1966–1980*, n.d. [1981]

Leicester: K M KENYON, *Excavations at the Jewry Wall site, Leicester*, Soc. of Antiq. 1948 (much out of date)

Trans. Leics. Arch. and Hist. Soc. xliv (1968–9), 1–10

+ E BLANK, *A Guide to Leicestershire Archaeology*, Leicester Museums 1970 (booklet)

Water Newton: + J P WILD, *Romans in the Nene Valley*, Peterborough 1972 (booklet)

Arch.J. cxxxi (1974), 140–70

Orton Longueville: *Durobrivae* i (1973), 20–1; *ib.* ii (1974), 4

Britannia vi (1975), 252

Northamptonshire Arch. x (1975), 94–137

Wall: + DOE *Guide*, HMSO 1958 (booklet)

Trans. Lichfield and S. Staffordshire Arch. and Hist. Soc. v (1963–4), 1–47; *ib.* viii (1966–7), 1–38; *ib.* xi (1969–70), 7–31; *ib.* xv (1973–4), 13–28; *ib.* xxi (1979–80), 1–14

Britannia iii (1972), 316; *ib.* vi (1975), 247; *ib.* vii (1976), 328; *ib.* viii (1977), 392; *ib.* ix (1978), 435–6

Great Casterton: P CORDER, ed., *The Roman Town and Villa at Great Casterton*, Univ. of Nottingham, 3 reports, 1951, 1954 and 1961

M TODD, ed., *The Roman Fort at Great Casterton*, Univ. of Nottingham 1968

Ancaster: M TODD, *The Roman Town at Ancaster: the excavations of 1955–1971*, Univ. of Nottingham and Exeter 1981

Horncastle: *Lincs. Hist. and Arch.* xviii (1983), 47–88

Arch. in Lincs. 1984–85, 56–8

Chapter Six

General: V E NASH-WILLIAMS, *The Roman Frontier in Wales*, 2nd ed., revised by M G Jarrett, Univ. of Wales, Cardiff, 1969 (consult for *all* military sites)

I A RICHMOND, 'Roman Wales', ch. VI of *Prehistoric and Early Wales*, ed. I W Foster and G Daniel, Routledge 1965

G SIMPSON, *Britons and the Roman Army*, Gregg 1964

R W DAVIES, 'Roman Wales and Roman military practice camps', *Arch. Camb.* cxvii (1968), 103–18

Caerleon: G C BOON, *Isca, the Roman Legionary Fortress at Caerleon*, National Museum of Wales, Cardiff 1972

J D ZIENKIEWICZ, *The Legionary Fortress Baths at Caerleon*, 2 vols., Cardiff, Cadw: Welsh Historic Monuments 1986

+ G C BOON, *The Legionary Fortress of Caerleon – Isca: a brief account*, Caerleon 1987

+ R J BREWER, *Caerleon-Isca: the Roman Legionary Museum*, Caerleon 1987

+ DOE *Guide*, HMSO 1970 (booklet)

Arch. Camb. cxix (1970), 10–63

Chester: D F PETCH, in VCH *History of Cheshire*, vol. I, Univ. of London 1987, 117–85

T J STRICKLAND and P J DAVEY, *New Evidence for Roman Chester*, Univ. of Liverpool 1978

+ T J STRICKLAND, *Roman Chester*, Chester City Council 1984 (booklet)

J. Chester Arch. Soc. lxvi (1983), 5–11

Britannia xiv (1983), 297; *ib.* xv (1984), 286

Archaeologia cv (1976), 127–239 (amphitheatre)

Brecon Gaer: + DOE *Guide*, HMSO (pamphlet)

RCAHM (Wales) *Brecknock: hill forts and Roman Remains*, London 1986, 135–46

Gelligaer: RCHM *Glamorgan* I.2, HMSO Cardiff 1976, 95–8, 103

Neath: *ibid.* 88–90

Castell Collen: *Arch. Camb.* cxviii (1969), 124–34 (practice camps)

Y Pigwn: *BBCS* xxiii (1968–70), 100–3

RCAHM (Wales) *Brecknock* (see Brecon Gaer), 150–3

Dolaucothi: + G B D JONES and P R LEWIS, *The Roman Gold*

Mines at Dolaucothi, Carmarthen 1971 (booklet)
> *Antiq.J.* xlix (1969), 244–72
> *National Trust Yearbook for 1976–7*, 20–35
> *BBCS* xix (1960), 71–84 (aqueduct); *ib.* xxxi (1984), 304–13
Tomen-y-Mur: *JRS* lix (1969), 126–7 (Braich-ddu)
> *BBCS* xviii (1958–60), 397–402 (Doldinnas)
Caerhun: *Trans. Caernarvonshire Hist. Soc.* xxxv (1974), 7–13
Prestatyn: *Britannia* xvi (1985), 252–3; *ib.* xvii (1986), 364
Caernarfon: +G C BOON, *Caernarvon-Segontium*, National
> Museum of Wales 1974 (booklet)
> *Arch. Camb.* cxxiv (1975), 65–7
> *Britannia* vii (1976), 292; *ib.* viii (1977), 356–8; *ib.* ix
> (1978), 404–6
Caer Gybi: +DOE *Guide to the Ancient Monuments of
> Anglesey*, HMSO (booklet)
Holyhead signal station: *Britannia* xiii (1982), 328
Cardiff: RCHM *Glamorgan* I.2, HMSO Cardiff 1976, 90–4
> *Morgannwg* xxv (1981), 201–11 (early forts)
Barry: *Britannia* xvi (1985), 57–125
Carmarthen: *Carmarthen Antiq.* v (1964–9), 2–5; *ib.* vi (1970),
> 4–14, *ib.* vii (1971), 58–63
> G C BOON ed., *Monographs and Collections, Cambrian
> Arch. Association* I, Cardiff 1978, esp. 63–6
Caerwent: +DOE *Guide*, HMSO (booklet)
> *Arch. Camb.* cxxxii (1983), 49–77 (with controversial
> dating of stone defences)
> *Britannia* xiii (1982), 334; *ib.* xiv (1983), 283–4; *ib.* xv
> (1984), 270; *ib.* xvi (1985), 259–60; *ib.* xvii (1986), 369–70
> (house and temple)
Tre'r Ceiri: *Arch.J.* cxvii (1960), 1–39
Holyhead Mountain, Caer Leb, Din Lligwy: +DOE *Guide to
> Ancient Monuments of Anglesey*, HMSO (booklet)
> *Arch. Camb.* cxxxiii (1984), 64–82

Chapter Seven

General: R M BUTLER, ed., *Soldier and Civilian in Roman
> Yorkshire*, Leicester Univ. Press 1971
> P R WILSON, R F J JONES and D M EVANS, ed., *Settlement and
> Society in the Roman North*, Bradford 1984
> N HIGHAM, *The Northern Counties to AD 1000*, Longmans
> 1986, 145–241

H RAMM, *The Parisi*, Duckworth 1978

N HIGHAM and G B D JONES, *The Carvetii*, Alan Sutton 1985

+ T GARLICK, *Roman Sites in Yorkshire*, Dalesman 1971 (booklet)

+ T GARLICK, *Romans in the Lake Counties*, Dalesman 2nd ed., 1972 (booklet)

+ D C A SHOTTER, *Roman North West England*, Univ. of Lancaster 1984 (booklet)

York: RCHM, *Roman York : Eburacum*, HMSO 1962

R M BUTLER, ed., *op. cit.* (see General), 16–17, 45–53, 97–106, 179–92

P V ADDYMAN and V E BLACK, ed., *Archaeological Papers from York presented to M W Barley*, York Arch. Trust 1984, 28–42

+ B HOPE-TAYLOR, *Under York Minster*, York Minster 1971 (booklet)

Britannia iii (1972), 265–6 (plaster)

Antiq.J. liv (1974), 204–17

A B SUMPTER and S COLL, *Interval Tower SW5 and the SW Defences*, Archaeology of York 3.2, Council for British Arch., London 1977, 57–95

Cawthorn: *Arch.J.* lxxxix (1932), 17–78

Wheeldale Moor: R H HAYES and J G RUTTER, *Wade's Causeway*, Scarborough & District Arch. Soc. 1964 (booklet)

Malton: + L P WENHAM, *Derventio (Malton)*, Cameo Books 1974 (booklet)

Ilkley: *Proc. Leeds Philosophical & Literary Soc.* xii (1966), 23–72

Britannia xiv (1983), 337

Castleshaw: *Popular Arch.* March 1986, 27–35

Greater Manchester Arch. J. i (1985), 13–18

Blackstone Edge: + I D MARGARY, *Roman Roads in Britain*, Baker 1973, 404

Ribchester: + B J N EDWARDS, *Ribchester, Lancashire*, National Trust 1972 (booklet)

B J N EDWARDS and P V WEBSTER, *Ribchester Excavations Part 1*, University College Cardiff Extramural Dept. 1985

Arch.J. cxxvii (1970), 277–9

Britannia xii (1981), 331

Piercebridge: *Trans. Arch. Soc. Durham and Northumberland* vii (1936), 235–77; *ib.* ix (1939–41), 43–68; (new series) i

(1968), 27–44; *ib.* vi (1982), 77–82

CA 40 (Sept. 1973), 136–41

Britannia vi (1975), 234; *ib.* x (1979), 285; *ib.* xi (1980), 362

Binchester: R E HOOPELL, *Vinovia, a buried Roman city*, Whiting and Co. 1891

Trans. Archit. and Arch. Soc. Durham and Northumberland xi (1958), 115–24; *ib.* (new series) ii (1970), 33–7

Arch.J. cxi (1954), 195

Britannia viii (1977), 379; *ib.* ix (1978). 425–6; *ib.* x (1979), 284; *ib.* xi (1980), 361

W S HANSON, and L J F KEPPIE, ed., *Roman Frontier Studies 1979*, British Arch. Reports, Oxford 1980, 233–54

Lanchester: *Arch.J.* cxi (1954), 220–1

Proc. Soc. Antiq. Newcastle, 4th series, iii (1927), 101–4

HARDING, ed., *op. cit.* (see General), 214–6 (aqueducts)

Ebchester: *AA* xxxviii (1960), 193–229; *ib.* xlii (1964), 173–85; *ib.* (new series) iii (1975), 43–104

Britannia xvii (1986), 438

Bowes: *JRS* lviii (1968), 179–81

Britannia ii (1971), 251

Yorks. Arch.J. xlv (1973), 181–4 (aqueduct)

ibid. xxxvi (1946), 383–6; *ib.* xxxvii (1948), 107–16 (Scargill Moor)

Bowes Moor: W F GRIMES, ed., *Aspects of Archaeology in Britain and Beyond*, Edwards 1951, 293–302

HANSON and KEPPIE, *op. cit.* (see Binchester), 211–31

Rey Cross: *CW* xxxiv (1934), 50–61

Maiden Castle: *CW* xxvii (1927), 170–7

Brough: *CW* lviii (1958), 31–56; *ib.* lxxvii (1977), 14–47

Brougham: RCHM, *Westmorland*, HMSO 1936, 54

Temple Sowerby: *ibid.*, 226

Whitley Castle: *Proc. Soc. Antiq. Newcastle* i (1924), 249–55

AA xxxvii (1959), 191–202

Old Carlisle: *CW* li (1951), 16–39

Arch.J. cxxxii (1975), 18, 24–5

Maryport: M G JARRETT, *Maryport, a Roman Fort and its Garrison*, CW extra series 1976; cf. review in *Britannia* ix (1978), 493–5

+ J COLLINGWOOD BRUCE, *Handbook to the Roman Wall*, 13th ed. rev. by C DANIELS, Harold Hill, Newcastle 1978, 273–8

Ravenglass: *ibid.* 284–6
> T W POTTER, *Romans in NW England*, CW Research Series
> I, Kendal 1979, 1–138, esp. 48–50
> *CW* lxxxv (1985), 81–5 (baths)

Hardknott: *CW* xxviii (1928), 314–52; *ib.* lxiii (1963), 148–52;
> *ib.* lxv (1965), 169–75
> + DOE *Guide*, HMSO 1972 (pamphlet)
> + T GARLICK, *Hardknott Castle Roman Fort*, Dalesman
> 5th ed. 1985 (booklet)

Ambleside: RCHM, *Westmorland*, HMSO 1936, 1–3
> + T GARLICK, *Ambleside Roman Fort*, Dalesman 1975
> (booklet)

Middleton: R G COLLINGWOOD and R P WRIGHT, *Roman
> Inscriptions of Britain* I, Oxford Univ. Press 1965, no. 2283

Lancaster: *Trans. Hist. Soc. Lancashire and Cheshire* cv (1953),
> 1–23
> *Britannia* v (1974), 418; *ib.* vi (1975), 239; *ib.* ix (1978), 429
> G M LEATHER, *Lancaster Roman Bath House*, Lancaster
> 1979

Manchester: S BRYANT, M MORRIS and J S F WALKER, *Roman
> Manchester: a frontier settlement*, Greater Manchester
> Arch. Unit 1986

Aldborough: + DOE *Guide*, HMSO (booklet)
> BUTLER, ed., *op. cit.* (see General), 155–63

Hull: + D J SMITH, *The Roman Mosaics from Rudston,
> Brantingham and Horkstow*, Hull Museums and Art
> Gallery, 1976 (booklet)

Beadlam: *Yorks. Arch. J.* xliii (1971), 178–86
> *Britannia* iv (1973), 279

Grassington: *Antiquity* ii (1928), 168–72

Ewe Close: CW xxxiii (1933), 201–26

Scarborough: + R G COLLINGWOOD, *The Roman Signal Station
> on Castle Hill*, Scarborough 1925 (booklet)
> + DOE *Guide*, HMSO (pamphlet)

Chapter Eight

General: + OS *Map of Hadrian's Wall*, HMSO 2nd ed., 1972
> + J COLLINGWOOD BRUCE, *Handbook to the Roman Wall*,
> 13th ed., rev. by C DANIELS, Harold Hill, Newcastle 1978
> D J BREEZE and B DOBSON, *Hadrian's Wall*, Penguin, 3rd ed.
> 1987

E BIRLEY, *Research on Hadrian's Wall*, Titus Wilson, Kendal 1961

+ A R BIRLEY, *Hadrian's Wall*, HMSO 1963 (booklet)

+ D J BREEZE, *Hadrian's Wall: a souvenir guide to the Roman Wall*, HMBC 1987 (booklet)

+ R EMBLETON and F GRAHAM, *Hadrian's Wall in the Days of the Romans*, Frank Graham, Newcastle 1984

J C MANN, *The Northern Frontier in Britain from Hadrian to Honorius*, Univ. of Durham 1969 (ancient texts)

D CHARLESWORTH, 'The Turrets on Hadrian's Wall', in M R APTED, R GILYARD-BEER AND A D SAUNDERS, ed, *Ancient Monuments and Their Interpretation*, Phillimore 1977, 13–26

B R HARTLEY, 'Roman York and the northern military command', in *Soldier and Civilian in Roman Yorkshire*, ed. R M BUTLER, Univ. of Leicester Press 1971, 55–69

B R HARTLEY, 'The Roman Occupation of Scotland: the evidence of samian ware', *Britannia* iii (1972), 1–55

G B D JONES, 'The Solway Frontier: interim report, 1976–81', *Britannia* xiii (1982), 283–97

M HASSALL, 'The date of the rebuilding of Hadrian's turf wall in stone', *ibid.* xv (1984), 242–4

B DOBSON, 'The function of Hadrian's Wall', AA^5 xiv (1986), 1–30

The first two works cited above give full details about how much of the Wall and its attendant structures are visible today, and should be consulted for all sites. Below are listed some items published since 1978.

South Shields: J N DORE and J P GILLAM, *The Roman Fort at South Shields*, Newcastle 1979

R MIKET, *The Roman Fort at South Shields: excavation of the defences 1977–81*, Tyne and Wear County Council Museums, Gateshead 1983

Britannia xv (1984), 277; *ib.* xvi (1985), 268; *ib.* xvii (1986), 374–6

Wallsend: *Britannia* vii (1976), 306–8; *ib.* viii (1977), 371–2; *ib.* ix (1978), 419; *ib.* xi (1980), 355–8; *ib.* xii (1981), 322; *ib.* xiii (1982), 340–2; *ib.* xiv (1983), 289; *ib.* xv (1984), 277–8; *ib.* xvi (1985), 268–70

Corbridge: *Britannia* xi (1980), 165–71 (on the possible form
   of the Roman name)
Chesters Bridge: *Britannia* xiv (1983), 289–90; *ib.* xv (1984),
   278
Chesters: *AA*⁵ vii (1979), 114–26 (new Hadrianic inscription)
Carrawburgh: L ALLASON-JONES and B MCKAY, *Coventina's
   Well: a shrine on Hadrian's Wall*, Trustees of the Clayton
   Collection, Chesters 1985
Sewingshields: *AA*⁵ xii (1984), 33–147
Vindolanda: P T BIDWELL, *The Roman Fort of Vindolanda*,
   HMBC London 1985
   + A BOWMAN, *The Roman Writing Tablets from
   Vindolanda.* British Museum Publications 1983
   A BOWMAN and J D THOMAS, *Vindolanda: the Latin Writing
   Tablets*, Soc. for Promotion of Roman Studies 1983
   JRS lxxvi (1986), 120–3
   Britannia xvii (1986), 378
Peel Crag to Highshield Crags: *CA* 96 (April 1985), 16–19
   Britannia xiv (1983), 290; *ib.* xv (1984), 280; *ib.* xvi (1985),
   271; *ib.* xvii (1986), 378–81
Willowford Bridge: *Britannia* xvi (1985), 271; *ib.* xvii (1986),
   381–2
Stanwix: *Britannia* xvi (1985), 271
Carlisle: *Arch.J.* cxxxv (1978), 115–37
   CA 68 (August 1979), 268–72; *ib.* 86 (March 1983), 77–81;
   ib. 101 (August 1986), 171–7

Chapter Nine
General: +G and A RITCHIE, *Scotland, Archaeology and early
   history*, Thames and Hudson 1981, 121–41
   + L KEPPIE, *Scotland's Roman Remains*, John Donald,
   Edinburgh 1986
   + *Exploring Scotland's Heritage*, RCHM (Scotland) and
   HMSO, 7 vols., 1985–6 (for all periods)

§1, *Between the Walls*
General: +J COLLINGWOOD BRUCE, *Handbook to the Roman
   Wall*, 13th ed., rev. by C DANIELS, Newcastle 1978,
   287–326
   K A STEER, 'Roman and Native in S Scotland', *Arch.J.* cxxi
   (1964), 164–7

Swine Hill to Chew Green: I A RICHMOND, 'The Romans in
Redesdale', *Northumberland County History*, xv (1940),
63–159

Pennymuir: RCHM (Scotland), *Roxburgh II*, HMSO 1956,
375–7

Woden Law: *ib.* 169–72
PSAS cxii (1982), 277–84

Lyne: RCHM (Scotland), *Peeblesshire I*, HMSO 1967, 172–5

Castle Greg: RCHM (Scotland), *Midlothian and West Lothian*,
HMSO 1929, 140

Bothwellhaugh: RCAHMS, *Lanarkshire*, HMSO Edinburgh
1978, 119–21
Glasgow Arch. J. viii (1981), 46–94

Birrens: A S ROBERTSON, *Birrens (Blatobulgium)*, Dumfries
and Galloway N.H. and Antiq. Soc., Edinburgh 1975

Burnswark: *Arch.J.* cxv (1958), 234–6
Historia xxi (1972), 99–113
Trans. Dumfriesshire and Galloway N.H. and Antiq. Soc.
liii (1977–78), 57–104

§2, *The Antonine Wall*

G MACDONALD, *The Roman Wall in Scotland*, 2nd ed.,
Clarendon Press, 1934
+ A S ROBERTSON, *The Antonine Wall*, Glasgow Arch. Soc.,
rev. ed. 1979
W S HANSON and G S MAXWELL, *Rome's North West
Frontier: the Antonine Wall*, Edinburgh Univ. Press 1983
+ OS *Map of the Antonine Wall*, HMSO 2nd ed. 1975
D J BREEZE and B DOBSON, *Hadrian's Wall*, Penguin, 3rd ed.
1987
J P GILLAM, 'Possible changes in plan in the course of the
construction of the Antonine Wall', *Scottish Arch. Forum*
7, Edinburgh 1975, 51–6
L J F KEPPIE, 'The Antonine Wall 1960–1980', *Britannia* xiii
(1982), 91–111

Kinneil: *Britannia* x (1979), 275; *ib.* xii (1981), 150–4; *ib.* xiii
(1982), 97

Cramond: *Britannia* v (1974), 163–224
CA 59 (November 1977), 378–81

Bar Hill: A ROBERTSON, M SCOTT and L KEPPIE, *Bar Hill, a
Roman fort and its finds*, Oxford, British Archaeological

Reports 16, 1975
Glasgow Arch. J. xii (1985), 49–81
Bearsden: D J BREEZE, ed., *Studies in Scottish Antiquity presented to Stewart Cruden*, Edinburgh 1984, 32–68

§3, *Romans in the Far North*

General: O G S CRAWFORD, *Topography of Roman Scotland North of the Antonine Wall*, Cambridge Univ. Press 1949
R M OGILVIE and I A RICHMOND, ed., *Tacitus' Agricola*, Oxford Univ. Press 1967, esp. 52–76
J KENWORTHY, ed., *Agricola's Campaigns in Scotland* (Scottish Archaeological Forum 12), Edinburgh 1981
W S HANSON, *Agricola and the Conquest of the North*, Batsford 1987
J K ST JOSEPH, 'Air Reconnaissance in Britain 1965–8', *JRS* lix (1969), 113–19
id., 'Air Reconnaissance in Britain 1969–72', *JRS* lxiii (1973), 228–33
id., 'Air Reconnaissance in Britain 1973–6', *JRS* lxvii (1977), 143–5
id., 'The camp at Durno and Mons Graupius', *Britannia* ix (1978), 271–88
Ardoch: + D J BREEZE, *Ardoch Roman Fort, Braco near Dunblane: a guide*, Stirling 1983
id., in A O'CONNOR AND P V CLARKE, ed., *From the Stone Age to the 'Forty-Five. Studies presented to R B K Stevenson*, Edinburgh 1983, 224–36
Britannia i (1970), 163–78
Kaims Castle: *Arch.J.* cxxi (1964), 196
Gask Ridge: *Trans. Perthshire Soc. of Natural Science*, special issue 1974, 14–29
Popular Archaeology (May 1983), 18–21
Britannia xvii (1986), 371
Inchtuthil: L F PITTS and J K ST JOSEPH, *Inchtuthil, the Roman legionary fortress*, London, Soc. for Promotion of Roman Studies 1985
Cleaven Dyke: *PSAS* lxxiv (1939–40), 37–45
Britannia vii (1976), 299–300
Kirkbuddo: CRAWFORD, *op. cit.* (see General), 97–100
Raedykes: *ib.*, 108–10
PSAS l (1916), 318–48

Normandykes: CRAWFORD, *op. cit.* (see General), 110–12

Chapter Ten

R MERRIFIELD, *The Roman City of London*, Benn 1965

    + P MARSDEN, *Roman London*, Thames and Hudson 1980

    + R MERRIFIELD, *London, city of the Romans*, Batsford 1983

    + A SORRELL, *Roman London*, Batsford 1969 (reconstruction drawings)

    J MORRIS, *Londinium: London in the Roman Empire*, Weidenfeld 1982

    G MILNE, ed., *The Port of Roman London*, Batsford 1985

    W F GRIMES, *The Excavation of Roman and Medieval London*, Routledge 1968

    + *Londinium, a descriptive map and guide to Roman London*, OS 2nd ed. 1983

    + *The London Wall Walk*, Museum of London 1985 (pamphlet)

    + J HALL and R MERRIFIELD, *Roman London*, HMSO/ Museum of London 1986 (booklet)

Military origins: *Trans. London Middlesex Arch. Soc.* xxiv (1973), 1–73

Forum: P MARSDEN, *The Roman Forum Site in London: discoveries before 1985*, HMSO 1987

Palace: *CA* 8 (May 1968), 215–19

    Trans. London Middlesex Arch. Soc. xxvi (1975), 1–102

Mithraeum sculptures: J M C TOYNBEE, *The Roman Art Treasures from the Temple of Mithras* (London and Middlesex Arch. Soc. Special Paper 7), 1986

Lower Thames Street house: *London Archaeologist* (Winter 1968), 3–5

    Antiq.J. lvii (1977), 54–6

Defences: J MALONEY and B HOBLEY, ed., *Roman Urban defences in the west*, Council for British Arch. 1983, 96–117

British Museum: K S PAINTER, *The Mildenhall Treasure*, British Museum Publications 1977 (booklet)

    id., *The Water Newton early Christian silver*, British Museum Publications 1977 (booklet)

    C JOHNS and T W POTTER, *The Thetford Treasure*, British Museum Publications 1983

    + T W POTTER, *Roman Britain*, British Museum 1983

Addenda

York (p. 227). An impressive section of the Roman legionary fortress wall still standing more than 2.5m high was discovered in 1987 during repairs to Granada Television's shop in Parliament Street. At the time of writing it is not clear whether this will be maintained as a feature in the refurbished premises.

South Shields (p. 398). The 'administrative nerve-centre' of the Severan supply-base, alluded to above (p.398), has now been located in the southern part of the unorthodox fort-cum-storebase of *c.* 208 (when the former HQ was converted to granary use). The new *principia* also has an underground strong-room approached by steps; it has a distinctive plan, currently being revealed (1988). Finds include a bronze finger from a life-size statue, probably of an emperor.

London (p. 354). The most exciting recent discovery is that of the amphitheatre of Roman London, located on a development site immediately next to Guildhall. At the time of writing (May 1988) it is not yet clear if the remains (part of the curving stone walls of the building and of one of the two entrances on the major axis) can be preserved within the modern development. The entrance to the arena is flanked on either side by a chamber, presumably both shrines (cf. that of Nemesis in a similar position in the Chester amphitheatre: p. 199). As at both Chester and Silchester, an early timber amphitheatre was replaced later by one with stone retaining walls, at London sometime around AD 100; it is estimated to have measured about 100m by 80m. Guildhall Yard lies wholly within the Roman amphitheatre's arena, and the shape of the early medieval structures constructed on the site (as happened for example at Lucca in Italy), including the first Guildhall and the church of St Lawrence Jewry.

Highshield Craggs (p. 401). The comments about the alleged idiosyncracy of the Wall-builders here in giving the Wall-face a white mortar rendering now stand in need of revision, in view of the very recent discovery of similar evidence for 'whitewashing' in a quite different stretch of Hadrian's Wall, at Denton Burn near Newcastle, which was recorded before destruction by road-works in 1988. Taken with another very recent discovery that the town walls of Colchester (p. 138) were also rendered in white mortar, it now seems likely that this practice was more widespread in Roman Britian than had hitherto been recognised.

Index 1—Sites

Only the main entries for each site is here given; passing references to these and other places with Roman remains, and all sites listed in Appendix One, are omitted.

Index 2 – Types of Monument

This index is designed for those interested in following up some particular category of building: the entry gives the page number(s) on which *begins* the description of each visible example of the type. Sites listed in Appendix One are omitted.